Cast List

Giacomo Agostini – legendary Italian bike racer who won 15 World Championship titles & 122 Grands Prix
James Allen – ITV F1 pit lane reporter who succeeded Murray as main commentator in 2002
Chris Amon – Le Mans winner & brilliant GP driver who, through bad luck, never realised potential
Rubens Barrichello – British F3 Champion, multiple GP winner & driver for Jordan, Stewart, Ferrari & Honda
Brian Barwick – former BBC Head of Sport & then ITV Controller of Sport & later CEO of the FA
Derek Bell – F1 for Surtees, McLaren, Ferrari & Tecno, 5-time Le Mans winner, legendary sports racer
Dave Bickers – motocross rider 1953-93, twice World Champion, 7-time British Champion
Matt Bishop – Editor of *F1 Racing* for 11 years before becoming head of PR for McLaren in 2008
Herbie Blash – former Lotus & Brabham mechanic, FIA Observer & close colleague of Bernie Ecclestone
Ross Brawn – former TWR, Benetton & Ferrari F1, & current Honda F1, technical supremo
Martin Brundle – World Sports Champion, Le Mans winner, F1 driver with 158 starts & 9 podiums, Murray`s F1 ITV pundit colleague and multiple Royal Television Society Award winner
Jenson Button – F1 driver since 2000, driven for Williams, Benetton, Renault, BAR & Honda, GP winner in 2006
John Button – leading rallycross driver & father of Jenson
Rod Chapman – very successful Ford works rallycross driver & 1985 European Truck Racing Champion
Peter Cleaver – BBC Producer on F1 and *Driving Force* programmes & photographer
John Cleland – great character & twice winner of the British Touring Car Championship
Norman Crofts - former senior colleague at advertising agency Masius & Ferguson
Mike Doodson – distinguished motor racing journalist who assisted Murray in commentary box during BBC F1 era
Tony Dron – very long-term successful racer, former Editor of *Classic Cars* & top motoring journalist
Daisy Duke – wife of Geoff
Geoff Duke – legendary bike racer, winner of 6 World Championships and 5 TTs
Neil Duncanson – CEO of North One, producers of F1 coverage for ITV
Vic Eastwood – motocross rider & multiple British Champion
Alan Fearnley – one of the world's finest motoring artists
Nick Fry – Team Principal, Honda F1 Racing
Richard Galvani – F3 team owner in 1980s
Robert Glen – MD of EP Barrus, suppliers of power boat engines, & founder of Formula Johnson series
Louise Goodman – journalist & former F1 PR, then ITV F1 pit lane reporter & presenter
Nick Goozee – former MD of Penske Cars & close friend of Murray's
Bryan 'Badger' Goss – leading motocross rider
Alan Gow – Chief Executive of TOCA (Touring Cars Association)
Stuart Graham – only man, post-war, to win TT on two wheels & four, son of 1949 motor cycle 500cc World Champion
Peter Gwynn – former senior colleague at Masius & Ferguson, now MD of successful car restoration company
Lewis Hamilton – promising F1 driver!
Tim Harvey – British Touring Car Champion & commentator
Paddy Hopkirk – winner of the Monte Carlo Rally & rallying legend
Christian Horner – Team Principal, Red Bull Racing
Tony Jardine – commentator, F1 pit lane reporter, pundit and PR supremo
Nigel Mansell – 1992 World Champion, 1993 Indycar Champion
Lord March – mastermind of the brilliant Goodwood Festival & Revival events
Jonathan Martin – BBC *Grand Prix* Producer & Head of Sport
Roger Moody – BBC *Grand Prix* Producer
Sir Stirling Moss – arguably the greatest all-round racing driver of all time
Lady Susie Moss – Sir Stirling's fantastic wife
Ros Nott – Editor of *Power Boat and Water Skiing* & co-commentator with Murray on power boats
Phil Read – extremely successful bike racer, winner of 8 TTs & 8 World Championship titles
Jim Reside – Producer & later Executive Producer of BBC *Grand Prix* series
John Rhodes – considered by many to be the greatest Mini racer of all time
David Richards – former top rally co-driver, co-founder of Prodrive, Team Principal of Benetton & BAR F1 teams, co-owner of Aston Martin
Keith Ripp – highly successful rallycross racer & founder of Rippspeed
Tommy Robb – rode for Honda & Yamaha during 15-year career, winning TT in 1973
Max Robertson – one of the BBC's legendary commentators, specialising in tennis
Andy Rouse – 4-time winner of the British Touring Car Championship & one of the most successful touring car racers of all time
Vern Schuppan – Le Mans winner, F1 driver & 3-time Indianapolis competitor finishing 3rd in 1981
Bill Smith – bike racer who competed in record 79 TTs, with 4 victories & 51 silver replicas
Steve Soper – versatile driver who raced sports cars & was one of the greats of touring cars
Sir Jackie Stewart – World Champion in 1969, 1971 & 1973 & much, much more
Paul Stoddart – owner of European Aviation & former owner of Minardi F1 team
John Surtees – only person ever to win World Championships on two & four wheels
Pat Symonds – Technical Director of Benetton & Renault F1 teams
Stuart Tallack – brother of Andy Tallack, BBC Outside Broadcast Stage Manager
John Taylor – ex-steeplechase jockey & first ever European Rallycross Champion in 1973 and much more
Owen Thomas – member of BBC *Grand Prix* team responsible for commentary box
Dave Thorpe – top motocross rider, World Champion 1985, 1986 & 1989
Stuart Turner – legendary BMC & Competition Manager
Derek Warwick – World Stock Car Champion, British F3 Champion, World Sports Car Champion & F1 driver 1981-93
John Watson – competed in over 150 F1 races, 5-time GP winner & TV commentator on F1 & A1 series
John Welch – leading rallycross driver
Hugh Wheldon – apple-farmer winner of the Wills Rallycross Championship
Charlie Whiting – ex-Brabham F1 Chief Mechanic & now FIA Technical & Race Director
Mark Wilkin – BBC *Grand Prix* Producer
Barrie 'Whizzo' Williams – very long term, incredibly versatile & successful racer
'Jumping' Jeff Williamson – very successful private & BMC works rallycross driver
Eoin Young – highly distinguished New Zealand motor racing journalist & much more

First published in April 2008

ISBN 978-0-9556564-5-3
ISBN 978-0-9556564-6-0 (de Luxe edition)

Published by
Porter Press International
an imprint of Porter & Porter Ltd.

PO Box 2, Tenbury Wells,
WR15 8XX, UK.
Tel: +44 (0)1584 781588
Fax: +44 (0)1584 781630
sales@porterpress.co.uk
www.porterpress.co.uk

Designed by Grafx Resource
Printed and bound through World Print Limited in China

COPYRIGHT

We have made every effort to trace and acknowledge copyright holders and we apologise in advance for any unintentional omission. We would be pleased to insert the appropriate acknowledgement in any subsequent edition. Further to those mentioned on the Acknowledgements page, we wish to thank the following, plus the Editors and publishers of the named publications, which we have managed to trace, for their kind permission to reproduce the cuttings and/or images – Charles Griffin, Sutton Images, LAT, Maureen Magee, Colin Taylor Productions, Salisbury Newspapers, Nick Goozee, Autosport, Motoring News, F1 Racing, Shropshire Star, Barry Foley and Solo Syndications. Extracts from Daily Mirror courtesy Mirrorpix. Punch Cartoon (p. 104) reproduced with permission of Punch Ltd., www.punch.co.uk. Extracts from The Sunday Post © and courtesy D.C. Thomson & Co., Ltd. Extracts from The Times © John Goodbody, NI Syndication. "Honours List is a thriller for novelist Rendell" Copyright: The Daily Telegraph, 15 June 1996. "Sad day when Murray is taken to the scrapyard" Copyright: The Daily Telegraph 15 December 1995. Without their co-operation, this publication would not have been possible.

Murray Walker Scrapbook

Murray Walker & Philip Porter

Design by Andrew Garman

Porter Press International

ACKNOWLEDGEMENTS

A book that covers over 80 years and is, hopefully, as comprehensive as this one is, and deals with many aspects of motor sport, is far from straightforward to write. Thus the support needed from experts in various fields is all the more important. I used to watch the scrambling, and later the rallycross, with Murray commentating but I was only a child, and thus am no great expert to say the very least.

The one person who has given more support and invaluable assistance than any other is, of course, Murray himself who has been exceptionally helpful, kind and, in line with what everyone says of him, incredibly enthusiastic. It has been a real honour and privilege to work with him.

I would like to very sincerely thank the approximately 70 people I have interviewed and who have contributed in various ways to this book. They are, of course, named within the book. The fact that most people made the time to talk to me, and were often very keen to be involved, is, of course, an absolute tribute to Murray.

In no order whatsoever, the following have very kindly helped with information, introductions, contact details or images: Jim Bamber, Marion Calver-Smith, John Colley, Tim Whittington, Brian Crighton (Associate Editor of *Classic Bike*), Graham Robson, Robert Glen, Carl McKellar, Jonathan Gill, Kerry Dunlop, Ellen Kolby, Eoin Young, Nick Nicholls, Jane Skayman, Dave Pickthall, Peter Higham (of *F1 Racing*), Jeff Whitaker, Peter Ferbrache, Margot Green, Margaret Cole, Gerard Kane (Editor of *Classic Dirt Bike*), Nicki Dance, Patricia Gregory, Pauline Hailwood, Sue Aston and Tom Whiting.

Although she is one of those extensively quoted within the book, I would like to single out Louise Goodman, who could not have been more helpful in providing introductions and opening doors. Mike Doodson has also given exceptional support, painting several vivid pictures and allowing us to quote from his writings. Talking of pictures, I would like to thank Alan Fearnley for permission to reproduce several of his fantastic paintings.

Chris Willows, who happens to be a good friend of Murray's and an old friend of mine, has been extremely helpful in providing photographs for the Touring Car and F1 chapters.

On our own team, my two closest colleagues, Claire Bryan and Abigail Humphries, have worked exceptionally hard and been brilliant at all times. Annelise Airey, Leanne Banks and Mary Fulford-Talbot have been a great help. Tim Parker, in the USA, has given wise counsel based on his tremendous breadth of experience in the motoring publishing world. My wife, and business partner, Julie has been as supportive as ever.

Working silly hours, you can easily miss a few howlers and create some prize Porterisms! One needs an exceptional person who not only has an eye for detail but is also highly knowledgeable about many motoring and motor racing matters. Such a man is Mark Holman, in New Zealand, and my unqualified thanks to him for reading all the chapters.

As ever with these books, Andy Garman, the designer, deserves the most enormous credit. He has combined very hard work with tremendous creative ability. I cannot stress enough the role Andy has played in creating this book.

As a number of people have mentioned to me, Elizabeth Walker is a quite exceptional lady who has given Murray extraordinary support for nearly 50 years. She has also entered into the spirit of this book with kindness and practical assistance.

Finally, my heartfelt thanks go to Murray himself. We have had enormous fun and I hope you will too as you leaf through these pages that recount, in a rather different way, the story of a truly remarkable man.

INTRODUCTION

This is a new experience for me - writing an Introduction to a book about myself which someone else has put together - and 'put together' are the key words for what charming workaholic and motor sport enthusiast Philip Porter has done.

As a great admirer of the superb 'Scrapbooks' that he has produced covering the brilliant careers of Sir Stirling Moss and Graham Hill, I was immensely flattered when he suggested that we do one together on me. 'Together' is the wrong word, though, for my involvement has been minimal whereas Philip's tireless application in assembling a unique words-and-pictures record of my long and happy life has been awe-inspiring. As he points out I have been around the motor sport scene for a long time and have been lucky enough to be at, and talk about, virtually every major form of competition involving engines and wheels. In the process I've travelled the world and been associated with countless outstanding personalities from Formula One immortals Juan Manuel Fangio to Michael Schumacher, motor cycle legends Stanley Woods to Mick Doohan, touring car champions Andy Rouse to Andy Priaulx, motocross heroes Arthur Lampkin to Dave Thorpe and rallycross stars John Taylor to Martin Schanche. Plus so many great people in their teams and the media. Oh, and power boats and trucks too.

One inevitably loses touch with people when so many of them are involved over such a long period but Philip has not only, patiently and industriously, found an amazing number of them but has persuaded them to reminisce about my involvement with their sporting lives. Some of the things they have said have even been news to me and they have reminded me, vividly and emotionally, of why I love motor sport and the very special people who inhabit it. This is a book whose illustrations, and the memories they recall, tug at my heart strings and will, I hope, amuse and interest you.

If you read Philip's Acknowledgements, you'll think we sound like a mutual admiration society. If you do, it will be because I am overwhelmed by what I regard as a 'Porter tour de force' and because in producing this book on my life and times we have got on like a house on fire. So, thank you Philip and thank you, kind reader, for investing your hard-earned money in your copy. If you enjoy it half as much as I've enjoyed my life, I shall be well pleased.

Murray Walker

Mutual Admiration Society – Part Two! Murray is too, too kind in his over-generous comments. Though it pains me, I do have to take issue with him on several points, not least of which is his typically modest statement about his minimal involvement. In reality, Murray, as you would expect of Murray, has been totally committed from his first email and has put a very great deal of time and effort into this book. He has dug deep into his archives to produce a welter of fascinating material that is as varied, not surprisingly, as his remarkable life.

We have conducted many long interviews. He has made copious suggestions as to victims with whom to talk. He has checked every single word and he has written 95% of the captions, as evidenced by the quote marks where appropriate.

He calls me a workaholic. It takes one to know one. While we have been working on this, Murray has been laid low on occasions by a nasty virus. Like a true trooper, he has stuck to it even when under the weather. Throughout, he has shown such patience, sensitivity and kindness.

Murray's oft-used phrase, "Unless I am much mistaken," was one of Sherlock Holmes's favourite sayings. Holmes said of Watson that he was, "The one fixed point in a changing age". It could be applied to Murray. Indeed, they were remarkably similar, having absolute integrity, being intensely patriotic, totally loyal, courageous and full of boyish enthusiasm.

Enough of the mutual back-slapping. As an author, I am very fortunate indeed to have such a wonderful subject to write about. Murray has packed many lives in his one long one. I hope this book will paint a vivid picture of the incredible variety of his first 84 years. Like all our 'Scrapbooks', you can dip in and out, or read from cover to cover. I very much hope that, thanks to Murray's amazing life and the tremendous contributions from over 70 people who have played some part in that extraordinary life, that you will find it very difficult to put down.

I must pay tribute to our mutual friend, Sir Stirling Moss. If Stirling had not kept wonderful scrapbooks, I would have never had the idea for this series. If he had not agreed to me doing the first 'Scrapbook' with him, the concept would never have become a reality and we would not be here now!

It has been an overwhelming privilege to write about Murray, a man who is adored, respected and loved by tens and tens and tens of millions around the globe.

Philip Porter

Early Years

Graeme Murray Walker was born on October 10, 1923. His parents, Graham and Elsie, lived in Hall Green, a suburb to the south of Birmingham city centre, neighbouring Moseley and Edgbaston. They lived in Reddings Lane, not too far from The Reddings, Moseley's well-known rugby ground and the world-famous Edgbaston cricket ground. However, the young Murray, as he was always known, would not take to either sport as, by his own admission, his hand and eye co-ordination was not one of his finer qualities. Sport, though, was to dominate much of his life for more than 50 years.

Little Murray was born into a comfortable middle-class lifestyle. His maternal grandfather, Harry Spratt, was a successful gentlemen's outfitter and draper in Leighton Buzzard in Bedfordshire and his attractive and intelligent daughter enjoyed a privileged upbringing. Murray's paternal grandfather, William Walker of Aberdeen, was equally affluent, holding the position of Company Secretary of the famous Union Castle shipping line. William, and his wife Jessie, had no less than four sons and two daughters. The youngest of the sons, Graham, was mad keen on motor bikes.

It was hardly surprising, therefore, that when he served with the Royal Engineers during the first world war, he was a despatch rider. Injured in France by a German shell, he was convalescing in Leighton Buzzard. There Graham met, and courted, Elsie and they were married soon afterwards. Murray then made a dramatic arrival for the doctor assisting his birth told Graham he had to choose between wife or son, as only one could survive. Graham decisively instructed that, at all costs, his wife must take priority but, happily, both made it. Indeed, Elsie lived to celebrate her century, plus one.

Graham, with his overriding passion for motor bikes, was carving out a successful career racing them and tuning examples for others. Due to his father's increasing success, Murray had the unusual situation of having a famous father. Though the son had not, at this stage, inherited the father's love of two-wheeled machines, he benefited from broadening his young horizons by visiting many European countries when such travel, especially for youngsters, was exceptionally rare.

As we shall see, much of Murray's life would revolve around the charismatic TT races in the Isle of Man which were integral to the history of motor cycle racing and would witness heroes and tragedies in full measure. Graham was to enjoy considerable success on this uniquely challenging course. He was a works rider for Birmingham-based Norton when Murray was born but in 1925 became Competitions Manager for the prestigious Sunbeam company which dictated a move to Wolverhampton. Three years later, the family moved again, this time to Coventry, to Rudge-Whitworth, where Walker became Sales and Competition Director. Shortly afterwards, with a sales office based in London, and Elsie's preference for the south, the family moved to Enfield in Middlesex where Murray was to live until he married 31 years later.

Murray's education began at home with a governess, followed by a brace of prep schools before moving to Highgate, the public school to which his father had gone.

When the second world war broke out, the school was evacuated to North Devon, where Murray remained until he left, aged 18, in 1941. He had done reasonably well academically, gaining his School Certificate and taken up shooting, at which he excelled, becoming Captain of Shooting and Company Sergeant Major of the School Corps. It was a pretty idyllic life, which Murray enjoyed to the full but, thanks to Mr. Hitler, it could not last.

Eager to fight for King and country, Murray reasoned that if you volunteered you had some choice as to which area of the services you served in, as opposed to the conscripts having no say in their destiny at all. Murray's eyesight precluded fanciful notions of being a fighter pilot so he chose the next best form of mechanised transport – tanks.

He was accepted but, curiously, there was a shortage of equipment on which to train and so he was told to fill his time until formally called up. This he did very successfully, winning one of just 12 annual business training scholarships awarded by the Dunlop Rubber Company. Then, about a year later, in October 1942, he reported to the 30th Primary Training Wing at Bovington in Dorset. The maturing process was about to be hastened and completed in no uncertain terms.

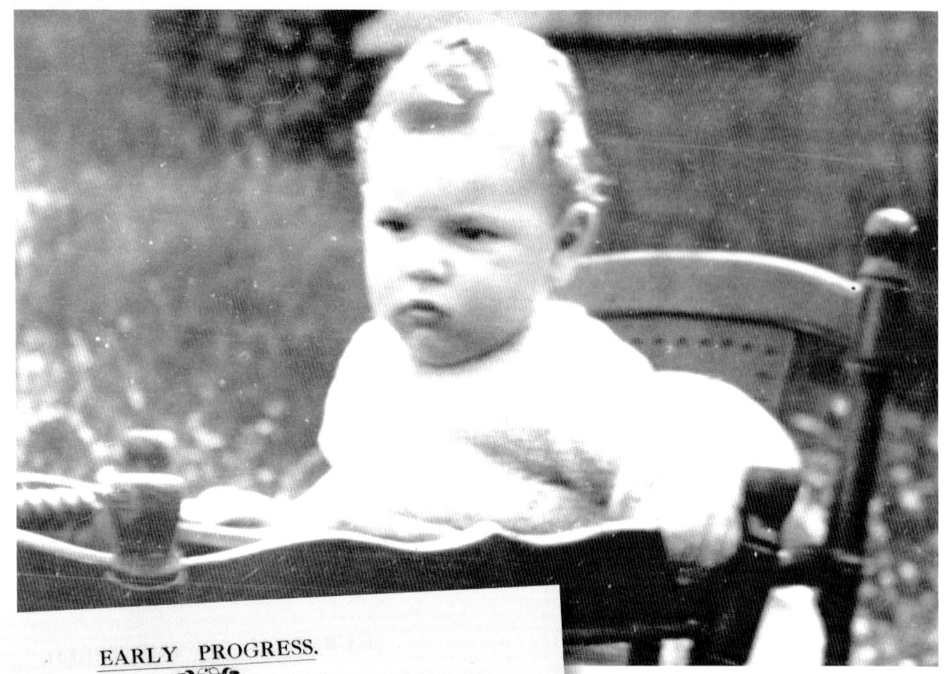

Murray, aged one, in his first commentary box. Although, he did not stand but sat in those early days, he still clearly had an impact

EARLY PROGRESS.

First Birthday Notes Spent at 9 Clarence Rd. Moseley O' Lawn

First Stood Alone 13 mths.

First Words 'Bang' 'Dada' Date 9 mths.

First Sentence 'Look Mummy pretty wow-wow!' Date

Favourite Expression 'Oh Bang!'

First Tune Date

Funny Sayings

Very fond of dogs, horses & any-thing mechanical.
Count 1-4 at 2 years.

25

A telling comment is made with reference to his interest, from a very early age, in 'anything mechanical'. He would employ his favourite phrase a good deal in later life and especially when commentating on rallycross!

Blotter

The commencement of solid food denotes an important "stepping stone" in baby's life. When about 9 months old "Ovaltine" Rusks may be given with the utmost advantage. Babies show a keen delight in nibbling these choice crisp Rusks. They break up readily and safely in the mouth, and give just the assistance needed to bring the little teeth through the gums.

OVALTINE
RUSKS

Deliciously crisp, appetising, easily digested and much more nourishing than ordinary rusks or biscuits.

By his third year, Murray was sporting a particularly fine head of hair, which would not be one his characteristics later in life. Here he is with his Uncle Leslie and his grandfather, both very snappily dressed for their time

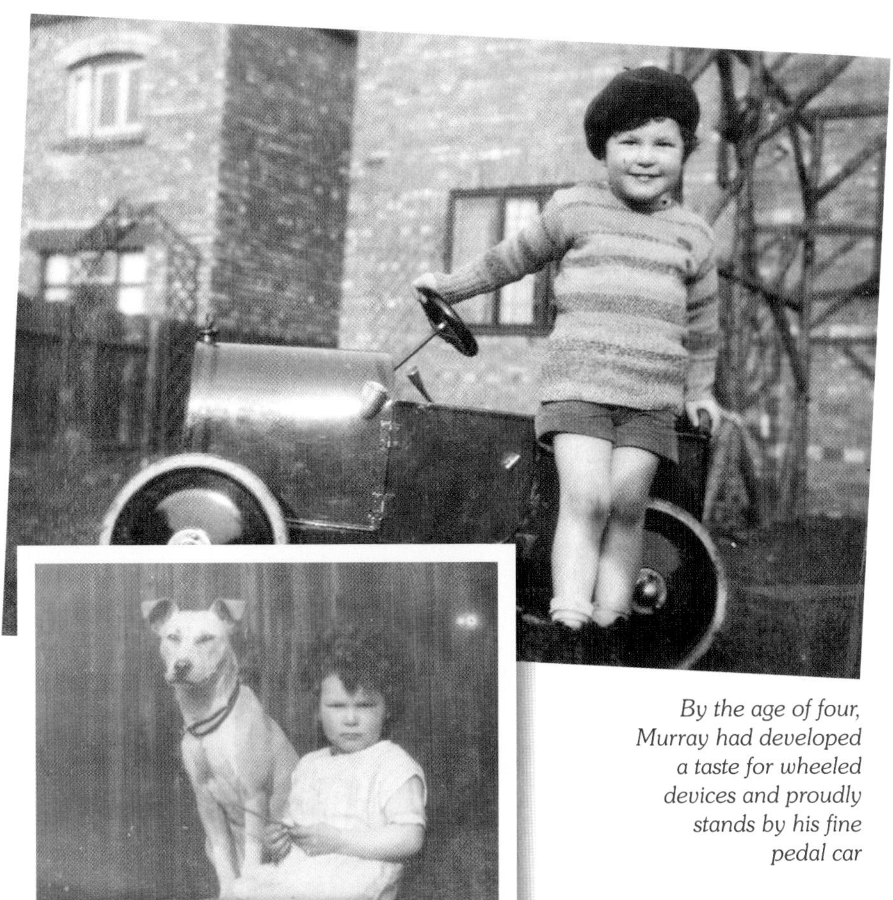

By the age of four, Murray had developed a taste for wheeled devices and proudly stands by his fine pedal car

One of Murray's earliest friendships was with Ben, the bull terrier and they became inseperable

Ben, The Bull Terrier

Murray Walker

"We had a white bull terrier and when we moved to Wolverhampton the next door neighbour came round and said to my father, 'I would advise you to keep your dog indoors as I have an Airedale which has killed three dogs'.

"So my father said, 'Well, if your dog has killed three dogs you ought not to have it. So, it is your problem, not mine'.

"To cut a long story short Ben, our bull terrier, and the Airedale had an inevitable confrontation. Bull terriers are very tough dogs and Ben killed him.

"But Ben was like butter in my mouth and he adored me and I adored him and he would let me do anything with, and to, him. One day, when I was about four, my mother said to the maid we had, 'Sophie, go out and see what Murray is doing and tell him to stop'. She knew something was amiss. The girl went running back to my mother who came rushing out, just as I had finished painting Ben green with a tin of paint I found in the garage!

"What happened to Ben? I think we got some turps or thinners or something – anyway he was okay!"

A Plumbing Problem

Murray Walker

"This was in the days when to have a motor bike in the 20s – my father was racing in the TT and doing very well as a motor cycle tuner and racer – was pretty big time, to have a motorbike and sidecar was big, big time, but to have a car was massive. Very few people had them.

"My father had a Bullnose Morris Cowley. My mother and I were about to set off from Wolverhampton to go to Liverpool and then on to Douglas in the Isle of Man for the TT races and I came running into the house – I was about five or six – 'Oh Mummy, come and look at the lovely water'.

"Mummy came out and I had been poking some pointed instrument through the radiator grille bars and into the radiator pipes and punctured them. The 'lovely water' was coming out as a waterfall from the front of the car. This was when my father worked for Sunbeam and my mother rang Sunbeam and said, 'Look I have this dreadful problem'. And, as happened in those days, they came round and fixed it – I am not sure how – and my Mama and I got to Liverpool and to the Isle of Man races in time, despite my best efforts."

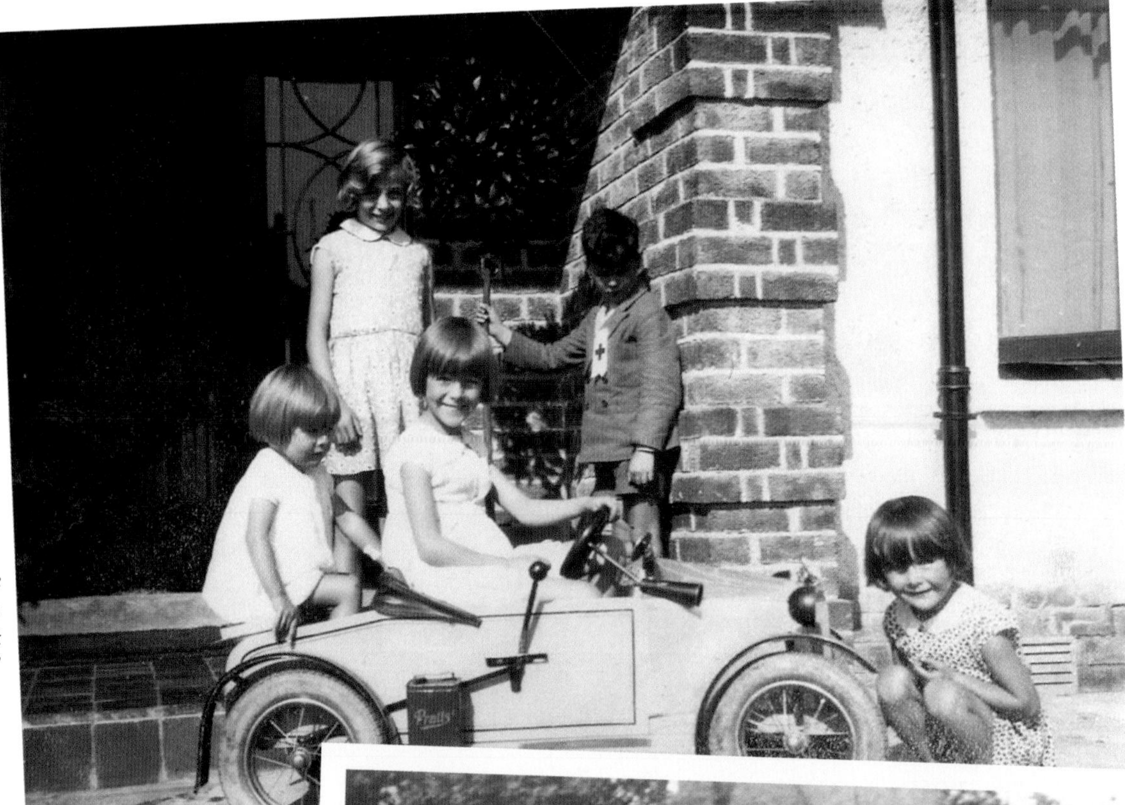

"In this picture, the tall one standing is Maureen, at the steering wheel is Joan, in the boot is Paddy, the one in front is Fay and the surly-looking chap leaning against the wall is me!"

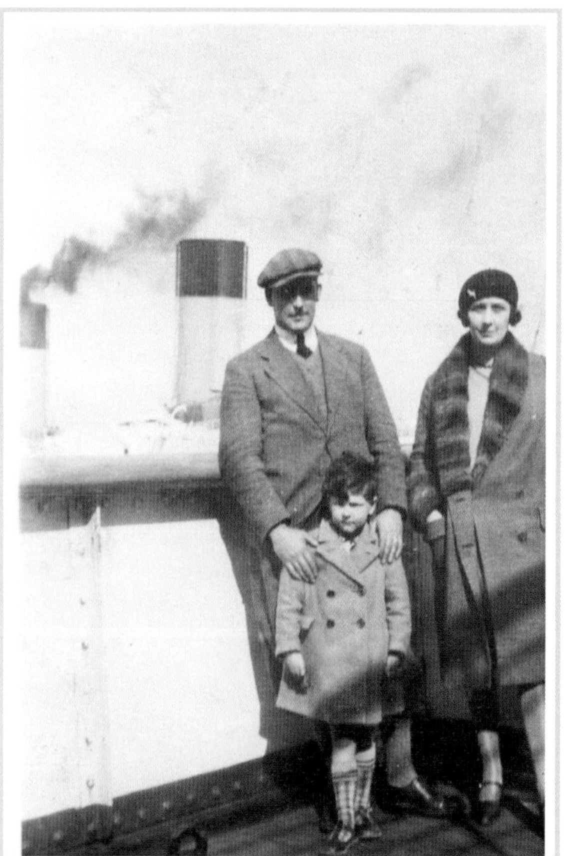

From an early age, Murray travelled extensively with his parents, which was rare for a child in those days

The Shaw Girls

Murray Walker

"My father raced in the TT and other races with an Irishman called Jimmy Shaw and they were both members of the Norton works team. Jimmy Shaw, and his wife Ethel, had a very prosperous motor business in Belfast. He was the Irish distributor for Triumph cars and for Lea Francis cars and he had a son, Wesley, plus Maureen, Joan, Paddy, Fay and Barbara – five daughters, two of which were older than me, one the same age and two were younger than me, and we grew together as a total family. Although we lived in North London and they lived in Belfast, there was a lot of travelling to and fro – I would go over there and they would come over here.

"Over the years, as I grew older and my hormones developed, I fell in love, or thought I did, first with Maureen, who rejected me to marry a chap in the American army, and then with Joan, who rejected me to go and marry a chap who was a BOAC pilot. Then I fell in love with Paddy, and when the war had finished, I went to America because Paddy had gone to America, and we spent six weeks driving from Yellowstone Park where she worked down to La Jolla and San Diego – right across America with me hoping to get the job done, in terms of getting her to marry me. I didn't succeed and, with the wisdom of hindsight, it was right that we didn't."

The Walkers' neighbour, Alan Emerton, built this motorised miniature car for his son Brian, and his friend Murray, to enjoy

One of the first places eminent motor cycle racer Graham Walker took his son was to the Isle of Man for the TT races. Multiple TT winner, Alec Bennett, is fixing Murray's model plane in the gardens of the Castle Mona Hotel where they stayed in Douglas. In the background, on the left, is Bill Mansell, Managing Director of Norton Motors and his son Derek - note the plus fours!

This young man is now aged 11

Motorised Transport

Murray Walker

"I had a great friend, Brian Emerton, who lived up the road, and his father Alan was a very good practical engineer and he built a little car with a Royal Enfield motor cycle engine in it. We had a very big garden and so did they and Brian and I used to charge up and down the road and round the gardens. This is my parents' friends, Joe Woodhouse and his wife, Rita, doing what Brian and I did, actually, with the trailer on the back."

Two of the Walker family's great friends were Joe and Rita Woodhouse. Joe was the MG car distributor for Germany and used to take Murray to the pre-war Grands Prix at Donington, so memorably dominated by the mighty Mercedes-Benz and Auto Union works cars

Ethel Shaw and Elsie Walker preparing a Triumph Dolomite for the Bangor Concours d'Elegance of August, 1931, and in which they finished first in class

With friends, Peter and Pat, in suitably sporting machinery in 1938. By now Murray was wearing spectacles, as they were then known

Floating friends on Southampton Water - Murray with Gordon Mitchell (centre), who was the son of R.J. Mitchell, the Spitfire designer, and best friend, Bill Galloway (right). The name of the third member on a postcard, please!

"Our strong-as-a-horse Labrador, Kem, used to pull me round our large garden on my Ski-Kar."

"The Highgate School OTC riflemen set to repel the German Wehrmacht at Westward Ho! The scruffy ones in blazers, in the front row, are Bill Galloway and myself."

Sound Advice

Murray Walker

"Although I am and was a very, very minor personality compared with the Beckhams, whom I met recently, I was always perhaps pompously mindful of what my father said to me when I was young on one occasion. My father, in his world, was very famous in his day.

"I remember him saying to me, 'I'll give you a bit of advice, son. Don't ever do anything that you wouldn't want to read about in the papers because, if you do, you will.' And I have often thought, 'My God, he was right'. I have seen so much stuff in the papers not just about Formula One people but about other people in life that they really would not have wanted to read about themselves."

"We lived in a private unmade road in Enfield, Middlesex and I used to ride up and down it endlessly on my Rudge Whitworth Autobyke. I also used it for my journeys to the Chase Farm Hospital Nurses' Home but that's another story!"

Graham Walker

To understand Murray, it could be said that you must first understand his remarkable father. They were to share a passion for motor cycles but what really made them extraordinary was their capacity for success in several fields, concurrently.

Graham had a strictly religious Scottish upbringing. His Aberdonian father, as well as being Secretary of the Union Castle steamship line, was friendly with Field Marshall Smuts, the South African military leader and politician. Apprenticed to a Clydeside shipyard, Graham also worked briefly on one of his father's liners as a steward. He had started competing on two wheels in 1912 and, with the outbreak of war, joined up, aged 18, as a Despatch Rider, which earned him a title of 'lance-jack'. At 20 he became the youngest Sergeant-Major in the British army.

A stray shell ended his active service, leaving him with a metal plate in his head and a damaged left leg which caused him to use a special brake pedal on some of his racing bikes. In spite of all this, between 1920 and his retirement in 1934, he raced throughout Europe with great success. In 1928 he very nearly won the most important bike race in the world, the Senior TT, retiring while in the lead, having covered some 268 miles and with just 14 more to go.

Two months later he had his revenge, winning the Ulster Grand Prix by a mere 11 seconds from the great Charlie Dodson. After racing, wheel to wheel, with their crude machines, for no less than two and a half hours, Walker won the fastest road race in the world and became the first to win at an average over 80mph. Furthermore, to combat the diminutive Dodson, the much bulkier Walker had tried to streamline his body by lying flat on the tank and sticking his legs straight out behind him, thereby overhauling Dodson on the Clady Straight on the very last lap. Thus, he not only took a great victory but could be said to have invented the prone riding position that was to be universally adopted.

Following Graham Walker's great victory, the production Rudge 500 was renamed the 'Ulster' and became an iconic road-going machine.

In 1930 the Senior TT eluded him again but he finished second and a year later won the Lightweight TT, which was extraordinary for a man who weighed 15 stone (210lbs/95 kgs). His tally of 15 TT Replicas was unmatched at one time.

While competing and clocking up a prodigious number of successes, he also held senior managerial posts at, successively, Norton, Sunbeam and Rudge. When he took up writing, he added a third career to his portfolio.

In 1934, his body having been subjected to a deal of abuse, he retired from racing and four years later became Editor of *Motor Cycling* in which position he waged many crusades on behalf of motor cycling, motor cycles and motor cyclists. At the time of his death, one obituary stated that it was Walker "who first made the public generally aware of the virtues and benefits of motor cycles".

He championed the cause of auto-cycles, which later became known as mopeds, and, with the outbreak of the Hitler war, his scheme for riders to enlist for special duties involving riding was officially adopted. Amongst the many who signed up were the great TT heroes, Freddie Frith and Geoff Duke.

Always a brilliant communicator, he adopted yet another career in 1935 when he became a commentator for the BBC, a role in which he once again excelled. Fourteen years later, he was to take on a certain apprentice and it is said that they made a fantastic double-act.

Always a worrier, Graham smoked too much and with the battering his body had taken, plus years of hard work, his health began to fail and he gave up the position of Editor of *Motor Cycling* in 1954 and took on a role at Lord Montagu's Motor Museum at Beaulieu. He was a tower of strength there until his sadly premature death, in 1962, at the age of just 66. Elsie and Murray had lost, respectively, a very special husband and father, and the motor cycling world had lost a colossus.

Graham Walker with a group of fellow motor cyclists. Achille Varzi, second from right, would become one of the greatest racing drivers of the pre-war years, beginning with Bugattis in 1928. He was Tazio Nuvolari's greatest rival and also drove for Maserati, Alfa Romeo and Auto Union

The Magic Of The TT

Murray Walker

"I first went to what I regard as the greatest motor sporting event in the world, the Isle of Man TT, in 1925. The Isle of Man is some 30 miles by 10 miles. The circuit is 37¾ miles of tarmac magic. It is country roads that blast through the Isle of Man, it goes up 1200ft Mount Snaefell, it goes down the other side, it goes through towns and villages, the riders doing, these days, up to 200mph. The lap record is 130mph. There is a magic about Isle of Man TT week that no other event I've been to has.

"I had a whole series of what I called 'uncles', the top riders of the day whom I used to meet at these events and would be staying in the same hotels as us."

"1927. Behind the TT grandstand in the Isle of Man. Racing kit was a bit different in those days - lace-up boots, horse-hide breeches, body belt and padded jacket."

"The 1928 all-conquering Rudge Whitworth team of Graham Walker, Ernie Nott and Irishman Tyrrell Smith. You can see that my dad was a big man."

Murray On Graham

Mike Doodson ...

"Murray's commentating bug was caught from Graham Walker, his widely respected father. Walker Snr had left the British army in 1918, badly wounded as a despatch rider, and become one of Britain's greatest motor cyclists. He won the first-ever international motorcycle GP at the Nűrburgring (1927), the world's first 80mph average speed Grand Prix in Ulster in 1928 and won a TT in 1931. He made a handsome living from other bike activities, from six day trials to sidecars and sand racing.

"'My father happened to be a peculiar mixture,' adds Murray. 'He was 100% a motorcycle man, and in his early career, in addition to racing, he tuned engines for people who wanted to compete against him. He also had a commercial career in sales and distribution with the great motorcycle companies of his day. When Enzo Ferrari set up his own motorcycle racing team in 1932, he chose Rudge-Whitworth bikes. And it was my father who sold them to him.

"'He became Editor of *Motor Cycling*. He was not a trained journalist, but although the magazine was on its uppers when he was brought in, he revived it. And then he went on to become a sports commentator. He was bloody brilliant: we worked together from 1949 until 1962, the year he died. Although we usually worked on the opposite sides of circuits, I think we were telepathic. It was a wonderful partnership.'"

Voices In The Night

Murray Walker

"In the Isle of Man, the Castle Mona Hotel was *the* place to stay. It was the six-star hotel, the ancestral home of the Derby family and I believe the Derby horse race actually started in the Isle of Man – not a lot of people know that. My father, my mother, and therefore I, always used to stay there. I had these legendary 'uncles' staying and they'd come down to breakfast in their leathers to ride in the TT – superstars like Freddie Dixon, Stanley Woods and Jimmy Guthrie.

"In the bedroom next to me was a chap called Denis Mansell, who was a Director of Norton motor cycles. These were the days when you had transoms over the bedroom doors and you could open the transom to let some fresh air in.

"So, I am sitting having breakfast with my mother next morning, surrounded by all the officials and the top riders. 'Mummy', I said, rather loudly, 'I think Uncle Denis is very mean.' 'Oh yes, dear,' said my mother. 'I think he's very mean,' I repeated even louder.

"Now children won't be put off and my mother thought, 'I'd better let him say what he wants to say. 'Why is that, dear?'

"I heard a woman in his room last night saying, 'If you don't give me five pounds, I am going to leave immediately.' Caused a bit of a stir!"

OCTOBER, 1928.
Mr. GRAHAM W. WALKER
Sales Manager of Messrs. Rudge-Whitworth Ltd., and WINNER OF FASTEST ROAD RACE EVER RIDDEN. A familiar figure at our West End Premises, where he is a frequent visitor.

"I know I am biased but I think my father was a very good-looking man - I still have his gold shirt collar bar. The premises referred to above were the Rudge Whitworth sales offices in London's Tottenham Court Road."

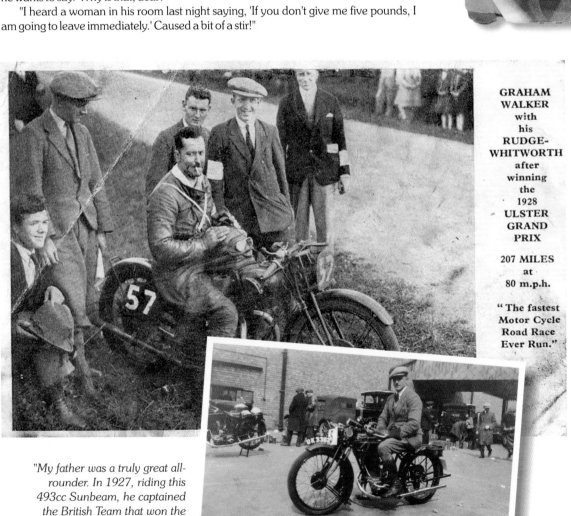

GRAHAM WALKER with his RUDGE-WHITWORTH after winning the 1928 ULSTER GRAND PRIX

207 MILES at 80 m.p.h.

"The fastest Motor Cycle Road Race Ever Run."

"I had my father's Ulster Grand Prix-winning Rudge Whitworth completely restored in the 1990s and it is now in the National Motor Museum at Beaulieu, on the gallery named in his memory."

"My father was a truly great all-rounder. In 1927, riding this 493cc Sunbeam, he captained the British Team that won the prestigious International Six Days Trial."

On Fame

Murray Walker

PP: "Did you always want to be famous, did that appeal?"

"I don't know. I grew up in the shadow of a famous father and I remember thinking, when people were always saying, 'That's Graham Walker's son', I recall thinking it would be nice if one day people looked at my father and said, 'That's Murray Walker's father'.

"I don't know to what extent, therefore, that 'being famous' motivated me. I don't think it has motivated me as such, just been part of what happened. I don't regard myself as famous; I regard myself as being very well-known in a very confined area of life which is motor sport and things associated with it. Yes, I love it. I am a ham. One of the reasons I performed the way I did on TV and radio was because I have a great passion for the sport which I wanted to communicate to the public. I did, and still do, get very excited about it and I like performing in public. I like after-dinner speaking, corporate things. It is a fact that you have got knowledge and experience, and it is very flattering that others want to hear it and I suppose to some extent you feel in a position of power because on radio or television they can't answer back and at after-dinner and corporate events they don't either. I have always been much more at ease on my feet and talking in public than I am in social conversations. At least, I have always regarded myself as being much better."

WE ARE NOT MAD!

By GRAHAM W. WALKER

The Famous Motor Cyclist.

MIDDLE-AGED fathers and mothers—lend me your ears! Possibly you have a son or daughter who desires, above all things, a motor cycle, but you hesitate to sanction the purchase lest peradventure your offspring should attempt to emulate the example of "those young madmen" who take part in motor cycle races. Give me a patient hearing and I will endeavour to make clear to you that you have misjudged us. Possibly your impressions have been gained from that curse of the suburbs and the seaside promenade, the brainless youngster who rides an unnecessarily noisy machine in an equally unnecessarily noisy riding kit. Truly Darwin suggested we have all descended from apes, and the psuedo-knut will be with us for all time, and this particular type loves to ape the racing man. Possibly the daily press has artfully undermined your judgment by referring in glaring headlines to "Pillion Deaths" and showing photographs of tumbles. They do *not* put headlines showing the thousands of riders who cover thousands of miles annually without mishap—this would, of course, not be sensational.

What manner of men are these "mad young fools"? Take a stroll down the aisles of Olympia Show. Do you see that quiet little man in a quiet lounge suit examining a machine? "Nothing remarkable about him," you say? That is Alec. Bennett, the world's finest road racer. He obviously is no "mad young fool." Indeed, he, like many of us, is married and has a family. He also manages a very successful motor business single-handed. Talk with him and you find a business man after your own heart.

Who is that good looking youngster talking with the accent of Dublin? That is Stanley Woods who runs a highly successful toffee business, despite his youth.

Graham Walker.

And that somewhat timid and depressed little man in the corner? That is Jimmy Simpson, the fastest man round a corner in the world and still one of the safest, as he never falls off.

You would never have thought that those every-day kind of fellows were your son's heroes?" The fact is they are business men in their own sphere of life as you are in yours. You take risks of one sort; they take risks of another. Both you and they develop a guard against the particular pitfalls of the respective businesses. But you ask, "What on earth is the use of all this speed?" That is the question most frequently asked by people outside the trade. Possibly you own a car or a motor cycle. It is entirely due to the racing of these "mad young fools" that you have a British-made magneto that you can forget all about instead of a foreign production upon which we were entirely dependent before the war. The sparking plugs you love to change if anything goes wrong are seldom the cause of the trouble. They have been developed purely by racing to their present wonderful reliability. That speedometer that enables you to tell "motorists' tales" to your friends and provides a check on petrol, oil and tyre consumption, has been developed in racing. Those tyres that give you many thousands of trouble-free miles of pleasure in place of two thousand miles of punctures as in pre-war days, have been developed through the necessities of "those mad young fools." Detachable wheels which enable you to mend punctures at leisure, were invented for racing in the first case. Those practically ever-lasting brake linings are due to the same cause, and so on throughout the entire machine. Racing has given you the present-day machine with its wonderful controllability, economy, reliability and lasting qualities, and has made safe for the million a wonderful means of pleasure. Riders are necessary for developing machines, as Robots will never be created for this purpose, and if I have convinced you that "these mad young fools" are really sane men acting as experimental engineers on your behalf, my object has been achieved.

Finally, I hope your son or daughter will get his or her wish, and the consideration of the tremendous labour that has gone into the product of their purchase will enable them to take a pride in what is the most flourishing of all British industries.

One last word—if they mould themselves in their riding on the typical racing man when the latter is "off duty," you need have no anxiety. Let them only beware of following the example of the brainless young promenade fop.

Graham's Mischievous Humour

Like his son, Graham had a great sense of humour. One of his tricks was to turn his foot 180°, a legacy of the war, to the consternation of those around. Once, when chased by a dog, which Graham had the misfortune to hit, he proved to the female owner of the unfortunate hound that he, Graham, had also come off badly with a foot that now pointed backwards. It successfully silenced her protestations!

Said, in racing, to be a bad weather specialist, during one TT, he rode out of a thick fog, slapped the great Stanley Woods, who was groping his way along, on the backside, and disappeared again, at a vast rate, into a wall of fog!

Graham Walker was not only good at riding a motor cycle, he was very gifted with words. Even before his retirement from racing, he was writing for the publications of the day. Later in his career, he became a great broadcaster

Father And Son

Murray Walker

PP: "Are you good at small talk?"

"No, I'm not good at small talk – not my scene and, funnily enough, while I was looking out material for this book, I found the most poignant letter from my father which I can't remember receiving. He was, in effect, apologising to me for being what he thought was an unsatisfactory father because he was away so much and worked so hard and he obviously felt he was not as close to his son as he would like to be and as he thought other fathers were.

"I idolised my father. I never thought of him in the way that he appeared to think of himself. I am a chip off the old block in many ways and that is one of them. If I am with a bunch of mates, motor sport journalists, I can give and take with the best of them, but in a social situation I'll hold my end up alright and hopefully even lead the conversation because I cannot abide being in a situation where people are not communicating with each other and if necessary I will jump in and take the lead, but I think I am better in a serious environment than a social environment, which makes me sound very dull."

Graham Walker (Rudge Whitworth number 57) rounding Clady Corner ahead of Charlie Dodson (Sunbeam) during their epic race-long duel in the 1928 Ulster Grand Prix. They were as close as this for some three-and-a-half hours

Just A Job But A Great Man

Murray Walker

"I think that, for a lot of sons with great fathers, growing up can be very difficult because they don't appreciate the situation they are in. I know I regard my father as a very great man, not only intellectually but in what he achieved in the motor cycle racing world, and the editorial world, and the broadcasting world. But when I was a little boy, we would go to the Isle of Man, we being my father, my mother and me. He would be riding in the TT races as one of the top men, and probably doing very well. My mother said I used to infuriate her because I sat in the grandstand reading a comic; I was totally unimpressed by the whole thing. As far as I was concerned my father might have been a plumber. Racing motor cycles was what he did. I didn't think there was anything special about it because I had nothing to compare it with."

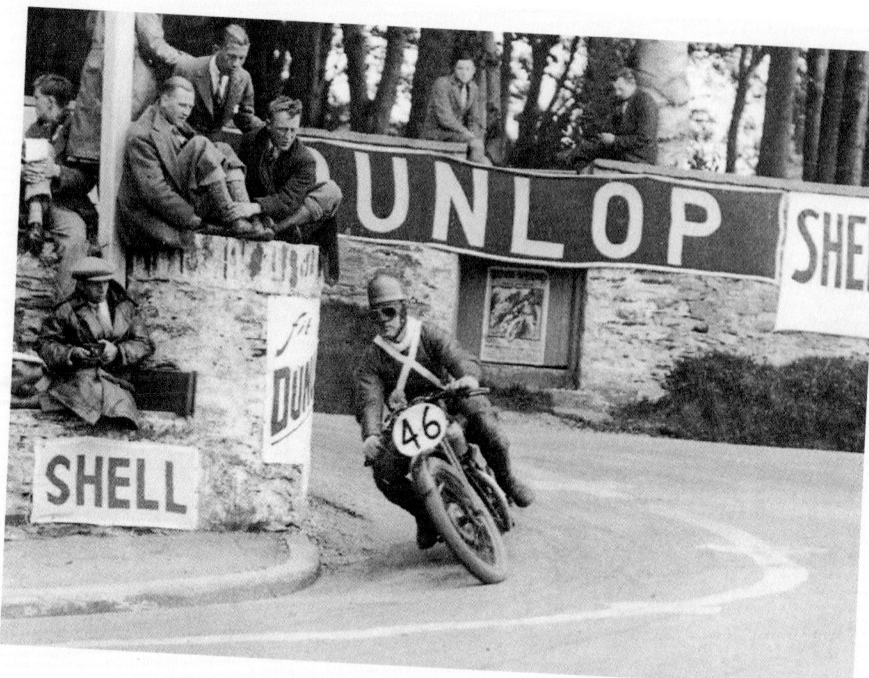

Graham rounding Governor's Bridge on his Rudge Whitworth in the Senior TT, 1929

"Victory at last! My father won the 250cc 1931 Lightweight TT, in spite of his weight, snatching victory from team mate, Ernie Nott, on the left."

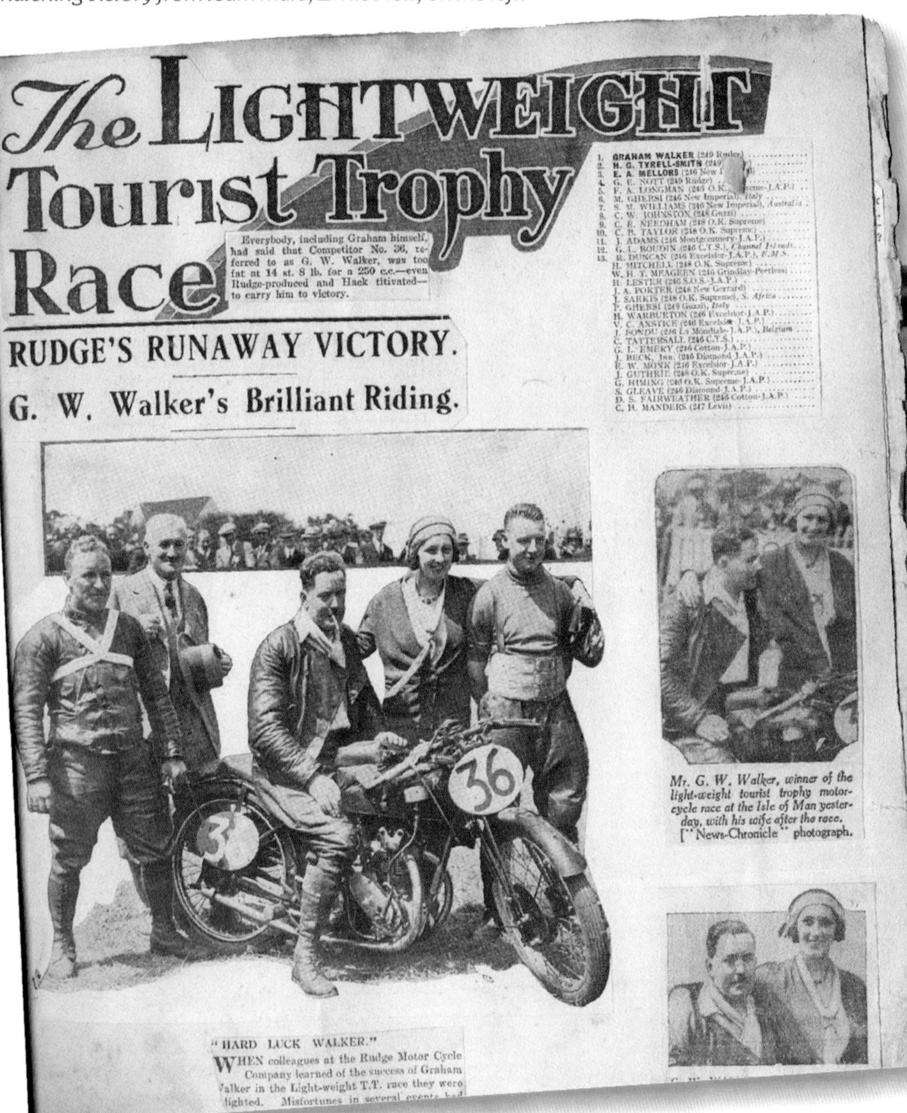

The LIGHTWEIGHT Tourist Trophy Race

Everybody, including Graham himself, had said that Competitor No. 36, referred to as G. W. Walker, was too fat at 14 st. 8 lb. for a 250 c.c.—even Rudge-produced and Hack titivated—to carry him to victory.

1. **GRAHAM WALKER** (249 Rudge)
2. **H. G. TYRELL-SMITH** (249 ...)
3. **E. A. MELLORS** (246 New ...)
4. G. E. NOTT (249 Rudge)
5. F. A. LONGMAN (246 O.K. ...-J.A.P.)
6. M. GHERSI (246 New Imperial), *Italy*
7. S. M. WILLIAMS (246 New Imperial), *Australia*
8. C. W. JOHNSTON (248 Guzzi)
9. C. E. NEEDHAM (248 O.K. Supreme)
10. C. B. TAYLOR (248 O.K. Supreme)
11. J. ADAMS (246 Montgomery-J.A.P.)
12. G. L. BOUDIN (246 C.T.S.), *Channel Islands*
13. R. DUNCAN (246 Excelsior-J.A.P.), *F.M.S.*

H. MITCHELL (248 O.K. Supreme)
W. H. T. MEAGEEN (246 Grindlay-Peerless)
H. LESTER (246 S.O.S.-J.A.P.)
J. A. PORTER (248 New Gerrard)
J. SARKIS (248 O.K. Supreme), *S. Africa*
P. GHERSI (248 Guzzi), *Italy*
H. WARBURTON (246 Excelsior-J.A.P.)
V. C. ANSTICE (246 Excelsior-J.A.P.)
J. FONDU (246 La Mondiale-J.A.P.), *Belgium*
C. TATTERSALL (246 C.T.S.)
G. L. EMERY (246 Cotton-J.A.P.)
J. BECK, Jnr. (246 Diamond-J.A.P.)
E. W. MONK (246 Excelsior-J.A.P.)
J. GUTHRIE (248 O.K. Supreme)
G. HIMING (246 O.K. Supreme-J.A.P.)
S. GLEAVE (246 Diamond-J.A.P.)
D. S. FAIRWEATHER (246 Cotton-J.A.P.)
C. H. MANDERS (247 Levis)

RUDGE'S RUNAWAY VICTORY.

G. W. Walker's Brilliant Riding.

Mr. G. W. Walker, winner of the light-weight tourist trophy motor-cycle race at the Isle of Man yesterday, with his wife after the race. ["News-Chronicle" photograph.

"HARD LUCK WALKER."

WHEN colleagues at the Rudge Motor Cycle Company learned of the success of Graham Walker in the Light-weight T.T. race they were delighted. Misfortunes in several events had

"In 1932 my father was no lighter than the previous year when he won but still took a close second in the 1932 250cc TT. I don't look too happy about it!"

Appearances Can Be Deceptive

Graham was always smartly dressed which could be at odds with the popular conception of the motor cyclist, especially amongst other riders. Apparently, one model of Rudge, with ML Maglita ignition, could catch fire if a precise starting procedure was not adhered to. When Graham, immaculately dressed, as ever, chanced upon a young chap struggling to start such a machine, he went up to this fellow to assist and warn him. Looking up at this pipe-smoking 'toff', the fellow told Graham to, "Bugger off. What would you know about bikes?". Apparently, the fire was quite impressive.

"In his early days, Graham Walker raced sidecars, as well as solos. Here he is rounding Ramsay Hairpin on his Norton on the way to finishing second behind the great Freddie Dixon (Douglas). My father designed and patented his outfit's unique sidecar and I have the piston from this engine in my study."

"Looking every inch as though he had done seven laps of the gruelling 37 ¾ mile course to win the 1931 Lightweight TT - as indeed he had. This was one of his greatest triumphs and he was very much my hero."

Wartime

Finally, the British army was ready for Murray. So, he left Dunlop where, ironically, he had been working at the famous Fort Dunlop building, and reported for duty on October 1 1942 at Bovington Camp in Dorset, between Bournemouth and Dorchester, as Private Walker, 14406224.

Bovington was the centre of tank training and the area was scattered with gunnery ranges, workshops, driving ranges, wireless schools and maintenance areas. For Murray it was all very different from the comforts of home life but he soon began to enjoy himself with the exception, that is, of sentry duty. Standing for two hours in every six, in full kit including tin helmet, in the freezing cold at the dead of night was monotonous in the extreme and not Murray's idea of fun. However, he quickly accepted the regime of strict army discipline, including the Orderly Officer's regular and fanatical inspections of kit, and was relocated, within Bovington, to Stanley Barracks as a Trooper in the 58th Training Regiment of the Royal Armoured Corps.

There proceeded six months of driving, gunnery, wireless and crew commanding instruction which included Murray's first taste of driving a four-wheeled vehicle. He had been riding the bike, a 1928 250cc Ariel Colt which his father had given him, for a while but his four-wheel baptism took place with a Ford 15cwt truck.

His training was now concentrating on tactics, weapons handling and enemy tank recognition. However, progress was interrupted when he caught pneumonia and had a long spell in hospital. Following this, he completed his training. Murray had always harboured ambitions to be an officer and he now went before the War Office Selection Board. To his great delight, he was successful and became an Officer Cadet.

This involved yet more training at Blackdown, before attending the world famous Royal Military Academy at Sandhurst, where they had been training elite officers since the 19th century. Murray was assigned to 115 Troop RAC OCTU, along with 23 other young men aspiring to be officers. Some six months later, after the extreme rigours of the intensive mental and physical training, 18 of the Troop passed out on April 8 1944 as Second Lieutenants.

With family and friends in attendance, it was a very proud Second Lieutenant Walker who marched past with the salute taken by no less than General Dwight Eisenhower, Commander-in-Chief of the Combined Allied Forces.

Now an officer in the Royal Armoured Corps, Murray sailed from Manningtree, near Harwich, to a prefabricated port at Arromanches. From here, he was assigned to a tank transporter column, heading for Brussels. In Holland he joined the Royal Scots Greys, which had been formed in 1678 and had one of the finest reputations in the British army.

The action started as the Greys pushed through Holland towards the Rhine. The fighting was very intense as the Germans, being forced back to their homeland, fought bitterly by demolishing bridges and employing snipers and Panzerfaust anti-tank weapons. At Udem, Murray had his extraordinary meeting with his father, described later in the chapter, and, on February 24, 1945, the Allied troops crossed the German border. Murray recalls how moving it was to see the crudely-written sign with the fateful words, "YOU ARE NOW ENTERING GERMANY".

After a massive 3300 gun bombardment across the Rhine, backed up by an assault from the 6th Airborne Division, they crossed the river on March 25. Slow but decisive progress was made towards the River Elbe and Hamburg. Then, with the Germans crushed, it was crucial the Allies reached the Baltic before the Russians. The Greys made a gallant dash for Wismar, reaching there on May 2 after 80 miles flat out and were the first British army unit to link up with the Russians.

With the cessation of hostilities, Lieutenant Murray, now promoted to Mechanical Transport Officer, was stationed in Rotenburg. In February 1946, he was promoted again, this time to Technical Adjutant. Around that time, he started a motor cycle club for the whole 4th Armoured Brigade, which did not go down well in the horse-oriented Royal Scots Greys. It was not the sort of thing that was done by a Greys officer! Following his clash of personalities, described elsewhere, with his Regimental Colonel, Murray was transferred to the British Army of the Rhine Royal Armoured Corps Training Centre at Belsen, of concentration camp infamy. Having achieved the rank of Captain, he was demobbed in May 1947 and returned to civilian life.

Murray has never actually taken a driving test, but all that was needed after the war was a certificate of proficiency from his Regimental Technical Adjutant, and that was him!

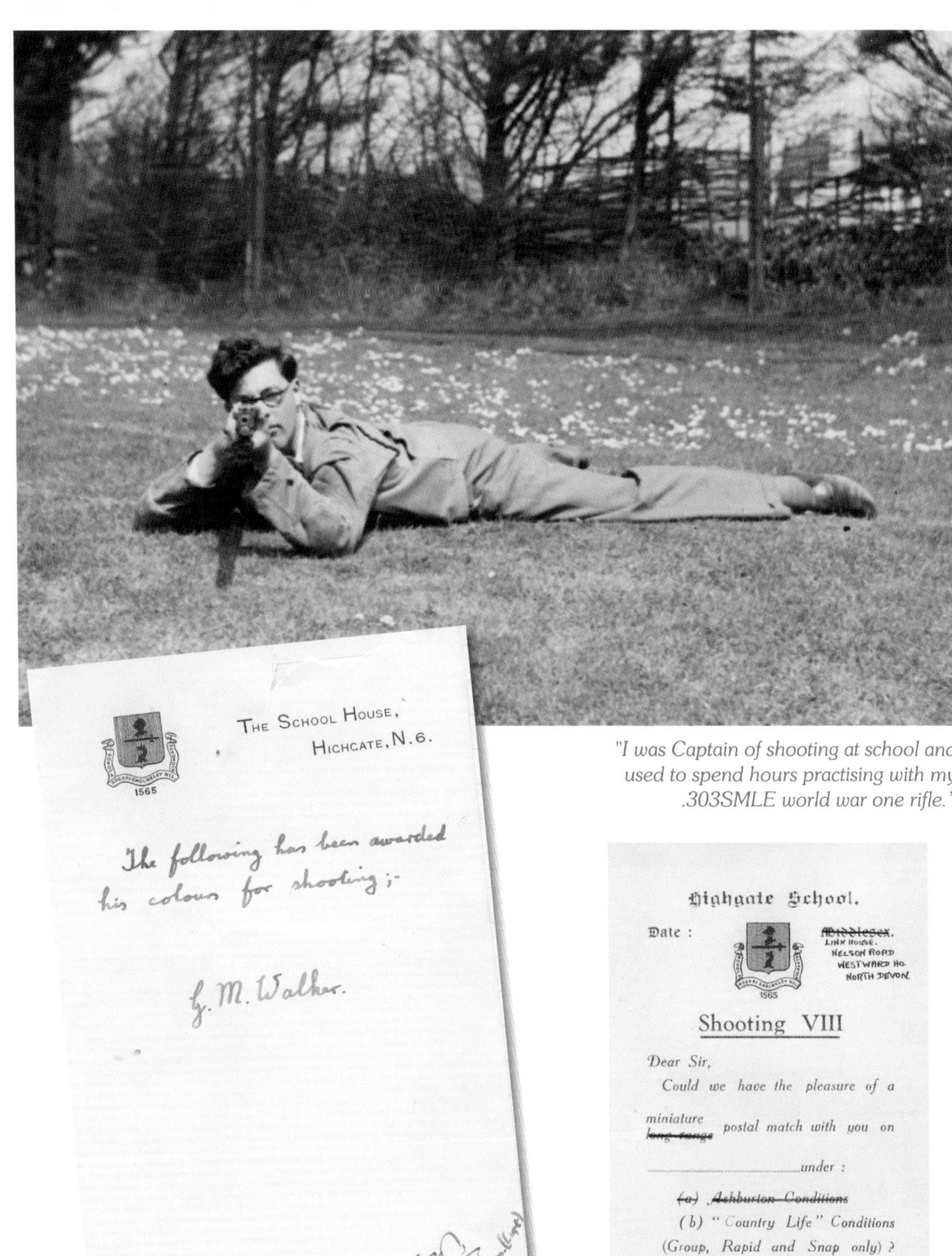

1565

THE SCHOOL HOUSE,
HIGHGATE, N.6.

The following has been awarded his colours for shooting;-

G. M. Walker.

21/X/40.

Highgate School.

Date :

~~Middlesex.~~
LINK HOUSE.
NELSON ROAD
WESTWARD HO.
NORTH DEVON.

1565

Shooting VIII

Dear Sir,

Could we have the pleasure of a miniature ~~long range~~ postal match with you on ________ under :

~~(a) Ashburton Conditions~~

(b) "Country Life" Conditions (Group, Rapid and Snap only) ?

Yours faithfully,

G. M. Walker.

Hon. Sec. Shooting.

"I was Captain of shooting at school and used to spend hours practising with my .303SMLE world war one rifle."

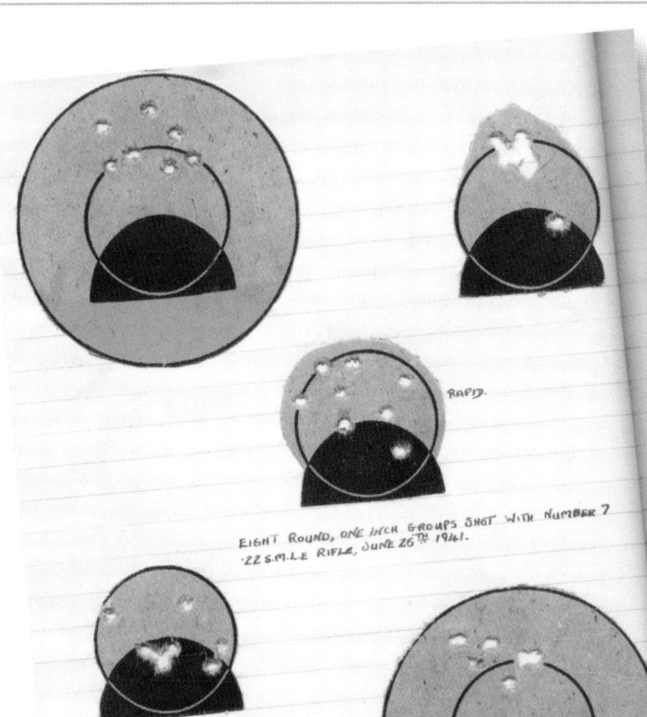

RAPID.
EIGHT ROUND, ONE INCH GROUPS SHOT WITH NUMBER 7
·22 S.M.L.E RIFLE, JUNE 26th 1941.

"I somewhat pompously kept a detailed record of just about every shot I fired on the .22 ranges. Here is a selection of my efforts - not brilliant, but not bad."

"Another extract from my shooting notebook; the Parker-Hale catalogue was my bible and their prices were not cheap, even then."

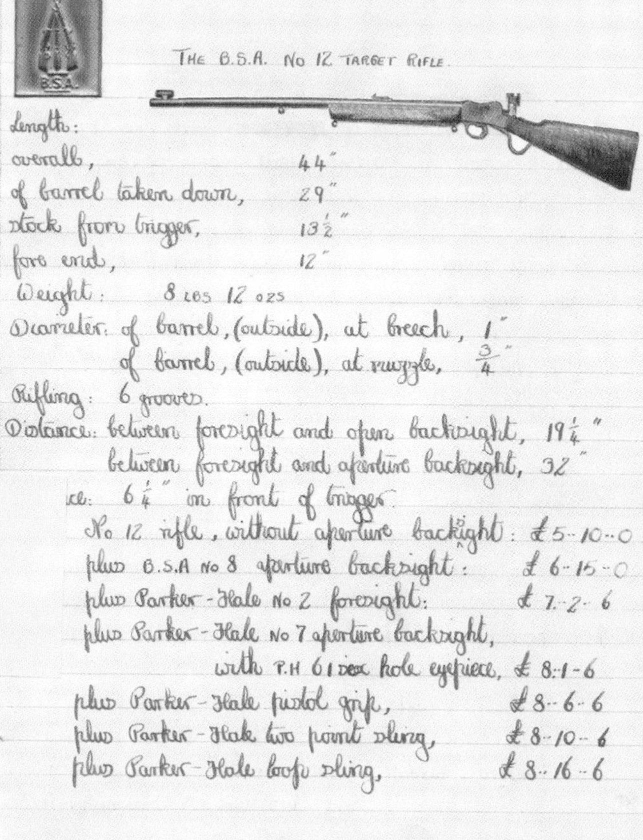

THE B.S.A. No 12 TARGET RIFLE.

Length:
overall, 44"
of barrel taken down, 29"
stock from trigger, 13½"
fore end, 12"
Weight: 8 lbs 12 ozs
Diameter of barrel, (outside), at breech, 1"
of barrel, (outside), at muzzle, ¾"
Rifling: 6 grooves.
Distance: between foresight and open backsight, 19¼"
between foresight and aperture backsight, 32"
ce: 6¼" in front of trigger.
No 12 rifle, without aperture backsight: £5-10-0
plus B.S.A No 8 aperture backsight: £6-15-0
plus Parker-Hale No 2 foresight: £7-2-6
plus Parker-Hale No 7 aperture backsight,
with P.H 61 six hole eyepiece, £8-1-6
plus Parker-Hale pistol grip, £8-6-6
plus Parker-Hale two point sling, £8-10-6
plus Parker-Hale loop sling, £8-16-6

"At home with my own .22 BSA Martini rifle and proudly wearing my shooting jacket, which was festooned with a achievement badges on the back."

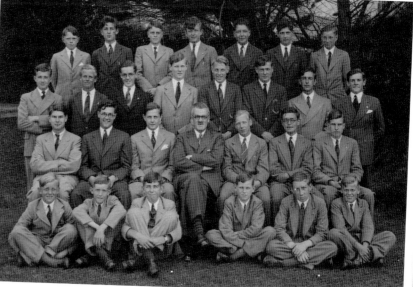

Sandhurst

Murray Walker

"I was there about a year and all the pre-war traditions still existed. We were in the same buildings and we had our own batman to look after us, and our clothing. The wonderful Sandhurst chapel was there, of course. I was instructed by the legendary Regimental Sergeant Major Brittain, who is one of the great characters in the history of the British army. It was extremely physical; you had to be fit. We used go on enormously long runs, in army boots with packs and rifles."

"1941 Highgate School Cordell House group. I am two to the left, as we look at it, of our formidable, but charming, housemaster, S. Kipping."

"1943 Sandhurst. The M23 side-valve BSA wouldn't pull the skin off a rice pudding but it got me to the top of the hill - just!"

The Last Laugh

"We did a battle course in Wales, where we spent a whole week out in the open in mid winter sleeping in pigsties and under hedges and all that sort thing. We ended up at the base of Mount Snowdon, and Captain Anthony Marsh, who was in charge, said, 'I want 10 volunteers to come and climb Snowdon'. I had been running round with a two inch mortar for the whole week and the two inch mortar is quite a heavy piece of military equipment with a hinge in the middle. The only way to carry it was with the hinge on the back of your neck, and a part on each side over your shoulder. Of course when you're running across country this thing was bouncing up and down on the back of your neck and your collar bones.

"So, I had had a week of this, but of course I volunteered and I was one of the blokes that got chosen. All of the others who had not volunteered were very smug about this because we had set off from a youth hostel in Capel Curig, a week earlier, then had been involved in all that unpleasant sleeping out and the rest of it. Those that weren't going to climb Snowdon were given a compass bearing which was going to take them straight back to the youth hostel at Capel Curig, where there were going to be hot showers and bed with sheets, and things we hadn't experienced for a week, while the rest of us were toiling up Snowdon. When we got to the top of Snowdon, we then went back down a goat track, a much easier way, to Capel Curig direct. The compass course, which the other people had been given, took them through swamps, bogs, across rivers with no boats, forests, and they got back about four o'clock in the morning, absolutely knackered. We were showered and in bed, and *we* were smug!"

"In spite of the fact that he was a daunting science teacher, and that he beat me in his study for some transgression, I had the greatest admiration and respect for my housemaster, Mr. Kipping, who wrote this charming letter to my father after I left school in 1943."

1565

Cordell House,
Highgate, N.6.

23rd June 1943.

Dear Mr Walker,

It was very sporting of you to bother to write, and also to send the tie, which I'm sure will come in most useful to someone in these difficult times. Thank you so much.

I was sorry to hear of your operation, on one of Murray's welcome visits to the House. The enforced inactivity must have been frightfully inconvenient and irksome for so busy a person as yourself. However, I trust the result is fully satisfactory and the inconvenience nearly over.

One of the most welcome features of our return to Highgate is of course the renewal of Old-Boy contacts now that we are in "calling radius". We have already been looked up by a large number of fellows, and it was particularly good to see Murray – and to see him looking so fit & happy. I'm sure his O.C.T.U. interview will [illegible] well; if he doesn't make the right impression there's something wrong with the Board! He knows how to speak for himself better, almost, than any fellow I've had. He knows what he wants to say, is perfectly definite about it, and gets it out without fuss or hesitation, but always with a modest deference which engenders confidence. I think his personal qualities will be a great asset to him in every situation of his life, – particularly as they are backed by a very sound fundamental common sense.

With kindest regards to you all, and again many thanks,

Yours sincerely,

S. F. Kipping.

Graham Walker, Esq.

Pirbright.
Gwyer-Gibbs
Royal Armoured Corps O.C.T.U., Sandhurst, 1943.

"This was 115 Troop at the Royal Armoured Corps OCTU - Officer Cadet Training Unit. I'm the one smiling in the middle. Seated (third from the left, as we look at this) is my great friend, Peter Johnson, with whom I joined the Royal Scots Greys, but sadly Ivan Troop (front row, third from right) was killed shortly after joining the 11th Hussars."

A Familiar Face

Murray Walker

"When the Greys were getting ready to take part in the crossing of the Rhine towards the end of the war, we had a particularly bloody series of battles fighting against crack German infantry regiments who were in their homeland, so they were really fighting like they had never fought before. And the Germans always fought very hard and extremely well. We were approaching the banks of the Rhine. I had a troop of tanks, which I was in command of. Every so often, of course, you had to pull out of the line, and go back to get refuelled and more ammunition. I was going back on one occasion and crossing a field, and I saw a party of chaps standing there, military people.

"I was sitting in top of the tank, on the top of the turret, with my legs dangling over the side. I looked at one of these people and thought, 'My God, he looks just like my father'.

"As we got closer, I realised it *was* my father. To say that it was unexpected is a masterpiece of understatement. A. what was my father doing there, and B. what was he doing in military uniform? So I jumped out and rushed over and said, 'What the hell are you doing here?'

"He had, as the Editor of *Motor Cycling*, got himself accredited as a War Correspondent, and had found out through contacts he had at the War Office where the regiment was, and had come to find me. This was on the eve of crossing the Rhine. I had about half an hour with him, while the tank was refuelled and took on more ammunition, and then off I went. It was, I would think, a unique experience. How many soldiers on the battlefield have been joined by their civilian father in military uniform, in extremely hazardous circumstances. That was the sort of thing my dad did."

Staying Alive

Murray Walker

"My war was a very different war to my father's. His was a very static war - trench warfare. Mine was just the reverse – an extremely mobile war, with tanks rushing across the country.

"On the day we met in the Rhine area, my mind was very fully occupied with staying alive. But it must have been a very emotional experience for him, A. to find me, B. to speak to me, and C. to leave me, knowing that we were going to be crossing the Rhine in a matter of hours, and that it was going to be a particularly bloody affair - and it was - and was I going to come through it? Thank God, I did."

"Paddy Shaw is the one that got away, but looks happy enough here. Not a very dignified posture for an officer in His Majesty's Army, though!"

Wartime Motivation

Murray Walker

"First of all, I have always led a very disciplined life, because I went to a public school and, though it's not like the army, public school life is pretty disciplined. You sleep in dormitories, have prefects and all that sort of thing. I think I have always respected authority, so that's part of my make-up.

"However, the thing that motivated me, and hopefully all of us, during the war was that we genuinely felt, indeed genuinely knew, that we were combating something dreadfully evil - Hitler and the Nazi regime - who had conquered Europe and his ultimate ambition was to dominate the world. He was an evil man, and he created and led and developed a thoroughly evil regime. Remember what they did to the Jews during the war, and I ended my war in Belsen, the concentration camp. So, there was colossal motivation to overcome evil, compounded by the fact that we were literally fighting for survival as a nation. France had been conquered, the whole of Europe from the French coast right through to the middle of Russia had been conquered. If they had got a foothold in Britain, I'm sure we would have fought like lions, but I'm equally sure we would have been beaten by the German military machine. Thank God they never got ashore.

"So, it was a compound of the fact that I'm naturally a respecter of discipline and enormously patriotic. I am very proud of being British, and I am even prouder of being English. The fact that I was part of something that was going to overcome evil, and enable us all to survive, plus of course the fact that I was in my late teens/early 20s, was colossally glamorous and exciting. I was very lucky in that whilst I had friends and colleagues killed and hurt, I came through the war unscathed. I went through exactly the same rigours they did, but I got away with it and they didn't. So I am not going to pretend that there wasn't an element of glamour and excitement involved, because there was. If you add all that up, it's a pretty heady compound."

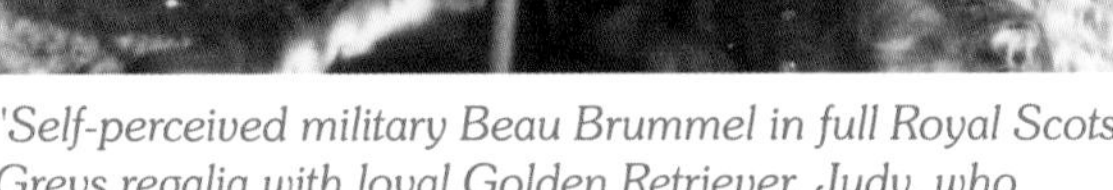

"Self-perceived military Beau Brummel in full Royal Scots Greys regalia with loyal Golden Retriever, Judy, who loved me as much as I loved her."

"Undoubtedly one of the proudest days of my life, that of my passing out parade at Sandhurst in 1944. Alongside me is my childhood friend, John Arthur, then in the RAF, who later became Judge John Arthur."

"Very few sons have had their father visit them on the battlefield but I have. Above, the very British War Correspondent shoulder flash he is wearing in the picture as we jointly examine my one-piece tank suit, which I later used while riding my motor cycle as a civilian."

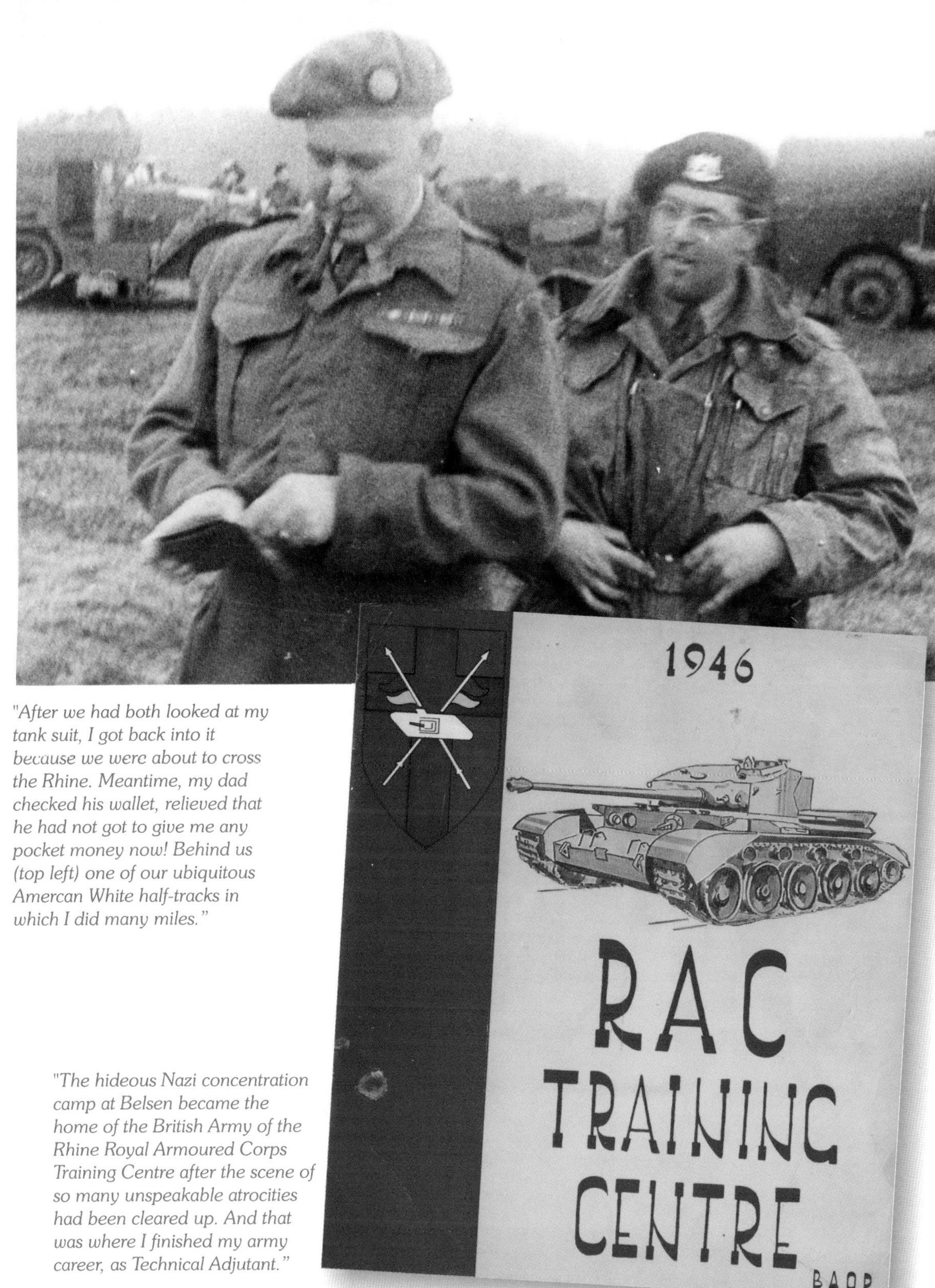

"After we had both looked at my tank suit, I got back into it because we were about to cross the Rhine. Meantime, my dad checked his wallet, relieved that he had not got to give me any pocket money now! Behind us (top left) one of our ubiquitous Amercan White half-tracks in which I did many miles."

"The hideous Nazi concentration camp at Belsen became the home of the British Army of the Rhine Royal Armoured Corps Training Centre after the scene of so many unspeakable atrocities had been cleared up. And that was where I finished my army career, as Technical Adjutant."

A Different Kind Of Fight

Murray Walker

"When I was fighting in the war, I was in the Royal Scots Greys, which is one of Britain's leading cavalry regiments. It was actually the last cavalry regiment in the British army to be mechanised. They were largely horsey people so, to some extent, I was a round peg in a square hole. But, on the other hand, because I did know about mechanical things and was interested in them, I was a bit of an odd man out in the regiment but a benefit to it.

"At the end of the war, I was made Mechanical Transport Officer and then was subsequently made Technical Adjutant. The Technical Adjutant carried a war establishment rank of Captain. We had a Colonel who was an extremely landed-gentry, horsey man and we were like oil and water, both in terms of social status and interests in life. I kept on saying, 'Colonel, the job I am doing carries the war establishment rank of Captain, and I am not a Captain'. He kept on finding reasons why I should not be promoted to the rank that I was entitled to have. This was in 1946.

"I was actually due to go on leave to the Isle of Man for its first post-war motor cycle race which was the Manx Grand Prix, which is in effect the amateur TT. The Colonel stopped my leave, which in my opinion was an act of vindictiveness. I put in an official protest. My father was an advisor to the Army Control Board and he managed to get my leave reinstated. It culminated with the Colonel and I having a colossal row and him losing his temper and putting in an official report that, in his opinion, I should be reduced in rank from Lieutenant to Corporal, a non-commissioned rank.

"At that time, as the war had ended, I was now negotiating with Dunlop, with whom I had been a scholarship student before I went in the army, to get a job there. I had had an interview there as an officer. It wasn't going to go down very well with them, quite apart from my psychological well-being, if I had turned up for my first interview as a Captain and turned up for the next one as a Corporal.

"I had to fight for my life now. You are entitled, as someone in this hazardous position, to write a rebuttal. I sat down and wrote one. As a result, Brigadier Mike Carver, who was the Brigadier in charge of the 4th Armoured Brigade, of which the Royal Scots Greys was a part - he subsequently became Field Marshal, Lord Carver, Chief of the Imperial General Staff - came to see *me* at the regimental headquarters - this was the mountain coming to Mohammed!

"He said, 'Look, you've been a bloody young fool, haven't you?' 'Yes, sir, I have.' He said, 'However, you are not to blame, but you can't stay in the regiment anymore because the atmosphere will be impossible. Therefore I am transferring you to the British Army of the Rhine Armoured Fighting Vehicles Schools at Belsen as Technical Adjutant and you will have the rank of Captain.'

"So, in the end I won, but it was a very grisly, unpleasant period. And, as a result, I left the regiment of which I was very fond, and had fought with, and missed being a part of. But I had no option but to fight for my life."

Road Racing

When Murray was demobbed, he rejoined Dunlop in Birmingham. The Midlands region, and in particular Birmingham, was the heart of the British motor cycle manufacturing world with companies such as BSA, Norton, Ariel, Villiers, Velocette, Royal Enfield and Triumph based there.

With his deep enthusiasm for motor cycles in all forms, Murray began entering competitions, fervently hoping he could follow in his father's footsteps. He entered off-road trials and raced at Brands Hatch when it was an anti-clockwise grass track, competing against future sidecar champion, Eric Oliver, and a young John Surtees, having his first outing. Murray also raced at the Cadwell Park circuit, amongst others, but two factors brought his fledgling career to a premature halt. Although he won a Gold Medal in the 1949 International Six Days Trial and competed successfully in the Scottish Six Days Trial and the Southern Experts event, being entirely realistic, he instinctively knew that he did not have the innate skill necessary to reach the top. However, something else occurred that would determine the course of Murray's life.

By now his father had become well established as the BBC's top motor cycle commentator, admired for his infectious enthusiasm and depth of knowledge. The Midland Automobile Club, which is second in age only to the RAC, had been running a hillclimb at Shelsley Walsh, near Worcester, since 1905, and it had become established as one of Britain's premier pre-war motor sport venues, along with Brooklands and Donington Park. In 1949, the MAC asked Murray if he would like to do the Public Address (PA) commentary for a combined car and bike meeting at Shelsley.

Graham was scheduled to commentate for BBC Radio but was forced to pull out at the last minute and the plan was, therefore, to substitute the chap booked to do the PA. Graham's advice was sought and he thought his son was probably up to it and was worth a try.

Even though the spectators could see the action, young Murray concentrated on describing every detail, laced with plentiful facts and figures, with a view to impressing the BBC producer. It worked; a week later the BBC asked him to audition to commentate at Goodwood. Following that, Murray was the BBC's second commentator at the 1949 British Grand Prix. Some 12 days later, he was in the Isle of Man commentating on the Empire Trophy and Manx Cup car races. In the latter, he witnessed a phenomenal drive by a young chap who would also make a name for himself, one Stirling Moss.

In parallel with his developing business career, Murray now became a regular, professional commentator, concentrating mainly on motor cycle sport. Indeed, he would be number two to his father at the BBC for the next 13 years.

That same year, 1949, saw Murray join the BBC's team for the Isle of Man TT races which he would cover for nearly 30 years. Most weekends would now be devoted to commentating and, if it was not for the BBC or ITV, then he would be doing the PA commentary for the spectators at circuits throughout the UK.

As the TT now had World Championship status, top riders competed from all over the world. In 1950 Murray commentated on Geoff Duke winning his first International TT on a Norton and the gradual emergence of the Italian machines that would dominate the '50s – Duke and Bob McIntyre on Gileras, Bill Lomas and Ken Kavanagh on the Moto Guzzis and Carlo Ubbiali and Tarquinio Provini on the MV Augusta and Mondial bikes, respectively. During the late fifties and early sixties, for many the golden era of bike racing, Murray was commentating on the exploits of pre-eminent riders Les Graham, John Surtees, Mike Hailwood, Giacomo Agostini, Phil Read, Jim Redman and Bob McIntyre. Japanese bikes were challenging the supremacy of the aging British machines and the dominant Italian makes and, led by Honda, would soon rule the bike racing world.

Murray was good friends with all the riders but he and Mike Hailwood had a special relationship. For Murray, he was the absolute best, both as a *bloke* and as a rider.

The mid-seventies saw the emergence of Mick Grant, who, in 1975 broke Hailwood's absolute lap record which had stood since 1967, Joey Dunlop, who would win an extraordinary 26 TTs, and the charismatic double World Champion, Barry Sheene, who Murray knew and befriended from his childhood until his tragic death in 2003.

It was an absolute pantheon of all the great road racing names and Murray was very much a part of it all.

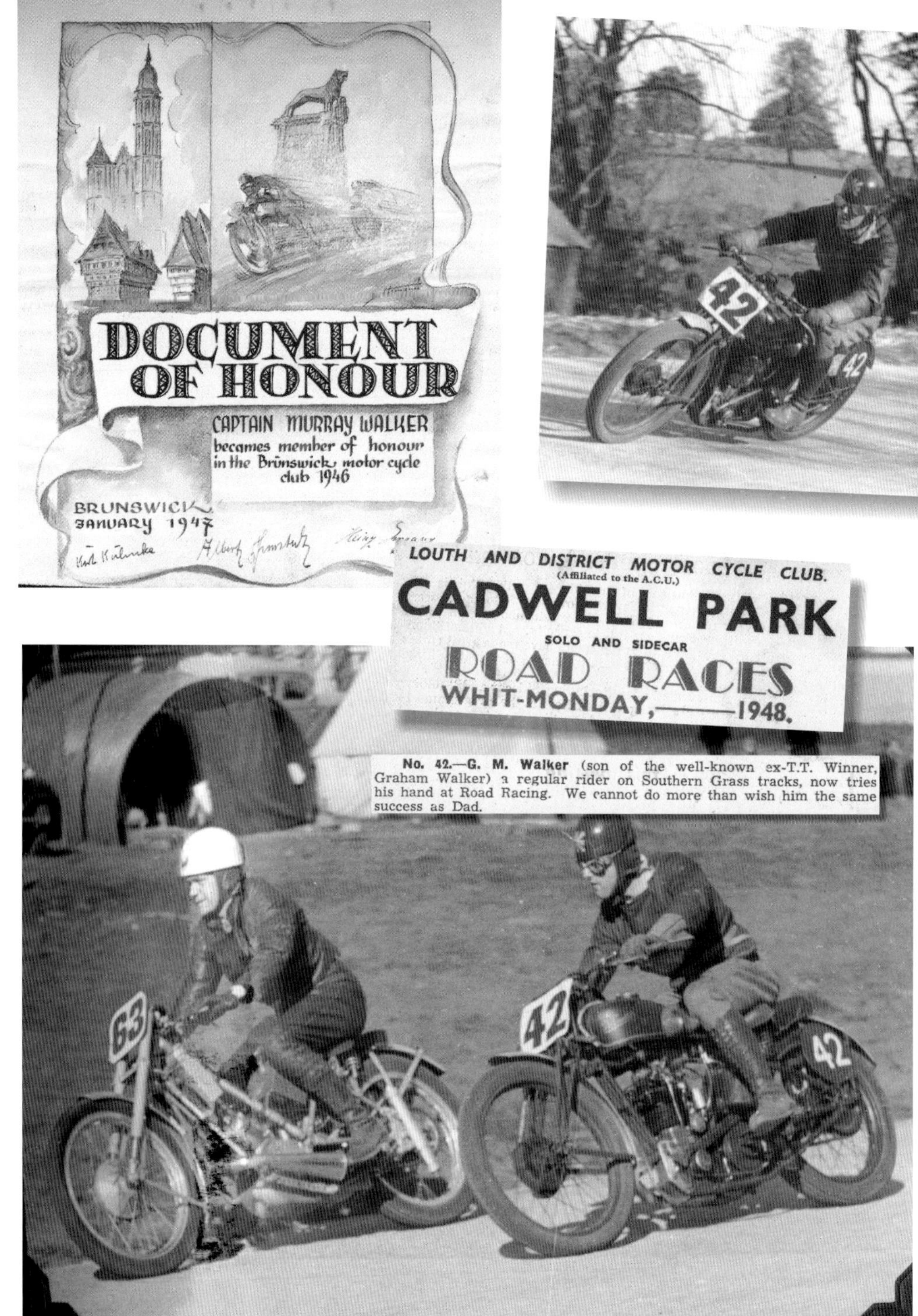

"After achieving the zenith of my Brands Hatch grasstrack racing career by winning a 250cc heat (!), on a dope AJS, I decided to become a star of the tarmac. Here I am failing to do so on an ancient KTT Velocette (note - rigid frame and girder forks) - can't remember who the bloke on the Scott was."

The Right Gear

Murray Walker

"After the war, when I was demobbed, I obviously continued with my motor cycle enthusiasm. I had a G3L Matchless, which my father had given me, a brand new army one in khaki paint, which I very proudly rode. The required clothing for a motor cyclist in those days was a tweed cap, with the peak at the back, a pair of Mark 8 fighter pilot goggles and a despatch rider's waterproof great coat, which literally came down to your ankles and had a very crafty series of press buttons, which enabled you to turn the coat into leggings, and a pair of waders - practically archaic.

"I was very avant garde, however, because I wore a brand new version of the tank over-suit, which I had used in the war in my Sherman tank, and a *crash helmet*. You may say, 'So what?' but in those days riders didn't wear crash helmets. My attitude, when my mates said, 'Do you think you're a racing motor cyclist?' was, 'No, I don't think I am a racing motor cyclist, but if both of us have a crash, and come off and bang our heads on the ground, I am more likely to get up than you are'. Although, to be honest, in those days crash helmets were pretty basic things, being just layers of linen gummed together to make a semi rigid cell. But, in the event of a very gentle tumble, it would have probably saved you."

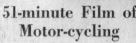

"The Walkers, father and son, test a 1948 prototype Sunbeam scooter which never actually happened."

51-minute Film of Motor-cycling

Midland Riders Among 300 Shown

More than 300 motor-cyclists appear in *Twist Grip*, a film made to give motor-cycling clubs a review, in 51 minutes, of their sport for the present year.

It begins with the Junior T.T. in the Isle of Man and goes on to the Scottish Six Days Trial of 900 miles, organised by the Edinburgh and District Motor Club.

Next comes the Victory (one-day) Trial organised by the Birmingham Motor-cycle Club at Church Stretton. A demonstration of riding technique is followed by the Sunbeam Point-to-Point, an exciting scramble organised by the Sunbeam Motor-cycle Club over a course of 1¾ miles at Liphook, and the film ends with the sidecar event in the Belgian Grand Prix, so completing the five different varieties of motor-cycle sport.

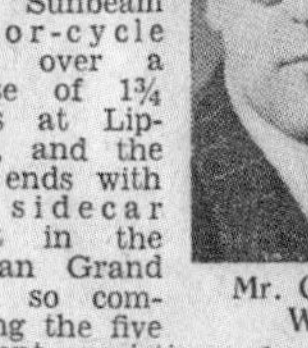

Mr. G. Murray Walker

Twist Grip has been produced by Jack R. Greenwood. Jo Ambor, Ken Ashfield, Roland Stafford, Norman Allin and A. T. Dinsdale have done the photography. The technical advisor and narrator is Mr. G. Murray Walker, son of Mr. Graham Walker, the former T.T. rider, and himself a coming man in motor-cycle trials. Both father and son are well-known for their broadcasts on motor-cycle events. The editor of the film is Mr. John Merritt; the sound supervisor, Mr. Richard A. Smith, and the recording is by Western Electric.

Midland motor-cyclists in the film are:—

Mrs. Briggs, Birmingham, B.S.A. (Scottish Six Days); Fred Rist, Birmingham, B.S.A. (Victory Trial and Sunbeam Point to Point); Arthur Frost, Birmingham, D.M.W. (Victory Trial); Ernie Nott, Coventry, Triumph (T.T. Race); Charlie Salt, Birmingham, B.S.A. (Junior T.T.); Eric Williams, Worcester (Junior T.T.); Jack Harding, Birmingham, A.J.S. (Junior T.T.); Pip Harris, Birmingham (Belgian Grand Prix); Cyril Smith, Birmingham, Norton (Belgian Grand Prix); Olga Kevelos, Birmingham, James (Scottish Six Days); Brian Martin, Birmingham, Francis Barnett (Scottish Six Days); Johnny [illegible], Walsall, Royal Enfield (Scottish Six Days); Johnny Lockett, Stretton, Norton (Junior T.T.).

"In 1949, my first ever motor cycle racing commentaries immediately followed my first ever car British Grand Prix commentary at Silverstone and they were on the TT races at the Isle of Man. I stood in the slip road at Ballacraine, seven miles out from the start, festooned with microphone harness, earphones and clip board. Superstar Les Graham nearly disembowelled me with his clutch lever when he overshot the corner. But I manfully stuck to my post!"

Parallel Enthusiasts

John Surtees

"Murray was playing with bikes at the same sort of time as I was starting. I had my first ever road race at Brands Hatch on the new circuit, which had just been built, which was 1950. At the same meeting a certain other person had his first road race and that happened to be Bernie Ecclestone, who was on a Norton-JAP and I was on a little 250 Triumph.

"Murray did bikes to start with and then went into cars, in the same way as I did. So, our lives ran parallel for a considerable amount of time. The biggest thing about Murray is that, however successful he has been, rather like Schumacher when he got up on the rostrum, there was a bounce about him, a sparkle and pure enjoyment. That's what I have seen in Murray. It all very much came from the heart – a genuine enthusiast.

"I haven't always agreed with him. I haven't always agreed with his assessment of other people, but at least he believed it and that is what comes across.

"He had a hard act to follow because his dad on motor cycling was very special."

"For years, with Stanley Schofield Productions, my father and I produced a series of 33.3rpm gramophone records (remember them?) of the TT races. We'd put sound crews all round the circuit, record the bike sounds, and stitch it all together with a linking script. Here I am interviewing my friends, the legendary Mike Hailwood (left) and 1962 250cc winner Derek Minter."

★

Graham Walker
(left)
and his son
Murray
will talk on Monday evening about the prospects of the British riders in the International Six Days' Motor Cycle Trial, which will be held this year in Austria

★

An Instinctive Partnership

Murray Walker

"My father and I were very close. We were more like brothers in many ways. When we were commentating, say at Silverstone, there were just the two of us, I was on one side of the circuit and he was on the other. We wouldn't need to say, 'Over to you Graham, over to you Murray'. We sort of had a telepathic instinct, and one would stop and the other would pick up immediately. We worked wonderfully well as a team."

Graham Walker

Geoff Duke

"Graham Walker was Editor of *Motor Cycling* after he gave up racing and he was a great writer. I used to follow his articles which were called 'Seen From The Saddle'. They were his personal experiences in racing. He was a bit unfortunate really because he came near to winning the Senior on more than one occasion but things went wrong and he quite surprised everyone by winning the 250cc race when he was a bit heavy for a 250.

"He was a very, very approachable man and he had quite a bit to do with me joining Nortons, in fact. Perhaps his enthusiasm for me as a potential road-racer made quite a difference. He was very friendly with Gilbert Smith, the Managing Director of Nortons, and there was this constant contact there because I worked at Nortons for quite a while and raced for them, of course. He was a very interesting man and wonderful journalist, and I think in many respects his son, Murray, has followed in his footsteps.

"They used to commentate together on the TTs for the BBC. It was terrific listening to the commentaries because they were so knowledgeable, the pair of them. They worked together so well because they worked instinctively. They will both be remembered as outstanding people and their commentating and journalistic abilities were just out of this world."

1960 signing records

Geoff Duke

Murray Walker

"Geoff Duke transformed motor cycle racing with his fluent style, with the fact that he was the first person ever to wear single-piece leathers, instead of those great big bulky things with padding all over the place. Geoff got a glove maker in his home town of St Helens, a chap called Frank Barker, to make a skin-tight, leather suit for him. We had this wonderful image of this young, good-looking, youthful, wavy-haired Geoff Duke in his tight-fitting leathers on his Norton – this was the dying years of the greatness of Norton. One of the reasons that Geoff was so successful was his bike, which was nicknamed the 'Featherbed' Norton, had this magical frame which allowed it to handle better than anything else. The frame was designed by a genius of an Irishman, called Rex McCandless, a great friend of mine who I got to know through the Shaw family in Belfast. He went on to design very specialised military vehicles for Harry Ferguson and transformed auto-gyro flight."

"The highlight of any TT, for me, was seeing my friend, the inspirational, multi-World Champion, Geoff Duke in action. For years, he dominated the TT riding Nortons and Gileras." (Mortons Media Group Archive)

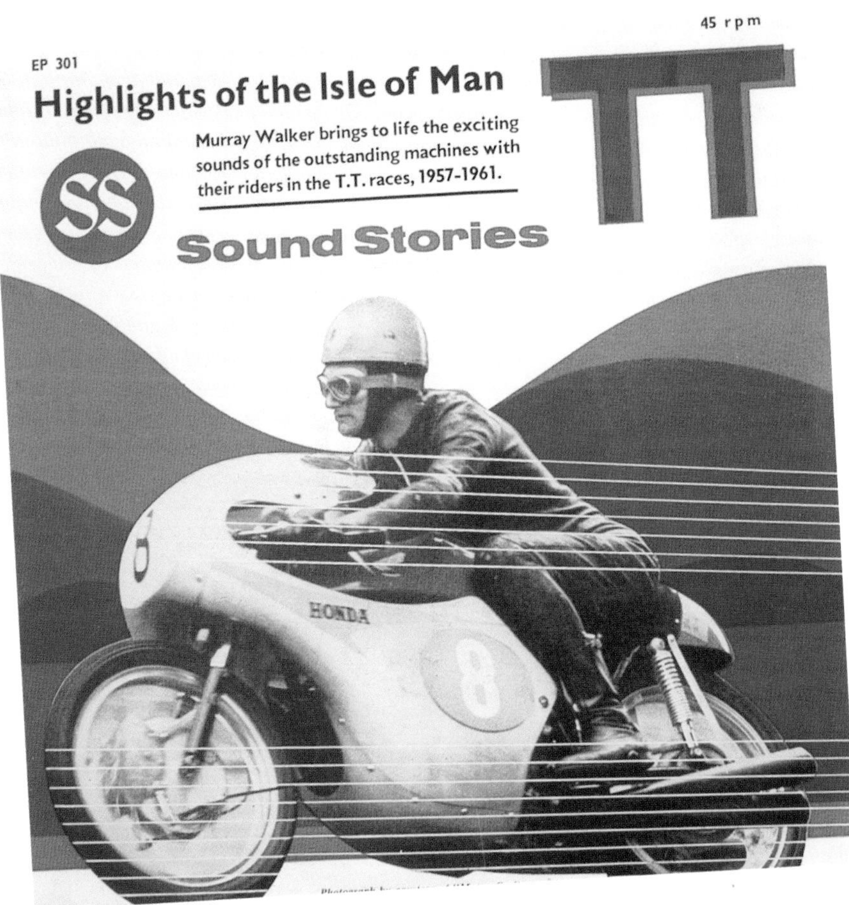

45 rpm
EP 301
Highlights of the Isle of Man
TT
Murray Walker brings to life the exciting sounds of the outstanding machines with their riders in the T.T. races, 1957-1961.
SS
Sound Stories
HONDA
8

"For years, the incomparable John Surtees dominated the Senior and Junior TT races on four-cylinder MV Agustas. This is his fourth win, the Junior race in 1959 where I commentated from Crag ny Baa. Its sound, as it yowled down to Brandish Corner, was fabulous." (Mortons Media Group Archive)

Sheer Music

John Surtees

"Graham was doing the commentaries at the TT and then in came Murray. In those days, you had no television and it was all radio and sound (on records). When myself and Bob McIntyre were in the '57 TT and coming off the mountain, Murray got so excited, and said, 'Just listen to this music'. We had a pair of four-cylinder machines, Bob on the Gilera and me on an MV, coming down to Creg ny Baa with the wheels slightly hopping and you heard the sound of the engine revs fluctuating and that was certainly a point when Murray excelled himself with excitement."

An Understatement!

Bill Smith

"In 1959, we had an horrendous race in the Isle of Man. There was the most incredible storm. I didn't have a face mask on and I finished the race with all my face bleeding because the hailstones had hammered Hell out of my mouth and all sorts. I came into the pits and Murray stuck a microphone under my nose and said, 'Was the weather rough out there?' And I was absolutely soaked to the skin and bleeding. I wasn't very amused!"

"After my father retired as Editor of Motor Cycling, *he helped Lord Montagu develop what is now the National Motor Museum at Beaulieu. My beloved parents lived in the East Wing of Palace House with their boxer dog, Clady, who was named after the Ulster Grand Prix circuit."*

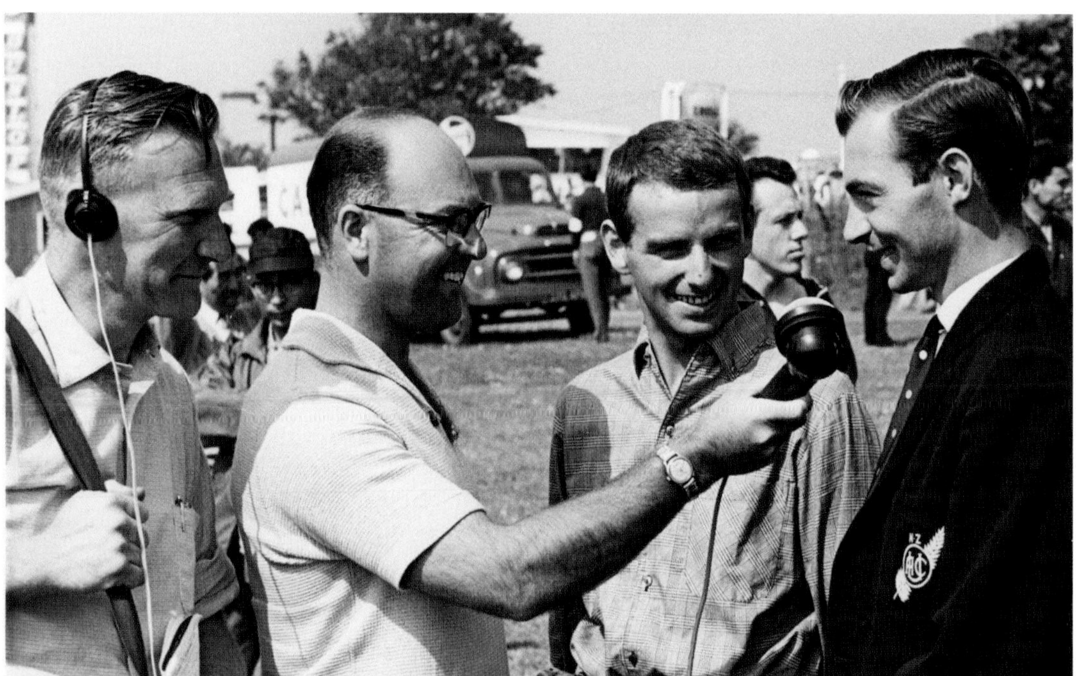

"Gordon Pitt, on the left, was the brilliant technician who put the Sound Stories records together. Canadian Mike Duff, on the right, later became Michelle Duff after a sex change operation. Ernst Degner, in the middle, is the man who defected from MZ in East Germany taking all their two-stroke secrets to Suzuki in Japan. They profited massively, and so did he. But MZ weren't too happy."

Mutual Admiration

Geoff Duke

"Murray was a fantastic commentator and he caused a lot of his amusement because of his occasional mistakes. He was quite a fan of mine, apparently, and I always found him extremely pleasant and very knowledgeable as far as motor cycle racing was concerned. In fact, I think his enthusiasm was more for motor cycles even than cars.

"He has a fantastic personality which obviously makes a big difference to his appeal to people in general and also his knowledge goes back so far, from the early days of his father really."

Murray's Tone

Tommy Robb

"Graham was doing the commentaries when I started my career way back in the '50s. Murray was a chip off the old block in that his love of motor cycles was second to none. He has never, in all the time I have known him, lost his enthusiasm for any of the sports. It's extraordinary when you think how boring travelling can become. People thinks it's a nice life and so on but you do get fed up staying away in hotels and airports and what-have-you.

"I always found Murray so amiable. He could talk on any subject – it didn't have to be just bikes or cars.

"I also, having done a bit of commentating myself, marvelled at the fact that Murray's voice was exactly the right tone, the right pitch and everything for the job that he was doing. The tone of his voice was probably one of the things that made him."

To The Point

Phil Read

"I think my first conversation with Murray was when I won my first TT in the Isle of Man, surprisingly on my private Norton, and my mechanic was pushing the bike up the finishing enclosure and Murray was standing there. 'Well done,' he said, 'you've won but why are you limping?'

"I said, 'If you'd changed gear 2000 times, you'd be limping!'"

14 MILES OF TAPE

Charlie Rous investigates the full production of LP records of the TT

THE "song" of a racing motorcycle engine is music to the ears of a true enthusiast. How true! At Christmas two years ago, demand for long playing records of the TT races at a leading West End store was three times greater than for the then current hit "My Fair Lady." And, if past sales are any criterion, there's going to be a big rush for the 1961 TT long-players released today.

However, when the idea of producing a sound story first occurred few people (including many experts) gave it much chance of success.

Producer Stanley Schofield nevertheless pressed on with the gamble, secure at least in the knowledge that he had made successful sound stories before in the motoring world. And, with Graham and Murray Walker in charge of the commentary and script, he came out with the first movement of his Isle of Man symphony in 1958.

The opportunity to re-live those fierce and thrilling moments time and time again made this record of the Senior TT a hit from the start.

Overture

The 1959 overture featured sound from four TT races—the Lightweight on the old Clypse course; the one-year-only Formula One events; plus the Junior and Senior.

Mention of the former events serves to illustrate the historical value of these discs, for these are sounds that can never be repeated. Indeed, to take this point further there is also that never-to-be-repeated crescendo of Bob McIntyre and John Surtees whanging it down to Brandish from the Creg on their Gilera and MV "fours," or the wail of the Guzzi Vee-8 with the late Dickie Dale aboard.

For 1960 the records were further improved by featuring sound from every race, and a thrilling moment occurs in the sidecar sequence as the microphone captures the instant Florian Camathias' BMW seized!

The illusion of actually being on the island is created long after the races are over at a studio in London. How else could Graham Walker flit around the 37¾-mile course in a moment, or be able to condense nearly two and a half hours of racing into twenty-odd minutes on a gramophone record.

However, apart from what goes on at the time of the racing, and after, just as important is the planning that goes into it beforehand.

Preparation for the current 1961 production began early in March with a planning conference. At this, Stanley Schofield, Graham and Murray Walker and chief recordist Gordon Pitt, outlined a scheme of cramming two weeks' practising and racing, interviews with personalities, plus the presentation ceremonies, into 88 minutes on two records!

This in itself is a monumental task, but with a rough idea of what they were after the party arrived in the Isle of Man.

Tape recorders are used to take the sound on the spot and days are taken up with searching out of suitable locations.

Here the difficulties start, for not only must the operator obtain a suitably balanced sound from the passing machines, he must also be in a position where he can see them clearly for the purpose of identification afterwards.

Another difficulty in this respect is that a location deserted on practice days will be crowded for the race and this affects the ingress of sound considerably, and similarly, may obscure the recordist's view of the road to spot the riders.

No fewer than 14 miles of tape were used in recording this year's events; this is equivalent to ten hours of continuous playing.

Gordon Pitt's first task on returning to the home studio is to listen to, and associate every sound with the written notes taken in the Island. From this he compiles a "sound cue" sheet which lists precisely the identity, duration and quality of every sequence from beginning to end.

From this master plan the production team selects the choicest sounds; bearing in mind that they are telling the story of the races lap by lap. There can be no margin for error for the team is well aware of the sensitivity of the racing enthusiast's ear which can identify the sound of any machine.

Condensed

Murray Walker now comes into the picture and he listens to the first condensed version of the overall recording. This may amount to a third or more of the total recording taken in the Island. He then writes a script to match the chosen sounds that will tell the tale, and this is recorded separately by Graham after considerable rehearsal.

Timed to the instant, the two separate recordings are then played into each other and picked up by a third machine; by manipulating a most complex arrangement of knobs and switches, Gordon Pitt fades in and out the sound of the machines with the voice of Graham Walker taken in the studio weeks after, and thus emerges an end product which sounds as if it were all done on the spot.

"Father, Graham, interviews Mike Hailwood, in my opinion, the greatest motor racing cyclist of all time, while Gordon Pitt masterminds the tape recorder. Look at the size of it."

The Distaff Side

Daisy Duke

"Murray Walker – what I think sums him up is his great love of life."

"It wasn't just the words and engine sounds that enabled the Sound Stories to sell so well. One of their great attractions was the superb sleeve artwork done by Ernest Wragg - like this one of brilliant Mike Hailwood winning the 1961 Senior TT on his Norton."

"Here I am excitedly delving into the depths of the great Tarquinio Provini's 250 Mondial at the 1961 TT, while my father tells me what it is really all about."

A Communicator

John Surtees

"Graham and Murray's styles of commentary were very different. His father was more like Raymond Baxter. Murray developed and projected this excitement. Let's face it, Murray ran away with himself at times. He certainly dropped a few clangers but got away with it in a superb manner. I think the advertising background was a very important factor. He had the knack of communication. Murray is someone special."

"I wrote my first book in 1960 and this is it - a pot-pourri of road racing and motocross. I loved doing it and it was to lead to many others, including this one!"

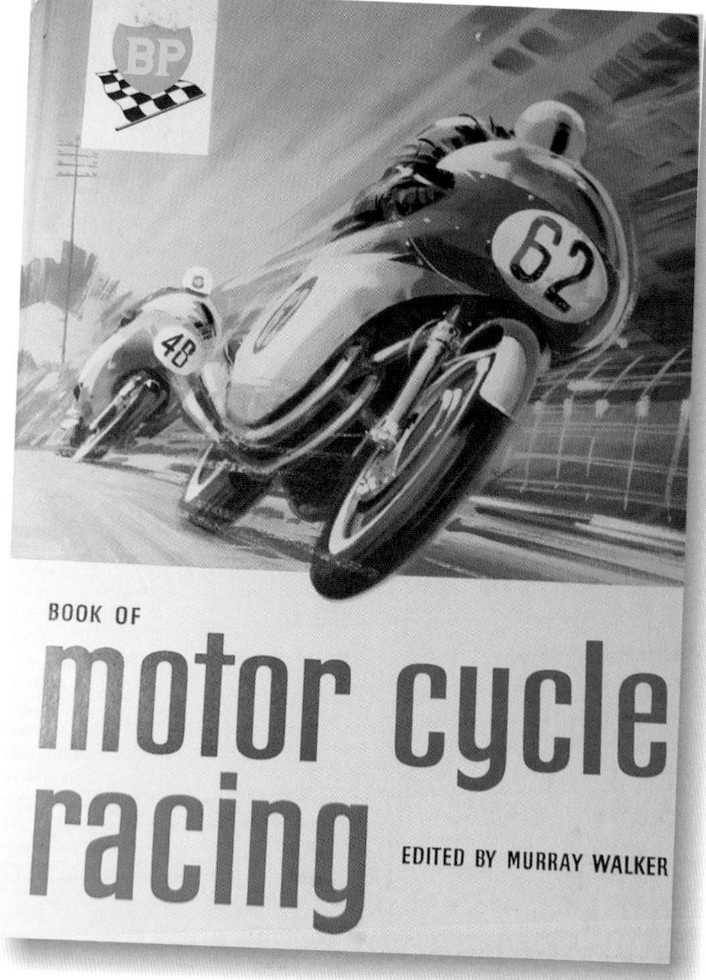

"Mike Hailwood's first TT win was the 1961 250cc race on number 10, the glorious four-cylinder Honda. I used to stop talking so that the listeners could hear its wonderful sound as it plunged down Bray Hill on its way to Quarter Bridge where Mike is heeled over here." (Mortons Group Media Archive)

A Unique Aspect?

Tommy Robb

"I cannot remember any other commentator doing both cars and bikes. Murray automatically followed on from his dad. In the early days of the TT, when I did the interviews with him for the various Stanley Schofield records, Murray was just following straight on from his father. Graham Walker was like Murray – he had dulcet tones, he had the right intonation in his voice to come over so well on the radio in those days."

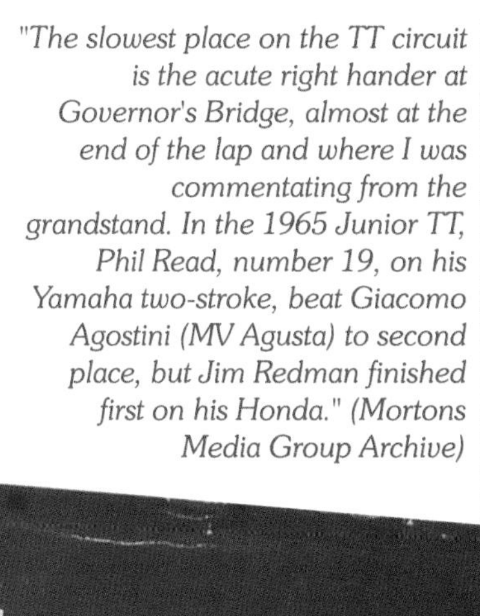

"The slowest place on the TT circuit is the acute right hander at Governor's Bridge, almost at the end of the lap and where I was commentating from the grandstand. In the 1965 Junior TT, Phil Read, number 19, on his Yamaha two-stroke, beat Giacomo Agostini (MV Agusta) to second place, but Jim Redman finished first on his Honda." (Mortons Media Group Archive)

Congratulations to Mike and Murray

Whether you are a seasoned road racing exponent or an enthusiastic recruit to the sport, you are sure to find plenty of valuable information tucked away in the newly published volume "The Art of Motorcycle Racing".

This 186 page cloth bound effort by Mike Hailwood and Murray Walker is a really splendid achievement and it fills a gap which has been vacant in the road racing library for far too long.

Without becoming too technical, the joint editors describe the whole process of the sport from well before arrival on the grid until long after the chequered flag has fallen. Starting with physical and mental requirements Hailwood and Walker touch on such aspects as finance, temperament, ability and mechanical prowess.

After this readers are told about joining a club and more than a dozen pages are devoted to clothing inclusive of boots, gloves, helmet and goggles. This section is particularly descriptive and there is some very useful information which will be of value to many a seasoned campaigner.

MIKE HAILWOOD.

NIGHT WORK

The choice of a machine is followed by some very interesting notes on preparation and routine maintenance. Then comes a short but important piece of advice about "learning the course." A quotation from this chapter tells us that "yet another way of learning a course and one which appeals to me even if it will not to most peoplel is to study it at night. This may at first seem an almost laughable thing to do but . . . it is not just an isolated theory of my own."

After this Hailwood mentions two riders who endorse these remarks—Mike Featherstone a former A.J.S. works rider and Libero Liberati who won the Ulster Grand Prix on his way to a world title in 1957.

The way to approach scrutineering and practice and a little bit about pre-race "butte:flies" is backed up by some well written suggestions for the starting grid.

TECHNIQUES

At this stage we are told about three different techniques and examples are given of Ernst Degnèr and Hailwood himself as well as an amusing little side-line on the late Fergus Anderson.

Riding techniques, pit-stops, signals and racing tactics are all dealt with in plain down-to-earth language and this highly entertaining volume concludes with some warnings and tips about adverse weather as well as the advisability of taking out accident policies.

The book is printed on good art paper and it contains more than 80 first class photographs most of which are attributed to Brian Nicholls. Priced at 21/- it is exceptional value for money and is published by Cassell & Co. Ltd., 35 Red Lion Square, London, W.C.1.

THIS IS YOUR BOOK

Mike Hailwood and Murray Walker

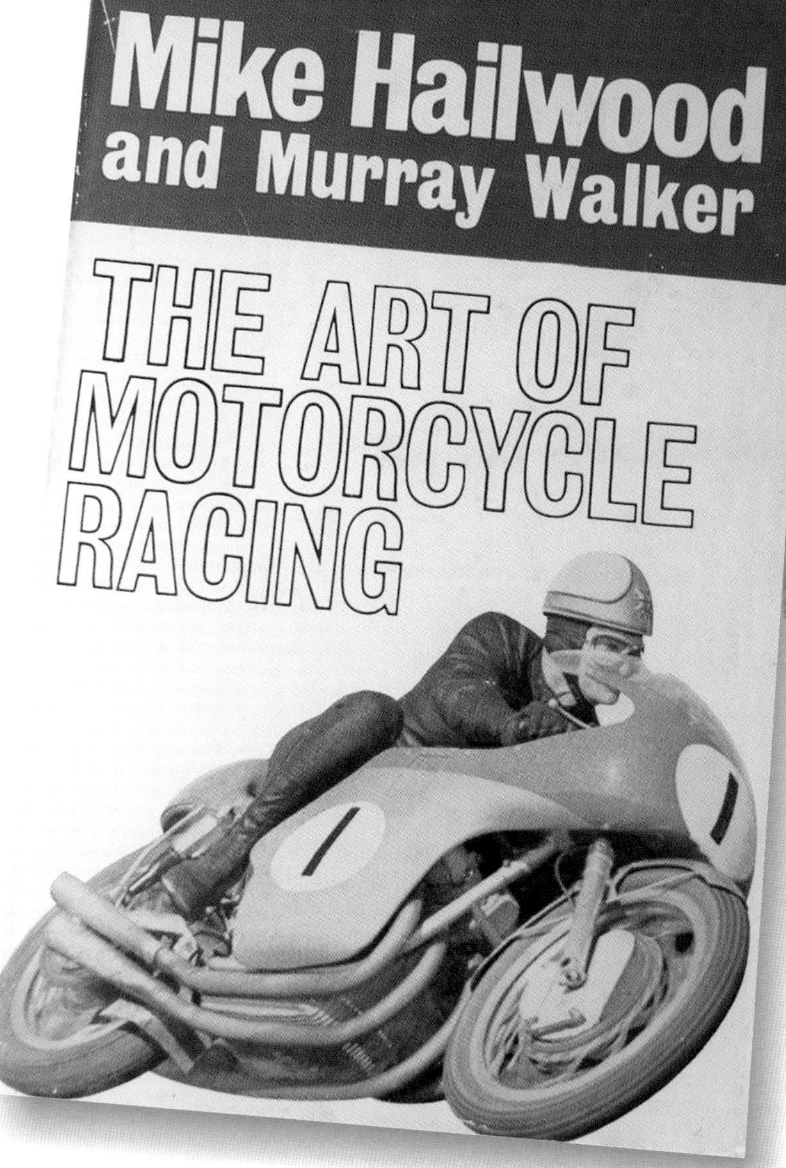

Mixing It With The Lads

Tommy Robb

"When Mike Hailwood and I were riding quite a lot together and we were thrown into various company, Murray really enjoyed the parties and the get togethers, and living with the lads in the paddock.

"Murray got on so well with everybody which probably allowed him to get a better insight into the type of person he was going to be talking about. He was so well accepted because he was such a nice person. He was one of those people who is such an easy mixer.

"He met every rider and was able to talk to them on their own level. He would ask riders very, very sensible questions about racing, probably because of his background."

Mike The Bike

Murray Walker

"Mike Hailwood was the closest friend I have lost. I wasn't there when it happened because it was a road accident. He was going out to get fish and chips with his two children and a truck did a 'U' turn across one carriageway to another and poor Mike didn't have a chance. He was the closest."

"I make no apologies for including another shot of the great Mike Hailwood (Honda), the supreme master of the TT at the height of the event's greatness." (Mortons Media Group Archive)

"One of the many unique aspects of the Isle of Man TT is that the riders start singly at 10 second intervals so that the race is, in effect, a time trial. In my day, they bump-started their bikes on the Glencrutchery Road, immediately beneath my commentary box, as Phil Read is doing here, before plunging full bore down the terrifying Bray Hill." (Mortons Media Group Archive)

Mike Hailwood

Murray Walker

"For me the greatest racing motor cyclist of all time, bar none, is Mike Hailwood, who was not only a lovely bloke, but a great personal friend of mine. I saw him in his first ever motor cycle race in 1957 and knew him right through to his tragic death.

"In 1963, I wanted to write a book about motor cycle racing but, to be honest, I wasn't sufficiently confident that my name would be enough to motivate sales. So I got Mike to co-operate with me by putting his name on the book as well. It was called *The Art of Motor Cycle Racing* by Mike Hailwood and Murray Walker, with Mike Hailwood in big letters, and Murray Walker in smaller print.

"In point of fact, Mike was the most laid back chap I have ever met in my life and he wasn't the least bit interested in either writing anything or contributing to anything. So I wrote the whole thing, including how to take the best racing line on a corner, and how to tune your double-overhead cam Norton engine. I was pretty deficient of knowledge on both those counts. I used to vainly try to get Mike to read the chapter and give it the seal of approval.

"I remember on one occasion I took the chapter dealing with racing lines, and said, 'Look, here's the latest chapter, have a look and let me know what you think'. 'Oh, do you think it's alright, Murray?' I said, 'Well yeah, I think it's alright. I wrote it so I am bound to think it's alright.' 'Well if you think it's alright, I think it's alright.'

"I won't say he never read a word, because on one occasion I wrote something about crash helmets, and how to pick a helmet and how to put it on - all sort of details - and I said, 'Of course, another good plus point is that a helmet keeps your head warm'.

"Mike looked at this and said, 'Bloody nonsense! It's there to protect your skull.' So I took that bit out."

Family Parallels

Stuart Graham

"Having known each other almost since childhood, he is a very special friend. We share a rather unique family history/background in that we both had famous motorcycle racing fathers (Les Graham, the 1949 500cc World Champion, and Graham Walker), we both followed on with successful careers of our own in the motorcycle world, me racing (Stuart won a TT), Murray as a commentator, and then we both forged new and successful careers in car racing (Stuart is the only person, post-war, to win the TT on two wheels and four), and both like to feel that our respective fathers, who were a hard act to follow, would have approved."

"Is this the most impressive racing motor cycle of all time? It is for me - the incredible four-valve, six-cylinder 20,000rpm Honda four-stroke. Mike Hailwood's eyes look way ahead of him - and look at his scruffy, taped-up leathers and boot. They didn't slow him down though." (Mortons Media Group Archive)

An Appreciation

Giacomo Agostini

"A very nice person, very professional. We don't meet a lot now but when we do, we are very good friends. He was fantastic for the sport because he loved the sport – he understood it so well."

Another Understatement!

Bill Smith

"In 1967 Tommy Robb and I had a big battle for the 250cc production race and I won it by a fifth of a second. Murray was interviewing us afterwards and said, 'Well, was it a close race?' You couldn't get much closer than a fifth of a second!

"But he was a great, infectious character to have round the paddock. His knowledge of bikes, much of which came from his father, was incredible. He was very, very popular in the sixties and seventies, particularly in the Isle of Man, and his commentaries on the Stanley Schofield records were absolutely wonderful."

Sheene's Salute

Jim Reside

"When commentating on motor cycle racing, Murray was probably at his most relaxed because he has always said motor cycling was his first love because of his dad and so on, and there was that great moment at Silverstone where Barry Sheene turned round and gave a 'V' sign to the guy behind, whom he had just passed, and Murray said, 'Oh, look, Barry Sheene's waving!'" [It was actually the great Kenny Roberts]

"No-one delighted me more during my motor cycle racing days than the irrepressible and brilliant Barry Sheene, whom I knew from the time when, as a little boy, he used to accompany his racing father, Frank Sheene, to the races at Brands Hatch where I did the public address. I commentated on countless of his victories, including very sadly his very last at Goodwood in 2002 - which typically he won, only a matter of months before he tragically succumbed to cancer."

"I was commentating for the BBC, standing on top of a road-mender's hut, just to the left of Phil Read, as he exited Parliament Square at Ramsay on his Yamaha in 1968 on his way to controversially beating his team mate Bill Ivy in the 125cc TT." (Mortons Media Group Archive)

Bikes Take Precedence

Jim Reside

"In the days of Barry Sheene, there were less egos than there were in Formula One. The bikers were always slightly more human in their response to the media and they didn't get upset if you wanted to get involved and do stories.

"Murray was always keen to do the motor cycle Grands Prix and frequently the BBC chose to send him the British Motor Cycle GP and miss a F1 GP on the same day."

The Special Relationship

John Surtees

"Although Murray didn't compete at the top level, the fact remains that Murray would have had that relationship with a piece of machinery. When you have created a relationship with a piece of machinery and felt it, this is something that is very, very special and bikes are very special that way. It's the same with me; they are my first love."

MOTOR CYCLE NEWS, January 18, 1978

THE STARS

"I don't know what you're drinking but it looks a bit like punch!" Murray Walker, commentator, takes the Mike our of Hailwood, winner of MCN's Man of the Year trophy in 1961, 63 and 67.

Working Together

John Surtees

"I worked with him for a while on the motor cycling side and, much as I didn't present the problems to him that James did, I always made a point of trying to communicate with everyone involved. You could be sure that Murray had already been around (the teams). He would try to get some insight rather than just scratch the surface. Luckily, he had enough respect from people that they communicated with him.

"He was not the easiest person to work with on the commentary side as he wanted to dominate. It wasn't possible to develop one's own style so it was not the easiest thing to do, but a good experience."

'Best wishes Murray'
Geoff Duke

"One of the immortals of motor cycle racing and, certainly for me, the supreme stylist was my great friend, Geoff Duke. I first got to know him just after the war when he was a Norton works trials rider and we both lived in Birmingham. A lovely man who hardly looked a day older, 34 years later, in 1981."

It Takes One To Know One

Phil Read

"He's just an incredible person, with a great memory and a wonderful voice. And he's a keen motorcyclist as well, which makes him human (laughter)! All the real people are motor cyclists and he knew the thrill and what danger and what skill one needs to race a motor cycle.

"Of course, he has a great background with his father and his connections with the Isle of Man. He also recounts wonderful stories, quite politely, about other riders!"

The Rough Stuff

Off-road motor cycle competitions have taken various forms over the years, including trials, scrambles and grass track racing. Today scrambles are more generally known as motocross, which was what the Europeans called the sport. Scrambling really developed after the war and was originally a summer sport, whereas trials were traditionally held in the winter.

Scrambles were races over the roughest terrain imaginable and required great skill to avoid a tumble which regularly happened to all but the best. The sport rapidly grew in popularity in the early fifties, the British Championships having been launched in 1951.

Murray effectively began his television career in 1957 when scrambles began to be broadcast regularly and he was the commentator. This exposure gave the sport an enormous boost. Compulsive viewing, it was shown on Saturday and Sunday afternoons, with many families glued to the set. As a result, names such as Les Archer, Geoff Ward, Jeff Smith, Arthur Lampkin, Vic Eastwood, Dave Bickers and Brian 'Badger' Goss became widely known throughout the UK. Murray, of course, with his trademark infectious enthusiasm brought the whole thing alive for armchair viewers of all ages, from children to grandparents.

Those who watched in that period remember the seemingly ever-present mud but that was not normally a scrambling ingredient, as the events were held in the summer. However, the televised scrambles were held in the winter as other sports had to take place in the summer and the television schedules were a bit sparse in the winter months.

As happens with every mechanically-based sport, the machinery gradually became more and more specialised and sophisticated. Most of the manufacturers listed a Competition model. The big four-stroke Matchless and BSA bikes were dominant in the top 500cc class in the fifties and early sixties. Other manufacturers represented included Ariel, Royal Enfield, DOT, Greeves, Norton, AJS and Triumph.

Scrambling gave Murray his big break and launched his television career. Initially, it was the commercial station, ABC, who covered the north and Midlands, which broadcast an event at Bentley Springs and retained Murray to commentate for them. As he was not exclusively contracted to the BBC, he was able to work for their rivals as well. The exciting sport very much moulded Murray's excited style.

Most of the events were in the north of England and Murray, together with his incredibly supportive wife, Elizabeth, would head off from London on a Friday evening and trudge north, long before the swift motorways of today. He would spend the morning wandering around the muddy paddock, talking to all and sundry, gathering his information before repairing to a modest hut bedecked with a small TV monitor and a microphone. To assist with commentaries, Murray had enthusiastic Yorkshireman, Denis Parkinson, and Elizabeth gamely keeping a lap chart, attempting to determine the mud-encrusted machines and their equally plastered riders!

Just to add to the challenge, different ITV regions took different slots during the afternoon and would come and go, irrespective of the stage in the action, and Murray would be instructed, in his headphones by the producer, to say good-bye to one region, then welcome another. It sounds like a veritable nightmare but such challenges honed Murray's innate ability.

This coverage, despite these challenges, was so popular that the BBC woke up to the potential, negotiated with the sport's governing body to put on events with consistently higher quality entry lists and offered Murray a long-term contract, provided he worked exclusively for the BBC in future.

The British Broadcasting Corporation did a fine job with scrambling and the high quality entries and courses around England and Wales, together with some spectacular riders, made superb television. Scrambles became an integral part of the much-loved *Grandstand* sports programme. Split into classes for 250cc and 500cc bikes, the riders were competing for the coveted BBC Grandstand Trophy.

Meanwhile, scrambling had become very popular in such countries as Sweden, Denmark, Belgium, Czechoslovakia and Russia. In 1966 the big four-strokes were challenged by Paul Friedrichs on a two-stroke CZ, and the writing was on the wall. Many would argue that Jeff Smith, who had won the world title in 1964 and 1965, was the greatest of his period, but Dave Bickers won the British crown seven times and was European Champion twice. Smith was the ultimate professional and was a fine athlete who trained with Maurice Herriott, a silver medallist at the Tokyo Olympics. The Swedes, Torsten Hallman and Rolf Tibblin on their Husqvarnas, had also arrived on the scene, were very successful and British dominance faded for a while.

Regular coverage by the BBC ceased in the late sixties but they showed the annual British Motocross GP and Murray continued commentating until 1985. By now a new generation of world class riders had emerged, including Graham Noyce, Neil Hudson and, considered by some to be the very best of all time, Dave Thorpe, who was World Champion in 1985, 1986 and 1989.

Scrambling had been good for Murray, establishing his television career, and Murray had been good for scrambling, establishing it as a cult sport that thrives to this day.

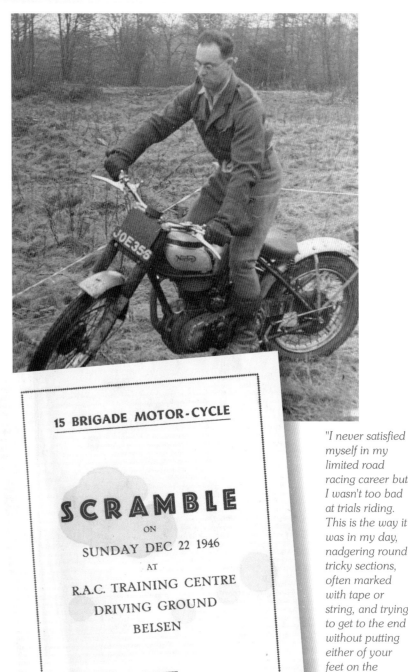

JOE 356
15 BRIGADE MOTOR-CYCLE
SCRAMBLE
ON
SUNDAY DEC 22 1946
AT
R.A.C. TRAINING CENTRE
DRIVING GROUND
BELSEN

"I never satisfied myself in my limited road racing career but I wasn't too bad at trials riding. This is the way it was in my day, nadgering round tricky sections, often marked with tape or string, and trying to get to the end without putting either of your feet on the ground. NB: no crash helmet in 1948."

Bikes Across Frontiers

Murray Walker

"When the war ended, the Royal Scots Greys were moved to a place near Brunswick, in what later became East Germany. We had been fighting the Germans, in one of the most bitter wars in the history of mankind since 1939 and I had been busy for years trying to rub out as many of them as I could. All of a sudden I found myself near Brunswick. There was a chap there called Kurt Kühnke, who had been a pre-war German DKW works rider. Somehow he knew about my motor cycle connections and invited me to make a visit to the *Brunswick Motor Cycle Club*.

"It's difficult to communicate, now, what it felt like to be contacted by a German, who was completely beyond the pale because we were understandably intolerant in those days and regarded all Germans as being evil. Being invited by a German to make a social call felt very strange to put it mildly and, to be honest, I was concerned about accepting it, as a British army officer, and wondered what the hell would happen to me when I got in amongst what I regarded as a bunch of Nazis who had been defeated by us. But I went over there, was treated like royalty and given an absolutely marvellous evening. At the end of it they gave me what they described as a Document of Honour, which had been specially painted. Quite amazing the way things could turn round so quickly."

"The Beggar's Roost Trial run by the Sunbeam Motor Cycle Club, of which my father had been President, was a great event and my single-cylinder Norton was ideally suited to the stony ground. I wasn't though and didn't do very well!"

ROUTES IN THE 1949 "SCOTTISH"

South Midland Review

"Six Days" Diary

October 1949 By A. C. WOOLLARD

Friday. Watched riders treating the old coach road through the Elan Valley as if it were the local byepass, a nasty water-splash being taken as if it just wasn't there. Basil Hall (Dunstable) riding nicely and looking as if enjoying himself; Murray Walker (Wood Green) (one of the few British riders wearing a crash hat—wise man) passed, nursing his front mud-guard in his lap. No-one appeared to have much time in hand and all were going like stink. Later in the evening came the tidings that Ray of the Trophy Team has suffered a crash but hoped to be running on the morrow.

"I borrowed a works Norton for the 1948 Press Trial but a fat lot of good it did me!"

For The Record

Murray Walker

"I started commentating in 1949 when television hardly existed. It did exist, of course, but hardly anybody had television sets in their homes and there wasn't much television coverage of anything. There certainly wasn't much coverage of sport and there was even less of motor sport. Those were the days when you had enormous cameras and everything was confined to how far you could get with land lines. For instance, when I was doing radio commentary on trials riding, I used to go out with a BBC Humber Super Snipe. The back had been converted into a sort of studio and the driver was also the engineer.

"When we got to somewhere that we wanted to talk about, I would get as far away from the car as the cable would allow. Now, if you're trying to talk about motor cycle trials, and you're in a Humber Super Snipe, it's very difficult to get to some of the sections. So I would talk, and my words would go into the microphone, down the wire, and emerge at a gramophone - not a tape machine and not a digital recorder or anything - a gramophone, on which was a plain wax disc, with no grooves. As I talked, my words went into the pick-up and through the needle and cut grooves in the record.

"At the end of the event, we would dash back to the studio in Birmingham. I would then read my script, interspersed with recordings from the disc. When I said, '...and this is what Harold Tozer and his sidecar sounded like going through the section,' they would have to drop the needle on to that section of the record - state of the art in those days!"

Majoring On Excitement

Vic Eastwood

"It was an eye-opener for so many people. Television was almost a new thing and it was really brilliant. It was all live. The main thing about Murray is that he made the racing exciting, even if it wasn't. He had quite a lot of input on who the cameras should follow because some people were exciting to watch and some people weren't. Nowadays I don't think they have anybody with any idea of what racing is. It's just film crews. Murray could see what *was* exciting and what *could be* exciting.

"It was the same when we were laying out the tracks. We had big jumps downhill – you don't get anything like that anymore. Unfortunately the tracks now are not very difficult whereas we would get in valleys with trees and twist through them and into bomb holes and jump out of 'em, and it was exciting to watch."

"The Scottish Six Days Trial is one of the greatest events of its type in the world. It is based at Fort William, takes in some truly breathtaking scenery and makes unique demands on man and machine. Wearing the loudest cap I could find, I was very proud to win a first class award in 1949 on my trusty Norton."

"This was my shining hour, the 1949 International Six Days Trial, based at Llandrindod Wells in Wales. I had just changed the engine sprocket on my one-day trials Norton, had a go, won a Gold Medal and was a member of the winning club team. But, look at this - number 185, Jack Blackwell on a works Norton, has already caught pedestrian me as we clear the water splash. You'll note that I'm very racy in a crash helmet now!"

THE Press Trial was run over a short course on private ground near Sevenoaks last Sunday. The Uncle Rowe Cup for best performance on handicap was won by C. E. (Titch) Allen, on a B.S.A. Bantam. Cyril Quantrill, using W. H. J. Peacock as human ballast on the latter's Matchless sidecar outfit, won the Charles Markham shield for the best performance in the opposite class. Best performance irrespective of handicap was made by Murray Walker (490 Norton), who lost only six marks. Competitors included T. H. Wisdom, the famous motoring correspondent; Denis Jenkinson and Phil Heath, the Continental Circus road racers; and John Bolster, the racing car driver.

The

No. 222 October, 1949

SUNBEAM CLUB NEWS

INTERNATIONAL 6 DAYS

WHAT a wonderful week, to be sure! The course was good, the weather was good, and the Sunbeam successes in the club team contest were overwhelming.

Last year, when we had fielded three club teams, it was widely suggested that such riders as Fred Rist and Charlie Rogers probably hadn't paid their subs. anyway, and, even if they had (which they certainly had!) the Sunbeam Club could hardly do otherwise than win the club team prize when their teams consisted entirely of Trophy and Vase men. Certainly it was a great deal easier then, but for 1949 the regs. were revised so as to permit no members of Trophy, Vase or Manufacturers' teams to participate in the club contest, and the general feeling seems to have been that we wouldn't stand a chance without our 'trade' riders to rely on.

That *was* the feeling—but not any more! There were nineteen club teams entered for this year's I.S.D.T. three of these being fielded by the Sunbeam M.C.C. In our 'A' team were Ray Petty, Murray Walker and Jim Powell (all on 490 Nortons), in our 'B' team were Alan Sanders (498 Triumph) and Jim Kentish and Ron Woolaway on 350 B.S.A.s. Our 'C' team was originally composed of Alec Fletcher (347 A.J.S.), Bob O'Neill (249 Velocette) and Peter Head (125 Enfield), but poor Peter fell ill with pneumonia just before the trial, and Alan Taylor (498 A.J.S.) took his place.

O'Neill had the cruel luck to crash on the second day, but the remaining members of his team finished the week intact. And what of the other two Sunbeam teams? Neither the 'A' nor the 'B' lost a solitary mark—and they had the magnificent distinction of being the only club teams to complete the course unpenalised! They rode with outstanding skill and determination throughout, and thoroughly deserved their 'golds' (to say nothing of the dinner Jack Whitfield stood them on the Saturday night). Their achievement has done an immeasurable amount of good to our reputation, and the whole Club joins in offering them very heartiest congratulations and thanks.

In all, 'golds' were won by no less than eighteen Sunbeam members (Rist, Ray, Powell, Walker, Mooney, Burnard, Mein, Fletcher, Sanders, Taylor, Petty, Viney, Alves, Hall, Woolaway, Kentish, Rogers and last—but by no means last—Olga Kevelos). I say again, what a wonderful week!

RALPH VENABLES.

How The Style Developed

Murray Walker

"I did radio for years. Radio is very different to television in terms of commentary because with television, they can see what you are talking about, and broadly speaking you have got to talk about what they can see, 'they' being the television viewers, and what they can see is decided not by the commentator but by the producer. So you talk to the pictures that the producer gives you. With radio, on the other hand, you are conscious of the fact that the people can't see what you are talking about, so you have to endeavour to paint a word picture. With radio, of course, if there is nothing in particular happening, you can't say, 'There is nothing much going on at the moment, but I will let you know when there is'. You have to keep talking.

"That is undoubtedly what conditioned my commentating style, because I commentated for years on radio where people couldn't see what I was talking about. That's what's developed my crash, bang, wallop, trousers-on-fire, all-action commentary style. I was trying to get through to radio listeners and it's very difficult to change your habits."

A Kindly Gesture

Bryan 'Badger' Goss

"In the old days, back in 1962 when I was riding for Greeves, one thing showed what a wonderful man he was. He knew I loved my scrambling. I'd won the 250, at Caerleon, Newport. The next race was for over 250cc bikes and I wasn't allowed in it. Do you know, he beckoned me up on to his commentator's box. He said, 'Come on, come and have a watch from here'.

"As soon as the next race went off, he started and his wife was jogging his memory with different things and, oh, it was just absolutely wonderful.

"For somebody like me, just an ordinary cattle lorry driver, who was able to ride a motor bike a little bit, to be asked up, by Murray Walker – I think that was absolutely wonderful."

"Superstar Walker (Norton) wins the 1950 Press Trial - and so he should, all the rest were drunk or ancient!"

"My very first TV broadcast was in 1949 at the Knatts Valley hillclimb and just look at the size of the camera. Fastest time of the day was by Wally Lock, who I am interviewing in the picture below. The producer was a stripling Peter Dimmock, who went on to achieve greatness with the BBC."

Lampkin's Leap

Murray Walker

"I had an enormous number of very happy days commentating on motocross for ITV, names like Arthur Lampkin, Dave Bickers, Jeff Smith… Arthur Lampkin is a dour Yorkshireman who rode a BSA Gold Star and the BSA Gold Star was *the* bike to ride – single cylinder, alloy engine, spring frame, telescopic forks – and motocross is really a sort of motor cycle steeplechase. They race across some very rough ground and you spend most of the time standing on the footrests, hanging on to the handlebars, letting your knees absorb the shock.

"So, Arthur hits an enormous bump – and this is live on television – his feet leave the footrests, he hangs on to the handlebars, and they had a thing called the 'bum pad' on the back mudguard, which their backside would occasionally hit when they came down over the bumps. Arthur landed with a sickening crunch between the saddle and the bum pad.

"'My God,' I said, 'he's trapped his knackers'. Now, while the words were actually on their way, from the brain to the mouth, I said to myself, 'Murray, they're not going to like this'. And what I actually said was, 'My God, he's trapped his knickers'. Not as good a line, but it kept me on TV!"

Covering The Angles

Vic Eastwood

"We first met when we were doing the TV races and we used to go out to the tracks together with the BBC producer. This was to get the right places for the cameras. I would take the bike to some of the tracks to make sure they had got the cameras in the right place, which they don't do now. They just stick the camera on a pedestal and make it follow 50% of the track and you don't get the feeling of it being difficult. That was one really good thing he did. If you set the camera up on the side of a hill, as the riders go past they go diagonally across the screen and you can actually see how difficult it is to get up the hills, rather than putting a camera at the top. That was what made TV racing so exciting then."

No Favourites

Bryan 'Badger' Goss

"People loved him for his mistakes. There'll never be anybody like him.

"You'd get to the meetings and it'd be cold and frosty and he'd be walking around with his wife and his dog. He always had time to come and say hello, not just to talk about the racing. He was a gentleman and he never favoured anybody, that's what I like about him."

"Commentating for ABC TV was not exactly a luxurious occupation - an open-fronted commentary box, a miniature black and white monitor and it was usually bitterly cold. Ex-road racer, Denis Parkinson, on my left, was my co-commentator, whilst Alan Collinson, in the dark glasses, tried to sort out which mud-covered rider was which. Often none of us knew, but then neither did the public!"

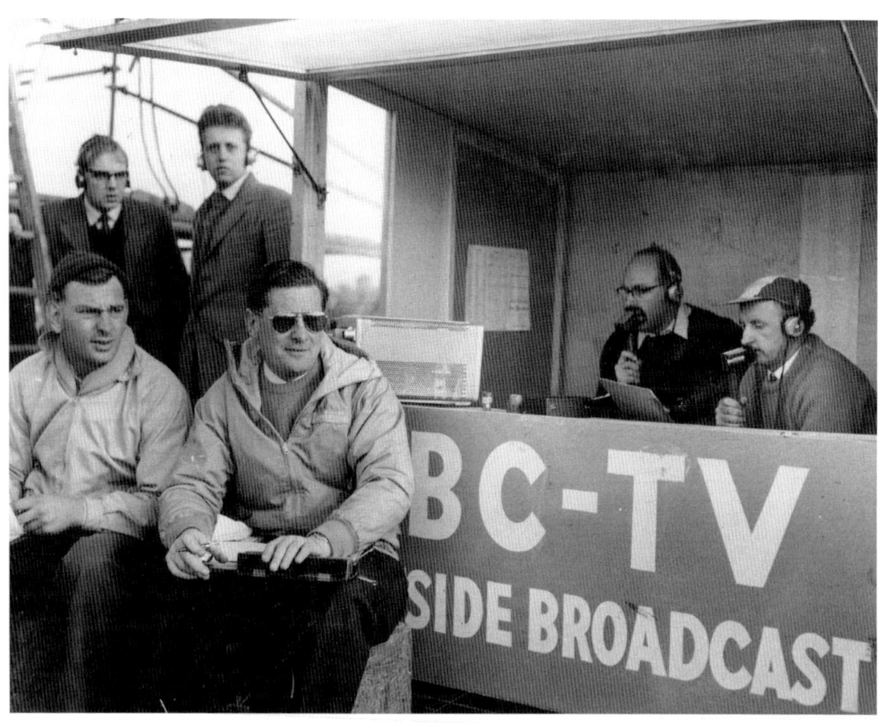

"In the background, wearing the monumentally unsuitable navy trilby, Crombie overcoat and snappy shoes, is Horace Saunders-Jacobs, the producer during my early BBC radio days in the 1950s. The subject of my interview was the great sidecar trials champion, Harold Tozer."

"Certainly, the greatest scrambles rider in my day was the World Champion, Jeff Smith, here ready to do a demonstration lap carrying an early, massive on-rider TV camera pack, as I give it some verbal wellie."

Walker Or Walker

Mike Doodson

"For some time, Murray was covering motorcycle scrambles both for the BBC and the ITV, and claims that several times in 1965 for half an hour one afternoon, there was nothing but Walker on both the available TV channels – one recorded and the other live!"

"'Here comes Dave Bickers,' I used to cry and the viewers sprang to attention!" (David Kindred)

A More Unusual Benefit

Dave Bickers

"I remember Murray in his Wellies on a cold winter's day in the mud but still full of enthusiasm, excitement and happy smiles. He brought a lot to the sport and he did us a world of good. Wherever I went, in the '60s, I was recognised. That was all because Murray had done all the shouting on the telly. So it did me a lot of good! It got me a lot of discount at places as well!"

Two Places At Once

Bryan 'Badger' Goss

"I was watching a television meet once. It was snowing and I was at home, having roast beef or whatever, and Bryan Goss finished fourth! I laughed to myself. He gave me good publicity but I wasn't even there. It was so funny. I finished fourth and yet I was eating my lunch at home!"

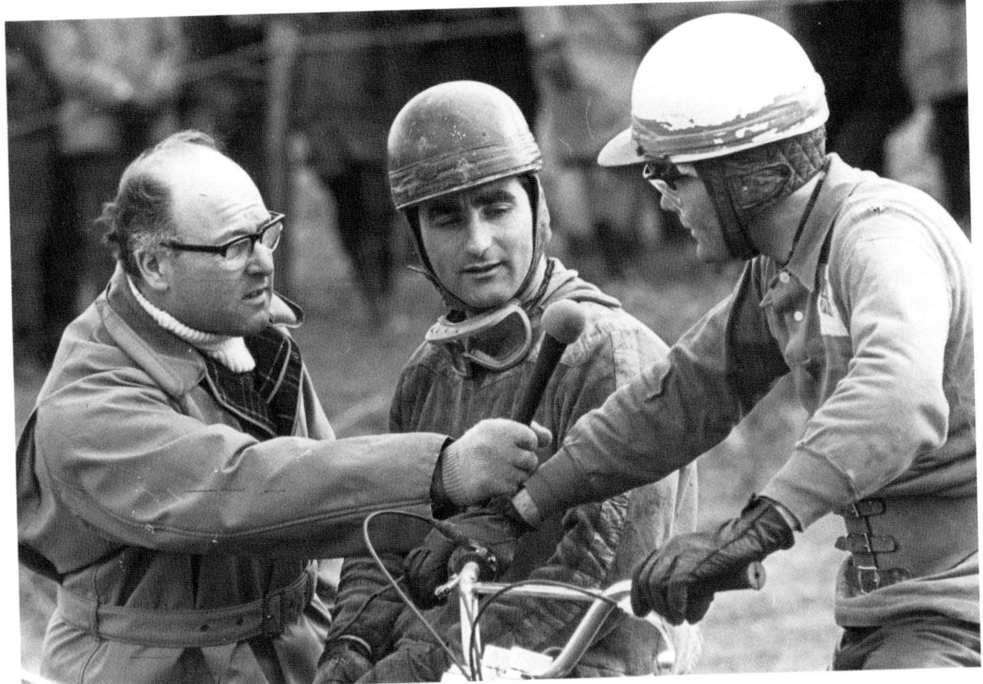

"Chris Horsefield, in the middle, rode a Matchless and Dave Bickers, on the right, rode a Greeves. Bickers's attacking style and winning ways made him the nation's top TV scrambles favourite, and gave me lots to talk about."

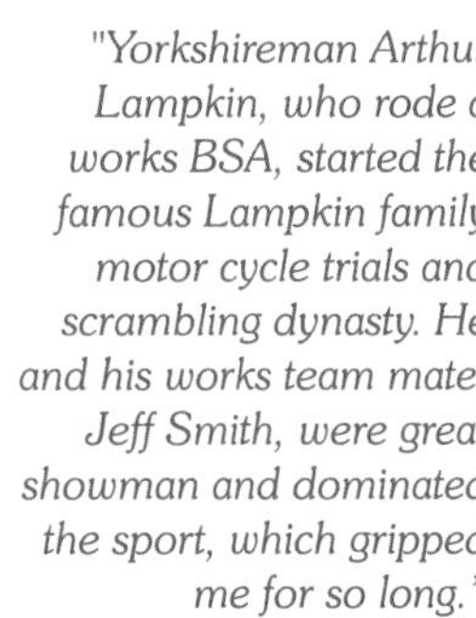

"Yorkshireman Arthur Lampkin, who rode a works BSA, started the famous Lampkin family motor cycle trials and scrambling dynasty. He and his works team mate, Jeff Smith, were great showman and dominated the sport, which gripped me for so long."

Badger's View

Bryan 'Badger' Goss

"As an ordinary country person, I feel privileged to be able to speak about such a wonderful man as Murray."

"Scrambling is really a summer sport which requires hard ground to get the maximum cross-country speed, but the needs of television required it also to become a winter spectacle where the problem was just as much about keeping going through glutinous mud as staying ahead of the rest. It never seemed to bother Jeff Smith, however, who almost invariably enjoyed the advantage of a clear track, thanks to getting away first. I remember once rabbiting away in my TV commentary about how much money he made from his high starting fees on his continental appearances, only to have him come up to me at the next meeting to say, 'For heaven's sake, don't talk about that again, Murray, my tax inspector is a great scrambling enthusiast'." (Action Library)

"To succeed in scrambling/motocross, as in all motor sports, you need to be supremely physically fit, to have superb balance and reactions, and to be fiercely aggressive and determined. BSA works rider, Jeff Smith, had all these attributes, but was also a very practical and skilled engineer. He built up his own B40 bikes using all the facilities of the enormous BSA factory at Small Heath, Birmingham." (Action Library)

MurrayismMurrayismMurrayism

"At the British GP meeting, he came up with one of his famous phrases in the heat of the moment. My father was my mechanic and Murray said we were 'an amazing trio'!"

... Dave Thorpe

The Murray Curse

Dave Bickers

"He lost me a couple of races. 'He can't lose now,' he said. Next thing I was arse over head. He put the mokkers on me!"

The Race Of My Life

Dave Thorpe

"I used to watch it with Murray on BBC Grandstand when I was growing up.

"For me, Murray is, and always was, nothing short of a legend. Murray was into cars and then the BBC took a little bit of interest in motocross for a short period of time during my racing career.

"He did a few commentaries on international events but the one most people remember is the 1985 British Grand Prix. I actually fell off at the beginning and came from last to first in four laps and Murray did the live commentary. Murray got extremely excited with his unique style of commentary.

"I now coach professional lads and our season starts in early November and we train for five months pre-season. So, when I crashed off in that race, which was in July and the ninth round of the 12-round series, when you make a mistake, you think the whole nine months you've been working up to for that day has gone. That's the frightening reality of it all. People don't appreciate the work and effort that has gone into the long build-up.

"Because it was the British GP, I had 40,000 plus people there cheering me on which was a tremendous help. Secondly, there was the adrenalin on the day because I was very motivated and, lastly, there was drizzly rain. When the ground is a little bit wet, but not muddy and not dry, it is, from a motocross rider's point of view, a lot more technical, you need a lot more throttle control and that was something I did excel in and that helped me come through the field quickly in the beginning because of the drizzle."

"Very few riders could beat the works BSAs but Vic Eastwood could on his works Matchless. Slight, light and wiry, he was incredibly quick. Even Arthur Lampkin, second in the picture, was left behind this time." (David Kindred)

"Just look at this for typical top level motocross style, speed and competitive action. Britain's great World Champion, and courteous gentleman, Dave Thorpe, aggressively leads the pack on his works Honda, as he usually did. He was an absolute joy for me to talk about in the TV commentary box, partly because he was British, partly because he was such a nice bloke and partly because of his effortless superority." (Action Library)

Instant Recall

Bryan 'Badger' Goss

"Many years after I'd known Murray, a friend of mine, who ran the Hawk team, was at Thruxton, at a big road race meeting. He could see Murray was being hassled by a lot of autograph hunters. When it quietened down, he invited Murray over to his hospitality area. I'd said to him, 'If you ever see Murray, pass on my regards to him'.

"He said to Murray, 'I speak to Bryan Goss every week and he never goes without mentioning you'.

"'Oh,' Murray said, 'Badger, the fastest cattle lorry driver in the west!'"

The Day Job

Though Murray is famous for his motor sport commentating, he actually had a very successful, and demanding, career in the 'real' world. It is quite extraordinary how he managed to combine the two, without compromising either.

As we have seen, he won a scholarship awarded by the Dunlop Rubber Company and joined the firm for a year or so before being called up in 1942 and serving with distinction in the Royal Scots Greys. Unlike his mother, Murray really liked Birmingham with its conglomeration of great motor cycle manufacturers and so managed to obtain a position back at Dunlop. Specifically, he became assistant to the Tyre Division Advertising Manager, based once again at imposing Fort Dunlop. During this time, Murray enjoyed his foray into motor cycle competitions, before having his commentating breakthrough at Shelsley Walsh.

The Dunlop job, for which he was paid a salary of £350 a year, was not stretching Murray, even though he had been promoted to HQ in St James's Street in the heart of London's Piccadilly and now reported to the group's PR supremo. Bored again, he gladly accepted an offer to join the Allied Group Advertising Department and became Advertising Manager for various specialist rubber divisions. After seven years with Dunlop, he felt he needed to broaden his horizons.

Through an interview with Masius and Ferguson, an ambitious London advertising agency, he was offered a job with Aspro, manufacturers of the world-famous analgesic, as a copywriter. His salary was now £1000 a year. Soon he found himself travelling around India and Pakistan, promoting 'the wonder cure'.

After various promotions, Murray was lured away from Aspro by McCann Erickson, then the world's largest advertising agency, and they doubled his salary and put him to work on the Esso account. After two years, he was less than enthralled by the work and had a yearning to join Masius, where he had made various friends. This agency was clearly going places.

Murray's new clients were Mars, who are famous for confectionary, but were venturing into something entirely new – pet food. Sold in cans, this was a new concept when people had always fed their cats and dogs on leftovers and such like. As with most innovative ideas, there was considerable resistance to be overcome because people were not accustomed to spending money on feeding their pets. To prove to sceptical retailers that the tins contained wholesome food, the company reps, and Murray who often accompanied them, would open a tin and sample it themselves!

In 1964 Murray's charismatic Chairman, Jack Wynne-Williams, made four employees, whom he considered to be his rising stars and the next generation of senior management, an offer. Each could buy £30,000 worth of shares, an enormous sum which Warburg, the company's bankers, would lend at a rate of 10% per annum. Murray discussed it with Elizabeth, whom he had married in 1959, and they decided to go ahead, risky though it was. The decision would prove to be one of the best they ever made. At that time, the agency had offices in London and Hamburg. When Murray left in 1982, it was a 53-office organisation with branches in 27 countries worldwide, including four in Australia, and an annual billing of more than one billion pounds.

DUNLOP RUBBER COMPANY LTD.

This Diploma is awarded to

Graeme Murray Walker

who, having by selection been the holder of a DUNLOP SCHOLARSHIP, has completed a full-time and comprehensive Commercial Course of Instruction within the Company's Organisation and has passed his examinations, both written and oral, satisfactorily.

The Course of Instruction commenced on September 1st, 1941 and terminated on June 27th, 1942

FOR DUNLOP RUBBER COMPANY LTD.

1942 — Director, General Sales Division

"Snappy sports coat. Yellow sweater. Smart cravat. You're lovely!"

"In 1947 the British Motor Cycle Racing Club held its first post-war Dinner, which I attended in my Captain's uniform. With his inevitable pipe in hand, my father stands behind me. On the other side, behind me, is family friend and ex-Brooklands star, Vic Horsman, whilst to my right, drink in hand, is Ruben Harveyson, great friend of TT star, Jimmy Simpson."

Not A Minor Matter

Murray Walker

"When I stopped riding competitively, I switched to four wheels. At that time my mother had a brand new Morris Minor, which was a highly desirable motor car in those days. I borrowed it one weekend to compete in a car rally. It was the *London Motor Club*. The rally took us right into Lancashire. The two people I wanted to do the navigating were unable to. I ended up asking a chap called Jack Greenwood, who had been the producer of a film that I had made with Dunlop.

"I asked Jack to be my navigator, not really knowing if he was any good at navigating or any good at driving. Turned out he wasn't any good at either. We were battling through somewhere between Lancaster and Preston in the dead of night. This was winter, and there was snow and ice. I had been driving all the way and not to be too modest, we were actually doing very well.

"I handed over to Jack at about 4am and we came to a place called Dunsop Bridge. The road forked and you could go to the left or the right, and straight ahead was a dry stone wall. Jack took neither left or right, and went straight into the dry stone wall. Smashed in the front of the car, and we were out of the rally. We managed to limp home all the way to north London.

"I got back on Sunday morning - I was living with my parents still at the time – and I went upstairs. It was early. My mother and father were in bed. I went into their room. My mother said, 'Hello dear, you're back much earlier than I expected you to be'. 'Yes mother,' I said, 'I have had a little problem. I will sit down and tell you about it.' So then I had to sit down and tell her that I had written-off her motor car. She got another and I bought my first car – a Standard 10."

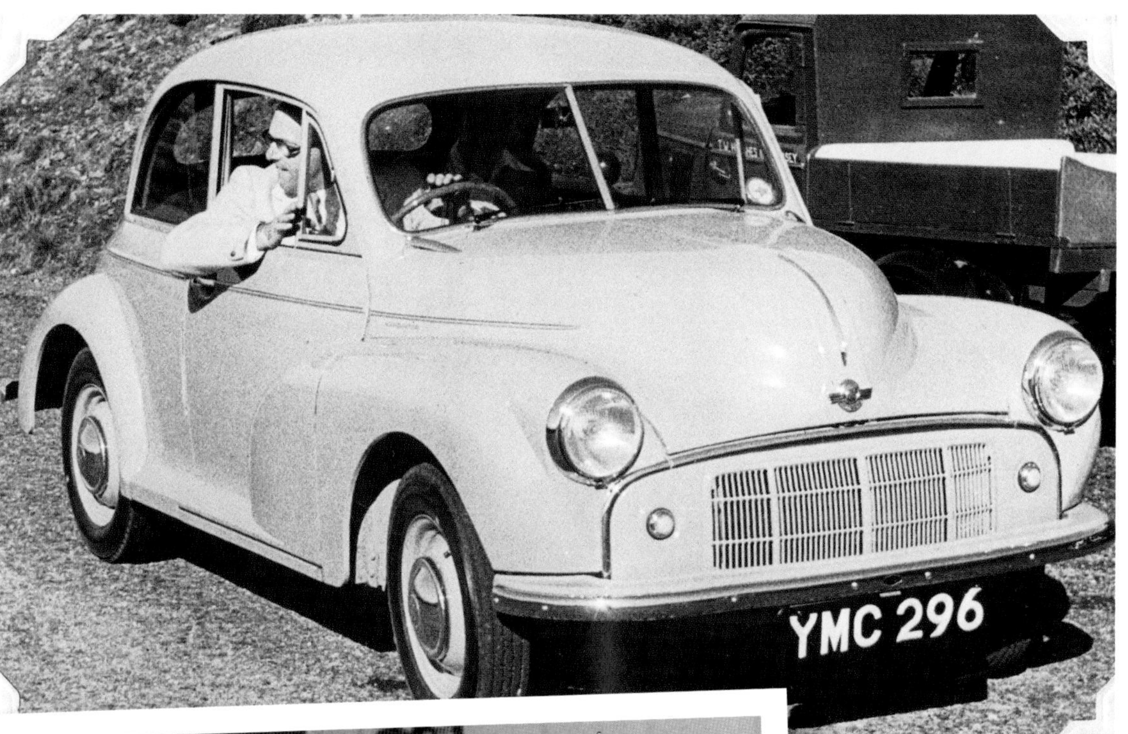

"This is my mother's prized side-valve Morris Minor which, on one occasion, I succeeded in persuading up to 72mph (downhill) with my friend Brian Emerton and two girls in the back. Brian and I wore crash helmets to heighten the effect, much to the amusement of the girls. YMC 296 suffered a tragic end, though, when my co-driver impaled it on a stone wall during a rally in Lancashire. My mother took it like a trooper."

Life After Dunlop

Murray Walker

"I got a job with Aspro and spent a marvellous time in India. It was a challenge, because there was no TV, no newspapers, and the only commercial radio station was booked up for a year. Since we wanted to command an audience, we formed a band of bagpipe-playing Indians in pink trousers, purple jackets and black busbies, who toured the villages. It was a pretty epoch-making way to gain attention, and the Indians loved it."

"Now as an eager, beaver advertising executive at Aspro-Nicholas, I harangue the sales force at a conference to get out and sell on the back of the fantastic campaign my colleagues and I have evolved for Lifeguard Disinfectant. Sales Director, Tom Peters, next to me, nods off in spite of my best efforts."

ASPRO PERSONALITIES

No. 36—MR. G. M. WALKER

Broadcaster, Sports Commentator, T.V. Consultant and Film Producer. Who is this personality in our midst ? None other than our own Murray Walker.

Murray, educated at Highgate School, London, won a business scholarship to the Dunlop Rubber Company, but after one year his business training was to be interrupted for some time because of the outbreak of war.

Murray, who was keen to get into the Tanks, joined the Young Soldiers' Battalion, a Pre-O.C.T.U. Unit, which enabled him to go to Sandhurst on an Officers Training Course. Having completed his training he was posted to the Royal Scots Greys as Second Lieutenant. Murray who was in the Normandy Landings on D-Day plus one, saw service in France, Belgium, Holland and Germany, and was with the troops when they made their first link-up with the Russians on the Baltic Coast. He finished his military service as a Captain in the Royal Armoured Corps, having spent his last eighteen months at the Armoured Division School at the infamous Belsen Camp.

In 1945 Murray re-joined the Dunlop Rubber Company where he was to remain until 1954, during which time he held the following positions—Assistant Advertising Manager to the Tyre Group, Assistant Public Relations Officer, Advertising Manager—General Rubber Goods Division, and Advertising Manager Dunlopillo.

When asked about hobbies Murray told us that broadcasting and motor cycle racing were his main interests, and although retired from racing himself his voice can be heard over the air from such places as the Isle of Man during T.T. week, from Ulster, Silverstone or any other part of Great Britain where International Motor Cycling or Motor Racing takes place. Murray has made over 300 Radio broadcasts and taken part in six feature programmes. He is the Motor Cycle Consultant to the Independent Television Authority and has just completed a film for them. Incidentally, his keenness for this sport has been passed on from his father, Graham Walker, who Motor Cycle enthusiasts will recall was internationally famous as Captain of the British team for some years, and a winner of the Isle of Man T.T.

On leaving Dunlop in 1954 he joined the Aspro organisation as a copy writer for overseas, then became Media Executive, and is now Advertising Manager N.P.L. Murray, truly a man of many parts, who in the two years he has been with us has become extremely popular with all who work with him.

What does he do in his spare time, you say ? Never a dull moment, says Murray. Driving in car rallies, and tinkering with his car. Well girls, he's not married—yet ! !

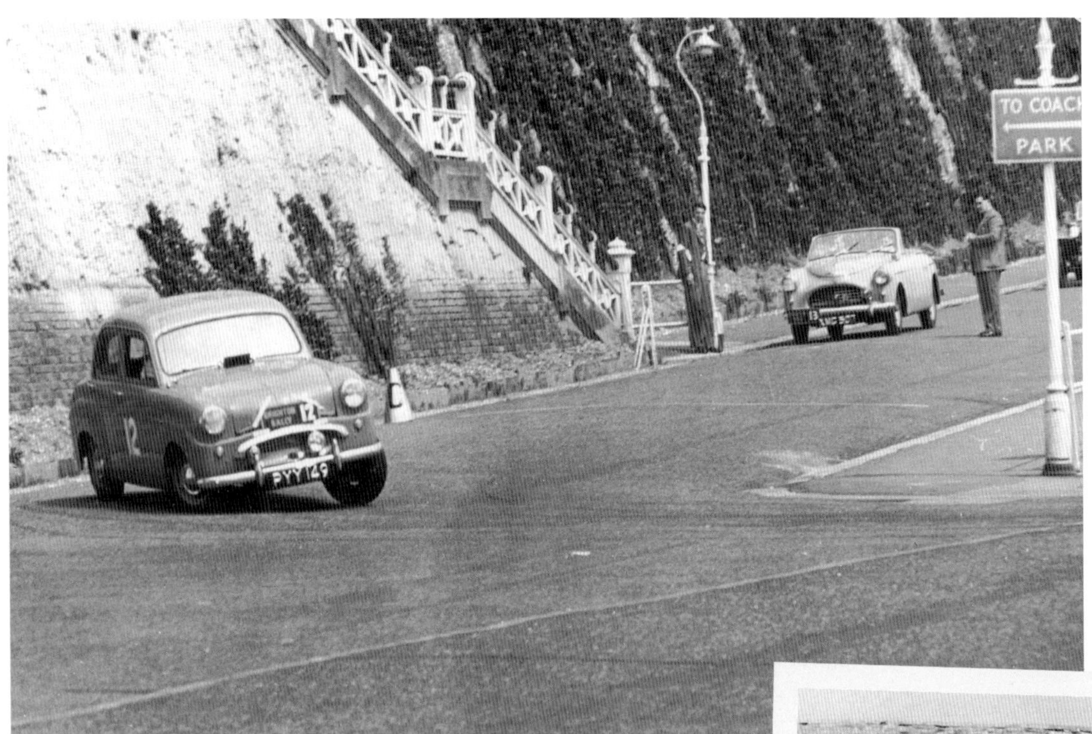

Murray On His 'Main' Career

Mike Doodson

"On weekdays, Murray Walker was a high pressure huckster, peddling Mars bars, Vauxhall cars, Smiths instruments, Dunlop tyres and the Co-op. Although he declines full responsibility for it, perhaps his best-known campaign was the one he conducted for a birdfood named Trill.

"'Birdseed is a very big market in England, you know. And we had built it up partly as a result of some memorable advertising: "Trill makes Budgies Bounce with Health -- because it contains Sunshine Grains". By the time we had 80% of the market, it was obvious that the solution to selling more Trill was not to get the remaining 20%, but to create more budgies.'

"A tough job, eh? But Murray and his men came up with the truly unforgettable slogan, 'An Only Budgie is a Lonely Budgie'. From TV and cinema screens across the nation, it touched the consciences of bird fanciers, put a smile on the faces of pet shop owners everywhere, and did no harm at all to the Masius balance sheet."

"With my very own money, I bought my first car, a bathtub Standard 10, which I looked after like a mother. To establish uniqueness, I had the roof painted scarlet and equipped it with an Alexander engine conversion and countless uselss but image-building accessories. I then proceeded to beat the hell out of it in rallies, including this one at Brighton. In my mind, Alberto Ascari had a great deal to worry about!"

Murray's Secret

Peter Gwynn

"Murray and I joined Masius & Ferguson, as it was then, in 1959 and worked together for 22 years. If you think of one word in relation to Murray, it's 'enthusiasm'. At board meetings, if anyone had good news, which happily we frequently did as we were a pretty good agency, Murray was the first person to say, 'Great. Well done.' He never hung back. I think the great thing about Murray is that you get what you see, he is what he appears to be. He is a lovely man, absolutely genuine, full of enthusiasm."

"Shortly before its sad demise, I drove my mother's immaculate Morris Minor in the Lancia Rally. My best mate, Brian Emerton, follows my wheel tracks through the ford in his superb Aston Martin with our mutual chum, George Tughan, bringing up the rear in his MG TD. Can anyone identify the brutal-looking device behind the barn?"

A Mars A Day Helps The Agency Work, Rest & Pay

Peter Gwynn

"The main account that he grew at the agency, although he handled many others, was the Mars pet food business. Mine was the Colgate Palmolive business – those were the two national, and then international accounts, we built the whole agency on."

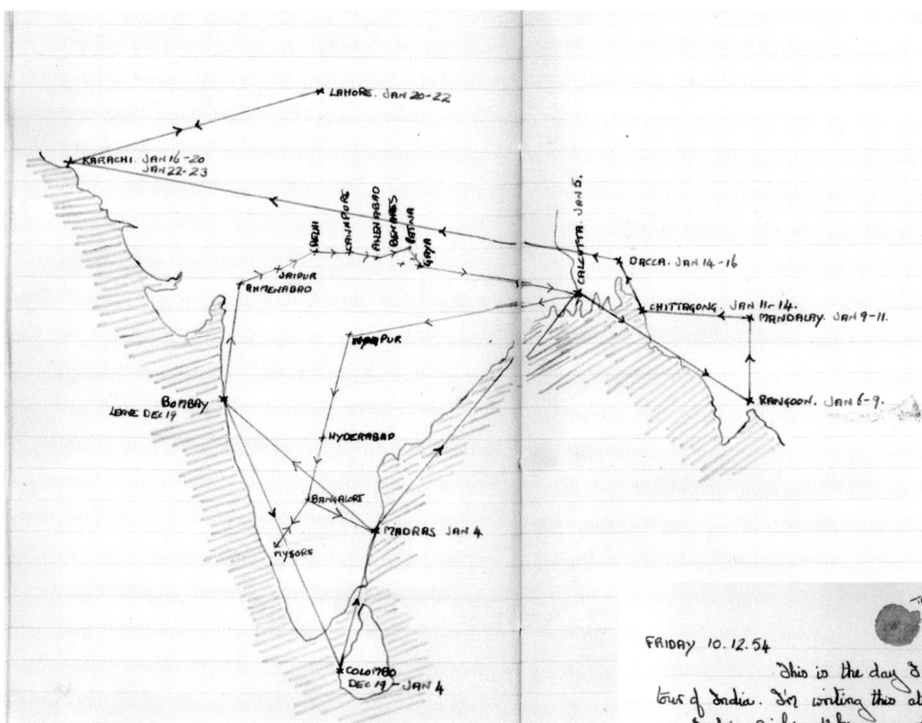

"During my time with Aspro, I was Overseas Advertising Manager and made a most incredible four-and-a-half month trip to India, and what were then East Pakistan, Ceylon and West Pakistan. I kept a detailed diary and these pages show the enthralling route I took. It was a long one."

THIS IS WHAT HAPPENS TO PENS IN AEROPLANES!

FRIDAY 10.12.54

This is the day I finish my tour of India. I'm writing this at one p.m in an Indian Airlines Viking somewhere between Madras and Bombay and by the time we land I reckon I'll have travelled 4,500 miles by rail, road, air and river in the six weeks since I left. Six wonderfully interesting weeks they've been too. I've learnt a lot and seen a lot but I've still got a long way to go and a lot more to see and learn before I get home. I'm pleased I'll be on my own from the 19th onwards for Jim is beginning to irritate me with his mannerism of riding every fiddling little item to death. However that's a small enough complaint and its quite a testimonial to all three of us that we've been able to live in each other's pockets day and night without any harsh words!

It hammered down with rain all night at Madras and was still at it when we took off at 11.50, an hour behind schedule. Now, at 1305, we've

The Cage Is A Stage

Norman Crofts

"I joined Masius the same year as Murray, in 1959.

"There was one Trill production meeting that Murray and I attended where the script called for the Budgie to perform tricks.

"The director listened in silence - repeated the script requirements – and then asked what we would like the budgie to do for an encore!"

"Here's another one who slipped through the net - Joan Hewson - looking very glamorous with a slim-sized me, both of us in our finery."

"Now this one, to my chagrin, was married! But Hyacinth Coombs, her husband Larry and I, had some great times together and went places in the scintillating Vauxhall Velox that I managed to pull the necessary strings for Larry to buy in the car-hungry post-war era."

To Work For A Rest?

Peter Gwynn

PP: "After a weekend commentating, did he arrive in the office shattered on Monday morning?"

"No! He was never shattered or, if he was, he never showed it. He reflected why the agency was such a good one. Everyone enjoyed it."

"Joan to my right, Hyacinth to my left... Didn't know which way to turn!"

"After Aspro, I joined famous advertising agency, McCann Erickson, as account executive on the Esso business, very much the agency's biggest client. I drove the Hillman Minx during a TV commercial shoot featuring the old Bullnose Morris. I could explain what the moustachioed bloke in the back is doing with the trombone but it would take too long!"

Modus Operandi

Peter Gwynn

PP: "Was he creative or did he rely on others to be creative?"

"We were known as 'The grocers of St James's Square'. That was supposed to be rather rude from our rival agencies. The fact of the matter was we handled a multitude of quick turnover products, a lot of which were grocery or pharmacy – that type of product. We never went after creative awards. We would never have won any because our advertising was very much to the point. Take PAL, for instance, you'd have a split screen - I'm exaggerating to make a point – you'd have an unhealthy dog on one side with Brand X and a fine, wagging-tail dog on the other with PAL – 'prolongs active life'.

"There was a Creative Dept and an Account Handling Dept but in fact they worked very closely together. In the highly creative agencies, the Creative Dept ruled the agency and, in our view, they produced many very beautiful, very memorable advertisements but no-one ever remembered what they were actually selling!

"So Murray world work very closely with the creative people but the creative people worked very closely with the account handlers."

"After joining advertising agency, Masius & Ferguson in 1959 to work on the Mars confectionery and pet foods accounts, I was instrumental in getting Dunlop to give us their major Dunlop tyre account business. The most memorable campaign we did for Dunlop featured a mythical wheeled animal which we called Groundhog. I am holding a visulaisation of our creature but it wasn't until I first went to Montreal for the Candian Grand Prix, years later, that I discovered there is a real live animal which they call the groundhog."

A Helping Hand

Norman Crofts

"At Christmas time, we used to take the secretaries and other down-the-line people out to lunch.

On one such occasion, we were in an Italian restaurant in Soho having a splendid time when one of the secretaries ordered a Zambucca liqueur with her coffee.

"As is usual, it came with sugar round the rim and floating coffee beans and the waiter set it alight. The secretary then asked how to put the flame out and Murray put the palm of his hand over the glass, which burned a ring on his palm, and we had to take him to hospital to get it dressed!"

Murray's Attributes

Peter Gwynn

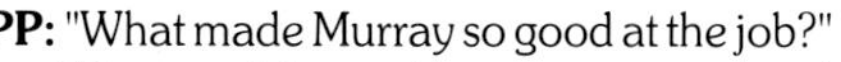

PP: "What made Murray so good at the job?"

"The usual things, like attention to detail. I would think the two most important things, and I speak with some experience as I ended up as Managing Director, were these. He was able to communicate on behalf of all the people working on the specific client's account – the agency's position, its recommendations – in his highly articulate manner but with immense authority. He was respected and liked by the clients.

"Equally important, people in the agency loved working with him and liked working for him. You take it as read that he had the ability to assess the marketing situations for many types of products and apply the various aspects of dealing with that. In fact, no-one would have reached the top of our, or any, agency if they hadn't got that."

"I go back to my first word 'enthusiasm' which overlaid everything he did with the clients and the people within the agency."

"We had models of our friendly Groundhog made and gave one to each of the Dunlop Board members who attended the presentation that we hoped would win us their business. When Managing Director, Bill Bailey, smilingly insisted on taking his model back to his office and said he was going to keep it on this desk, I knew that we were several million pounds better off!"

"What on earth am I up to here? I seem to remember it was part of a TV commercial for a builders' supplies company. Looks like I needed their help."

"At one point, I missed a couple of weeks at Masius through illness and was sent a brilliant get well card showing me roaring out of my hospital ward on my BMW motor cycle and ignoring the planitiff cries of the people who were trying to make me better. I liked it so much I had it framed for my office wall."

Wooing The Clients

Peter Gwynn

"Apart from developing the Mars pet food business, he worked on Vauxhall and Dunlop. He was with Aspro before he joined the agency and he looked after that account which he brought with him, and many others.

"After the war he had worked for Dunlop and he kept that contact going and he was largely instrumental in bringing the Dunlop business in to us.

"The fact that he was damn good at the job and had the personality he had was a great combination. We were an agency who kept our clients. Part of that was the director and the team, the director in charge of that business and the team under him. As a business, there's no machinery; it's just people. Murray, as he does with everyone, just wooed his clients – they loved him."

A Brace Of BMWs

Peter Gwynn

"Our office was in St James's Square and he used to arrive on his BMW motor cycle every morning wearing a totally enveloping orange track suit, which always appealed to everyone!

"Years ago, when we were still with the agency, we were going up to Donington together. I called to pick him up and we were having coffee. He said, 'Come out to the garage, I must show you something.' So we went out to the garage. All the cars were outside. Inside was not one BMW bike but two. I said, 'Murray, I didn't know you'd got two. What do you want two for?'

"He said, 'Because I love them so much,' which sums up his whole approach."

"By 1982, I found that trying to cope with the joint demands of a very busy life at Masius and the BBC at weekends was becoming too much so I decided to retire from my proper job. Masius gave me all sorts of wonderful presents, including two superb models of pre-war Mercedes-Benz and Auto Union Grand Prix cars which you see in front of me at one of my many retirement parties."

Absent Without Leave

Norman Crofts

"My office was next door to Murray's on the sixth floor and to keep costs down we shared a secretary, who had a small office the other side of the corridor. Late one night when I was in bed at home, I received a telephone call from Elizabeth, Murray's wife, asking me if I knew our secretary's home telephone number. In conversation it transpired that, very unlike Murray, he had not arrived home and, most unusually, he had not contacted Elizabeth, and she was getting worried.

"I told her to try to relax and I would find out where he was. I then phoned the janitor who had a flat on the sixth floor at the end of the corridor from our offices. The janitor was an ex-army Sergeant-Major by the name of Jock Cameron with a very broad Scottish (Glaswegian) accent and one of the best addresses in London at 2 St James's Square. He was in bed at the time and his false teeth were in the bathroom. His accent was so broad I had difficulty understanding him at the best of times but without his teeth...

"I asked him to go along the corridor and check that Murray was not in his office and ring me back which he did. However, he also checked with the night porter on the front door who remembered Murray going out earlier with a man he was able to describe so well that I knew it to be the European Manager of GM Service Division. I telephoned Elizabeth back and, just as I did, she said, 'He's just walked in'.

"The first person in my office the next morning was Murray apologising but I was able to assure him it happens to us all!"

"Desperately seeking to regain my long-distant youth, I bought myself this absolutely brilliant BMW R90S - the one with the sensational orange paint job. Needless to say, I had to make it different - hence the alloy Lester wheels which were very unusual in those days."

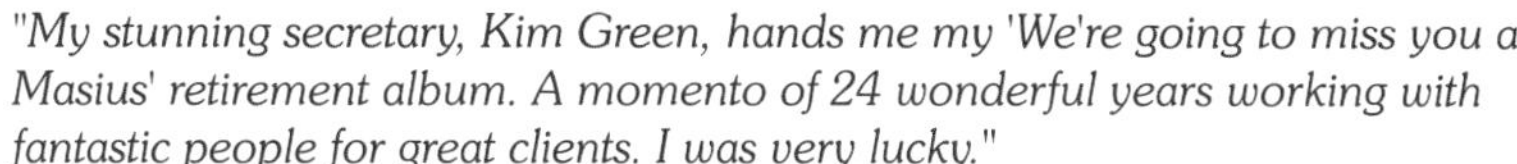

"My stunning secretary, Kim Green, hands me my 'We're going to miss you at Masius' retirement album. A momento of 24 wonderful years working with fantastic people for great clients. I was very lucky."

The End Of The Fun

Peter Gwynn

"The agency got into bed with an American company and everything changed. We were always an agency with, as far as it ever can be, no internal politics. We all got on like a house on fire, it was fun and I know I speak for Murray when I say we really enjoyed Masius and were proud of being part of it. While we were there, we built it up from being really quite small and for at least a year we managed to knock J. Walter Thompson off the top.

"Jack Wynne-Williams, who was our great Chairman, died and I think we both got fed-up with it at the same time. It became highly political. People were spending more time worrying what was going to be happening to them rather than looking after their clients. Murray and I decided we had had a great time but it wasn't as much fun as it used to be and we had other things in mind."

"Sadly the ravages of time have faded this fake 'Bayeau Tapestry' depiction of my life and times which Masius gave me when I left."

BOOK I

Best wishes from all at McCann's

THE MAN FOR MARS

Behind Every Great Man...

Peter Gwynn

"Murray and I were both great dancers at the agency Christmas party. We all enjoyed each other's company. I had immense admiration for him at the agency; I've had it ever since. Also great affection for him. And he had a great back-up from Elizabeth over the years. She's a tough lady and she's given him immense support. They're a great couple."

Rallycross

As Paddy Hopkirk describes below, an event was concocted by Raymond Baxter for BBC Television and run at Brands Hatch in 1963. This did not have all the elements of the later events and was not called 'rallycross'. In fact, it was named the Mini Monte and was organised by the *London Motor Club*.

It was actually some time later that an ABC Television producer Robert Reed came up with the idea for an event that combined a variety of surfaces but principally was a blend of tarmac track and various off-road conditions. Being run over a short circuit and not being dependent on the weather made this new type of event ideal for televising. ABC was one of the franchisees that made up the independent commercial network, under the ITV umbrella, the only rival to the BBC at that time. There was pretty fierce rivalry between them.

The first rallycross event was held at Lydden Hill on February 4, 1967 and was shown on the *World of Sport* programme that was ITV's answer to the BBC's *Grandstand*. Though it was intended to be a one-off, the event was so successful that another was held and gradually the concept took off and a new form of motor sport was born. For the first events, cars were run singly and timed.

It was John Sprinzel, prolific racer and one of the founders of Speedwell, who thought up the term 'rallycross'. These early events were organised by Bud Smith of the Tunbridge Wells Centre of the 750 Motor Club and were very much driven by him and Lydden owner, Bill Chesson.

The first *international* rallycross event was planned for the Saturday after the 1967 RAC Rally when all the big names would be in the UK. Unfortunately, the RAC Rally was cancelled that year due to foot and mouth disease. The rallycross event went ahead but without most of the international stars. Notably, rally legend, Roger Clark, shared a Ford Cortina GT with GP driver, Graham Hill.

Around this time, the BBC did a deal with the Thames Estuary Automobile Club, headed by Sid Offord, to run a series of events at Lydden which would be shown on *Grandstand* and this is where Murray came into the picture as the BBC's commentator. He had become known to audiences the length and breadth of the land for his commentaries on scrambling. Rallycross again suited his excitable style and further established that style and his name.

Lydden, which is near Dover in Kent, was created in 1955 by Bill Chesson and the track was originally used for grass track racing and stock cars. However, by 1965 a tarmac surface had been laid and the circuit then hosted a variety of car racing up to Formula Three. In 1989 the track was acquired by Tom Bissett and two years later it was purchased by the TAG-McLaren Group.

Initially rallycross was populated mainly by hot Minis, which revelled in the conditions and were relatively cheap to prepare and tune. These were supplemented by Escorts, in various guises, Hillman Imps and VW Beetles, usually Porsche-engined. Such names as 'Jumping' Jeff Williamson, Hugh Wheldon, Barry Lee, Tony Drummond, John Welch, John Button (Jenson's father), Keith Ripp, Rod Chapman and John Taylor came to be TV stars. A number of top rally drivers had been involved in the early events and by 1970 Roger Clark was driving a works four wheel drive Capri. As happens with every aspect of motor sport, the cars became more and more specialised, powerful and expensive. Four wheel drive was increasingly employed, to obvious advantage. There were V8 Minis, Saabs, Porsches, Volvos, Ford Fiestas, BMWs, VW Golfs, Renault 5s, DAFs, Skodas and Audi Quattros to name just some of the mud-splattered motor cars that were subjected to the rough and tumble of rallycross, and there were certainly some spectacular tumbles!

These usually took place when the car was leading and Murray was talking about the virtues of having a clear track ahead!

One of Murray's most famous, and oft repeated, gaffes involved a driver called Stan Hastilow. Murray had been diligently doing the rounds of the paddock earlier in the day and spoken with Hastilow and discovered several interesting facts. Later, when commentating with Hastilow in the lead, Murray was able to inform the viewers that Stan was a computer programmer who had cleverly used such skills to cut a series of holes of differing diameters, ensuring he could see, however mud-splattered his windscreen might be.

As Murray was just imparting this fascinating information, Hastilow left the circuit, mounted a bank and flew though an advertising hoarding!

From 1982 the BBC restricted their coverage to the annual British Rallycross Grands Prix at Brands Hatch which were dominated by the increasingly sophisticated Group B cars, such as the Metro 6R4, the Quattros and Ford RS 200s. Such pilots as Martin Schanche and Will Gollop were now the guys to beat.

Rather like motocross, rallycross had had a good run but the coverage peaked and then dropped away. Once again, Murray helped to make the sport the success it was, and still is, and the sport had been the perfect medium for Murray and his unique style.

"When the BBC, ITV and the public sadly got bored with over-exposed motor cycle scrambling, it was replaced with what was, in effect, the same thing in what looked like everyday saloon cars. Things like Minis, VW Beetles and Hillman Imps. The public took to it in a big way and it wasn't long before the rallying and saloon car racing works driver stars, conscious of the publicity potential, were appearing on the box. Two of them were Monte Carlo Rally winner, Paddy Hopkirk, on the left, and Mini racing sensation, John Rhodes. Funnily enough, though, neither of them set the world alight in competition with the rallycross specialists."

Murray's Curse

Hugh Wheldon

"Once he was saying how reliable my Mini was and how well I was doing.

"At that very moment, it ground to a halt."

"Here is another momento in my study - a cross-section of all the going that made the Lydden circuit such a stunner - bits of gravel, sand, chalk and tarmac - add water and you've got Lydden in a bottle!"

Soft Foundations

Paddy Hopkirk

"Rallycross was a new invention and I think it was influenced by Raymond Baxter. After we came back from the Monte Carlo Rally, he wanted a way of showing some action, rather than doing an interview with people just sitting around a table. I remember we did something at Brands Hatch. Pat Moss and Timo Makinen were involved.

"Instead of being on the track, we went across a bit of a field so we could see the cars sliding around in the slippery conditions. It was a foggy day in the middle of winter and it was the first time I realised that cameras can see through fog much better than the human eye. So the event, even though I thought it would be a washout, was in fact very good on television. All these cars were banging into each other and sliding around on the mud, and we were having a bit of fun.

"Then someone decided this was a good idea for a new sport and it was set up at Lydden Hill and then became quite a serious sport."

"My friend, John Batty, who was one of the leading lights of the Thames Estuary Automobile Club, who organised the TV rallycross meetings at Lydden, made this up to remind me of the great times I had had there - which it does."

"One of the better drivers at Lydden was the ever-cheerful Chris Coburn whose incredibly unlikely car was a Vauxhall Viva - the original biscuit tin on wheels which it was my misfortune, in my advertising executive capacity, to try to persuade the unsuspecting British public to buy. I even did in-car commentary on fast laps with Chris. What a hero!"

"Ouch! The ebullient 'Jumping' Jeff Williamson makes a crash-landing in his pristine Mini. Note, he has ingeniously saved weight by dispensing with the windscreen. Why bother, it only gets in the way of the mud!"

First Memories

Paddy Hopkirk

"I think I met Murray Walker for the first time at Lydden Hill. I remember being impressed by him because he was quite posh! He was not the usual sort of chap who followed motor sport but was with a top advertising agency in London. He was a great enthusiast, spoke English properly and was a very good commentator.

"I remember thinking how nice he was. He has always been a nice guy and never got up himself. He never talks down to people, he always recognises people and is very friendly. That is not always the case in our sport."

"Here are two rallycross greats. Roger Clark in the special-for-rallycross 4WD works Ford Capri having fun as a change from winning World Championship rallies and Mini-mounted Brian Chatfield. Meantime, I was shouting my head off in the commentary box as they started to climb Hairy Hill." (Kerry Dunlop)

"Here Williamson's Mark 2 Mini, now with hole-infested, mud-resisting windscreen and snazzy bracing bars."

"And they called it fun! But bumping, boring, slipping and sliding round Lydden in indescribable conditions used to generate massive entries and audiences of millions."

Nickname Takes Off

'Jumping' Jeff Williamson

"I was always known in rallycross by my nickname, 'Jumping' Jeff. Although Murray wasn't the one who christened me that he was certainly the one that brought it to millions of viewers. I didn't play on it much then but 40 years later I play on it more now! I'll always be grateful to Murray!"

Un Murrayism Francais

Paddy Hopkirk

"I did a lot of rallying in France with the Alpine, the Tour de France and Le Mans, and the French couldn't get their mouths around h-o-p-k-i-r-k and they used to call me Monsieur Hoprick. Quite a few joked about that but whether Murray called me that, I don't recall!"

Spot Of Misinformation

'Jumping' Jeff Williamson

"To be honest, we always used to have a bit of a laugh with Murray. He was always beavering about the paddock, asking this and that, and wanting to know what was going on and who was doing what.

"We were using a new type of race tyre, a Dunlop CR65. These always had a green spot on them and, for our own amusement, we used to paint them a different colour. We put on a red spot and then told Murray we'd found this new tyre that was worth two or three seconds a lap – the red spot that Dunlop had developed for us.

"Murray would take this information and use it in his commentary!"

Wills champion Hugh Wheldon chats with Murray Walker of the BBC.

Ground Work

John Taylor

"I first met Murray at Lydden Hill when the BBC used to broadcast rallycross on *Grandstand*. We'd get there at half past seven in the morning, and Murray would be there, clipboard in hand, pen poised and he would go to every person and quiz you and take notes. Then, during his commentary, all these little tit-bits that one had given him would be used in his commentary."

MOTOR week ending March 28 1970 67

Well done Hugh Wheldon for giving the works entrants the works.

Against the might of the Works entered teams, Hugh Wheldon drove his privately entered Mini to victory in the Wills Rallycross Championship.

Murray Walker, of the BBC, described it as "A fairy tale ending to an event held in a fairy tale setting."

We don't believe in fairies.

"The Lydden rallycross events were held in the winter months when the conditions were almost invariably cold, wet, foul and muddy. If you were racing and could see, you had more than a head's start and there were all sorts of weird and wonderful attempts at overcoming the challenge. They didn't make for a cosy interior though!"

The Downsides

Paddy Hopkirk

"I didn't really enjoy rallycross that much because there was so much dirt that it all came down to windscreens getting covered in mud and not being able to see where you were going. So the guys were putting huge windscreen washers that pumped gallons of water on the windscreen, people had holes cut in their windscreens – it became quite a different sport and I wasn't so enthusiastic about it.

"I didn't think it was a sport that involved actual driving skills as much as clever ideas. There was quite a lot of bumping and bashing so it was probably a very good spectator sport because a camera could stay in one place and watch a car going round in circles, which is rather different from special stages. That has always been the problem with rallying. It's hard to sell because you can't have an arena and can't sell tickets."

Totally On Board

Rod Chapman

"I first met Murray in the early days of rallycross. He used to arrive on his motorcycle, in all weathers. What can you say about such a gentleman? He is an absolute gem.

"He was so professional, had always done his homework. He went round to every team on the Saturday and got all the information before it went out live. We saw a lot of Murray in those early days.

"It was a very, very popular sport in those days and Murray came over extremely well. I think we all took him out in our cars. That was the way he liked it; he liked to be totally on-board."

MurrayismMurrayismMurrayism

"And the first three cars are all Escorts, which isn't surprising as this is an all-Escort race."

"In the car or out of it, they didn't call him 'Jumping' Jeff Williamson for nothing."

BMC's Attitude

Paddy Hopkirk

"For the BMC works team it was more a case of making guest appearances because we weren't going to take it up as a sport in any way. That may sound a bit snobby but it wasn't getting international publicity, whereas winning the Alpine or the Monte Carlo was, and BMC wanted to sell cars around the world. It got a bit of publicity for the UK market but rallying was much more international."

Wind-up Suspension

'Jumping' Jeff Williamson

"We'd been testing the week before at Lydden Hill with the works Minis and Murray was asking me what we had actually been testing. I said, 'Well, one of the things I was trying to decide was whether the Hydrolastic suspension or dry suspension was quicker round Lydden. So, we have been testing two cars, back to back.'

"He asked what the outcome had been.

"I said, 'Well, we couldn't really decide. So, we've gone for half and half – we've done one side Hydrolastic and one side dry!'

"It was all done in a light-hearted way because Murray, of all people, always did his homework."

Preparation's The Secret

John Rhodes

"Preparation was his secret. I was told years ago that there are four Ps in 'preparation' – 'poor preparation means poor performance'. At Lydden Hill, he'd be there at eight o'clock in the morning interviewing people."

"One of Lydden's superstars was Rod Chapman who literally made his living out of a hole in the ground. Landfill they called it." (Kerry Dunlop)

What woke me again, as it must have shattered the sleep of thousands, was the mild shouting of Murray Walker in the Pits for the BBC. Now there is a voice that could down a bat at 2000 yards. The screen as far as I could see was full of Fords and Volkswagens behaving almost precisely as they do in the Old Brompton Road. But Murray's excitement knows no bounds. He composed the following which I jotted down and will one day translate into the Chinese:

"Down is coming the rain.
Off has come de Lanière.
Off has come his bonnet-top."

"Tough and out-spoken, Ford works driver and rallycross's first European Champion, John Taylor, used to be a steeplechase jockey. He broke his back, falling off a horse, and he broke my ribs taking me round Lydden - sideways like this!" (Kerry Dunlop)

So Near And Yet Such A Wallop!

John Welch

"We had one incident which was always being shown on BBC. I was overtaking Tony Drummond for the lead and I only had to just overtake Tony and I would win the British Championship. He caught me just at the wrong time and the car didn't carry on going forwards; it just went sideways into the bank and spun round. Scrapped the car, scrapped my ribs and so on.

"Murray just said, 'Bang! Bang! Wallop!' Biggest wallop I ever had."

"Which way is quicker? The oversteery way or the understeery way? Leader Rod Chapman, in the Ford Escort, tries the former and rallycross's first BBC TV Champion, Hugh Wheldon in the Mini, tries the latter. Looks like Rod is right." (Kerry Dunlop)

Cutting Through The Fog

Stuart Tallack

"I remember seeing Murray in action at a rallycross Grand Prix at Brands Hatch and it was so foggy it was like an old-fashioned pea-souper. Murray could only see the cars for about 200 yards per lap and yet you wouldn't have known it. He was just commentating the whole time and when they briefly came back into view again, and if the order wasn't quite as expected, he would just seamlessly adjust and cope with it without anyone knowing. It was just incredible."

Action!

John Taylor

"They decided to introduce the *Grandstand* programme from Lydden Hill on a very wet, cold, miserable day and Murray did an intro to camera beside my car. He had the door open and the idea was that as soon as he finished his piece he would jump in the passenger seat of my car and then I would roar off and do one lap with Murray giving a description.

"I don't know whether he'd ever been in a car going that quickly on that slippery a surface, that sideways, seemingly out of control, and in his book he says I broke his ribs! He says he fell out of the seat or something. Well, I'm not sure that's quite true! I suspect it was the real tension of trying to commentate and experiencing being thrown round Lydden Hill at a fair rate of knots."

"Motor accessory tycoon, Keith Ripp, used only the most sophisticated machinery for his rallycrossing and always treated it with the utmost consideration."

"Note the maximum vision, high technology windscreen on Keith Ripp's Mini which enabled him to retain the lead. Getting off the line well helped too - which he invariably did."

Tongue-Twisters

John Welch

"He'd always have a wander round the bar, he'd have a chat with somebody, get all the foreign names totally mixed up but everybody knew who he meant. It didn't matter. Wonderful guy."

"Never mind mudguards - they only add to the weight. The spectacular Keith Ripp negotiates the slippery chalk at Chesson's Drift."

Wires Crossed

'Jumping' Jeff Williamson

"I always used to fill in the Commentator's Information Sheet. I got some feedback from my family after one event, that he'd described me as a GPO technician from Newcastle, whereas I was actually a garage mechanic, a grease monkey, from Retford!"

MurrayismMurrayismMurrayismMurrayismMurrayism

Murray speaking, of Martin Schanche's 420bhp turbocharged Escort, and John Welch in a similar machine – "The car in front is absolutely unique, except for the one behind it, which is identical."

"Without a shadow of doubt, the two most specatacular drivers, during my rallycross days, were the irrepressble, overwhelmingly excitable Norwegian Martin Schanche (left) and the craggy John Taylor who guaranteed me fireworks every time they hit the track. (Kerry Dunlop)

A Classic

Keith Ripp

"I competed in rallycross in the '80s with Murray commentating. One sequence was so funny that it became famous on television, was shown as the opening sequence for the BBC *Grandstand* programme for two years and has been aired on *Auntie's Bloomers* with Terry Wogan.

"Murray's words were as follows: "One lap to do and Keith Ripp is way ahead of the other drivers and should achieve fastest time of day. Keith Ripp is streaking away with just half a lap to do to finish, avoiding Mabbs Bank, which he does *not* do! Keith Ripp rolls his Mini over and over again."

"Superstar Will Gollop cut his rallycross teeth in a Saab, but despite his careful and considerate driving, he found it didn't hold together too well!"

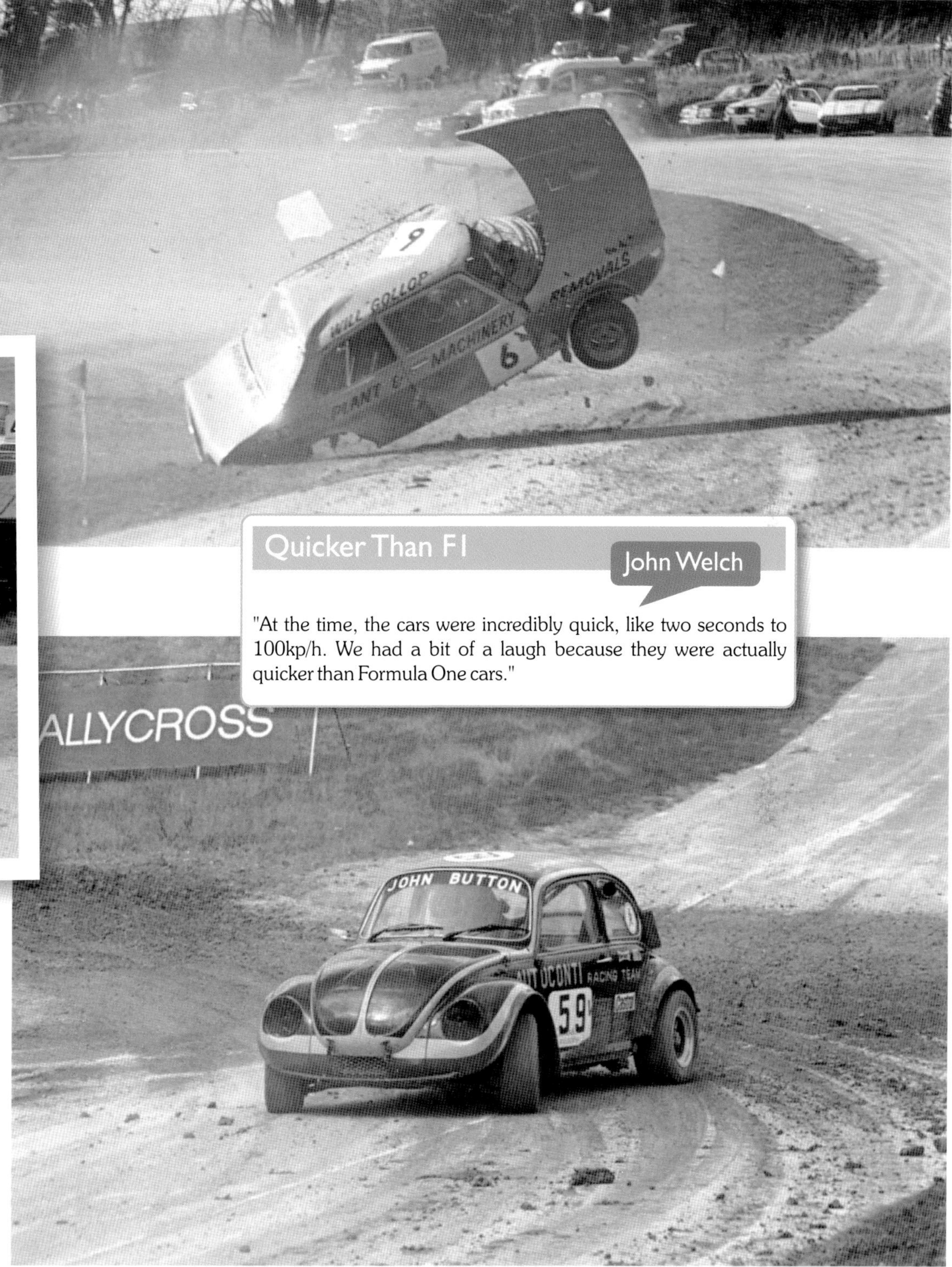

Quicker Than F1

John Welch

"At the time, the cars were incredibly quick, like two seconds to 100kp/h. We had a bit of a laugh because they were actually quicker than Formula One cars."

"This is where Jenson got his speed. Father John Button in his self-tuned VW Beetle was one of rallycross's top drivers and a mighty popular one too." (Kerry Dunlop)

Down To Earth

John Welch

"At the time, he was doing Formula One and knew all the Sennas and such like and yet he still found the time to talk to you and make you feel very important. And he would understand the sport and then be able to explain it to viewers.

"I last competed when Murray was commentating in about 1990 and yet at events today, you can be 20 yards away, but he'll still recognise you and give you a big smile and a wave. He can remember people's faces – that's nice."

"In time the saturation coverage of rallycross by the BBC outlasted its welcome, as had motor cycle scrambling. More's the pity because it was great stuff. However, the BBC gave welcome TV time to the newly-instituted British Rallycross Grand Prix at Brands Hatch on a specially built track that incorporated part of the tarmac Grand Prix cicuit. I actually had a decent commentary box there where I was able to rhapsodise about Keith Ripp in the lead - again, as he was at both these events." (Kerry Dunlop)

Modest Means

Jim Reside

"I used to work with him on the rallycross at Lydden Hill, and it was live so anything Murray said was there for all time. And we used to be in hysterics.

"It was very different because we didn't have the vast resources that Grand Prix racing demanded and indeed had. At Lydden, we did it with four cameras and it was a bit skimpy in terms of the investment the BBC put into it."

A Thump On The Back

Keith Ripp

"I was easily leading the BBC *Grandstand* Rallycross GP at Brands Hatch in a Ford Fiesta. The two works Audi Quattro 4WD cars had been given a 5% handicap and started at the back of the grid. They came storming through the field and then pushed me into the Armco barrier at Paddock Bend.

"Murray Walker interviewed me on TV after the crash. He said, 'I was standing about six feet away from the Armco at Paddock Bend, which you hit with a huge thump'.

"The works Audis were black-flagged for causing an incident and were excluded from the event."

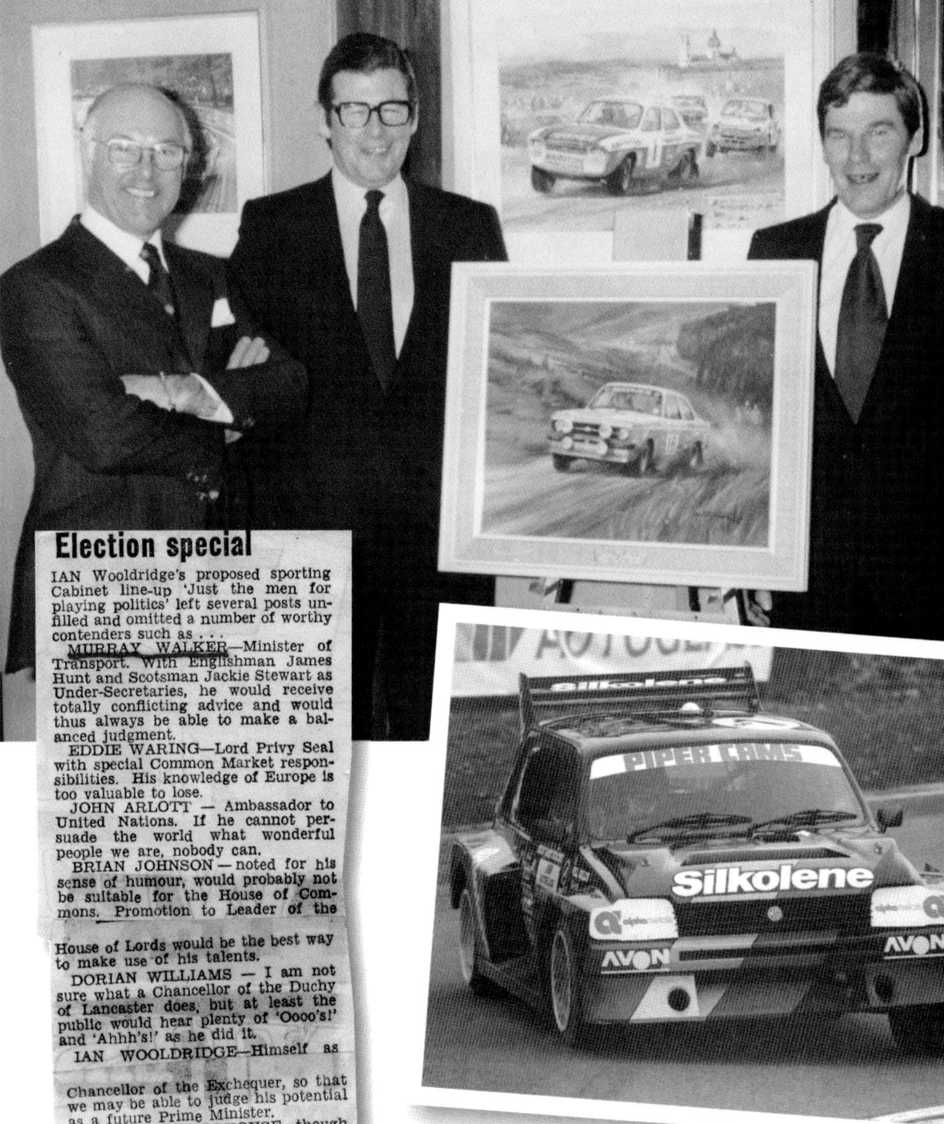

Election special

IAN Wooldridge's proposed sporting Cabinet line-up 'Just the men for playing politics' left several posts unfilled and omitted a number of worthy contenders such as . . .

MURRAY WALKER—Minister of Transport. With Englishman James Hunt and Scotsman Jackie Stewart as Under-Secretaries, he would receive totally conflicting advice and would thus always be able to make a balanced judgment.

EDDIE WARING—Lord Privy Seal with special Common Market responsibilities. His knowledge of Europe is too valuable to lose.

JOHN ARLOTT — Ambassador to United Nations. If he cannot persuade the world what wonderful people we are, nobody can.

BRIAN JOHNSON—noted for his sense of humour, would probably not be suitable for the House of Commons. Promotion to Leader of the House of Lords would be the best way to make use of his talents.

DORIAN WILLIAMS — I am not sure what a Chancellor of the Duchy of Lancaster does, but at least the public would hear plenty of 'Oooo's!' and 'Ahhh's!' as he did it.

IAN WOOLDRIDGE—Himself as Chancellor of the Exchequer, so that we may be able to judge his potential as a future Prime Minister.

BARBARA WOODHOUSE—though not a sports reporter—Speaker of the House. She'll be able to maintain discipline among the more rowdy elements.

DAVID COLE,
Oakham, Leicester.

First Meeting

John Button

"Murray was a big name to me because I used to listen to the Isle of Man TT and, even more importantly, he was painting the picture then [because it was on radio] so I was a big fan.

"I first met him at the Kentagon at Brands Hatch. I went over and introduced myself, bit terrified to do so because he was such a big name. But he was such a lovely, lovely chap, and it was absolutely wonderful to see him when we got into Formula One."

"Ford dealers, Haynes of Maidstone, sponsored European Rallycross European Champion, John Taylor. Here's David Haynes (next to me) with John Taylor (second from right) and the famous Ford Competitions Manager, Stuart Turner."

The Enthusiast In Murray

Paddy Hopkirk

"It was quite unusual to get somebody as high up as he was in business coming down to commentate on such a funny sport. That made him stand out in my mind. But he was always a very nice man, who couldn't have been more humble and friendly."

MurrayismMurrayismMurrayism

"Here at Brands Hatch, Will Gollop has a clear lead over Will Gollop."

"After he had switched to his Metro 6R4, Will Gollop became almost unbeatable. Nice bloke, too." (Kerry Dunlop)

"Another great rallycross champion was literally a giant of a man, Trevor Hopkins, who drove massive earth-moving devices when he was wasn't winning in his distinctive Ford RS200. Either way, he was a top man for me behind the microphone." (Kerry Dunlop)

Childhood Hilarity

Jenson Button

"What I most remember about Murray was that he used to commentate on my father's rallycross days. I remember once when my father hit this Mini at the first corner and the Mini barrel-rolled into the wall. I just remember Murray's voice. I thought it was hilarious at the time but obviously it wasn't, but I was very young!

"It was just Murray's voice: 'He's going over! And over! And over! And over! And over again!' Fantastic. He was so good to listen to."

And A Few Other Things...

Though most famous for his Formula One commentaries, Murray actually worked on a wide variety of different forms of motor sport, not all of which involved wheels.

In its earlier days of broadcasting Grand Prix racing and beforehand, the BBC also embraced the lower echelons, including Formula Three and the often mad antics of the Formula Ford brigade. These were, of course, the proving grounds for many a big name of the future.

Power boats did not have wheels but they most certainly had engines, and so Murray was dropped in at the deep end and given the job of commentating on this exciting, and highly dangerous, sport in the mid-'70s. Diligently doing his homework, as ever, he soon became a natural and took to the sport in the manner of a duck to the wet stuff.

Robert Glen of EP Barrus, the concessionaires for Johnson powerboat engines, was the catalyst and Murray often shared a commentary box with journalist and expert, Ros Nott. Venues included Bristol Docks, Fairford, the River Thames and, in the mid-'80s, Loch Vaal, near Johannesburg for South African television.

When someone had the crazy notion of racing trucks and it took off, the BBC turned to their man and Murray commentated on the likes of Steve Parrish, Barry Sheene, Martin Brundle, Alan Jones and Stig Blomqvist hurling the monsters around. Murray's expert co-commentators included bike racers Parrish and Sheene.

The *Driving Force* programmes broke new ground for television. Pairing a well-known driver with a 'personality', the teams were set various tasks, using vehicles of one form or another, like doing a timed cross-country lap in an army tank which included crushing a derelict car on the way. Much copied since, this annual programme was the first of the genre. Murray appeared originally as a competitor and thereafter became one of the presenters.

The breadth of his experience, to say nothing of his work rate, was awesome. In 1983, the year after he retired from his 'proper' job, Murray commentated on karting, power boats, Formula Ford, rallycross, Formula Three, motor cycle racing, motocross and Formula One.

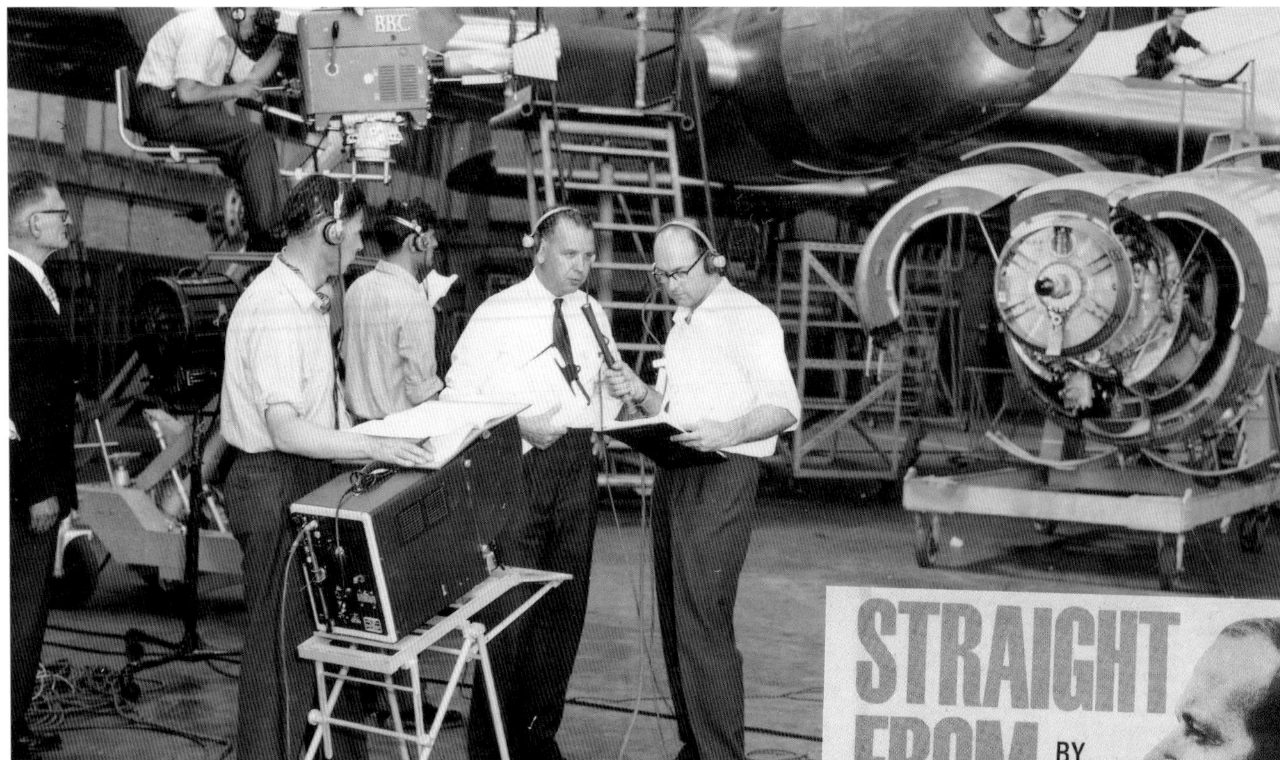

"In my early days, the BBC gave me all sorts of odd jobs to do, some of them nothing to do with sport. This one shows me getting ready to present a programme about the British Overseas Airways Corporation servicing base at Heathrow."

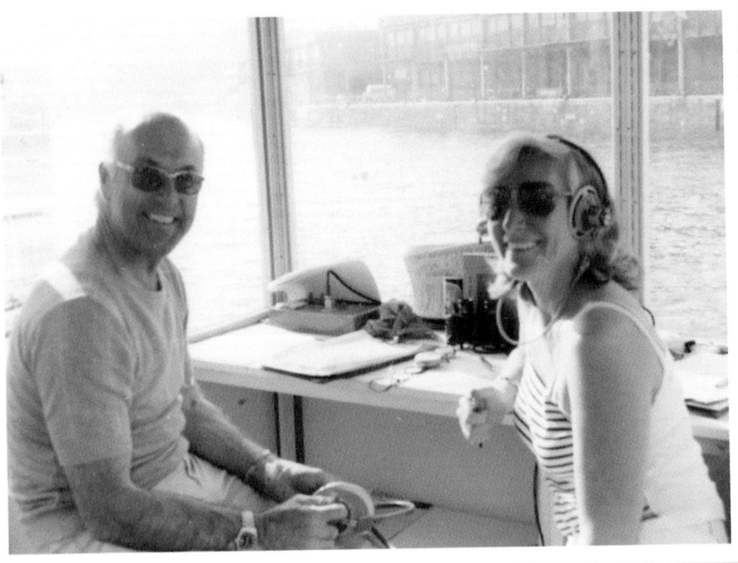

"Some of the most spectacular racing of any kind that I have ever seen was at the Embassy Powerboat Grand Prix at Bristol Docks. As you can see, the whole 'circuit' was bounded by high stone walls and it was incredibly dangerous."

STRAIGHT FROM THE GRID

BY EOIN YOUNG

GRAHAM HILL, talking about his stint as a television commentator at Thruxton on Easter Monday, was amazed that he had come across so well. "It really is extremely difficult. I must say I admire a chap like Murray Walker. You wouldn't believe how hard it is to identify cars on the little monitor screen we had in front of us. You've got to do your homework very well in practice or you can't tell which car is which, never mind rattle on about them. We were cramped shoulder to shoulder in this little box trying to watch what was happening on the track in front of us, what was happening on the monitor, and all the time listening to the chap directing the cameras who was rabbiting away doing a little commentary of his own. This was coming through our headphones the whole time, so we really had to be on the ball." It sounds like being a racing driver is a lot easier!

think this sort is quite rare isn't it? I mean, they didn't make many with four wheels, they were mostly 3-wheelers. . . ."—Isetta bubble-car painted a regal shade of dark blue with gold piping. Lady Sarah is afraid he'll get run over by a bus, but Piers says it's just the job for driving and parking in London. "You can just drive in at right angles to the kerb and park in the same meter space as a Mini." I'm not exactly sure of my ground on this point of law, but I have an idea you can get booked for doing things like that. Some of the traffic wardens these days have fairly heavily concealed senses of humour.

ITALIAN DRIVERS on the *Autostrada* from Turin to the mountains must have been mildly perplexed at the string of new Fiats that whistled by them all doing a crisp 100 mph or more if they happened to be the latest version of the front-engined

Grass Roots

Tony Dron

"Murray could walk up to some club driver, who might have been a mate of mine but would not have been known to the wider world, and he just always knew everybody's name and what they were doing. He'd say to my mate, Terry, 'How's the Mini going?' and it would astonish Terry that someone of that stature would know what he was up to.

"An amazingly well-informed, genial bloke."

"I was a busy chap in 1980 because not only was I continuing to do motor cycles, Formula Ford and Formula Three but I was now deeply into Formula One as well. But I loved the cut and thrust of Formula Three because that was where the Formula One drivers of the future were going to come from. So Brands Hatch saw a lot of me to talk about battles like the one on the right with Irishman Kenny Acheson leading in his March Toyota." (Chris Willows)

"Nigel Mansell had had a pretty dreary Formula Three season in the Unipart March in 1979 but things started to come together for him in F3 in 1980, racing against the likes of Stefan Johansson, Roberto Guerrero, Eddie Jordan (yes, the Eddie Jordan) and Brett Riley. In fact, in August that year Nigel made his now legendary debut for Lotus in the Austrian Grand Prix where he drove in agony, soaked in petrol, for most of the race." (Chris Willows)

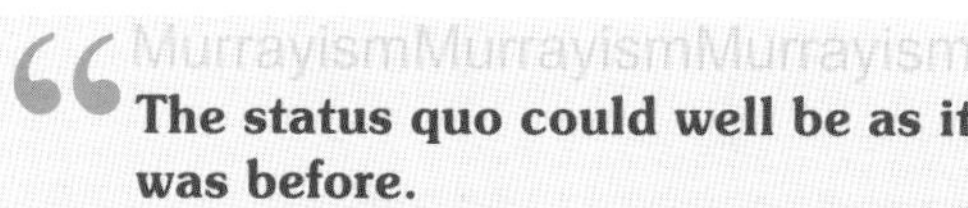

MurrayismMurrayismMurrayism
The status quo could well be as it was before.

Atlantic Crossing

Vern Schuppan

"I remember Murray from my very early days when I was doing Formula Atlantic, back in 1971, and I was always amazed he could remember so many people back then. He always knew you by name and he was always padding around the paddock and finding out what was going on. Over the years, he became such an icon but back in my early days he just seemed like this really nice bloke. As with so many, I came to like him very much as a person and we have certainly had a lot of laughs over the years."

"In 1981 Renault were still struggling to make their Formula One turbo car into a winner with Alain Prost and Rene Arnoux in the cockpits. But they capitalised on their Grand Prix involvement in every way possible, including flying Arnoux into England for a garden tractor race against myself. As this picture shows, I tried his tractor first and found it to be quicker than mine. Driver's excuse number 54!"

A Revealing Answer

Murray Walker

"Peter Gethin - great name from the past. His claim to fame is that in a BRM V12 in 1971 he won the fastest Grand Prix of all time until Montoya broke the record a couple of years ago. An average speed at the Italian Grand Prix at Monza of something like 151mph. I am subsequently, some years later, interviewing Peter Gethin at Oulton Park, at a F5000 meeting, live on BBC Grandstand, probably four million viewers.

"I said, 'Well Peter, great past, you've done Formula Ford, F3 and, of course, F1. You won the fastest Grand Prix ever but, tell me, what is the most exciting thing you ever did in your Grand Prix career?'

"He paused and said, "Well Murray, I suppose it was those red-headed twins in Bradford'."

Backs To The Wall

Stuart Turner

"I can recall Murray and I once speaking at a marshals' club dinner and busily rearranging the microphone arrangements so that we had our backs to a wall when we spoke. That was just professionalism on his part - and probably cowardice on mine so that they would only be able to throw things from one direction."

30TH MACAU G.P.
20·11·83
(STARTED 1954)
PAST WINNERS:
V. SCHUPPAN x 2.
R. PATRESE x 2
G. LEES x 2

RESULT = AGGREGATE & TIMES

F3 = CONTROL TYRES: YOKOHAMA
MINIMUM 455KG
2000cc / 4 CYLS (MAJOR PARTS FROM PON CARS)
24MM AIR RESTRICTOR
160 BHP:

* LAP = 3·8 MILES
* 15 LAPS = 57 MILES
* LR = TO BE SET: (1982 ATLANTIC GUERRERO 2·20·64 (97·5)
* 1983 POLE = SENNA 2·22·02 = APPROX 96·33
FIRST = £1,000 & MACAU CUP.

					F3 CHAMP
1	ROBERTO GUERRERO	24	RALT TOYOTA (E. JORDAN)	MEDELLIAN & DATCHET: 21 GPS: 2x KART CHAMP COLOMBIA: FF 76: F3 ARGO '80 5x1: F2 MAURER '81 1x1: ENSIGN 82/83: KATIE: CART TESTING: 83: HOLL 12: EURO 12: ITAL 13: GB 16: BRA 17: DNQ MON: DNF x 8	
2	MARTIN BRUNDLE	24	RALT TOYOTA (E. JORDAN)	KINGS LYNN: MOTOR BUSINESS: RALLY DAD JOHN: BRO SALOONS ROBIN: 6x1 F3 83: 1ST T.T. JAGUAR WORKS: McLAREN & TYRELL F1 TESTS: SALOONS/FF2000 1982 GROVEWOOD PREMIER. EURO F3 3x1 1 3: S'STONE/Donington	2 B
3	AYRTON SENNA	23	RALT TOYOTA (D. BENNETTS)	MENORCA: 2ND KART WC 79 & 80: 2x FF1600 CHAMP 81: BRIT & EURO FF2000 CHAMP 82: BRIT F3 CHAMP 83: WILLIAMS & McLAREN F1 TESTS '83 & BRABHAM 12x1 '83 (9 CONSECUTIVE) THEODORE	1 B
5	DAVY JONES	19	RALT VW (M. TAYLOR)	Mc GRAW (UPPER NY STATE): DAD SHIPPING & GRAIN: 3RD '82 USA FV CHAMP. FF CHAMP CANADA '81: 3RD BRIT F3 CHAMP 83: BRABHAM F1 TEST '83: 4x FL 83:	3 B
7	EJE ELGH	30	~~RALT~~ HAYASHI TOYOTA	KARLSKOGA SWEDEN: SUPERVEE 73-75: F3 '76/77 - 2ND BRIT CHAMP. F2 78-81: 1ST VALLELUNGA '81: 1983 JAPANESE F2 CHAMPIONSHIP & DOME GPC	
8	TIFF NEEDELL	32	~~RALT~~ HAYASHI TOYOTA	WEYBRIDGE: PRO & JOURNALIST & COMMENTATOR: NEARLY WON MACAU 82: 1971-75 FF1600/FF2000/F3: 1976-78 F5000: 1979/GP ENSIGN '80: 1981/82 SPORTS CARS/F2/ATLANTIC: LE MANS NIMROD: DOME JAPAN GPC	
90	J-LOUIS SCHLESSER	30	RALT VW ~~TOYOTA~~ (D. PRICE)	PARIS: JEWELLER: 1973-76 FORM RENAULT: 1977-81 F3: 1982 F2. 1983 RAM MARCH F1 & GPC: "MOROCCAN DESERT CROSS" ON HELMET (LIVED MOROCCO LONG TIME)	
39	DAVID HUNT	23	RALT VW (D. PRICE)	FARNHAM: 4YRS IN KARTS: BRO JAMES: SOME FF1600 SUCCESS: ENTERPRISE IAN TAYLOR & OH SCHOOLS: FIRST TIME VW MOTOR:	12 B
11	MARIO HYTTEN	23	RALT TOYOTA (NEIL TRUNDLE)	GENEVA: 5YRS: EX KARTS & FF: 6TH BRIT F3 CHAMP '83: 4 LANGUAGES: AXXESS = POP GROUP (ELECTRONIC SOUND) FIRST RECORD JUST RELEASED.	6 B
12	CLAUDIO LANGES	21	ANSON ALFA ~~VW~~ ALFA	LAKE GARDA: 6YRS: KARTS/F ABARTH/F3: ITALY KART CHAMP & JUNIOR WC PAPER IMPORT/EXPORT BUSINESS: V GOOD ANSON DEVELOPER '83: 83: LA CHATRE 4: MISANO 6: JARAMA 4: IMOLA 5: DON'TON 5:	9 E
14	TOMMY BYRNE	24	ANSON ALFA-R	BLACK ROCK: 6YRS: MONDELLO PARK SCHOOL: 2x FF CHAMP '80: BRIT & EURO FF2000 CHAMP 81: 1ST FFF '81: THEODORE F1 '82: 4TH EURO CHAMP F3 '83: 83: ZOLDER 4: M-COURS 5: AUSTRIA 1: S'STONE 2: MONZA 3: MISANO 1:	4 E
15	FRANZ CONRAD	31	~~RALT~~ ANSON VW	GERMAN: SPORTS CARS: PARTNERED WARWICK KREMER PORSCHE 956 SPA 1000K '83 WON 83 GERMAN F3 RACE & 3RD 78 WEC RACE	
16	CATHY MULLER	21	RALT VW	21 TOMORROW! 8YRS: KARTS 1975: KART WC '80 & LADIES CHAMP EURO 79: 1981 R5 GERMANY & WINFIELD SCHOOL MAGNY COURS (WON FREE YEAR FORM REN) '82 5TH FORM REN CHAMP: 1983 TO F3. SEPPOIS-LE-BAS	
17	PIER-LUIGI MARTINI	22	RALT ALFA-ROMEO	RAVENNA: F3 EUROCHAMP '83: BRABHAM F1 TEST '83: 2ND MISANO F2 '83 EURO F3 '83 4x1: EX KARTS (3YRS)/F. ABARTH/TO F3 '81. DAD SUPPLIES PARM 83: VAL 3: AUSTRIA 4: MISANO 2: Z'VOORT 2: NOGARO 1: JARAMA 1: IMOLA 1: CROIX 1:	1 E
18	KRISS NISSEN	23	[illegible] RALT ALFA	ARNUM DENMARK: KARTS 1974-77: FF2000 1979-82: F3 1983: PRO: 2x KART CHAMP DK: 1981 2ND FF2000 EUROCHAMP: 1982 FF2000 DK CHAMP, SCANDINAVIA CHAMP, 2ND GOLDEN LION: 1983 GOOD F3 PLACES: 83 M-COURS 4	
19	JO ZELLER	27	RALT TOYOTA	SWISS: FIRST TIME MACAU.	
21	GERHARD BERGER	24	RALT TOY ~~ALFA-ROMEO~~	WÖRGL: AUSTRIA: GERMAN F3 1982: F3 DEBUT 1981: HELMUT MARKO PROTEGE GREAT SUCCESS 1983 STARTED ALFASUD LIKES MACAU! 83: ZOLDER 3: M-COURS 6: AUSTRIA 2: KNUTSTORP 2: IMOLA 6:	7 E
22	LEO ANDERSSON	27	RALT TOYOTA	GOTHENBERG SWEDEN: 6YRS: 1983 F3 CHAMP SWEDEN: '78 SWEDISH FF CHAMP: 81/82 3RD & 2ND SWEDISH F3 CHAMP. CARPENTER:	
55	GARY GIBSON	33	RALT TOYOTA	COMBER: NI: PROPERTY DEALER: 11YRS: FF & F ATL: F ATL IRISH CHAMP 79/80 & 2ND 82: SECOND TIME HERE:	
66	VERN SCHUPPAN	40	RALT TOYOTA (MARLIN)	USA: 1ST LE MANS '83: FF 1969: F ATLANTIC BRIT CHAMP 71: BRM/ENSIGN/EMBASSY F1 1970/75: 1976-82 F5000 SUCCESS: ATLANTIC, INDY & SPORTS CARS WORLDWIDE (1ST MACAU '76 AT 92MPH & 74 AT 82MPH)	2x1 MACAU
72	BOB EARLE	33	RALT TOYOTA (ALAN DOCKING)	NOVATO: CALIFORNIA 1ST MACAU GP 1981 AT 94MPH: MOTOR RACING INSTRUCTOR EX FSV: DRIVEN SUZUKA: FLYING TIGERS. 15YRS:	
74	PRICE COBB	28	RALT TOYOTA (ALAN DOCKING)	FIRST TIME MACAU. FLYING TIGERS. USA FSV CHAMP: ATLANTIC/CANAM 9YRS: TURBO ENGNR:	
75	STANLEY DICKENS	30	ANSON TOYOTA	SWEDISH: FIRST TIME MACAU: 1980 EURO F2 & F3:	
76	COR EUSER	24	ANSON TOYOTA	HOLLAND: FF1600 DUTCH CHAMP: FF2000 82/83: F3 MAGNUM 1x1 '83 1ST EURO SPORTS 2000 & F3:	5 B
77	ALLEN BERG		RALT VW DANEM	2YRS: '83 NZ F PAC CHAMP. 5TH 83 BRIT CHAMP: MILTON KEYNES 83 1x1: 2x3: 2x4	

"I commentated on the brilliant Macau Grand Prix for many years but 1983 was a classic. Look at the names on my crib sheet. Number two Martin Brundle and number three Ayrton Senna battled for the British Championship for the whole season with Senna winning the Championship and Macau. Number 55 Gary Gibson was a mad Irishman whose exploits were only matched by those of number fourteen Tommy Byrne. On the Monday after the race, we all went out in the Mandarin Hotel's luxurious junk and Byrne, and future F1 star Gerhard Berger, threw most of us into the China Sea. I got away with it when Gary Gibson shouted, 'Not Murray, he's old!'."

Messing About With Boats

Ros Nott

"I did some stuff with him down at Bristol, at the Embassy Grand Prix which, in those days, was very famous but it eventually got dropped because so many people died. We had a couple of JPS [John Player Special] boats and he was brilliant because he was saying, 'Here we have Nigel Mansell going into the first turn buoy and I'm waving a piece of paper saying. 'No, not Nigel Mansell. We're at a boat race'!

"He went, 'No, no, I'm in the wrong place, I mean it's Tom Percival going…' Absolutely brilliant. But his research was so fantastic; that was something I always remember about him. He spent so long talking to everybody and making sure he got as much information as possible. Whether he got it right or not on the day, didn't really matter! And, bless him, most of the time, he didn't!

"He did all the groundwork; he didn't just roll in, like so many do these days and think, 'I know what I'm doing here'. He was an out and out professional."

"Always anxious to demonstrate my incompetence at the wheel, I whistled this strange device up the famous Prescott Hillclimb in 1983."

Drowned Out

Ros Nott

"I was Editor of *Power Boat and Water Skiing* magazine for 14 years and held the women's world water speed record, so they used to rope me in. Generally, Murray and I did the commentary between us. I tried to do the more technical side of it, while he did the actual race commentary. I shared lots of very small spaces with Murray! And it was absolutely hilarious.

"Murray, as you know, always does his commentaries standing up. Whether that ruins his vision of what he is supposed to be looking at, I don't know but we had a boat that was literally falling apart lap by lap in front of our eyes, and I couldn't catch his attention. Once he gets on a roll, you can't interrupt him, because he gets completely lost so you have to let him go. And I was pushing up all these bits of paper in front of him, 'Number eight is sinking'. 'Number eight is going to sink in front of you in a minute.'

"He must have gone past us four times before Murray grabbed the bit of paper and went [shouting], 'AHH, AND NUMBER EIGHT, LOOK, HE IS BEGINNING TO SINK...' Crowds of people clapped. Hilarious, just hilarious."

"Occasionally I love to wallow in nostalgia by getting out my bits of paper and reminiscing around them. For instance, look at my notes on the incredible line-up for the 1989 Race of Champions at Macau, all of whom were in Maxda MX5s. All of them great, great names in their various categories with but one exception. Who the hell was Grant Wolfkill? Incidentally, it's worth noting that in that galaxy of superstars, the man who took pole position was our very own Andy Rouse, who I used to rhapsodise about in the British Touring Car Championship."

30TH MACAU G.P.
20·11·83
(STARTED 1954)
PAST WINNERS:
V. SCHUPPAN x 2.
R. PATRESE x 2
G. LEES x 2

RESULT = AGGREGATE & TIMES

F3 = CONTROL TYRES: YOKOHAMA
MINIMUM 455 KG
2000cc / 4 CYLS (MAJOR PARTS FROM PDN CARS)
24MM AIR RESTRICTOR
160 BHP:

* LAP = 3·8 MILES
* 15 LAPS = 57 MILES
* LR = TO BE SET: (1982 ATLANTIC GUERRERO 2·20·64 (97·5)
* 1983 POLE = SENNA 2·22·02 = APPROX 96·33
FIRST = £1,000 & MACAU CUP.

No.	Driver	Age	Car	Notes	F3 CHAMP
1	ROBERTO GUERRERO	24	RALT TOYOTA (E. JORDAN)	MEDELLIN & DATCHET: 21 GPs: 2x KART CHAMP COLOMBIA: FF 76: F3 ARGO '80 5x1: F2 MAURER '81 1x1: ENSIGN 82/83: KATIE: CART TESTING: 83: HOL 12: EURO 12: ITAL 13: GB 16: BRA 17: DNQ MON: DNF x 8	
2	MARTIN BRUNDLE	24	RALT TOYOTA (E. JORDAN)	KINGS LYNN: MOTOR BUSINESS: RALLY DAD JOHN: BRO SALOONS ROBIN: 6x1 F3 83: 1ST T.T. JAGUAR WORKS: McLAREN & TYRELL F1 TESTS: SALOONS/FF2000 1982 GROVEWOOD PREMIER. EURO F3 3x1 13: S'STONE / DONINGTON	2 B
3	AYRTON SENNA	23	RALT TOYOTA (D. BENNETTS)	MENORCA: 2ND KART WC 79 & 80: 2x FF1600 CHAMP 81: BRIT & EURO FF2000 CHAMP 82: BRIT F3 CHAMP 83: WILLIAMS & McLAREN F1 TESTS '83 & BRABHAM 12x1 '83 (9 CONSECUTIVE) THEODORE	1 B
5	DAVY JONES	19	RALT VW (M. TAYLOR)	McGRAW (UPPER NY STATE): DAD SHIPPING & GRAIN: 3RD '82 USA FV CHAMP. FF CHAMP CANADA '81: 3RD BRIT F3 CHAMP 83: BRABHAM F1 TEST '83: 4x FL 83:	3 B
7	EJE ELGH	30	RALT HAYASHI TOYOTA	KARLSKOGA SWEDEN: SUPERVEE 73-75: F3 '76/77 - 2ND BRIT CHAMP. F2 78-81: 1ST VALLELUNGA '81: 1983 JAPANESE F2 CHAMPIONSHIP & DOME GpC	
8	TIFF NEEDELL	32	RALT HAYASHI TOYOTA	WEYBRIDGE: PRO & JOURNALIST & COMMENTATOR: NEARLY WON MACAU 82: 1971-75 FF1600/FF2000/F3: 1976-78 F5000: 1979/GP ENSIGN '80: 1981/82 SPORTS CARS/F2/ATLANTIC: LE MANS NIMROD: DOME JAPAN GP C	
90	J-LOUIS SCHLESSER	30	RALT VW (D. PRICE)	PARIS: JEWELLER 1973-76 FORM RENAULT: 1977-81 F3: 1982 F2. 1983 RAM MARCH F1 & GPC: "MOROCCAN DESERT CROSS" ON HELMET (LIVED MOROCCO LONG TIME)	
39	DAVID HUNT	23	RALT VW (D. PRICE)	FARNHAM: 4YRS IN KARTS: BRO JAMES: SOME FF1600 SUCCESS: ENTERPRISE IAN TAYLOR & GH SCHOOLS: FIRST TIME VW MOTOR:	12 B
11	MARIO HYTTEN	23	RALT TOYOTA (NEIL TRUNDLE)	GENEVA: 5YRS: EX KARTS & FF: 6TH BRIT F3 CHAMP '83: 4 LANGUAGES: AXXESS = POP GROUP (ELECTRONIC SOUND) FIRST RECORD JUST RELEASED.	6 B
12	CLAUDIO LANGES	21	ANSON ALFA	LAKE GARDA: 6YRS: KARTS / F ABARTH / F3: ITALY KART CHAMP & JUNIOR WC PAPER IMPORT / EXPORT BUSINESS: V GOOD ANSON DEVELOPER '83: 83: LA CHATRE 4: MISANO 6: JARAMA 4: IMOLA 5: DONINGTON 5:	9 E
14	TOMMY BYRNE	24	ANSON ALFA-R	BLACK ROCK: 6YRS: MONDELLO PARK SCHOOL: 2x FF CHAMP '80: BRIT & EURO FF2000 CHAMP 81: 1ST FFF '81: THEODORE F1 '82: 4TH EUROCHAMP F3 '83: 83: ZOLDER 4: N-COURS 5: AUSTRIA 1: S'STONE 2: MONZA 3: MISANO 1:	4 E
15	FRANZ CONRAD	31	ANSON VW	GERMAN: SPORTS CARS: PARTNERED WARWICK KREMER PORSCHE 956 SPA 1000K '83 WON 83 GERMAN F3 RACE & 3RD 78 WEC RACE	
16	CATHY MULLER	21	RAG VW	21 TOMORROW! 8YRS: KARTS 1975: KART WC '80 & LADIES CHAMP EURO 79: 1981 R5 GERMANY & WINFIELD SCHOOL MAGNY COURS (WON FREE YEAR FORM REN) '82 5TH FORM REN CHAMP: 1983 TO F3. SEPPOIS-LE-BAS	
17	PIER-LUIGI MARTINI	22	RALT ALFA-ROMEO	RAVENNA: F3 EUROCHAMP '83: BRABHAM F1 TEST '83: 2ND MISANO F2 '83 EURO F3 '83 4x1: EX KARTS (3YRS) / F. ABARTH / TO F3 '81. DAD SUPPLIES PARTS 83: VALL 3: AUSTRIA 4: MISANO 2: Z'VOORT 2: NOGARO 1: JARAMA 1: IMOLA 1: CROIX 1:	1 E
18	KRISS NISSEN	23	RAG ALFA	ARNUM DENMARK: KARTS 1974-77: FF2000 1979-82: F3 1983: PRO: 2x KART CHAMP DK: 1981 2ND FF2000 EUROCHAMP: 1982 FF2000 DK CHAMP, SCANDINAVIA CHAMP, 2ND GOLDEN LION: 1983 GOOD F3 PLACES: 83 M-COURS 4	
19	JO ZELLER	27	RAG TOYOTA	SWISS: FIRST TIME MACAU.	
21	GERHARD BERGER	24	RALT TOY	WÖRGL: AUSTRIA: GERMAN F3 1982: F3 DEBUT 1981: HELMUT MARKO PROTEGE GREAT SUCCESS 1983 STARTED ALFASUD LIKES MACAU! 83: ZOLDER 3: N-COURS 6: AUSTRIA 2: KNUTSTORP 2: IMOLA 6:	7 E
22	LEO ANDERSSON	27	RALT TOYOTA	GOTHENBERG SWEDEN: 6YRS: 1983 F3 CHAMP SWEDEN: '78 SWEDISH FF CHAMP: 81/82 3RD & 2ND SWEDISH F3 CHAMP. CARPENTER:	
55	GARY GIBSON	33	RALT TOYOTA	COMBER: NI: PROPERTY DEALER: 11YRS: FF & F ATL: F ATL IRISH CHAMP 79/80 & 2ND 82: SECOND TIME HERE:	
66	VERN SCHUPPAN	40	RALT TOYOTA	USA: 1ST LE MANS '83: FF 1969: F ATLANTIC BRIT CHAMP 71: BRM / ENSIGN / EMBASSY F1 1970/75: 1976-82 F5000 SUCCESS: ATLANTIC, INDY & SPORTS CARS WORLDWIDE 1ST MACAU '76 AT 92MPH & '74 AT 82MPH 2x1 MACAU	
72	BOB EARLE	33	RAG TOYOTA (ALAN DOCKING)	NOVATO: CALIFORNIA 1ST MACAU GP 1981 AT 94MPH: MOTOR RACING INSTRUCTOR EX FSV: DRIVEN SUZUKA: FLYING TIGERS. 15YRS:	
74	PRICE COBB	28	RALT TOYOTA (ALAN DOCKING)	FIRST TIME MACAU. FLYING TIGERS. USA FSV CHAMP: ATLANTIC / CANAM 9YRS: TURBO ENGNR:	
75	STANLEY DICKENS	30	ANSON TOYOTA	SWEDISH: FIRST TIME MACAU: 1980 EURO F2 & F3:	
76	COR EUSER	24	ANSON TOYOTA	HOLLAND: FF1600 DUTCH CHAMP: FF2000 82/83: F3 MAGNUM 1x1 '83 1ST EUROSPORTS 2000 & F3: 77 ALLEN BERG RALT VW (DANEM?) 2YRS: '83 NZ F PAC CHAMP. 5TH 83 BRIT CHAMP: MILTON KEYNES 83 1x1: 2x3: 2x4.	5 B

Slowest To The Fore

Robert Glen

"We had a reverse grid. In other words, instead of having the fastest boat at the front, we had the slowest at the front. So, in the 11 minutes of racing, the winners had to pass the rest of the field. It was pretty fraught but produced excellent television.

"He was very studious in how he went about collecting all his information. No fact was too small to get down and then he assembled all the facts. He grabbed the essence of it in a very short time and was very enthusiastic about our reverse grid. Because we were able to get cameras down, virtually on the waterline, we had some remarkably good shots for him to work with.

"His commentaries were very much like his motor racing commentaries but we gave him another dimension to comment on because the boats were going up and down on the screen, as well as left to right. He brought it much more alive than the rather amateur commentators who had previously done the job. He was in a league by himself."

Right Royal Drenching

Ros Nott

"Roger Jenkins was World Formula One Champion. We had one dreadful year in 1984 when five drivers were killed in four Grands Prix and he just said, 'Enough' and got up and walked away and never came back. He was a great character, though.

"We did the commentary, Murray and I, for the Marlboro GP on the River Thames which Princess Margaret started. She'd done a walkaround in the pits and hadn't spoken to Roger Jenkins, even though he was World Champion. So when she dropped the flag while standing on the pontoon, he, I'm afraid, started with his engine jacked right out – he absolutely drenched the entire VIP party. Murray and I were having terrible problems trying to keep a straight face and talk at the same time, as all the Ladies-in-Waiting had dripping straw hats. And I'm afraid Princess Margaret was pale blue on the back and dark blue on the front – it was the funniest thing I have ever seen and he did it absolutely on purpose!"

"Two shots at the same place but two very different drivers - 77 is the great Ayrton Senna who, having won Formula Ford and Formula Three championships, went on to win three Formula One World Championships and number 11 is Martin Brundle with whom I was later to form such an enjoyable partnership in the commentary box. The classic 1983 Formula Three season saw a titanic fight for the Championship between Ayrton and Martin in which Brundle gave the Brazilian a very hard time. I've always felt that Martin could have achieved Formula One greatness if he had had the cars that Senna drove." (Chris Willows)

That Sinking Feeling

"It was the only time they ever closed the Thames for a power boat race, and it didn't work. They put the barriers up to stop the driftwood going down, but that was never going to work. Inevitably, the barriers broke and I think nearly every boat was sinking when it was brought in. They were only 3mm marine plywood doing 120mph – it doesn't take much to sink those. It was an absolute unmitigated disaster."

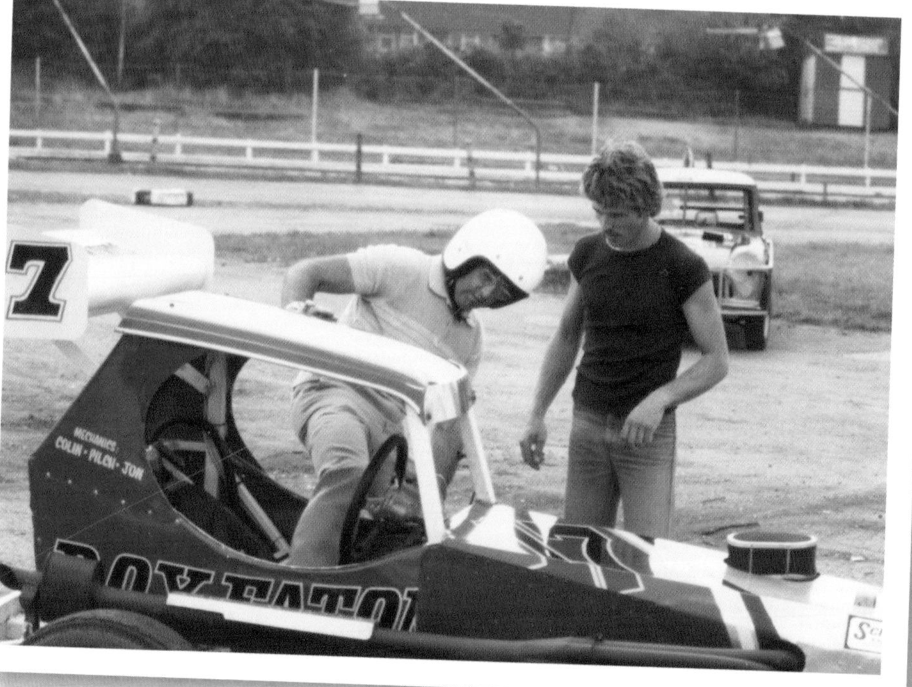

"Not a lot of people know that amongst the great Derek Warwick's many outstanding motor sport achievements was the Stock Car World Championship. I did a feature for BBC TV in 1983 which took me to Aldershot Stadium to find out what it was all about. It mainly consisted of a flat out 360° power slide and was the most enormous fun."

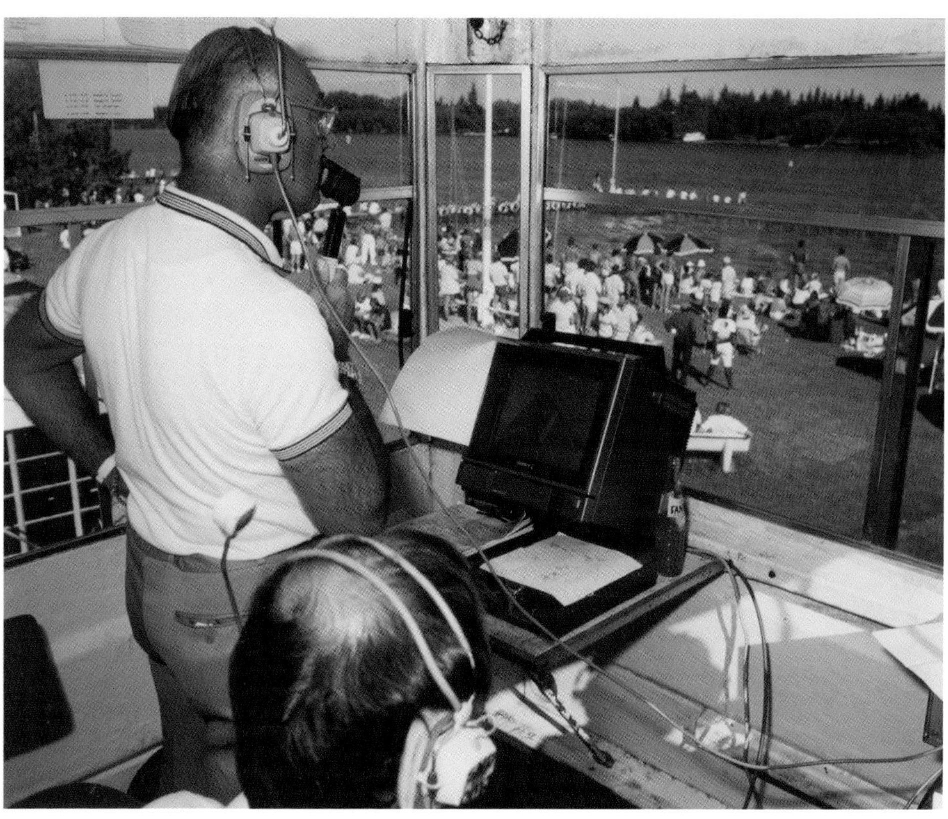

"In the commentary box at Loch Vaal, near Johannesburg, for an international power boat race in South Africa in 1985. I stayed with a very wealthy family who lived on 'Millionaire's Bend' of the Vaal river and vividly remember going to work at 60mph in a powerboat. It certainly got the adrenalin flowing."

Investing In The Future

Murray Walker

PP: "You have always done a lot of preparation work."

"It was thoroughness and enthusiasm but it was also, to be quite honest, self interest. My attitude was that I talked to people when they were in karting or Formula Ford. First time I met Nigel Mansell was when a friend of his called John Thornburn, who has been with him throughout his career, came up to me at Silverstone and said, 'There is a young Formula Ford driver I would like you to meet who I think is going places'. I said, 'Oh yeah, who is it?' He said, 'Nigel Mansell'. I said, 'Oh yes. He is in one of the races I am doing.'

"So I went and met this bloke, Nigel Mansell, and I sat on the front wheel of his Formula Ford car, and he was in the cockpit, and I talked to him. And I kept talking to him and to all the other Formula Ford, F3, F3000, F5000 drivers because I knew that some of them would get into F1. My theory, which proved to be correct because drivers have remarked on it to me, was that if I showed an interest in them when they were a nobody, they would have more interest in me when they were a somebody. That proved to be the case because I have been able to get interviews and talk to people because I have known them all the way through, when I wouldn't have been able to get to them if they were in F1 and didn't know me."

First Meeting

Nigel Mansell

"My first impression of Murray was of a dynamic commentator who made even the most boring race seem exciting.

"We first met about 1976 when he was commentating on a Formula Ford race. He came and spoke in the pits. He was a consummate professional."

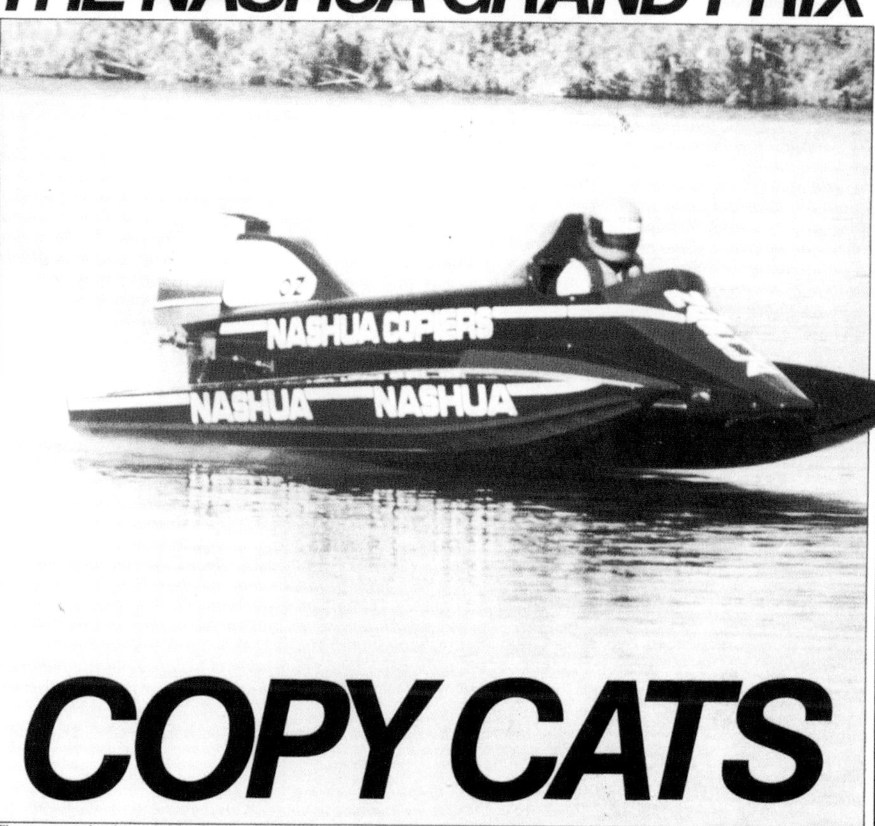

THE NASHUA GRAND PRIX

COPY CATS

The sponsors decals carried by Cees van der Velden

by Murray Walker

'Hello' said the voice, 'this is Rod Murphy of Marine Distributors in Johannesburg. Our Nashua Power Boat Grand Prix's happening at Loch Vaal soon and South Africa TV and I wonder if you can come out and handle the commentary for us?' 'I'll think about it Rod,' I said, 'I've thought about it – I'll come!'

That was how one of the most enjoyable weeks I've spent for a long time happened and as I settled down in great comfort for the non-stop thirteen hour flight with South African Airways (ten out of ten for service and comfort, incidentally) I wondered what I'd let myself in for. Where was Loch Vaal? Who exactly was going to be competing? What sort of equipment would they have? How competitive would they be? What would the organisation be like? And so on.

Well Loch Vaal is an absolutely stunning stretch of water about an hour or so down the motorway from Johannesburg and surprise, surprise, it's an extension of the Vaal River on the banks of which are some of the most impressive homes I've ever seen. The Loch waters are wide, deep and calm – or at least they're usually deep but this time down a lot due to the two year drought from which the whole of Africa seems to be suffering. But, no problem. The obliging Water Board took the bung out somewhere to adjust the levels and, come race day, all was well.

The indefatigable Rod Murphy, who seemed to be everywhere all the time, had worked with the organising Loch Vaal Club to put on the best possible OZ race which was strongly supported by classes for virtually everything that floats! Petrol Hydros, R3 Inboard Hydros, OC Hydros (and don't they go!), ROO, ON, OE, SN, TU, TN, TA. Hot Dogs and Formula 40's. Hot Dogs? Formula 40's? Hot Dogs are Hydroplane-based 9.9hp standard engined boats for two children's classes and Formula 40's are V shaped hulls with 40hp standard production engines.

So you can imagine that it was all go on Saturday, March 10th. A big, big crowd. Superb weather. Clear blue skies. Blazing sunshine and a 6,000ft altitude which thins the air and, I can assure you, promotes a very rapid tan!

Rod had imported three of the world's top OZ jockeys – Cees van der Velden, Arthur Mostert and Francois Salabert who, like the rest of the entrants, had limited themselves to V6 motors – as opposed to the 'light the blue touch paper and stand well back' V8's.

So what had South Africa got to offer against top class opposition like this? Answer: Peter Lindenberg! A confident 28 year old who runs a successful boat business in Johannesburg and who has amassed a stupifying number of awards for achievements ranging from the World's Barefoot Ramp Jump record (17.4 metres would you believe?) to multiple South African and State Colours for Powerboat successes – including past SAGP wins. Those of you who were at last year's London GP may wonder if it's the same Peter Lindenberg who took off, flew, crashed and ended up in hospital in less time than it takes to write it. It is! 'That thick air threw me Murray. I'm

APRIL 1984 7

'Driving Sheep'

Murray Walker

"For some years, we did an annual programme called *Driving Force*. It consisted of teams of alleged personalities, teams of two, doing competitive things with an 'automotive' theme. One year we had to dig a hole with a JCB, and fill it in again. I did that with Derek Bell. We had to drive on a trials course, manoeuvre an articulated truck, do a race lap at Thruxton. *Driving Force* went to Australia in 1990. We went to some pure white sands on the outskirts of Perth, miles and miles and miles of sand with steep cliffs and enormous drops. We had to do incredible things on Honda quads.

"We also had to take a Ute [utility], an Australian pick-up truck with an open back, and get six sheep out of a pen and into the Ute, drive the Ute about half a mile to a rail head, and then unload them from the Ute into a rail truck. All this was done against the clock. We were doing it with some of the Australian test match cricketers, including Ian Chappell, and Barry Sheene was in one of the teams. It was the most gigantic fun. All of them were show business people, like the cast of *Flying Doctors*, all of them very extrovert. Peter Brock, arguably the greatest Australian motor sport driver who has ever lived, nine times winner of Bathurst, was also in one of the teams. We just had the most gigantic fun in glorious weather, in wonderful surroundings."

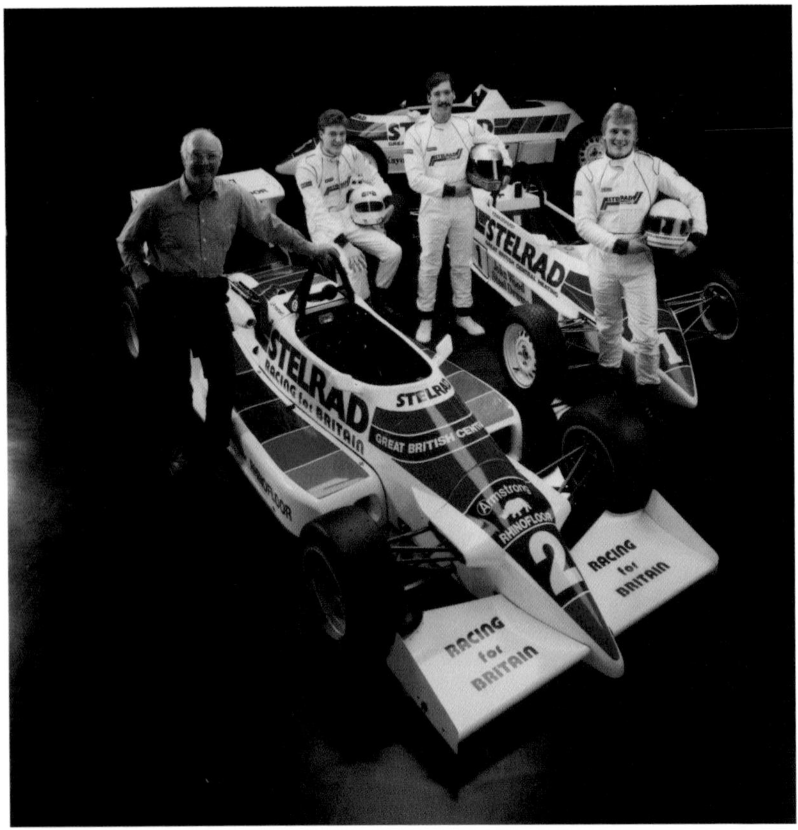

"Stelrad was a company which, unsurprisingly, made steel radiators for home heating and in 1987 they sponsored the cherubic Johnny Herbert, seen here on the right. I used to chat up the guests in the Stelrad hospitality unit and interview Johnny who later became a Formula One and Le Mans 24-hour race wiunner. Sadly the other two drivers, Chris Pullman and Rowan Dewhurst, fell by the wayside in their efforts to reach the top, as the majority of drivers do."

"The Formula Johnson Grandstand Trophy was the brainchild of ebullient EP Barrus boss, Bob Glen, and included a reverse grid where the fastest started from the back. It made for fabulously spectacular racing with the stars carving their way through the field with great roosters of spray leaping up behind them. This shot shows the formation lap and even that is full of action." (EP Barrus)

Tanking Along

Derek Bell

"It would be early eighties, we went to a tank proving ground and it was bloody freezing. Murray and I were pitched together, as a team – a driver and a personality. Anneka Rice was partnered by Tony Pond. Nigel Mansell was there and Rowan Atkinson.

"We had to drive the tanks on a track and then go into this water splash, which was full of foul, foul water. If you went too fast, the water would come over the tank and in the hole where I was sitting. Murray was up above me. We'd heard that Barry [Sheene] had gone into the water a little bit too fast and a wave just comes and blows over the poor bastard who's driving! Murray was calling out the orders and it was so funny.

"We had to go up to what they call 'the knife edge', up to the top of a hill like a pyramid, and virtually stop the thing, and it rocks over the crest and then you go down the other side. I was thinking, 'We've really got to make up some time here'. We got up to the top and Murray's screaming orders to me in that wonderful voice and we charged down the other side and I kept my hoof in it when we got to the bottom, because we had a left hander to negotiate before the finish line. I just dug in, full throttle, the thing's belching out smoke and the sheer mass of this thing and laws of physics meant it didn't bite at all, I just drifted out and went through all the sponsor's banners and wrapped them all around the tank because I just kept my foot in it. We all made bloopers and it was just great fun.

"The funniest part was driving this big pantechnicon. We had to drive these bloody great trucks through a handling course, with drums. We were doing this on the Thruxton circuit. Murray was driving and this time I'm calling out the orders to Murray. As we went through the slalom, I was sitting alongside him in the cab, screaming out, 'Little more to the left, Murray, little more to the right'. Murray actually hit every single drum. My idol TV commentator hit every 50 gallon drum! It was hilarious."

In-depth Coverage

Peter Cleaver

"I remember we attached a camera to the front of the barrel of the tank, telling them to drive very carefully, and they promptly ploughed straight in to the ditch and this very expensive camera went through six foot of mud, which bent it to smithereens, and reappeared!"

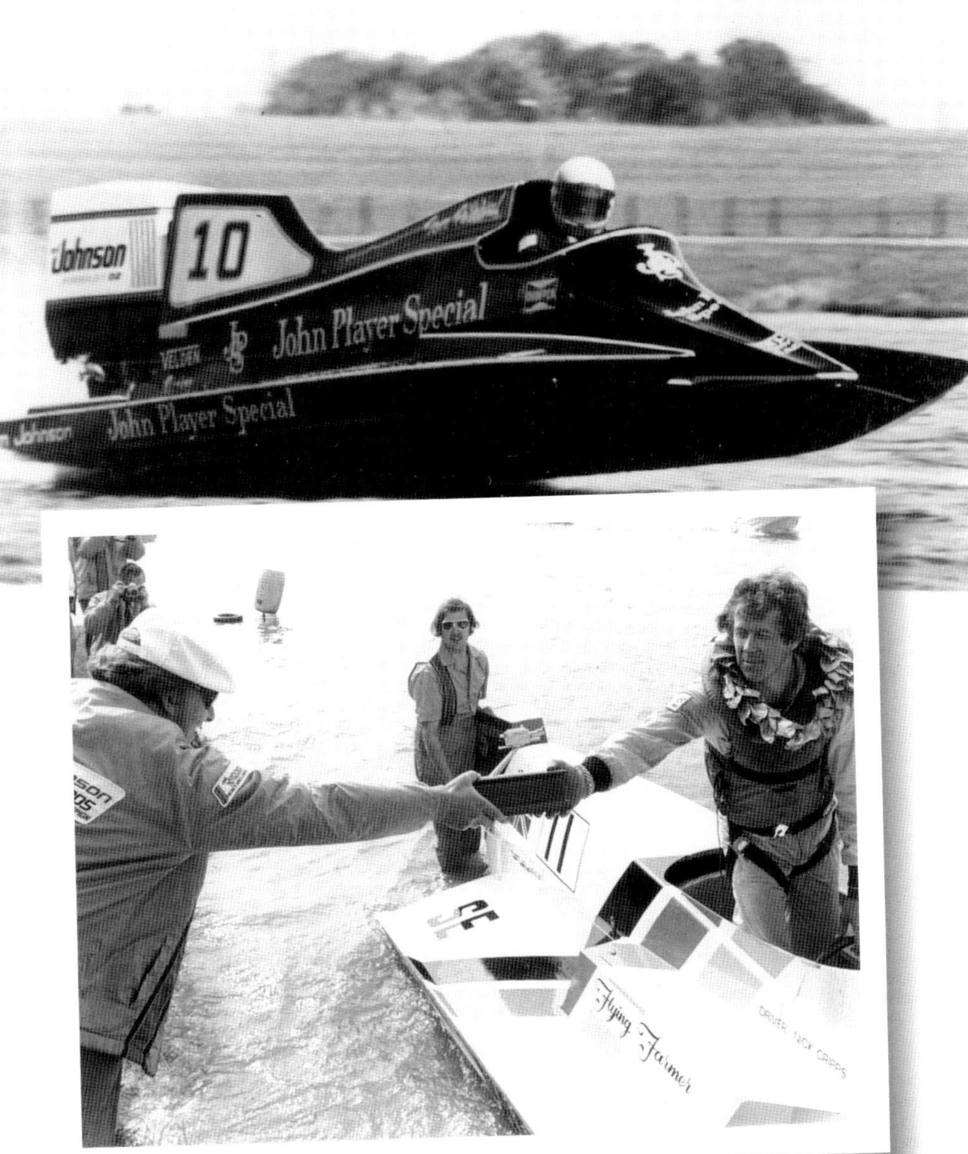

"One of the truly great powerboat drivers was Tom Percival, well up on the step here in his stunning Johnson-powered John Player Special."

"Jovial Nick Cripps was a top man in the Formula Johnson category and won the 1975 BBC TV Grandstand Trophy." (EP Barrus)

Making A Splash

Louise Goodman

"I first met Murray in the early '80s, long before I became involved in motor racing, during an event called the *Round London Inflatable Marathon* [for inflatable water craft]. It left from Putney, went up to Limehouse Basin, they dragged them up the wall, stuck them in the canal system, round and back into the river somewhere upstream and then back down to Putney. Murray was presenting the prizes but for me it was like, 'Wow! Murray Walker – the man off the telly'. So, I was really quite star-struck meeting him!"

"I was both a presenter and a competitor, at different times, for the 1980s and 1990s BBC TV 'Driving Force' series which set teams of two personalities against each other, doing strange things in powered-vehicles. This is the briefing session for the one in Perth, Australia with, on the right (yellow shirt), Australia's ultimate hero, Peter Brock, and the ever-cheerful Barry Sheene."

Senna

Murray Walker

"Formula Ford at Brands Hatch, which was where I first met Ayrton Senna. This young chap came up and said he's going back to Brazil the next day, having won virtually everything in Formula Ford in his first year. 'How can I get a video of this event?' he said. I said, 'I'll send you one, if you win'. He didn't win, he finished second but I sent him a video just the same and that started a very long association I had with the amazing, the incredible, the absolutely unique Ayrton Senna.

"I covered that fantastic F3 season of 1983 when it was nip and tuck between he and Martin Brundle all season and Senna just won."

And A Few Other Things...

First Memories

Martin Brundle

"I first remember him from when I was in Formula Three actually. Obviously I had listened to him a lot late night on a Sunday for the Grands Prix, when I was younger. Never really expected to be a Grand Prix driver; I was just racing for fun at the time. I used to obviously enjoy James and Murray. But of course it was only highlights; they didn't show it live. The first time I met the man would have been in F3 in 1982. He used to come along on his BMW motorbike. It always impressed me, because he'd just come and find out what was going on with the next generation. He was just as keen to see who would be in F1 next. Certainly, in the year I was up against Senna in F3, Murray was around quite a lot and very supportive."

"This is how close it could get in Formula Johnson and I'm sure it was not a staged finish because Roger Jenkins, who later became World Champion, and Nick Cripps (number 11) were great rivals. Sadly, the Formula Johnson series did not last very long on BBC TV which always mystified me because it made for great racing in very spectacular circumstances by a super lot of competitors."

"This is what they were racing for. The BBC TV Grandstand Trophy. Producer Bob Duncan in the middle is the man who claimed to have thought of using Fleetwood Mac's 'The Chain' as the theme music for the BBC TV 'Grand Prix' series. If he did, he deserves a medal. On the left is the larger-than-life Bob Glen, the boss of EP Barrus who masterminded the whole Formula Johnson concept with great aplomb. I wore a pair of those funny spectacles, which always go dark at the wrong time, in those days. They made me look at though I needed a white stick." (EP Barrus)

"The skill in powerboat racing is to get the majority out of the water and riding on the step to minimise friction. Tom Percival did it to perfection." (Colin Taylor Productions)

The Complete Pro

Richard Galvani

"In 1982 I was running a Formula Three team, one of the top six teams along with Eddie Jordan, Dick Bennetts, Murray Taylor, Neil Trundle and Alan Docking. Murray was always very good at coming round, talking to all and sundry. Particularly if we were at Brands Hatch or Silverstone for the Grand Prix-supporting race. I'm sure he had a lot to do but he always found the time to meet the new drivers and talk to the teams. He had an amazing way of coming into a room or a pit and talking to you as if he's known you for ages. I remember the first time he came in, it was so easy to talk to him. He didn't make us feel like we were inferior to the F1 teams.

"Occasionally he would turn up at a Formula Ford meeting as well. So, even down in the lower echelons, he was showing his interest. And you felt it wasn't just being very professional and keeping an eye on drivers who might come up in the future, but it was a genuine interest in motor racing.

"I remember we sent him a Christmas card, as a lot of the teams and drivers did – to be frank, a lot of them did it just to keep on the right side of Murray because they knew that if ever they got to F1, he could be quite influential depending on what he said on television – but what surprised me was when I got a Christmas card back. I'm sure he had many hundreds to send to his many friends round the world but there was always a card back, signed Murray and Elizabeth."

Chinese Whispers

Tony Jardine

"I remember doing various Macau Grands Prix with him and he had a Chinese producer. He did it for the BBC but he also did it for Star and all the Asian networks. He never saw this producer guy – I think he met him about once – and he just said, 'Mister Warrrkaar, you go to box'. Murray always talked about this mysterious Chinese producer. He'd get notes so he'd know what he was doing but he used to laugh his socks off because all this guy would ever say to him [over the headphones], when he wanted him to start, he'd just say, 'Torrrk Warrrkaar, Torrrk Warrrkaar' and that was it. We were off!"

"I partnered five-times Le Mans 24-hour race winner, Derek Bell, in the first 'Driving Force' programme and one of the things we had to do was perform miracles of manoeuvrability in a Trials car. Derek gets ready to shift his weight to the right place." (Peter Cleaver)

"'Driving Force' again and standing in front of the tank gun muzzle, with the camera slung underneath it, is BBC TV producer, Peter Cleaver, whose attention to detail was awesome. Competitor, Stock Car Champion, Barry Lee, sorely tried Peter's patience when he stuffed the gun barrel into a bank and wiped out the gigantically expensive camera." (Peter Cleaver)

Blakesley Soapbox GP

Murray Walker

"There was a hill on the outskirts of Blakesley and they had this soapbox derby every year. It is a bloody steep hill and the BBC wanted me to report on it and the organiser said, 'We are prepared to give you a run in Bloodshed, which is the name of the soapbox which holds the course record. If you have the balls to do it, we can guarantee you can go downhill without brakes, but you have to be pretty determined.' You can see I had a microphone on my chest to do commentary on the way down. Well, I thought, 'I'm going to do this if it's the last thing I do'. I did and I made the third fastest time of the day, doing commentary all the way. So, I was pretty pleased with myself!"

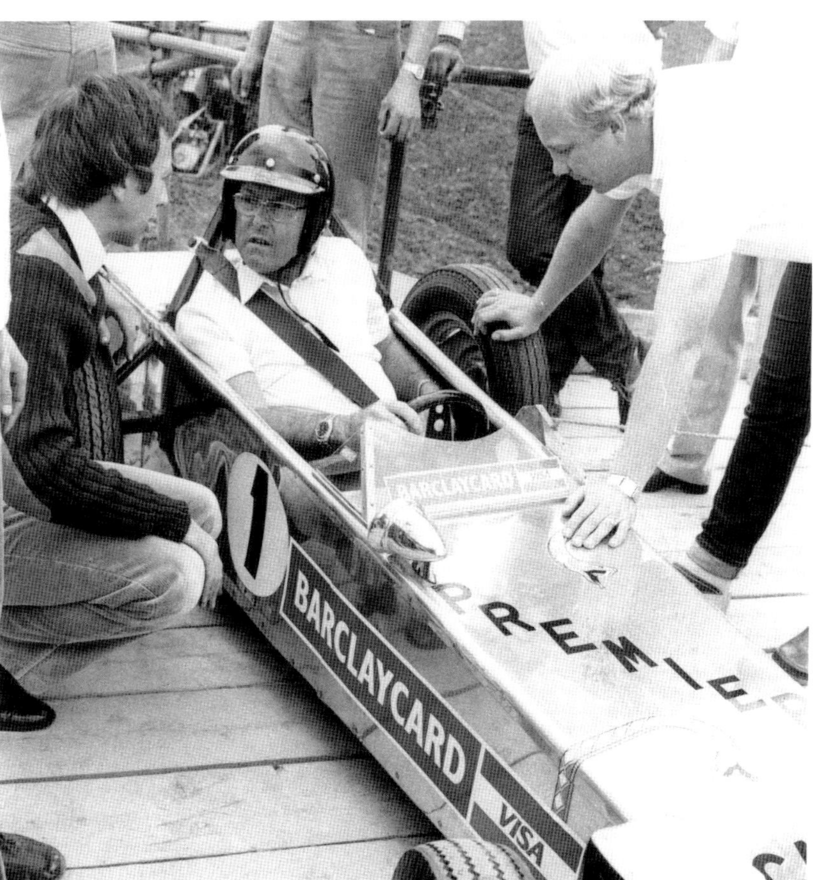

"This is me about to 'compete' in the Blakesley Soapbox Derby during British Grand Prix week, 1984. 'We've put you in our quickest car, Bloodshed' they said. 'Don't touch the brakes and you'll be quick.' I didn't and was third fastest. What a star."

Making The Effort

Richard Galvani

"When we raced at Monaco, the paddock for Formula 3 was actually in France, it was outside Monaco over an imaginary border but territorially it was France. There was no room in those days for other than the F1 cars in Monaco. It was quite a hike to our paddock and the cars had to be driven through the streets. But I remember Murray turning up and walking around, doing his preparation very thoroughly, despite the fact that it was not at all convenient to go out that far."

And A Few Other Things...

Be Upstanding

Vern Schuppan

"Murray used to come out to the Adelaide 500. A couple of times we went out for meals during the events and I remember we went to a well-known, very popular Chinese restaurant in Adelaide and when Murray walked in everyone stood up and gave him a standing ovation. He has become such a legend around the world."

"The chauvinistic male competitors in 'Driving Force' argued a lot but at least agreed on one thing and that was that the Barry Lee/Anneka Rice partnership hadn't got a chance because Anneka hadn't been able to practice any of the disciplines and anyway she was a woman, wasn't she? 'Pride goes before a fall, gentlemen.' Anneka was absolutely sensational, excelled at everything and with the help of superstar, Barry Lee, blew us all away to win the competition. In the picture, left to right, Derek Bell, me, Anneka, Barry and presenter, Mike Smith." (Peter Cleaver)

One Hoarse Race

Barrie 'Whizzo' Williams

"1985 European Grand Prix at Brands Hatch, I was lucky enough to drive one of the works Rothmans Renault Alpines, because no-one else would drive it, and I managed to win. But I had a lovely race up through the field and Murray was doing the commentary on it with James Hunt and it was absolutely hilarious because they both came up to me afterwards, 'We both lost our voices'.

"He knows everybody, he always says, 'Hello Barrie', he never misses a soul. His dad was the same. With my father, they all raced under the Castrol banner before the war. Great. Tremendous family. Wonderful."

"The years rolled back when I clambered into the driving seat, although it was actually some 40 years since I had driven a tank. I guess it's like a riding a bicycle, though, because I not only succeeded in driving over the rusting hulk of a Fiat 128, which was part of the challenge, but actually made fastest time of the day. The hills at Tidworth are a lot steeper than they look in this picture and Derek was screaming 'Faster, faster' at me, while I testily answered back, 'I can't go any bloody quicker - we're absolutely flat out!'"(Peter Cleaver)

Mass Mobbing

Ros Nott

"I have been doing Public Relations for the *Autosport Show* for some eight years, and we've hired some top name drivers to come to the Show. But, I can honestly tell you that if you can get Murray to come, he is the one that is the most mobbed by miles."

Murray Performs Sex Change

Christian Horner

"I grew up listening to Murray every other Sunday afternoon. I first came across him when I was racing in British Formula Three and he was commentating on it for the BBC at the time. I think he once referred to me as 'Christina Horner'!"

The Voice

Ros Nott

"We were debating whether he is one of the most famous voices in England and I think he must be. And hugely missed.

"He occasionally comes round for a kitchen supper. He was sitting here the other night and he suddenly went into Murray mode. 'And here I have my lamb chop, followed closely by my Brussels sprout, which is racing my new potato…' He just suddenly switched into this voice and it was just the funniest thing on this planet!"

"Sleek, black and gold, and menacing. I think the John Player Special livery, which was also used by Lotus in Formula One, is the greatest ever." (Colin Taylor Productions)

MurrayismMurrayismMurrayism

"You might not think that's cricket. And it's not, it's motor racing."

"In mid-80s Tom Wheatcroft, the owner of Donington was approached to promote a truck race. At that time, no-one had even thought of such a thing. So Tom, convinced that nobody would turn up, said, 'Okay, you can hire the circuit and I won't take a cut'. Imagine the universal consternation when over 100,000 people absolutely swamped Donington and brought a whole new audience to this exciting and novel sport, which I rapidly became involved with on television. Enormous truck tractors thundering wheel-to-wheel at over 100mph round Brands Hatch were a mind-boggling spectacle. This evocative Alan Fearnley painting shows ex-motor cycle racer, and Barry Sheene's great mate, Steve Parrish, at Brands Hatch in his European Truck Championship-winning Mercedes-Benz."

Universal Passion

Rubens Barrichello

"I first remember him back in 1991 when I was doing Formula Three. Sometimes he was commentating live, sometimes recorded but I think we were very lucky because he definitely made the races more entertaining. He was loud and he was fun. I was living in England and a big fan of Formula One and I saw him doing the same thing there. He didn't differentiate between Formula One and Formula Three; he used the same emotion and I thought he was very good."

Touring Cars

The British Saloon Car Championship was started in 1958 but would later evolve into the British Touring Car Championship. The very first winner was 'Gentleman' Jack Sears in an Austin A105, who won it on a tie-breaker from Tommy Sopwith in a 3.4 Jaguar Mark 1. The list of subsequent winners reads like a roll call of great names. In the '60s there was Doc Shepherd, Sir John Whitmore, John Love, Sears again, Jim Clark, Roy Pierpoint, John Fitzpatrick, Frank Gardner (twice) and Alec Poole. The '70s opened with a trio of titles for Bill McGovern, followed by Gardner again and Bernard Unett. The great Andy Rouse took his first title in 1975, followed by Unett again (twice) and the decade concluded with a brace of wins for Richard Longman.

In those days, the title was based on the highest points scored in one of the four classes rather than overall race winners. This was far from ideal, made it confusing for followers and favoured the smaller-engined cars. Just five drivers shared the spoils in the '80s with the great Win Percy taking the first three, followed by Rouse taking the next three, Chris Hodgetts annexing the next two and the decade being wrapped up with titles for Frank Sytner and that great character John Cleland.

In the '90s honours were taken by Rob Gravett, Will Hoy, Tim Harvey, Jo Winkelhock, Gabriele Tarquini, Cleland again, Frank Biela, Alain Menu, Rickard Rydell and Laurent Aiello.

Touring cars have always been highly popular with motor racing fans and when the BBC began to broadcast a few races on *Grandstand* the following just grew and grew. In 1988 the BBC made the decision to show a 20-minute edited compilation of the highlights of every round, and gave the job of commentating to Murray. The formula – touring cars and Murray – was an instant success.

As a result, everyone upped their act. TOCA, the *Touring Car Association*, was formed in 1992 by the teams run by Andy Rouse, David Richards, Dave Cook and Vic Lee, and was led by the redoubtable Alan Gow who made a brilliant job of packaging and promoting the series.

Apart from TV coverage, Murray, TOCA and Gow, the other magic ingredient that helped to make touring cars such a success was the adoption, from 1991, of a 2-litre limit for all cars. Super Touring, as it was now known, brought in a plethora of manufacturers, including overseas makes, much closer racing and a heightened spectacle.

Murray's touring car reign began in 1988 and was to last nine years. For many it was the golden age of touring cars with more makes competing than at any other time with BMWs battling with Fords, Rovers, Vauxhalls, Mazdas, Alfa Romeos, Toyotas, Audis, Nissans, Peugeots, Renaults, Hondas and even Volvos! Though a British championship, a sprinkling of overseas drivers began participating with great success and this all added to the flavour. In the '90s Brits won only four of the titles and the new millennium opened with the Swiss driver Alain Menu taking his second Championship.

Murray loves Australia (and it seems it is mutual) and so he was especially delighted when he was invited to join the commentary team for 'The Great Race', as they call the legendary Bathurst 1000 locally. He thoroughly enjoyed the experience in 1997 and went again the year after. Both years the organisers had adopted the BTCC formula for 2-litre cars but the Aussies missed their big V8s and, though it had produced some great racing, they returned to their beloved V8s in 1999.

Back in Britain, it had all worked out superbly. The racing was close – sometimes too close – and superbly presented with in-car filming and even commentary. There was controversy to spice up the series and the ever growing audiences loved it. The BBC reacted by giving increasing amounts of airtime to the touring cars and thus Murray was booming out of the nation's television sets more often than ever.

"I never commentated on the great Stirling Moss in his Grand Prix days because I was the BBC's motor cycle man then but when he made a bit of a comeback in Touring Cars in 1980, it looked as though I was going to have the chance to do so. I really looked forward to that but his time with Audi did not last long enough." (Chris Willows)

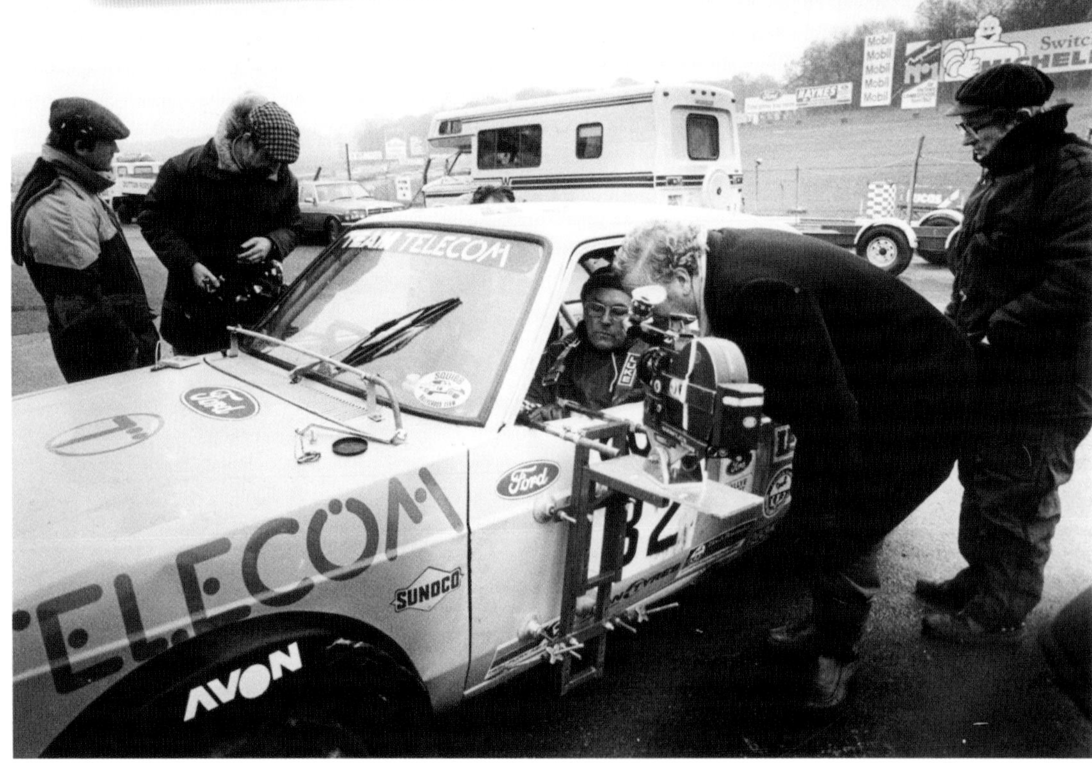

"What's that? You call this an on-car camera?" (Colin Taylor Productions)

Down To Earth

Andy Rouse

"What always amazed me about him, when we started appearing on TV, back in the late '80s with the Sierra Cosworths, was how friendly he was. But he was a motor racing enthusiast. We were amazed to see Murray Walker walking around the paddock talking to everybody. He was a big name but there he was at Thruxton, or wherever, just going round, chit-chatting, picking up his bits of gossip.

"Whatever he did with motor sport, he did well. He wasn't just a commentator, he was a very special commentator."

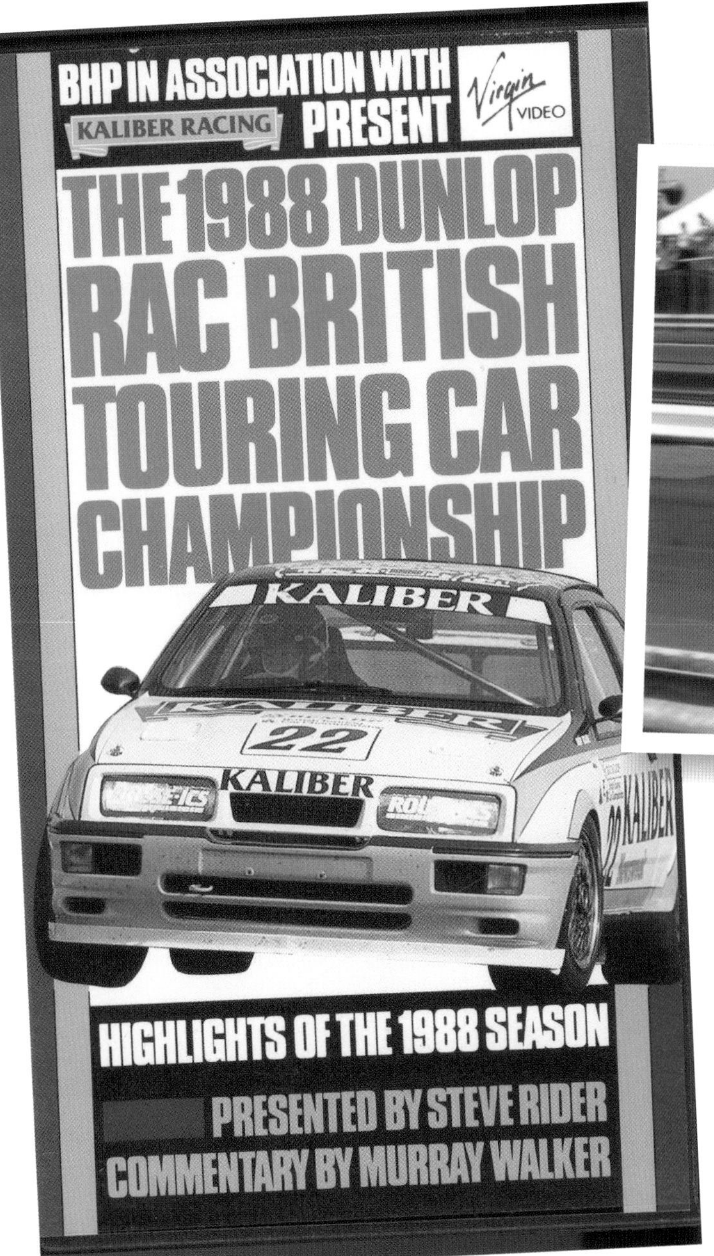

"Now here's a couple of mysteries that I found in my files. Of course, I know Frank Sytner, who sold the brilliant BMW and Alpina business he built up for a zillion pounds and now races very successfully in historic events, but I don't remember doing anything on him in 1983 when he obviously drove this 6-Series BMW. The other one's a puzzle too, but I reckon it's Dave 'I gold-plate my carburrettors' Brodie in a Mitsubishi at Brands Hatch. Get a grip Walker!" (Chris Willows)

Professionalism And Dedication

Alan Gow

"In 1991 TOCA was formed and took over the rights to run the British Touring Car Championship and obviously took over Murray as part of that as Murray was contracted to the BBC and we entered into a new agreement with the BBC to continue coverage of the Championship. Murray was, and still is, an incredibly enthusiastic supporter of the Touring Cars, not only as a commentator but he just loved watching the racing.

"In the early 90s it wasn't live on the BBC. It was recorded and shown about a week later. Murray would come in the week after the race, usually on a Wednesday. He would spend literally all day putting together a 20 minute segment – that's the professionalism he showed. That incredibly impressed me. So many people would have a look at the final edit once and then babble their way through it on the second run through. Murray would sit there and takes notes and go over it and over it and over it and over it, and literally spend all day doing that. He would finally put his voice to it at the end of the day. That showed the incredible professionalism and dedication that he put into it.

"He could have just waltzed in, spent just an hour there and just walked out."

Easing The Transition

Andy Rouse

"Barrie Hinchcliffe was employed by TOCA to film the Championship and Steve Rider was a partner in Barry Hinchcliffe Productions. Steve was very keen on touring cars and he was probably the person who did the most to get it on TV. Barry filmed and Murray commentated on it, and off we went. It was a great success story for some time.

"We were running the Sierra Cosworths but then in 1991 the rules changed for the simple reason that the Sierra Cosworth was running out of homologation. Cars were only homologated for five years. We could see a crisis coming up because there was nothing else to take its place. In the interests of protecting our position on television, we devised the 2-litre formula, which actually came from my offices in the first place. That was really the start of Super Touring.

"Murray helped us a lot because it was quite a transition from RS500s to front wheel drive Toyotas. So it needed treating quite carefully because the grids weren't that great to start with. It grew rapidly and Murray's input was crucial in keeping the TV audience interested and making it look good enough to interest the other manufacturers. About 1994 we had nine manufacturer teams in the Championship. Television was the driving force that made everything else work. Manufacturers wouldn't have been there without the TV, and the TV wouldn't have been very good without Murray.

"So he was a pivotal part of the success of the whole thing."

"For me, Mr Touring Car Racing is without doubt the great Andy Rouse who has not only won more British Touring Car Championship races than anyone else but who won the Championship with four different constructors. If I had a fiver for every one of his laps that I commentated on, I'd be a wealthy man. And he's a lovely bloke too." (BTCC Archive)

Hand Signals!

John Cleland

"His commentaries are just classic. I would wave my arms about in the car and stick up the 'V' sign or one figure or something like that. I remember a particularly heated battle between myself at Silverstone and a BMW driver. He'd given me a bit of a graze and I'd stuck one finger up at this guy ... and I had a camera in the car and it witnessed everything!

"Murray said, 'And John Cleland is just letting everyone know he is going for first place'! Only he could think of that!"

"Number 45, Rob Gravett, is a man who caused me more than a few seizures in the commentary box, thanks to his speed, style and determination. He's in a Peugeot 405 here but, in my opinion, his best period was driving the Ford Sierra Turbo." (BTCC Archive)

"Australian Alan Gow is the man who made the British Touring Car Championship one of British TV's top attractions and the public switched on in their millions to watch paint-swapping, curb-hopping battles like this. That's ex-Grand Prix driver Julian Bailey at the back trying to get into the Peugeot's boot." (BTCC Archive)

Instant Credibility

Steve Soper

"He had been involved in Grand Prix racing for about two decades so when he became involved in touring car racing, it gave us quite a bit more credibility. We eventually got on TV, which we'd been trying to do for years and years, and the fact that Murray Walker was, for most of the time, the commentator just raised it to a different level. Okay we were touring cars, not Formula One, but there wasn't someone banging on that didn't know what the hell he was talking about."

Spontaneous Scripts

Alan Gow

"Some of his comments were off the cuff and some of them were incredibly well rehearsed. The quips were often scripted because that's what people expected of Murray Walker. Some of it was just rampant enthusiasm getting in the way and other times he would sit there and think of a line to use.

"During the '90s the BBC increasingly gave it more vision – we went from 20 minutes to 30 to 40 to an hour. And Murray was a very important part of the success of the BTCC in that era. Both off screen and on screen, he was an incredibly enthusiastic supporter of the Championship. He would come to races, when he could, just as a spectator."

"Here are a couple of British Touring Car Champions who gave me in the commentary box and the public in their homes an enormous amount of pleasure. In BMW number eight, it is Tim Harvey - now a BTCC commentator himself - and on the left, Switzerland's Alain Menu." (BMW UK)

"You might think this is the North Circular Road on any typical work day but it's actually multiple Champion John Cleland in the Vauxhall at the back trying to muscle past Tim Harvey and the late, sadly-missed Will Hoy - all three British Champions." (BTCC Archive)

Timing Is Everything

John Cleland

"One lovely memory I have – we were at Donington Park for the Touring Car race in '92. I was going to do a live feed back to Murray during the race. It was before proper radio systems in the helmet. I was testing mid-week and had this microphone in my chin strap. I had a bit of an accident, hit the wall and, as my head snapped forward, the microphone actually broke my sternum. I also broke my lower back in the same accident and I always kinda blamed Murray for having that bloody microphone!

"We then went on to use it in a race some weeks later and I said, 'Right Murray, you are going speak to me at some stage during the race – try and choose a time when I'm not in the depth of a battle, let's try and do it when I am coming down the pits straight and not working quite so hard'.

"Part way through the race I'm in the monster of all battles. I think I'm third in the race and I've got two guys in front of me, I'm clambering all over them, I've got a couple of guys behind me, clambering all over me, down the side of me and everything. And it goes, ping-pong, 'It's Murray here. Can we have a chat about how the race is going?'

"I remember saying to him, 'Well, actually Murray, I'm a wee bit busy at the moment.'

"It was classic Murray. I thought, 'I can't believe this'. There was so much going on and he wanted me to talk to him!"

Live Coverage A Week Later

Andy Rouse

"The Touring Car races were always edited and shown a week later. Murray used to go into a studio and do his stuff. Nobody knew. We used to have an open pit lane at lunchtime and the spectators would come round for autographs. They all thought it was live when they watched it on television! Nobody ever let on that it wasn't!

"That did make a bit of a problem for us because there was a bit of a credibility gap between what people saw on TV and what they saw when they came to the racetrack. That was something we were always trying to address and it did improve the more cars we got. Alfa Romeo turned up with their Italian drivers and that sort of thing. There was a helluva buzz to it at the racetrack after a while. It was an international championship run on a national basis.

"It was incredible - some manufacturers were spending between £5m and £10m on what was a national championship, which was another reason it went into decline."

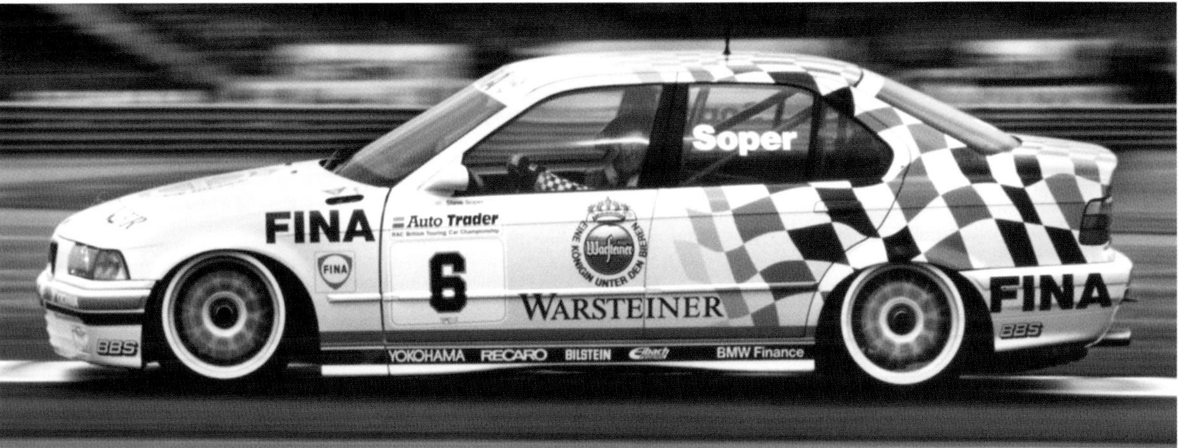

"I made so many friends when I was doing the British Touring Car Championship and one of them was certainly BMW's Steve Soper, in my opinion one of the really great all-round drivers." (BMW UK)

No Haven

John Cleland

"He seemed capable of always being in the right place and of asking the right questions because he knew so much about everything. Everybody pestered him at race meetings. I remember one day talking to him about it. I said, 'How do you cope when you are trying to get ready for a race and you can't even walk from the motorhome without getting attacked by everybody that wants your autograph?'

"He said, 'That's the way it is. It's what we're paid to do.' He said, 'I remember a time, I was at Silverstone and I went into the loo, locked the door and a wee hand with a programme and marker pen comes under the door. 'While you're sitting in there doing nothing, Murray, could I have your autograph, please?'

"That was brilliant, brilliant Murray!"

"Feisty Scotsman, John Cleland, was a Volvo dealer but his racing success, and there was a lot of it, was with Vauxhall. Not content with winning the British Touring Car Championship once, he did it again in a Vauxhall Cavalier and, for me, was just as much of a star to interview as he was to commentate on." (BTCC Archive)

"This is Steve Soper again, with John Cleland alongside him in the adjoining picture but so often they were alongside each on the track, especially in 1992 when their controversial coming together nearly led to blows, and enabled BMW's Tim Harvey to win the Championship. Scotsman, John Cleland, colourfully used some Anglo Saxon phraseology to describe his feelings but, as the BTCC was a family show, we were sadly not able to use them!" (BTCC Archive)

Mistaken Identity

Tim Harvey

"My young son who was, I should think five or six at the time, knew Murray's voice very much from watching and listening to all the touring car races but had never met Murray. I had him at Brands Hatch once and Murray was in a garage talking to another gentleman. I said to Jamie, 'Would you like to meet Murray Walker?'

"He said, 'Yes, definitely'. So, I took him into the garage and when there was a convenient break in the conversation, I said, 'Oh Murray, would you like to meet my son, Jamie? He'd very much like to say hello.' And Jamie held his hand out to the other gentleman, not realising what Murray actually looked like. Of course, Murray took all in great fashion and thought it all highly amusing. He's just a delightful man."

"I fondly remember Tim Harvey racing for BMW, for Renault, for Volvo and especially in the spectacular, flame-spitting Ford Sierra Turbo. He always gave great value for money to his team and sponsor, and to me as a commentator." (BTCC Archive)

"Such was the attraction of the British Touring Car Championship because of its worldwide television coverage which, to be honest, didn't do me any harm, that in 1994 and 1995, the fabled Alfa Romeo team entered a couple of cars, one of them driven by ex-Grand Prix racer, Gabriele Tarquini, who not only brought a touch of Italian flamboyance and style to the series, but also glory to Alfa by winning it in 1994." (BTCC Archive)

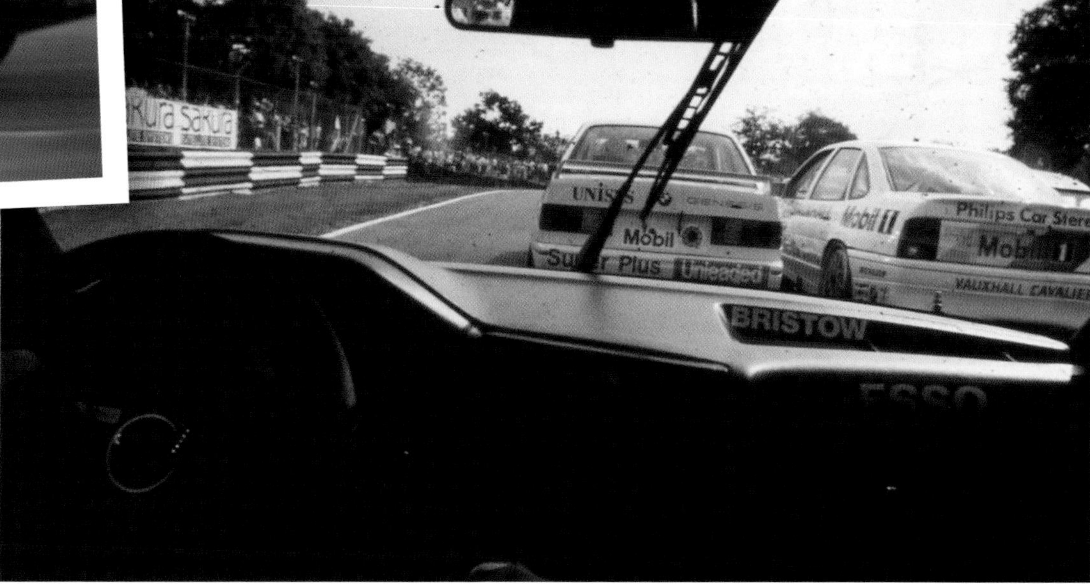

"One of the main reasons for the astounding success of the BTCC was the film editing brilliance of BHP's Steve Saint. Thanks to the innovative use of in-car footage, like this, he was able to make what had actually been a processional race look absolutely rivetting on the box. A very rare skill." (BTCC Archive)

Sending Up Oneself

John Cleland

"The thing about Murray is that he always managed to poke fun at himself, which I thought was brilliant. I think that was a lesson for a lot of us. I used to try and aim things back at myself and it then didn't sound quite so pretentious sometimes!"

"Twenty-three on the grid. All of them with virtually identical performance and driven by skilled stars determined to win. Put them on the Brands Hatch Indy short circuit and you are guaranteed sensational, spectacular panel-banging and paint-swapping action. The public loved the racing and the manufacturers loved the TV ratings. Me? I loved all of it." (BTCC Archive)

Instant Recall

Steve Soper

"The first thing that struck me about Murray was that he always had a smile on his face, and secondly, he never forgot a name. I am diabolical with names. But you could walk up to him, even after several years and out of context – not necessarily at a motoring event – and he would immediately recognise you and remember the name. Just imagine the number of people and the drivers, not just British drivers, he has met but he always had a fantastic recall for who was who, and what they did. There was never a blank look on his face. Straight away it was, 'Hi Steve, and how are you?'"

"At the time, people thought that staid old Volvo were pushing their luck by entering the BTCC but the Tom Walkinshaw-prepared cars, particularly Rickard Rydell's, transformed the Volvo image. Rickard had transformed his Volvo's bodywork here, too!" (BTCC Archive)

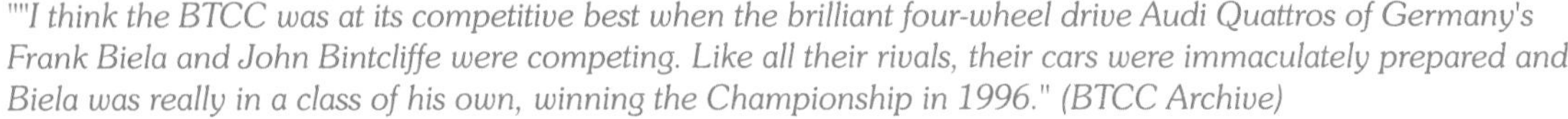

""I think the BTCC was at its competitive best when the brilliant four-wheel drive Audi Quattros of Germany's Frank Biela and John Bintcliffe were competing. Like all their rivals, their cars were immaculately prepared and Biela was really in a class of his own, winning the Championship in 1996." (BTCC Archive)

Ongoing Homework

Steve Soper

"Other commentators would garble their way through but Murray, being a professional, would walk round the paddock and around the pits. If he hadn't done a touring car race for six weeks, he'd make sure he was up-to-date on all the latest things, he'd see the teams, he'd see the drivers and say to John Cleland or Andy Rouse or myself, 'Right, anything I need to know, anything changed?' A total professional before the event started, before he got in the box – he was making sure he didn't miss something. I know he is famous for his blunders but actually it's more through excitement."

Just Don't Say It

John Cleland

"There were one or two situations where championships had gone down to the wire and I remember saying to him, 'Please, please, if I am in the lead, don't say anything along the lines of, 'Well, Cleland is certain to win this race,' because that would be the Murray Walker-kiss-of-death. 'For God's sake, don't say it'."

"From my apprehensive expression, it looks as though Tim Harvey is giving me a bit of stick. But he is much too nice a chap to do that." (BTCC Archive)

"This is the technical bit of television that I never really grasped. The control room was an electronic mystery to me but BHP certainly made it all work brilliantly." (BTCC Archive)

"They came from far and wide to compete in the BTCC, including Australian Sir Jack Brabham's son, David." (BTCC Archive)

"People used to think that Vauxhall and Renault mainly made pretty ordinary cars for sales reps. That's why they both entered the BTCC and they've certainly reaped the reward in image terms, helped by battles like this between Vauxhall champion John Cleland and Renault champion Alain Menu." (BTCC Archive)

Sticking To The Facts

Tim Harvey

"I think it's important to stress that Murray wasn't just a commentator, that he was somebody that was up and down the pit lane, talking to the drivers – he was very much part of the scene as an enthusiast and as a commentator. There are so many journalists now in motor sport that we never even see at the meetings. Yet they write race reports with quotes and everything else, and you've never even spoken to the chap over the weekend. That wasn't Murray's style at all. He was on the ground and always had the right information, even if he didn't always (laughing) say it in the correct manner!

"He didn't have favourites. He had drivers that he liked more than other drivers, perhaps, but he said it as he saw it. He didn't pass judgement too much on rights and wrongs of incidents in touring cars, of which there are plenty. He reported the accident and said it as he saw it."

"1996. What a carve-up! Five in together. Alain Menu leads in the Renault, followed by John Cleland's Vauxhall, with Frank Biela's silver Audi diving up the inside. David Leslie, Honda Accord, and James Thompspon, Vauxhall, make up the numbers, while I poured out a babble of excitement!" (BTCC Archive)

The Golden Era

"He was the voice of motor sport and having him do the commentary, when he was doing Formula One, endorsed the credibility of touring cars, and it was the halcyon period of touring cars with up to eight or nine manufacturers involved. So, they were the best days in a lot of ways."

"Patrick Watts, who drove for Peugeot, never really achieved the success that his ability deserved. In his flaming 405, he valiantly tries to take John Bintcliffe's Audi." (BTCC Archive)

"One of the fabulous perks of my job was to get high-speed rides round the circuits, driven by the stars of the day. But why the camera?" (BMW UK)

Wish I Was There

John Cleland

"He was great fun and I really miss hearing his voice on the Touring Cars coverage. There's not anyone near the same.

"It was always live and he would do the voice-overs afterwards. I would go home and sit down on the Saturday afternoon and watch a race I had competed in the previous weekend, fully knowing it was the most boring race I think I'd ever taken part in. I'm watching this, and I'm listening to Murray, and the way they've cut and shut, and pushed in some in-car stuff, and I'm thinking, 'What a phenomenal race – I wish I'd been there'. 'Cos it sounded much more exciting than when I was in it!

"He had the knack of making things sound exciting and he has a passion, a real passion for it and a real buzz for the sport. I just wish there were more folk like him involved in it, and that view applies to the competitors as well as the commentators. There are some competitors who say (in flat monotone), 'It was really nice to win the race today and I'd like to thank Nissan…' or whoever it was – bullshit!

"With Murray, it was a passion. You felt it from his shoelaces all the way up, that he just enjoyed being there. He just had a ball.

"The gaffes that he made were part of Murray Walker and I don't think anybody would have wanted anything else. He just took it on the nose and I think that's what made him so popular."

"While you sat at home watching from your comfortable living room, BBC TV cameramen had to be all-weather heroes at times." (BTCC Archive)

The Murray Effect

Alan Gow

"It was *one* of the golden eras. If you measure it by the number of manufacturer teams in the Championship, it was the best we ever had. I honestly don't think we would have had the public following that we had in that time if it hadn't been for Murray."

A Right Charlie

Alan Gow

"Then we started doing some live broadcasts. They started with one or two a year, then three or four, and Murray was still doing it.

"We teamed him up with a guy called Charlie Cox. Charlie is a fellow Australian and was racing in the Championship in the early '90s and then had an horrendous accident at Thruxton that really finished his racing career. But Charlie has the gift of the gab and I thought he would be a perfect foil for Murray, and he proved to be. He'd never done any commentary work or TV before but he just took to it like a duck to water and those two got on famously well. It was serious racing and serious commentary but there were some very, very funny quips between them."

"Until 2007, there is little doubt that BMW driver, Italian Roberto Ravaglia, was the world's greatest touring car driver with multiple national and international touring car championships to his name. But now it is another of BMW's seemingly limitless succession of superstars with Guernseyman Andy Priaux having uniquely achieved four successive World Championships - if you regard his 2004 European Championship success as being a 'world' title which I do. It has been my enormous pleasure to commentate on them both at their very best." (BMW UK)

"What a monumental privilege. To be driven round Australia's legendary Mount Panorama, scene of one of the world's greatest touring car races, the Bathurst 1000, by the even more legendary, all-time Australian hero, Peter Brock, in his incredible three-litre racing Holden engine-powered Austin A30."

Being Driven By Peter Brock

Murray Walker

"I went out to cover the famous Bathurst 1000. Went to see the producer, and he said, 'We have arranged for you to go round with Peter Brock'. Now in Australia saying that is like saying we have arranged for you to be driven round by God - Peter Brock was that much of a hero. I went and found Peter; I had met him in the past. 'Glad to hear I will going round with you, Peter. What will we be going round in?' He said, 'I thought we would go round in my A30'. I said, 'Austin A30?' 'Yes,' he said. I said, 'That's nice. My mother had one of those.' He said, 'Not like this one. It has a three-litre race-tuned Holden engine in it.' They put cameras in the car, microphones on both of us, helicopter following us around, fixed cameras all around the circuit. We couldn't move a wheel without being covered. There was one lovely shot as we are going down Conrod Straight, fast downhill, very long straight. I looked across, 'How fast are we going, Peter?' and he said, '150mph'. In an Austin A30!"

Enhancing The Show

John Cleland

"There is absolutely no doubt that he did more to popularise Touring Cars than anybody else. He was there at the right time. There were a number of characters involved in it in those days and he just made it all possible. He plucked the best out of those characters and made something of them. He was very astute and observant in the way that he managed to pick some of those things up.

"Without Murray I don't think British Touring Cars would have been quite as World-renowned as they became. His ability to make it sound, in many cases, better than it was was responsible for its success. I thought he was great."

LAP = 6.213 KM = 3.86M

161 LAPS = 1,000KM = 621.5M

LAP RECORD: JASON PLATO (LAGUNA) 2M 16.8034 (1997)

36TH AMP BATHURST 1000: 4.10.48

$123,000 CASH PRIZES
1ST = $50,000
* ROOKIE OF YEAR
* SAE TROPHY (TOP OZ UNDER 30)
* TOCA TROPHY = TOP BTCC D/R
* 7 NETWORK TPHY = HIGHEST INDEP

TOP 10
1
2
3
4
5
6
7
8
9
10

POLE:
97: P. MORRIS (BMW) 2M 16.5958
98: ~~RYDELL~~ J. RICHARDS 2M 14.9265

		Driver	Age	Car	Notes
1	*	BRAD JONES	38	AUDI (YELLOW)	ALBURY NSW: 28YRS: 7X: FF: 2x AUST TCC: 2ND BATHURST 97 & 94: 3RD BATHURST 93: 12x B/HURST
		CAMERON OZCH2 McCONVILLE 98	24	(RED)	MELBOURNE: 17YRS: FF & TC CHAMPS: KARTS/ FVEE/FF 3RD BATHURST 97: 2ND AUS TCC 98 TO B. JONES 4x B/HURST
2	*	PAUL MORRIS	31	AUDI (BLUE)	GOLD COAST: 12YRS: 5x BATHURST: PAC WEST INDY LIGHTS '98: AUS TC CHAMP 95-97: 24x1 AUS STCC: BATHURST CLASS WINNER 91-94
		PAUL RADISICH	36	(RED)	WORLD TC CHAMP 93/94: MULTIPLE BTCC WINNER: FORD/ PEUGEOT BATHURST x7 (2ND '90): F.PACIFIC/ F3 /F.SUPERVEE
4	*	JAN NILSSON	38	VOLVO	1xB/HST: SWEDISH TC CHAMP 96/97: SCAN FF CHAMP 88/89 B/HURST 5TH '97:
		TIM HARVEY	37	(BLUE STRIP)	1x B/HST: BTCC CHAMP 92: BMW/ RENAULT/ VOLVO/ PEUGEOT:
8	*	DEREK WARWICK	44	VECTRA	JERSEY: B/HURST 6TH '97 (VECTRA): WORLD SC CHAMP 92: 1ST LE MANS '92: 2ND EURO F2 CHAMP 80: F1 ARROWS/ TOLEMAN/ RENAULT LOTUS
		JOHN CLELAND	47		GALLASHIELS: B/HURST 6TH '95: BTCC CHAMP 89 & 95: 2ND '91 BTCC: 3 & 4 BTCC 92 & 93: 4x B/HURST:
10		TONY NEWMAN	42	PEUGEOT 406	SYDNEY: 18YRS: 1ST MANFIELD 3HR 94/95: 1x B/HURST:
		MARK WILLIAMSON	33		WOODFORD NSW: F.VAUXHALL (BRITAIN): BATHURST x2:
11		MILTON LESLIGHT	!	TOYOTA CARINA	SYDNEY: 25YRS: AUS GT PDN CHAMP (C CLASS) 95 B/HURST DEBUT:
		DENNIS CRIBBIN	54		MOSS VALE NSW: 30YRS: CLUBBIES: SEVERAL BATHURST
12	*	CAMERON OZCH McLEAN 4/98	30	BMW 1997 WINNER!	BRISBANE: 5TH BATHURST 97 (VOLVO): 97/98 AUS SUPER TC INDEP CHAMP: 14YRS KARTS & TC: 1x B/HURST: INDEP CH '98
		TONY SCOTT	41	4x B/HURST	BRISBANE: LOT TC EXPERIENCE: TRUCK WORKSHOP OWNER: CLASS 1ST WELLINGTON & PUKEKOHE 500S '92: 1ST CLASS B/HURST 12HR '93
14		JIM CORNISH	27	NISSAN PRIMERA	SYDNEY: 7YRS:
		BLAIR SMITH (NZ)	34		CHRISTCHURCH: NZ: FURNITURE IMPORTER: 5YRS: FF & TC
15		MARK ADDERTON	31	HONDA ACCORD	SYDNEY: DRIVING INSTRUCTOR: 4YRS (TC): 1x B/HURST INDEP CH 2/98
		JAMIE WALL	21		CHESTER: KARTS/ JRRDS/ FIESTA: BTCC 97 CAVALIER
16		PAUL ALAN NELSON	34	BMW	7TH B/HURST 97: 1X B/HURST:
		JUSTIN MATHEWS	32		SYDNEY: BUILDER: 4YRS: 1ST BATH INDEP '97: 7TH B/HURST '97
		BOB HOLDEN	56	29x B/HST	BOOTAWA: NSW: ENGINEER: 35YRS: 1ST BATHURST '66
18		AARON McGILL	35	PEUGEOT 405	MITTAGONG: DRIVING SCHOOL: B/HURST 97 (MONDEO) 1998 PDN CHAMPIONSHIP 2 IN CLASS
		CLAYTON HAYNES	31		SYDNEY: PRO: KARTS: 98 PDN CAR CHAMPIONSHIP.
20		DENNIS CHAPMAN (NZ)	44	BMW	8TH B/HURST '97: NZ ENDURO SUCCESS: 1x B/HURST
		BRIAN BRADSHAW (NZ)	48		8TH B/HURST '97: 1ST CLASS NZ ENDURO SERIES '66: 1x B/HURST:
22		ROD WILSON	27	BMW	B/HURST DEBUT:
		RODNEY FORBES	31		FF LAP RECORD HOLDER SYDNEY: COMPUTER ANALYST B/HURST 1000 DEBUT (BUT F.FORD) 97 STATE FF CHAMP. 4TH 98 AUS PDN CAR CHAMP

Murray's 1998 crib sheet

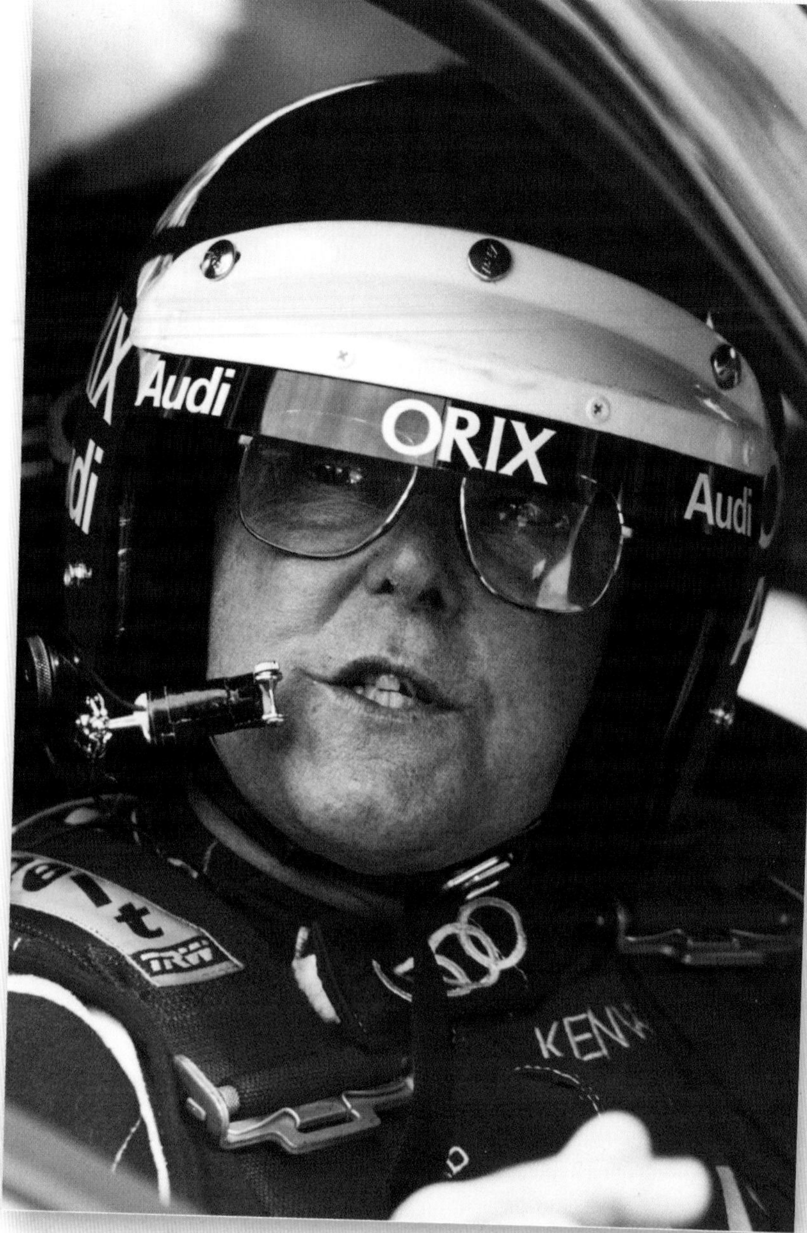

"In 1998 I achieved one of my life's ambitions by commentating on Australia's Bathurst 1000. Two-litre Champion, Brad Jones, took me round in his Audi Quattro." (Sutton Images)

Always The Pro

Steve Soper

"In about 1999 he was involved in a motor sport event at my BMW dealership in Lincoln for me. BMW asked him if he would do it and he did it out of the goodness of his heart, he didn't even charge a fee, *and* he was wasn't well, *and* he was flying off to Canada next day. We had a motor sport quiz and a big opening of the dealership. He was very ill and halfway through the day we got a doctor for him. The doctor basically said he was not dying and he came back downstairs and performed like Murray Walker always performs, and didn't even leave early. A great man."

I love Panorama

Murray pushes for mountain World Cup

Call of the wild: Murray Walker

By CAMERON BELL

LEGENDARY motor racing figure Murray Walker, in Australia to call his second Bathurst 1000, is pushing for a World Cup Super Touring race on Mt Panorama.

Walker, the voice of Formula One, said such a race could be one of the great international events of the year.

"People know me from calling Formula One but my work with the BBC in England involves calling the British touring cars," the 75-year-old said.

"I rate the touring car drivers very highly and I would love to see a World Cup race consisting of all the top touring car drivers in the world on Mt Panorama. That would be sensational."

Last year, when Walker first arrived in Bathurst, he was taken on a drive of the circuit by Allan Moffat, Brad Jones and the King of the Mountain, Peter Brock.

He fell in love with the course, which he rates as equal to any he has seen in the world.

"The idea of a World Cup race here is one that I have come up with — but wouldn't it be great to see the Alfas from Italy going head-to-head with the BMWs, Toyotas, Nissans, Renaults and Vectras. That would be fabulous."

Almost as good as listening to Walker's call of today's race on Channel 7.

Walker certainly doesn't need much winding up when it comes to talking about his passion for motor racing.

A question on how he's enjoying his second Bathurst gets his mouth racing faster than Michael Schumacher's Ferrari. So, how are things at Bathurst, Murray?

"Well, young Steven Richards has just got the fastest lap time at 2:18.46 in the Nissan and is looking particularly good," he said.

"But the Vectras will be on the track shortly and I'm looking forward to seeing the Audi of Brad Jones."

Walker said he still got the same buzz calling the Super Tourers at Mt Panorama as he did calling the F1 boys at Monaco.

So, how does he rate Bathurst on the scale of the world's great races?

"Bathurst to me is one of three great races I always promised myself I would get to," he said.

"The first one I would have loved to have seen was the Mille Miglia, which was a 1000km race through public roads in Italy — but they stopped that race in 1955 and I never got to see it.

"The second I was always interested in was the Targa Floria race in Sicily, but they stopped that, and the third was Bathurst and here I am.

"When Channel 7 asked me to come out last year I had no hesitation — and they didn't need to ask me twice for this year's event."

Does he have a tip for this year?

"Well, there are a number of cars and drivers who could win and I never have a very good track record when it comes to tipping the winner of a race," he said.

"But if I'm absolutely forced into making a selection then I would go for the Audi of Brad Jones."

It wouldn't be right to let Murray Walker go without asking him about the Formula One season, which has come down to the wire with the last race being held in Japan later this month.

"This year's season has been absolutely fabulous," he said.

"At the start of the year the McLarens were so dominant and everyone was dreading the five-week break between Luxembourg and Japan because we thought the season would be over.

"It wasn't as if the McLarens came back to the field ... it's just that Ferrari caught up.

"But we've really got something to look forward to at Suzuka and I would have to say Mika Hakkinen is looking good. Schumacher can still win but he has a lot of work to do and ..."

We're sure, by now, you have the picture.

114—THE SUNDAY TELEGRAPH, www.news.com.au October 4, 1998—114

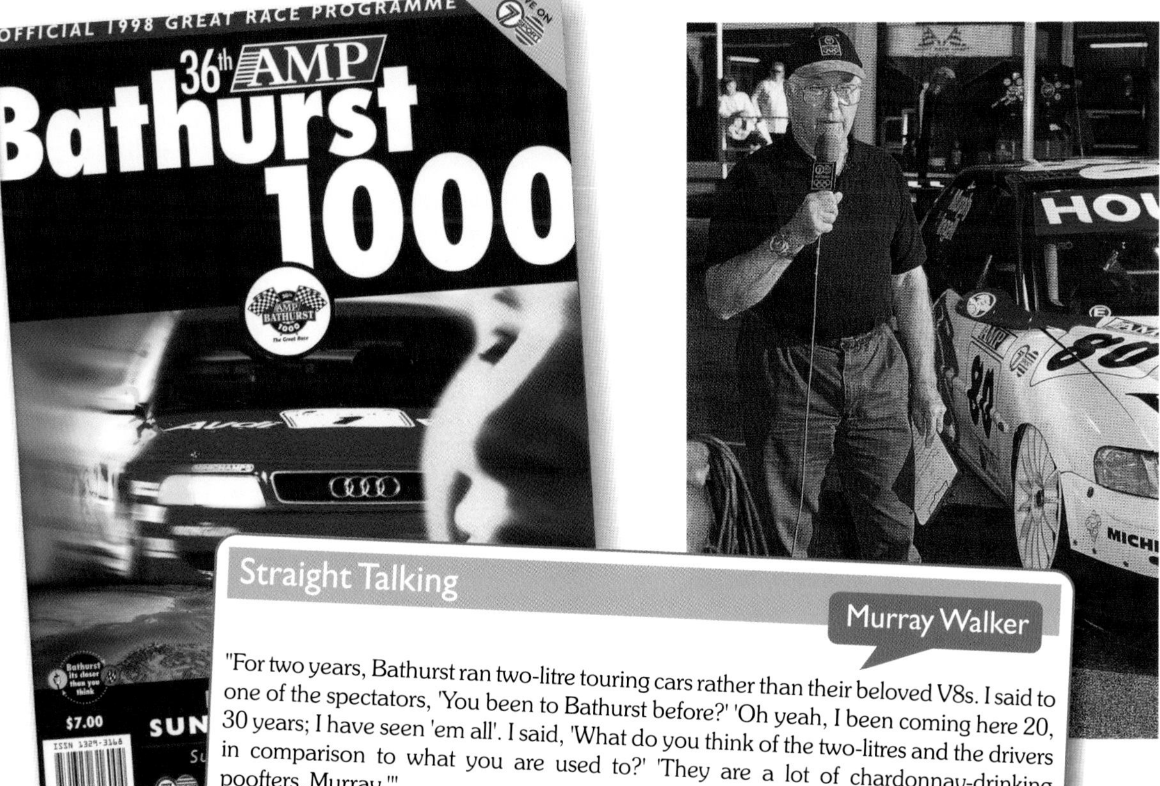

Straight Talking

Murray Walker

"For two years, Bathurst ran two-litre touring cars rather than their beloved V8s. I said to one of the spectators, 'You been to Bathurst before?' 'Oh yeah, I been coming here 20, 30 years; I have seen 'em all'. I said, 'What do you think of the two-litres and the drivers in comparison to what you are used to?' 'They are a lot of chardonnay-drinking poofters, Murray.'"

> MurrayismMurrayismMurrayism
>
> **"The European drivers have adapted to this circuit extremely quickly, especially Paul Radisich who's a New Zealander."**

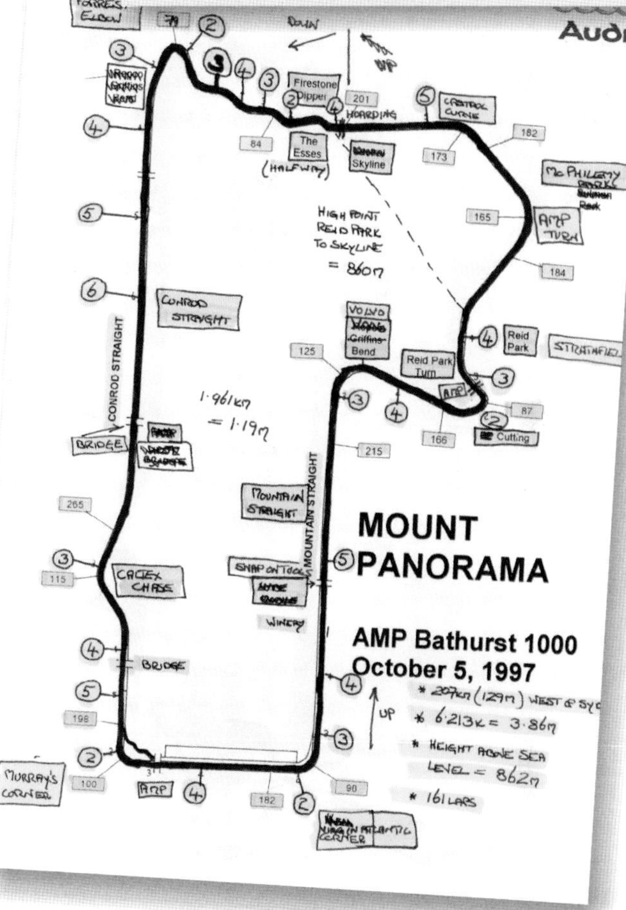

All Or Nothing

Alan Gow

"A lot of people just take the money, sit back and just turn up when they have to, but that's just not Murray. My enduring memory of Murray during his time with the BTCC was just his rampant enthusiasm for it.

"It was a very, very sad day when Murray decided to hang up his microphone. Because the BBC were increasingly giving us more airtime, the one day that he spent in post-production became two days. It was becoming fairly onerous. I hasten to add that he chose to do two days – he could have done it in one day but he was not like that – he was such a perfectionist. That was the downfall of the arrangement. Whilst it was fantastic that we enjoyed extended BBC coverage, the workload proved to be too much for Murray with his F1 commitments and everything else.

"One day he said, 'Alan, I just can't dedicate the time I want to it,' and he wouldn't take shortcuts. It is all or nothing with Murray."

F1 With BBC

Murray did his first television broadcast on a Grand Prix, the very first British GP in 1949, and, several decades later, Grand Prix racing was to make his name known on a truly international basis.

During the 1950s and 1960s, the BBC merely showed occasional short snatches of the more charismatic Formula One races. The BBC's resident commentator for such events was the great Raymond Baxter. The BBC's *Grandstand* programme was wont to make several visits during the race and one has fond memories of Baxter's standard opening remarks, in RAF/BBC voice, 'Twenty three laps gone, forty seven laps to go…'.

When Colin Chapman, of Lotus, and the infamous Louis Stanley, of BRM, introduced sponsorship to Formula One, the BBC found itself in difficulties for the Corporation had strict guidelines which forbade advertising. However, it finally took the view that motor racing was a special case. Everything came to a climax in 1976 when the immensely popular James Hunt won the World Championship.

With the added British interest, the BBC reacted to this catalyst and made the momentous decision to cover the entire GP season from the beginning of 1978. With Baxter now PR Director of BMC and no longer available and Murray's vast experience of commentating, top BBC producer, Jonathan Martin, offered him the job. This was, for Murray, very rich icing on an already sumptuous cake!

The F1 coverage was not to be as we know it today – far from it – but it was a massive step forward for motor racing enthusiasts. For years, they had had the agony of the occasional coverage breaking off to return to the 4.15 at Catterick, or wherever, and watching a lot of four legged creatures parading, seemingly meaninglessly and incessantly, and then cantering round a field! How we hated horse racing!

As explained elsewhere, the first couple of years were a compromise before the coverage became rather more ambitious. For Murray and the very small BBC support team, the conditions under which they laboured were often challenging in the extreme and explained a few of the errors for which Murray gained a certain notoriety.

The theme music – *The Chain* by Fleetwood Mac - was a brilliant choice and became, for many an enthusiast the aural equivalent of, say, Castrol 'R'! When, for the 1980 season onwards, James Hunt was brought in to play the 'expert' role alongside Murray, the die was cast. Although Murray, as he explains, was both wary of Hunt and at odds with his attitude and demeanour, the viewers were blissfully unaware of the off-screen friction, and grew to love the pairing. Gradually, the tensions eased, Hunt avoided the drugs, gave up drinking and learnt to appreciate his hallowed position. Tensions eased and respect, admiration and even fondness became mutual.

Lotus and their number one driver, Mario Andretti, dominated the 1978 season with the revolutionary 'ground effects' Lotus 79. Ronnie Peterson, the loyal number two, dutifully followed Andretti and took two wins of his own before tragically dying after an accident at Monza. Lotus failed to score a single victory the following year and the Championship was fought out by Ferrari team mates, Gilles Villeneuve and Jody Scheckter, the crown going to the latter. The beginning of the new decade saw Williams dominant with Australian Alan Jones taking ultimate glory.

In 1981 Nelson Piquet, in a Brabham, took his first Championship by a point from Carlos Reuteman. A close 1982 season saw Williams, Renault, McLaren, Ferrari, Brabham, Lotus and Tyrrell all take wins and Keke Rosberg the Championship in spite of clocking up only one victory. In '83, Piquet won by two points from Alain Prost. The 1984 season was even closer when Niki Lauda took his third Championship by half a point from Prost, who won the following year in a McLaren. Just three points separated winner Prost, Nigel Mansell and Piquet in 1986. The next season saw Piquet take another title from Mansell and Ayrton Senna. Total domination by McLaren, bar one race, was the story of the 1988 season as Prost and Senna shared the victories and the Brazilian took the Championship. The decade closed with McLaren Honda once again supreme and the drivers' positions being reversed.

As the nineties began, Senna beat his bitter rival who was now in a Ferrari. In 1991 it was Senna from Mansell, for whom it all came right in 1992, the Englishman winning nine of the 16 races in his Williams. Michael Schumacher scored his first win in 1993 and that year Prost beat Senna to the title, but Damon Hill registered three victories.

During 1993 Murray and the motor racing world were rocked by the sudden death of James Hunt at the sadly early age of just 45. The 'odd couple' had entered many people's homes and touched their hearts. His sudden and premature passing was a blow to many and Murray paid a moving tribute to his eccentric partner on television and at James's memorial service.

The '94 season will be remembered for Senna's tragically fatal accident and Schumacher controversially colliding with Hill at the final GP to take his first title by a point. Retired GP pilot, Dr. Jonathan Palmer, had taken over from Hunt in the 'com box'. Schumacher, still with Benetton, dominated the '95 season with Brits, Hill, Coulthard and Herbert taking the next three positions.

During this period Bernie Ecclestone had transformed Formula One, making the circus an exceptionally professional one and gaining incredible television audiences. He dropped a bombshell at the end of 1995, when he told the BBC that ITV had won the contract to broadcast F1 from 1997. As the New Year dawned, Murray started what many thought would be his final year of commentating on the pinnacle of motor sport. If it was to be his last season, it was a good one to go out on. Schumacher had moved to Ferrari, who were then uncompetitive, and Damon Hill took the World Championship, the first time a father and son had achieved this feat. For many, it also marked the end of an era.

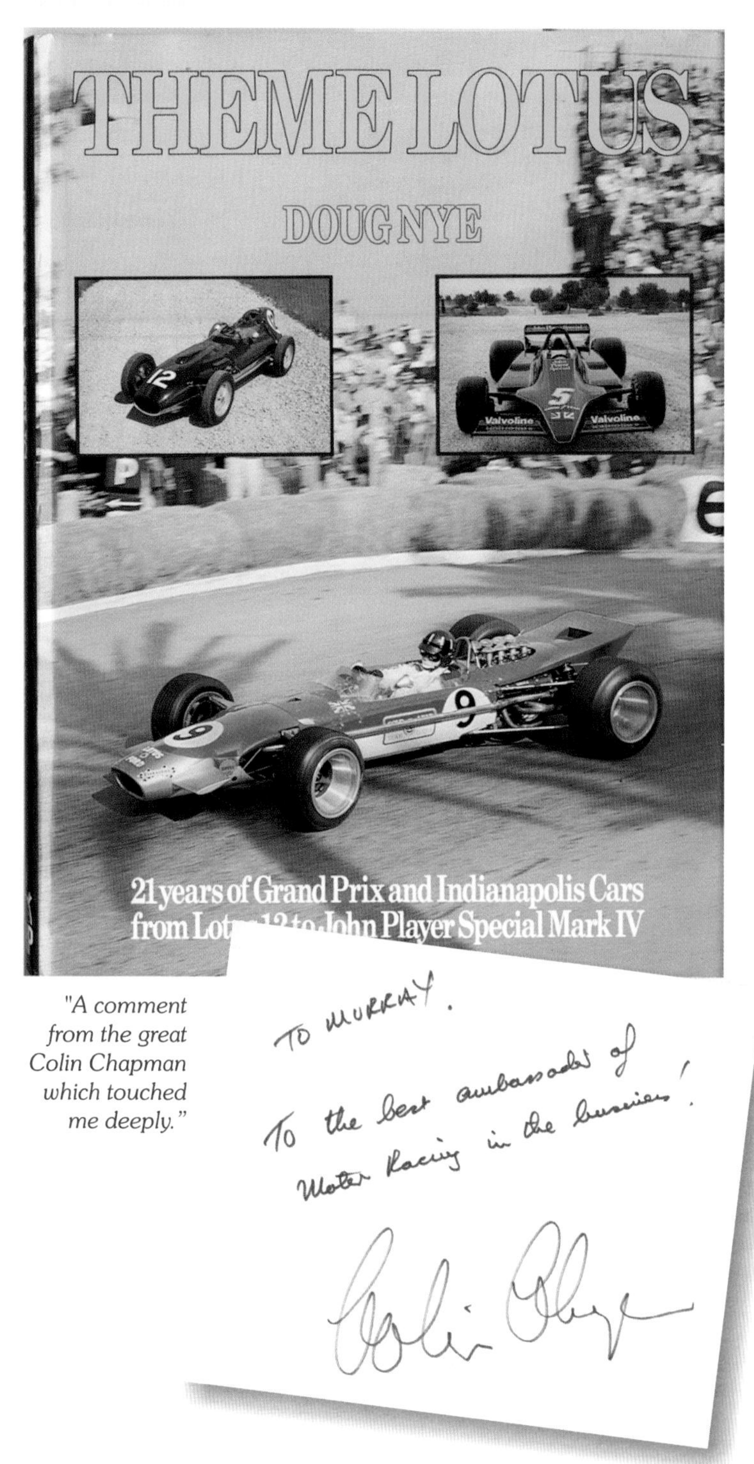

"A comment from the great Colin Chapman which touched me deeply."

MurrayismMurrayismMurrayism

"That's history. I say history because it happened in the past."

That Very First Broadcast

Max Robertson

"I used to talk fast. I was the only person who could do tennis on radio. They gave me these other jobs as well because I was on the staff and that meant they didn't have to pay me a fee. There were a lot of producers who were new to television. They were looking at these screens, not knowing what they wanted, and they needed someone they could trust. And they could trust me to do an accurate commentary. And I wouldn't cost them anything!

"I didn't know anything about motor racing. I hated the sound of the bloody engines but I certainly did the British Grand Prix with Murray Walker. He was very new to it all but he put up a good performance and I think I told him so, or someone else did. I am sure he got a commendation for it.

"The way we worked was that I would commentate on someone up to a certain bend and then he would take over. There are always a few glitches.

"It was a challenge with the crude technology of those days, but great fun."

Pioneering Stuff

Murray Walker

"I was totally overwhelmed when, in 1949, the BBC invited me to be the second commentator on the British Grand Prix. It was, of course, at Silverstone, though a very different Silverstone to the one we are used to now. I was in the commentary box at Stowe Corner and tennis commentator, Max Robertson, who, with the greatest of respect, knew as much about motor racing as I knew about tennis, was in the main commentary box, overlooking the start/finish straight. We batted it backwards and forwards between the two of us. I have a recording and when I listen now, it all sounds terribly stilted and formal, but that's the way it was in those days.

"I remember an incident where John Bolster, who was driving an ERA, came barrelling down the Hangar Straight, towards me, lost control and the car cart-wheeled end over end, over end, over end at horrifying speed, threw Bolster out and deposited him in a bleeding heap at the base of my commentary box. I looked out, absolutely horrified, honestly thinking that he was dead, and I thought to myself, 'They didn't tell me what to say about this,' and I blurted out, 'Bolster's gone off,' which was perfectly true but a masterly understatement!

"Happily Bolster recovered completely and became the BBC's very famous pit lane commentator, known for his outspoken comments, throaty voice and deerstalker hat."

A Promising Start

Max Robertson

PP: "Did you ever expect Murray to go on and do so well?"

"Yes, I think I did. It was quite clear that he knew what he was talking about. He had a passion in those days and this is what I couldn't understand because I hated the bloody things! He really loved it, the noise and everything about it."

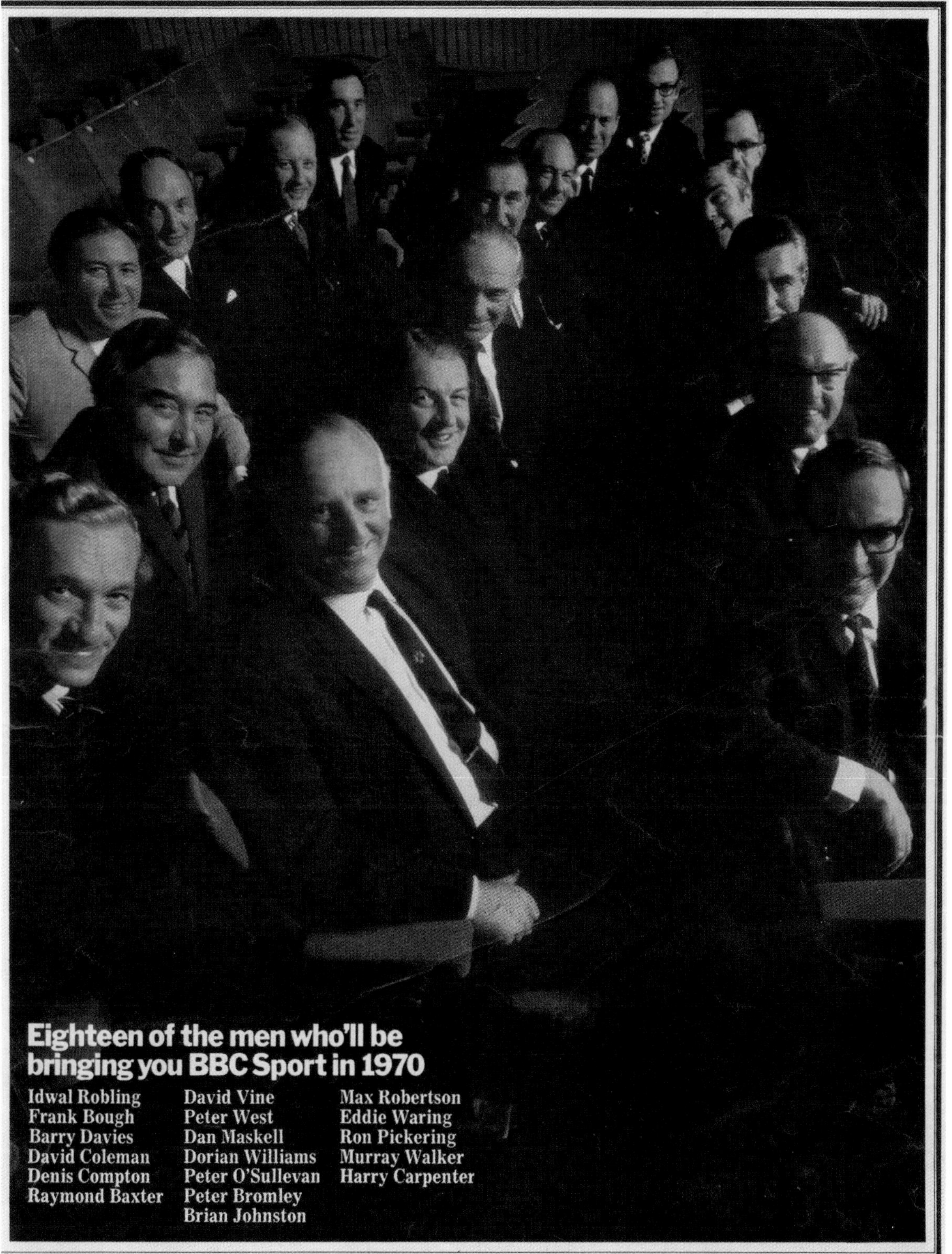

Eighteen of the men who'll be bringing you BBC Sport in 1970
Idwal Robling
Frank Bough
Barry Davies
David Coleman
Denis Compton
Raymond Baxter
David Vine
Peter West
Dan Maskell
Dorian Williams
Peter O'Sullevan
Peter Bromley
Brian Johnston
Max Robertson
Eddie Waring
Ron Pickering
Murray Walker
Harry Carpenter

Modus Operandi

Murray Walker

"After I had done one-offs with, for example, Clay Reggazoni winning in a Ferrari at the Nűrburgring, Jacky Ickx winning in the Brabham also at the Nűrburgring and the 1976 British GP, the BBC decided they were going to do all the Grands Prix on the box. They weren't going to do them live, they were going to record them. I was going to go out to the event on Thursday, watch Friday practice, watch practising and qualifying on Saturday, would then fly back to Britain, watch the race on what was then called Eurovision and they would edit it down from the full length to half an hour, and I would put the commentary on, usually beforehand, but sometimes it had to go out live."

Remarkably Early Memories

Jenson Button

"I remember back in the early Williams days listening to Murray commentate when they were sponsored by Saudia, which is a long time ago – probably two or three years into the Williams team." [This was actually 1978 – two years before Jenson was born. Is this a Buttonism?]

"This superb Alan Fearnley painting depicts two truly great drivers, and gentlemen, rounding Mirabeau Corner in the 1973 Monaco Grand Prix. Sweden's Ronnie Peterson in the Lotus 72 leads Jackie Stewart's Tyrrell. This was to be Stewart's 25th Grand Prix victory, out of 27, with Ronnie in a fighting third place behind team mate Emerson Fittipaldi. Jackie was to retire at the end of the season, following the tragic death of his team mate Francois Cevert. He later achieved even more success, including a knighthood, but, sadly, the modest and self-effacing Ronnie Peterson was to die in hospital following a startline crash at the 1978 Italian Grand Prix at Monza, which was a terrible experience for me and his many thousands of other followers."

Ronnie Peterson

Murray Walker

"A lot of people think Ronnie Peterson was the greatest driver who has ever lived and he was certainly a very good one. In September1978, I was following my usual routine. I went out to Monza for the Italian Grand Prix practice. When the race was held, I was back in London of course, because I had gone back on the Saturday afternoon as usual. So we watched the crash at the beginning of the race.

"That was the crash where James Hunt developed his hatred of Riccardo Patrese, whom he regarded as being responsible for the Ronnie Peterson crash, which he wasn't actually. So we saw this dreadful crash on television and they held the race and I did the commentary. I went home having checked because we phoned through to Monza that in fact Ronnie Peterson was going to be alright. He had broken his leg, been taken to hospital and was going to be okay. So you can imagine how shocked I was the next day when I learnt that he had in fact died because there had been an embolism. He had died of that."

MurrayismMurrayismMurrayism

"If that isn't a lap record, I'll eat the hat I don't normally wear."

A Happy Gift

Murray Walker

PP: "Did you ever, ever dry?"

"No. There is no such thing as a dull F1 race. There are processional F1 races but that doesn't mean they are dull because there is always drama and excitement and something worth drawing attention to if you look hard enough and know enough about it and are interested enough in finding it. I am naturally eloquent in that sort of situation and I was always bubbling with enthusiasm to tell everybody about this wonderful thing that was happening and why it was affecting me so much and why I wanted it to affect them so much. No, I never dried up."

"In 1976, after he had become a double World Champion, for Lotus and McLaren, Emerson Fittipaldi was no longer a leading contender in Formula One, having courageously but inadvisedly decided, with his brother, Wilson, to build their own Formula One car, the Coppersucar in Brazil. Emerson and I chat in the pit lane at Monaco, 1978, in its old location after the Gasworks Hairpin. An amazing 28 years later, we were to chat again in the pit lane as driver and commentator during the 2006 Grand Prix Masters series."

MurrayismMurrayismMurrayism
"...and I interrupt myself to bring you this..."

"1979 was the first year in which the BBC covered all the races and at Monaco to celebrate the occasion was my BBC boss and mentor, Jonathan Martin, to whom I owe so much. Pity about the shirts! Jonathan deservedly went on to become BBC TV's Head of Sport and I was to be happily responsible to him until my switch to ITV in 1997 when the BBC lost the franchise."

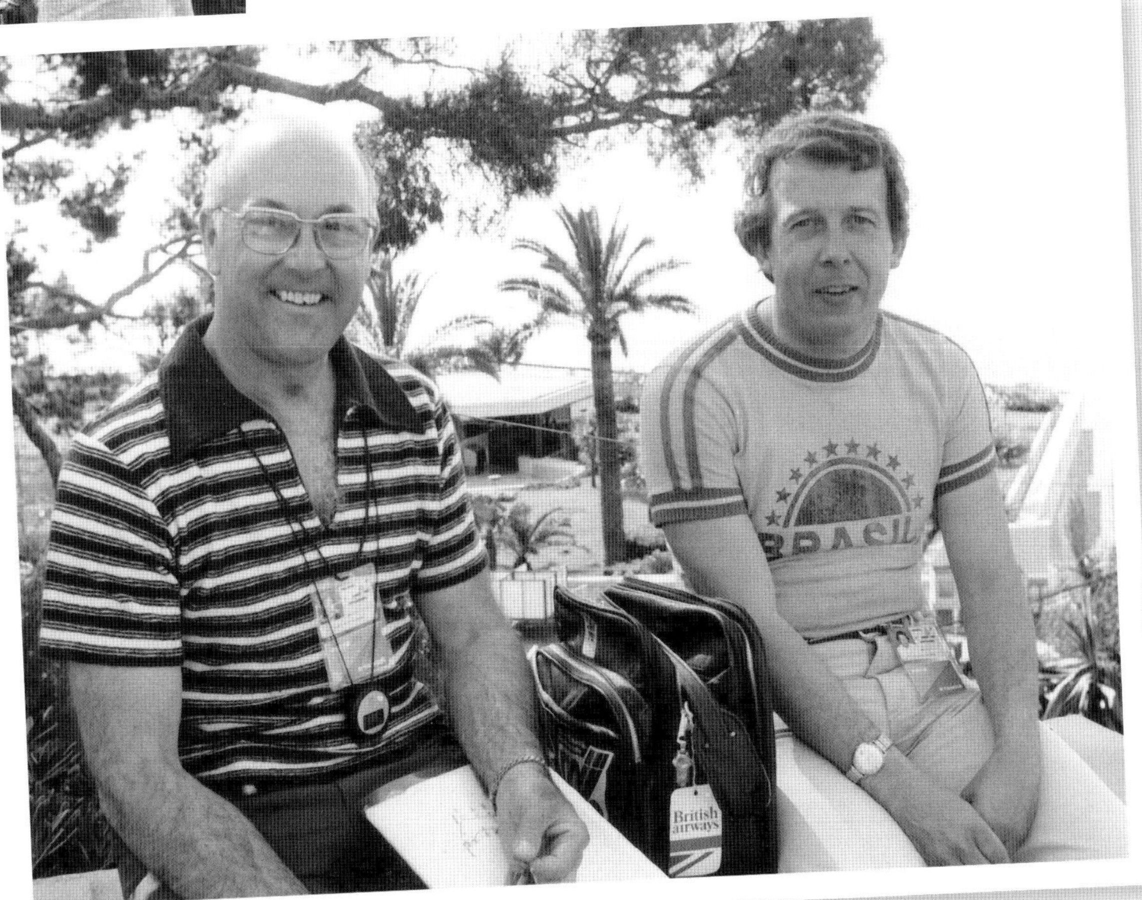

Commentating With Graham Hill

Murray Walker

PP: "Do you have any recollection of what it was like commentating with Graham Hill, which you did on one occasion?"

"I can remember it was at Silverstone. Graham Hill was in the box with me, and Colin Chapman. I think it must have been the British Grand Prix, from which he had presumably retired. He was interjecting with comments. I do remember that, when we finished, he said, 'Blimey, it's not as easy as I thought it was'."

"Some people, like me, have never actually participated at the highest level in the sport they love but Frenchman Jacques Laffite most certainly has. Against a background of 176 Grands Prix and six wins, he now commentates for French television. This is him in a Ligier at Brands Hatch but I commentated on him as recently as 2006 when he drove in the Grand Prix Masters series." (Chris Willows)

The Sunday Post, June 10, 1979. 17

CHIP OFF THE OLD BLOCK

ENTHUSIASTIC, knowledgeable and a bit of a character—that's Murray Walker, whose commentaries on Grand Prix racing are a highlight of BBC sports coverage.

It takes a lot of experience to sort out the positions of a field of hurtling Formula 1 cars, but Murray's been doing it for 30 years.

His father, Graham Walker, was one of Britain's top motor cyclists, and winner of the TT races in 1931.

Murray, born in Birmingham, tried his hand in motor cycle racing for a while, too.

Though he won some races, he always found himself in his father's shadow.

MURRAY WALKER.

"I decided I wasn't going to be very successful at competing, so I thought I'd have a go at talking about it."

Once more he found himself in the same field as his father.

They broadcast side by side from 1949 to 1962, a unique record.

When Raymond Baxter moved over to "Tomorrow's World," Murray stepped into his shoes as the BBC's top motor racing commentator.

Yet commentating is only his hobby.

He's a director of one of Britain's biggest advertising agencies.

Murray, 58, lives with his wife, Elizabeth, in North London—when he's not travelling all round Europe.

Ghastly Prospect

Roger Moody

"I worked for the BBC from 1970 though to 1999 and in 1978, I was asked by the Head of Sport, Jonathan Martin, to be the Assistant Producer on *Grand Prix*. I thought, 'My God, I can't think of anything more boring than watching cars hurtling around at hundreds of miles an hour in formation'. I took that on in 1978 and went up into management in 1988. I worked on virtually all the GPs, first as Assistant Producer and then as Producer.

"Murray was a wonderful man to work with. I don't really recall Murray ever losing his temper or being cross with anybody."

The Passion

Murray Walker

PP: "Raymond Baxter was a consummate professional but he didn't bring any theatre to it."

"Raymond Baxter was a lovely, lovely chap with a wonderful voice, a complete command of the sport, respected and admired by everybody. I am obviously coming to a 'but' and this is it. I always felt, as part of my remit as a TV commentator on motor sport, a need to entertain as well as inform and in my opinion Raymond Baxter informed people in an extremely authoritative way but did not entertain people - there was no passion, no excitement, no drama. That is the way he was, I am not being unpleasant about him.

"It is because I have this passion and excitement about the sport that I got this reputation of producing what people call Murrayisms because I would be talking 15 to the dozen about the picture people were looking at and people didn't know that I didn't have 16 monitors which gave me a total command of the circuit. I had one monitor which would give me the picture that the public were looking at and it was my job to interpret the race, inform them what was happening and entertain them about what was happening by bringing out the drama and excitement. That's why the words sometimes came out in the wrong order, sometimes I made a mis-identification, sometimes I just said the wrong thing. But the difference between sitting at home dispassionately looking at a TV monitor and not having to say anything about what you are looking at, and having to stand there with adrenalin pouring out of you by the bucketful and also having to look at a telemetry monitor and interpret all the figures it is giving you and having to read the race is the difference between night and day, chalk and cheese."

"Just because you have not been World Champion does not mean to say that you are not one of the greatest ever drivers. Stirling Moss never won the World Championship and nor, here, did French-Canadian Gilles Villeneuve. But Gilles won races for Ferrari in cars that were not really good enough and to a commentator, he was manna from heaven." (Chris Willows)

Gunnar Nilsson & George Harrison

Murray Walker

"Almost every weekend George Harrison, the Beatle, used to come and sit with us while we were editing the programme.

"Towards the end of 1978, Gunnar Nilsson, the Swede who drove for Lotus and won the Belgian Grand Prix, came in. The reason Gunnar came in was that he had been diagnosed with cancer. He had had the chemotherapy and he was as bald as an egg, and he was dying, and he knew he was dying. But he still came in and watched the programmes, talked to us and was full of fun and good humour, and actually started the Gunnar Nilsson Cancer Treatment Trust Fund. After the last race of the year, I left the commentary booth and Gunnar and George Harrison were in the editing room outside.

"Gunnar said, 'Goodbye Murray, I won't see you again'. I knew what he meant, but I said, 'Don't be silly, Gunnar. I will see you next season; you must come in again next year, we have enjoyed having you.' I never saw him again." [George Harrison released a single to raise money for the Fund]

"'He's behind you!' FIA President Max Mosley is an extremely contentious personality but Formula One needs a strong man at the top and, in Max, it certainly has one. As a successful single-seater driver, a Formula One car manufacturer (March), a successful barrister and Bernie's friend and confidente, the much-feared, charming and urbane Mosley has led a tremendosuly distinguished life. Unlike many, I have a gigantic admiration and respect for him and for what he has achieved."

"My friends, the stars! Future World Champion, Nigel Mansell, Grand Prix driver and later to be my co-commentator Jonathan Palmer and five-times Grand Prix winner, John Watson, now TV commentator for the A1 series, and a jolly good one too. We were at the BBC Sports Review of the Year."

MurrayismMurrayismMurrayism

I make no apologies for their absence. I'm sorry they're not here.

"1980 was a wonderful year for me, for Williams and for Britain. BBC TV's Formula One coverage was going like gangbusters and outspoken Australian Alan Jones won the World Championship for Williams in spite of the efforts of his brilliant Argentine team mate, Carlos Reuteman (here), to stop him doing so. They were not the best of chums." (Chris Willows)

Well-Intentioned Hospitality

Jonathan Martin

"Quite often we'd have guests in to watch the race live. I think the Petersons lived somewhere in the south of England and Ronnie's wife Barbro came in to watch the Italian GP. When the accident happened, it was a very difficult experience for all of us. We vowed after that that we'd work without guests. It was not a happy experience to say the least because we obviously still had to get on and produce a television programme."

On The Other Line

Jim Reside

"The technology in those days was nothing like as good as it is today and the pictures used to flash and bang from the other side of the world, and the commentary circuit that Murray was talking on, even in European races in France or Italy, frequently used to disappear and Murray had to commentate on the telephone. In those days, commentary circuits were bits of wire like our telephones at home and required somebody in a technical room somewhere in Europe to plug in this big jack plug that connected it to Paris. Then somebody in Paris had to take the other end and plug it in to pass it through to London. So, it just needed one person to pull out the wrong plug somewhere in Europe and you lost Murray!

"This used to happen with annoying frequency and we always had a telephone standby and Murray quite often had to commentate over the phone. If you listen to some of those from the eighties, it sounds as though he is commentating from the moon."

> Murray: "And there are flames coming from the back of Prost's car as he enters the swimming pool."
> James: "Well, that should put them out then."

"More of my friends, the stars! This time, it is the brilliant Formula One journalist, Nigel Roebuck, seated left, Frank Williams and his driver, the ebullient Irishman Derek Daly. This was, of course, before Frank had his terrible accident leaving the Paul Ricard circuit which put him into a wheelchair for the rest of his life and was a special tragedy because he was one of the fittest people I ever knew and a superb athlete. Derek Daly later raced successfully in America where he subsequently, like me, became a TV commentator. Being Irish, he's never short of the appropriate phrase!"

Telling it how it is!

by BBC TV motor racing commentator Murray Walker

MAN-ON-THE-SPOT: Walker (left) keeps viewers throughout the world informed with the help of James Hunt's pertinence, and a lap chart by motoring journalist Mike Doodson. It isn't always easy . . .

The Eyes And Ears

Mike Doodson

"When Murray started commentating for the BBC, he needed a spotter. There were no electronic screens in those days and he needed someone to do a lap chart for him, and that was me. So I sat alongside him through all the great years. I got slightly deafened!

"For quite a long time, the BBC didn't send Murray to very distant places, so I was the eyes and ears of the BBC in those distant places. James Hunt always deeply resented having to go to Shepherd's Bush at 3 o'clock in the morning for the Japanese Grand Prix instead of actually being there."

"My friends the stars, part three! I can't remember the occasion but I can remember the people and what a line-up. Left to right - rally stars Tony Pond, Pentti Airikkala and Jimmy McRae (Colin's dad); ex-touring car racer and rally organiser Nick Brittan; a tieless John Watson, Nigel Mansell, an amazingly youthful-looking Derek Warwick and later winner of the Indy 500, American Danny O'Sullivan."

MurrayismMurrayism

"And now Jacques Laffite is as close to Surer as Surer is to Laffite."

A Murray Spoonerism

Vern Schuppan

"One Murray memory that always come to my mind was when Rene Arnoux was having that great dice at Dijon with Gilles Villeneuve and they were famously banging wheels. Murray got so excited he starting calling Arnoux, 'Arne Renoux'!"

Vicious Attack

Murray Walker

"One of the most outstanding people I met in my F1 career and the last really of the great private owners was Ken Tyrrell. In the early days of my second year of commentating on F1 I went out to Jarama for the Spanish GP. I was spectating and looking up a hill to a hairpin bend. As Didier Pironi, who was one of Ken's drivers, came round the hairpin and started going down the hill, his front wheel came off and came bounding down the circuit, straight at me. A front wheel and tyre, and everything that goes with it, weighs a lot, and it was carrying an enormous momentum. I watched this wheel very carefully and moved aside. It just clipped me on the shoulder as it went past.

"So, I thought it was pretty fantastic that I had been hit by Didier Pironi's wheel. I strolled off into the pit lane. I said, 'Hey Ken, do you know what just happened?' I told him. 'Oh,' said Ken, 'Didn't hit you hard enough did it?' He *was* joking!"

"Every so often, I got to sit in a Formula One car to do a piece to camera. Here I am smirking happily out of the cockpit of Nelson Piquet's World Championship-winning Brabham BMW in spite of the fact that I thought I had just lost my gold Rolex watch."

Hunt The Hedonist

Mike Doodson

"He [James Hunt] still had a close relationship with the Marlboro people, some of whom shared his hard-partying enthusiasm, and he stayed in the same hotels as them. They were known as 'FOFA' (Formula One Fun Association). If only half of what we heard about their activities was true, then they must have been living life very hard. James was so decadent that his capacity to shock wore off quite quickly."

"I always stood up to do my commentaries. James Hunt, alongside me, always sat down. A source of non-stop friction."

"My friends, the stars - part four. See if you can identify them all. There are five World Champions and eight Grand Prix winners, including Juan Manuel Fangio, Stirling Moss, Jack Brabham and John Surtees."

Murray's Idiosyncrasies

Jackie Stewart

"Of course he stands up all the time. That hasn't changed in all the years that have passed. He is still a very fit man, a remarkably fit man for his age.

"The energy that he produces on the mic is quite extraordinary. He is never standing flat footed, he is always on the edge of everything. I always went in and sat down in the normal way, as one does. In my time with ABC's *Wide World of Sport*, all the commentators sat.

"Then of course he also liked to use a lip mic. which is the old-fashioned, very heavy cabled mic with a sort of metal frame around it which almost fitted on to your lip, your top lip. With the modern medical problems that go round the world, that was something that everybody looked at rather suspiciously! But that was his first love, and of course he always had a strong delivery, and with a mic glued to your upper lip you never turned your head away from the mic so you never lost the momentum of an explanation or a move.

"His abilities were many, and so were his errors! (much laughter) But never to a point where anybody would ever be either insulted and angry. It was 'doing a Murray' in quotes. It was always quite amusing to be the other part of the commentary team!"

Working With One Mic

Murray Walker

"The BBC were always worried that if you gave two egotistical commentators a microphone each they would be talking over each other. The only way to stop this was to give them one microphone and let them fight over it, which is what James and I did. I always used to stand up to do my commentaries, because I was very excited. It is a lot easier to commentate standing up rather than sitting, because when you sit down your shoulders go forward, and your chest is deflated. When you stand up your shoulders go back, and your chest is inflated and you can project your voice better. Psychologically you feel much freer. The dilemma for my co-commentator was what does he do. James always used to sit in a sort of scrunched up heap, languidly waving his hand if he wanted the microphone."

Spoiling The Effect

Tony Jardine

"I worked with him when I used to do the guide commentaries for the BBC. He has these amazing, meticulous notes. He does all his homework where he has drivers' best results, their worst results, all the histories of the drivers and he tapes them all over the walls of the commentary box.

"When I was doing the guide commentaries from Canada, or the States or South Africa, he would be in the studio in London. So, I would do the build-up and give him all the information live during the race to feed back to the studio and he and James would always pretend to be in Canada or wherever. James Hunt hated it and every time Murray would say, 'Here we are in Canada…', literally 10 minutes later James would go, 'From the window of my BBC commentary hut here at White City…' He would always give the game away and Murray would be crestfallen by this. James would do it to him every time, every time!"

"In 1985, we started to become truly aware of what a sensational driver Ayrton Senna was. In his previous debut year, he had worked wonders in the tardy Toleman, nearly winning the Monaco Grand Prix, but now, driving for Lotus in a superior car, he won his first two Grands Prix against the likes of Alain Prost, Nigel Mansell and Nelson Piquet." (Chris Willows)

MurrayismMurrayismMurrayism

"I should imagine that the conditions in the cockpit are unimaginable!"

"I'M SORRY TO SAY THAT WE WILL NOT AFTER ALL, BE ABLE TO BRING YOU THE INTERVIEW WITH CATCHPOLE, DUE TO A RATHER UNFORTUNATE ACCIDENT."
BBC
FOLEY.

Dear Murray

I understand from Simon Taylor that I may have upset you a little with my 'Catchpole' cartoon in Autosport last week. I hold your commentaries in high esteem and would certainly not wish to offend you – my cartoon was not meant to be anything other than an affectionate dig, so I do hope you are able to take it in the spirit it was meant.

The real irony (considering the joke I was having at your expense) was that the cartoon was printed by mistake – I had done another that was supposed to replace it.

I enclose a small cartoon by way of an apology.

Regards. Barry Foley.

"I knew better than to take offence at some of the well-meant barbs that were fired at me but was deeply hurt by one Barry Foley carricature for Autosport about which I moaned to the publishers. For Barry's amusing response, see left."

Fooling The Public…

Jim Reside

"The early Grand Prix races (when the BBC first covered them) were run on a tight budget. We used to only commentate on the European races from the track. The races in Canada, Japan and Australia were all done by Murray in a broom cupboard in the Television Centre.

"Murray used to famously says things like, 'I can't actually see the final corner from my commentary position…' We used to raise our eyebrows and worry that someone would find out that the reason for that was that he was in a broom cupboard in Shepherd's Bush! So, though we didn't actually say we were there, we hinted we were there."

An Uneasy Partnership

John Watson

"When I do my broadcasting, I still approach it the same way I would have done if I was a racing driver. I still realise I have an opportunity, which is not dangerous, but there are dangers, and the dangers come from doing a poor job or being unprepared, or being casual or dismissive about it.

"When James Hunt joined the commentary team, I know that Murray was very concerned and thought this was the slippery slope. For the BBC anybody over 40 was old and Murray was considerably over 40. But I think Murray realised very quickly, and I'm sure the BBC did as well, that James did not have the same appreciation of having the opportunity to broadcast around the world on Grands Prix.

"James had a totally contradictory attitude, as well as approach, to the job. I know that irked Murray considerably because he didn't respect that kind of attitude to the job that he was doing. There were occasions when James turned up at the commentary booth and he wasn't as coherent as he ought to have been."

"I've shown similar shots of two very different cars here to demonstrate that one team's wind tunnel results in a given year will be much the same as another's. At the top, Alain Prost's Driver's Championship-winning McLaren TAG with below Keke Rosberg's race-winning Williams Honda, but Alain achieved nearly double Rosberg's points. Look at Keke's glowing carbon fibre brake discs." (Chris Willows)

MurrayismMurrayismMurrayism

"There is nothing wrong with the car except that it is on fire."

Stirring Jenson's Blood

John Button

"Jenson was born in 1980 so he grew up with Murray as a Formula One commentator. Jenson started watching the Grands Prix when he was really tiny. He would be handed to me when I was watching! So he grew up with it and it's in his blood."

Start As You Mean To Go On

Mike Doodson

"James regularly pushed the producer to the limit, though. I have dined out several times off the following exchange at Monaco in 1983, the year that Keke Rosberg's Williams-Cosworth beat all the turbos because he gambled on slicks on a damp track (the turbos with their huge power would have gone off the road) and didn't have to change tyres when the track dried.

"The Scene: James arrives at commentary point, moments before transmission starts, scattering other commentary teams aside as he staggers past, clearly the worse for wear.

"Me (nervously): 'I saw you crossing the grid to get here, James. Did you notice who was on slicks and wets?'

"JH: 'No, I've been having lunch.'

"Me: 'So, not too much to drink, obviously...'

"JH: 'Doods, I've never reported this race sober, and I have no intention of starting to do so now.'"

Livewire Walker busier than a Beirut bricklayer

By MIKE KABLE

IF Murray Walker is not grand prix racing's foremost ambassador, then he is assuredly its most fervent supporter.

This affable Englishman is to world motor sport what the incomparable Alan McGilvray has been to cricket – its No.1 disciple, whose voice is very familiar with the millions of fans who watch the regular telecasts of the Formula One world championship series.

Walker, an extremely fit 62, is the doyen of motor racing commentators, whose part-time career behind a microphone spans the entire 419 races that have been run since the championship started in 1950.

It began in fact, before then – in 1949, when he broadcast the British Grand Prix at Silverstone and was momentarily startled when a driver later to become a fellow radio commentator, John Bolster, was involved in an enormous accident which deposited him a crumpled heap at the foot of the commentary box.

And he saw grand prix racing before World War Two, in the golden days of the 1930s, when legends like Tazio Nuvolari, Rudi Carraciola, Dick Seaman, Hermann Lang, Berndt Rosemeyer and Achille Varzi were battling for supremacy in their mighty Alfa Romeos, Mercedes-Benz and Auto-Unions.

The doyen of motor racing commentators, Murray Walker . . . thinks Adelaide Grand Prix will be 'marvellous'. Picture by BOB FINLAYSON

Walker arrived in Sydney this week, en route to Adelaide for the inaugural world championship Mitsubishi-sponsored Australian Grand Prix next Sunday, to take his customary role for the BBC in front of a television monitor and relay to the world at large what is happening in the SA capital's tree-lined streets.

He is busier than the proverbial bricklayer in Beirut, because grand prix racing is just one facet of the motor sport scene he covers, which ranges from humble club meetings at Britain's lesser-known circuits to motorcycle racing, motorkhanas and car rallies.

But he took time off in Sydney to meet motoring writers at a function hosted by Alfa Romeo and captivate them with his infectious enthusiasm in an entertaining after-dinner discourse.

Then, over three days, culminating in a final appearance tonight, he has taken further time to visit the Sydney International Motor Show to meet a cross-section of his Australian audience, who have besieged him with curly questions about the latest state-of-the-art and comings-and-goings in Formula One.

Murray Walker, as any grand prix expert knows, makes his fair share of gaffes on the screen, for reasons he is only too happy to elaborate.

They include being forced to commentate, on occasions, before a mini-sized black and white monitor, while viewers are sitting back in the luxury of their lounge rooms, watching the action on large colour TV sets.

At last year's Monaco Grand Prix for example, he did not even have a monitor. It was extinguished by torrential rain, and he was forced to compromise by listening over his headphones to information from the BBC's nerve centre in London, then relaying it as best he could, out of synchronisation with the picture.

Motor racing journalist Mike Doodson compiles the lap charts which are Walker's main reference material. Doodson says he is a Walker fan.

"To be honest, it is no discourtesy to Murray to suggest he should count to three before making a positive identification of a crashed or blown-up car.

"But his enthusiasm is so great, his excitement is so intense, that he has difficulty restraining himself."

Off the screen, Murray Walker is exactly what you would expect him to be – a walking, talking encyclopaedia of motor sport, especially grand prix racing.

"Did you know," he told us cheerfully, "that Australian drivers have won a total of 26 grand prix races?

"This corresponds to 6.2 per cent of the 419 championship races that have been run.

"And 11.4 per cent of world champions have been Australians."

I was not aware of the percentages, nor the astonishing fact that the worldwide Formula One multi-lingual telecasts are relayed to 47 countries with a potential audience of 10,500 million people.

"No other sport combines so many factors – speed, colour, noise, international spectacle, mind-boggling finances, intrigue and politics.

"Nor the sheer technology, not to forget the discipline, organisation and co-ordination of moving more than 40 cars and hundreds of tonnes of equipment from country to country, 16 times a year, between April and November.

"Formula One is a mammoth undertaking."

Walker has nothing but praise for the man who has masterminded the modern concept of world championship racing; Bernie Ecclestone, boss of the Brabham-BMW team and president of the Formula One Constructors' Association (FOCA), which puts on the show.

"Bernie is pedantic on the one hand, but on the other he has tremendous organisational skills.

"He has bullied and cajoled the world championship from being an amateur six-race European series to one which spans the five continents.

"There are 23 countries vieing now for the 16 GPs next year – and we'll be seeing the first ever championship grand prix run in a communist country, in Hungary, round the streets of Budapest."

Walker inherited his love of commentating from his father, Graham Walker, a champion motorcyclist who became internationally known for his BBC broadcasts of the annual Isle of Man Tourist Trophy week classic.

They worked together from 1949 to 1962, the year his father died.

Murray continued the family tradition, despite having carved out a successful career in advertising and buying a substantial share in the agency for whom he worked, Masius and Ferguson, now an international organisation with branches in 27 countries, including Australia.

He cites the best grand prix race he has seen (one I was also lucky enough to attend) as the 1981 Spanish GP won by the late Gilles Villeneuve after a race-long, seven-car battle at the Jarama circuit near Madrid.

His favourite drivers in terms of co-operation (contrary to the expectations of long-time viewers who assume he is the founder of Nigel

Continued on Page 71

A Drop (Or Two) Too Much

Roger Moody

"At the French GP at Dijon – the commentary facilities were quite appalling. We had scaffolding and planks of wood to sit on, and another plank in front of us on which we had our TV monitors. I think it was raffia over the top of us. That would have been alright if it had been a blazing hot summer's day but, halfway through the meeting, the heavens opened and the raffia wasn't able to cope with the downpour. Everything blacked out.

"So Murray said, 'I've lost my pictures but I'm sure you're still getting them at home so I shall continue to commentate'. But, of course, he had nothing to see apart from the odd car coming round every 90 seconds. I was seconded to go off and find the engineer. No names, no pack drill but this particular engineer enjoyed a drop of red wine. When I got to the OB [Outside Broadcast] trucks, he was blissfully unaware that we had lost our pictures and he was lying, semi-comatose with a bottle of wine in his hand. Fortunately, the pictures came back so we survived that one!"

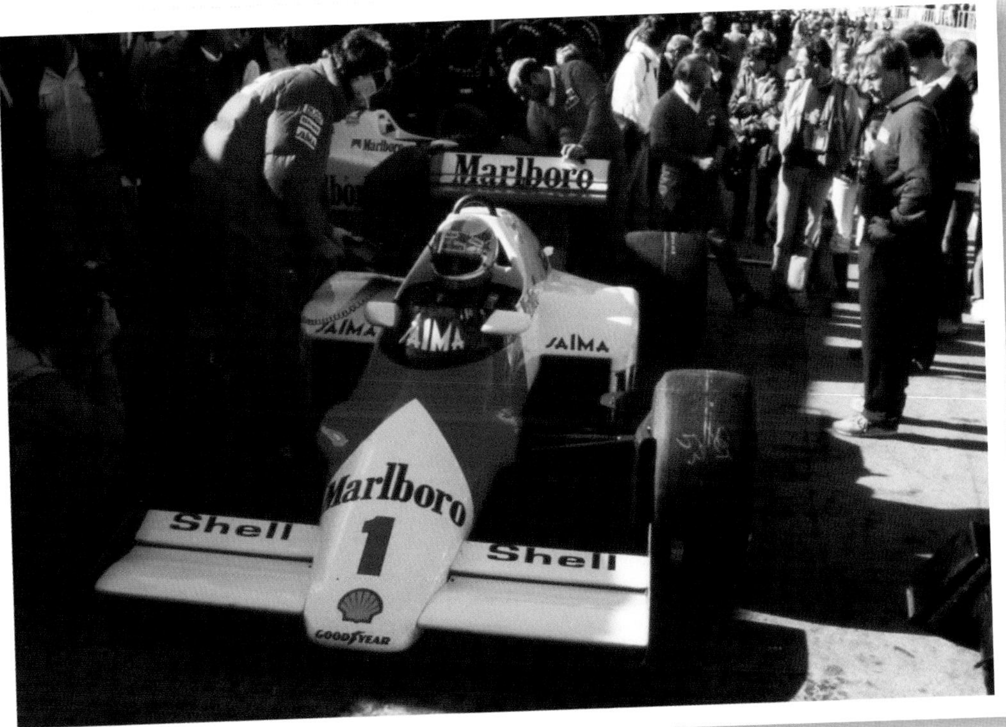

"Good old Wattie. It was a delight to be able to talk about such a successful British driver and two of John's five Grand Prix wins for McLaren were well-nigh unbelievable - the 1982 American Grand Prix at Detroit and the following year at Long Beach - because on both occasions, he started from the back of the grid. And I'll never forget his emotional victory at Silverstone in 1981 where, from the commentary box, like the rest of the crowd, I was willing him to win."

PP: *"And so was I, in that crowd!"*
(Chris Willows)

Down And Outs

Jonathan Martin

"Murray and James used to sit on the pavement in Monaco with the sun beaming down on them. You had a much better view at home that they did on the monitor."

"My friends, the stars - part five. I know I am not in this picture but Beatle George Harrison on the left used to come into the studio in London when we were putting together the early Grand Prix programmes. Gordon Murray in the centre is, I humbly submit, the most ingenious Grand Prix designer of all time. And singer Leo Sayer is a true Grand Prix fan with whom I have shared many happy hours." (Chris Willows)

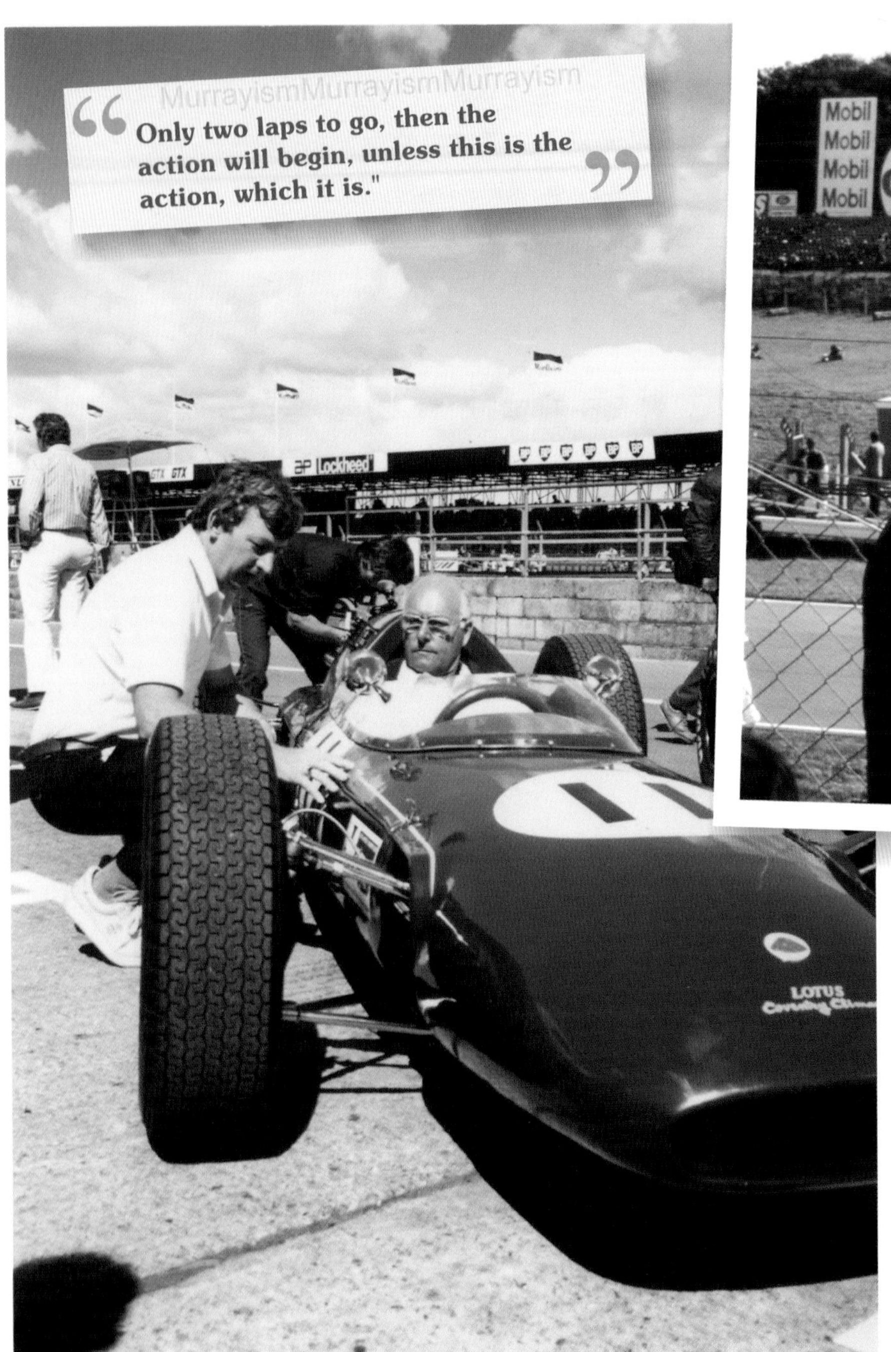

MurrayismMurrayismMurrayism
"Only two laps to go, then the action will begin, unless this is the action, which it is."
Lockheed
LOTUS

"I've been lucky enough to sit in some truly great Grand Prix cars but none greater than Jim Clark's Lotus 25 - to the left, BBC producer Roger Moody gives me another earful."

Deflating Murray

Mike Doodson

"Even when stoned out of his mind, James managed to be pretty sharp.

"One year at Detroit, Nelson Piquet's Brabham slowed dramatically while leading the race, which sent Murray into a long dissertation about a gearbox problem which Piquet had been having in practice.

"'Poor Piquet, it's terrible for him. It must be more gearbox trouble,' screamed Murray.

"Having wrestled away the microphone, Hunt intoned, 'If you look at his left rear tyre, Murray, you'll see that it's going flat.'"

That Rascal Hunt

Jackie Stewart

"I think Murray's best 'errors' were always the ones he did with James Hunt, because James never, ever let him off the hook. James would draw the public's attention to the error. Mum and dad, even the hardcore enthusiasts, as well as uncle and auntie, had never even noticed that there was anything wrong in the first place!"

"In 1983, I cheered Nelson Piquet home to victory at Kyalami in South Africa when he defeated Alain Prost's Renault to win his second World Championship in the Brabham BMW turbo. Things didn't so well for him in 1985. Eighth in the Championship with only one win. Nelson loved life, loved the women, was sometimes embarrassingly outspoken and was an irespressible practical joker, much loved by his team. After Formula One, he became a very wealthy man, in his native Brazil, thanks to his commercial acumen and his son Nelsinho is proving to be a very handy pilot too." (Chis Willows)

MurrayismMurrayismMurrayism

"Just under 10 seconds for Mansell. Call it 9.5 seconds in round figures."

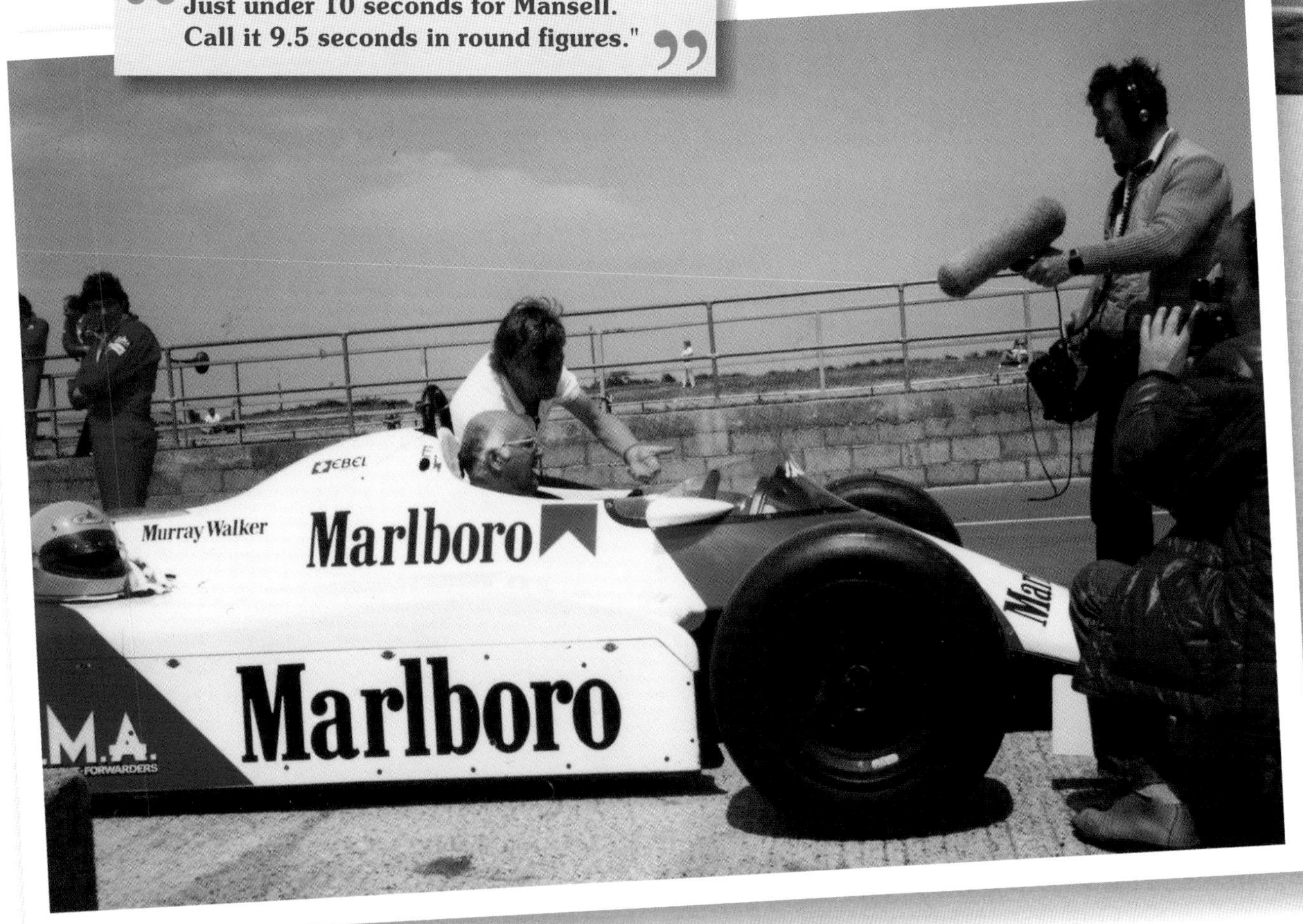

The Drive Of My Life

Murray Walker

"In 1983 I was at a function and Ron Dennis, the McLaren boss, said to me. 'Have you ever driven a Formula One car, Murray?' 'No,' I replied, 'I haven't, Ron. Not many people get to do that.' He said, 'Do you want to drive one?' I said, 'Yes, I would love to'. He said, 'I will be in touch'. So I thought, 'Oh yeah, I bet you will. I have heard that before.'

"But Ron isn't like that. He is a man of his word. He phoned me the next week and he said, 'Get to Silverstone on Thursday and you will have a drive'. So I jumped on my BMW motor cycle and when I arrived I was given a spare set of Niki Lauda's overalls. James was there to help with advice and a BBC crew to film it all. It was a Goodyear tyre testing day with Lauda and Watson driving their McLarens and all the teams were there. I was due to go out in the lunch hour, which I did and loved every second of it.

"I was driving John Watson's MP4 and judging by the revs I saw, he told me I was doing 150mph down Hangar Straight!"

"My tutor, James Hunt, explains that the two things I must not do is stall the engine on leaving the pit lane or stop at the wrong garage. Shortly after this piocture was taken, I ran over the sound engineer's foot. You can't win 'em all."

Murray's Missed Vocation

John Watson

"McLaren invited Murray to drive one of our cars and Murray had the fulfilment of a lifetime's dream to get in to a current F1 car and drive it. And he drove it extremely well. Believe me, even though the cars are nothing like they are today, to go stone cold into a F1 car was very, very impressive indeed.

"He was given an opportunity that not many broadcasters have ever had.

"I know what it's like to get into a single-seater race car, the expectations, the tensions and the nervousness that goes with it, and that's as a racing driver. I've had a background of being a racing driver so all you are doing is rekindling and reawakening your senses but Murray never had that. You don't just get into a competitive F1 car at a high speed circuit like Silverstone. I think he acquitted himself very, very well indeed."

Background To The Challenge

Roger Moody

"I went all over the world with him and sat in commentary boxes which were, by and large, pretty ropey. When anyone criticised Murray for not being able to recognise a car hurtling around at 180mph, it was only because Murray actually had worse positions than the average viewer at home. The commentary boxes in those days sometimes had black and white monitors, and you had to distinguish between a red and white McLaren and a red and white Alfa Romeo. You had four cars that looked very similar and on a black and white monitor were almost impossible to distinguish. Murray did all this, most times, to perfection – standing up, dancing around like a maniac, mostly getting it right.

"I bet that no-one could have done it as well as Murray did in the circumstances."

MR GOLDEN VOICE COMING

Murray Walker . . . energetic and friendly man

James Hunt . . . former world champion

The king of grand prix commentators, the BBC's Murray Walker, is headed Down Under for the first Australian Formula One Grand Prix in Adelaide.

The man whose voice lights up all the thrills and spills of Formula One races for Network Nine viewers on Sunday nights, is an energetic and friendly man of 62.

Walker and former world champion, James Hunt, form the English odd couple commentary team.

They will come to Australia late this month to cover the Australian Mitsubishi Grand Prix, which will be run on a spectacular street circuit through the City of Adelaide on Sunday, November 3.

But this time Murray's enthusiastic commentary and James' cool analysis of the race will be supported by a massive Nine Network coverage of the event.

Murray became a BBC commentator 36 years ago, after he realised that he would never become a top-class racer.

His family is steeped in motor sport. He said recently: "I really started in motor racing when I was born, because my father was a professional motorcycle racer at world championship level.

Murray toured Europe going to the big motor cycle races with his parents. Then, when he left school, he went straight into a tank regiment. He began motorcycle racing himself after he was demobbed.

But he also followed his father's career in other ways by going into broadcasting.

"When my father retired (from motor racing), he became the editor of a motorcycle magazine and he did a lot of sports commentary on motorcycle racing for the BBC. I just followed on.

"I very rapidly came to the conclusion that I was either going to race motor cycles or talk about it, which I enjoyed, and

Walker, Hunt an odd pair

hopefully make a bit of money.

"The first event I ever covered was a radio commentary of the British Grand Prix, but I also did my first TV commentary in 1949."

At the start commentary was only a hobby. Murray's normal working week was spent trying to guide the fortunes of Britain's largest advertising agency.

Three years ago he retired from that rat-race to cover the Grand Prix circuit and other motor racing—bikes, Formula Two, rallycross and go-karts—full-time.

So far he has covered about 200 GPs around the world.

Murray and James visit all of the GP races, except for those in Brazil, the U.S. and Canada. They cover these from a TV monitor located in the heart of the BBC in London.

Apart from Britain and Australia, their race coverages are seen in Eire, Canada, parts of the U.S. on Belgian and Dutch cable television, NZ and South Africa.

While Murray concentrates on calling the progress of the race, James, in his dry, English public-school voice, interposes every so often with analysis of the race from a driver's viewpoint. He also discusses driver strategies and team tactics.

He's been working with Murray since he retired from motor racing in 1979, after winning one world championship and 10 GPs.

Keep eye on scoreboards

Grand prix spectators will rely on four electronic lap scoreboards to keep abreast of both practice and race runs.

The boards have been manufactured in SA by Werner Electronics Industries.

They consist of displays with three identical faces forming a triangle, mounted on top of specially prepared towers.

The largest tower, 20 metres high, is located on the Fullarton Rd side of the Victoria Park racecourse, visible from the main grandstand area.

The other three are all mounted on overpasses on the pit straight, Dequetteville Tce and Rundle Rd.

The digits are clearly visible in sunlight from 200 metres.

All the display panels are controlled in unison by an in-built custom-made micro-processor and connected to a central control computer via Telecom lines.

There are two modes of operation for the lap board display system, RACE or PRACTICE.

During the race, the lap boards will display the lap number at the top and then the place-cars in order through car ment of the fastest six numbers.

During the practice and qualifying runs, the boards will display the previous fastest and second fastest cars, with the fastest car's lap time and the current challenger with his lap time.

Dining-out 'in' thing

Dining out will definitely be the in thing during grand prix week.

Celebrations, reunions, business meals and time to simply get out and enjoy the "electric" atmosphere will be the order of the period.

The Olde London Tavern, in the heart of the city in Stephen's Place, will no doubt be popular.

The variety of entertainment and dining facilities at the complex will ensure the Olde London becomes a new friend for many people.

Food is available continuously from 11 am to 9 pm in Her Majesty's Restaurant, where more than 70 dishes can be ordered.

Loud And Clear

Martin Brundle

"I had a bit of a relationship with him [from F3], and then I got into F1. Ken Tyrrell signed me up after the Rio tests in early '84 but kept it a secret – classic Ken Tyrrell. I drove to the Mayfair Hotel for the announcement. The press were there. Many of them are still around - Murray and Maurice Hamilton, Nigel Roebuck, Alan Henry and the other usual suspects.

"Tyrrell created a bit of drama with trumpets or something – 'And the new driver for 1984 is…'. I remember walking into the room to great cheers and applause, unquestionably the loudest of which was Murray. He had been very supportive throughout '83, the Senna year, and with *Racing for Britain* when we were getting funding together. I can remember hearing his voice above everybody else's. So that was nice."

"My friends, the stars - part six! On the left, Stirling Moss's sponsor, the great Rob Walker of Johnnie Walker whisky fame, whom I persuaded to write his engrossing autobiography. On the right, Sir 'Black Jack' Brabham, Australia's finest, who I really am honoured to call a friend." (Chris Willows)

THE NEWS
JUBILEE
Murray Walker's
International grand prix commentator
GRAND PRIX
REPORT
Souvenir Poster
No.1

"I'd love to say that this is my friends, the stars - part seven, but I can't because I was fawningly in awe of Enzo Ferrari's son Piero at a visit to the Ferrari factory in Maranello. But certainly not in awe of my mates, top journalists bearded Maurice Hamilton and Bob Constanduros."

MurrayismMurrayismMurrayism

Do my eyes deceive me, or is Senna's Lotus sounding rough?"

Name Swapping

John Watson

"At the European GP at Brands Hatch in 1983, I'd completed 150 Grands Prix and a small trophy was given to me as an acknowledgement. It was done in front of television and Murray did the presentation, and I think this went out on the PA as well. Murray is so professional in his preparation that it seems totally seamless but he had one of those moments when a subliminal thought got in the way.

"He did his lead-in and called me 'John McLaren'. I said to him, 'McLaren's the car, I'm John Watson!'

"It was a light-hearted moment in a very poignant part of my career. Murray immediately said, 'Oh my God…' and everyone laughed.

"Part of Murray's charm as a broadcaster was his Murrayisms. And Murrayisms come in many forms and fashions. To me, the thing that stands out as a broadcaster, aside from all his other qualities as a human being, is that he always brought sincere and genuine enthusiasm and honesty to his broadcasting. The Murrayisms were part of his endearment to his audience and that is missed. There was an element in the audience who enjoyed the odd slip-up."

Abnormal Service

Mike Doodson

"Emotions were not calmed by some of the little stunts pulled by the gremlins in the local equipment. I remember only too well an Imola race where our TV monitor produced nothing but flashes of lightning for five minutes. And what about the memorable Monaco GP in the rain in 1984 when our monitor got soaked and Murray had to talk, *live* as the London producer, who was getting perfect pictures, described the race to him down a crackly telephone line?

"For technical and other reasons, at the North and South American races it was necessary for the commentators to do their job from a London studio, operating with the help of a 'guide' commentator in Rio, Detroit or wherever. This deprived Murray and James of the opportunity to absorb local colour, such as the celebrated fights which have broken out in the TV stand between rival commentators. Perhaps the most famous of these was a bruising France v Sweden affair at Monaco which ended with a technical KO in the third minute. And Murray was sitting between them, stoically ignoring the fisticuffs!"

"Okay Nige, let's see who can do the cheesiest grin, as you receive the prestigious BBC TV Sports Personality of the Year *trophy, 1986. Well done, Nige, you deserved it."*

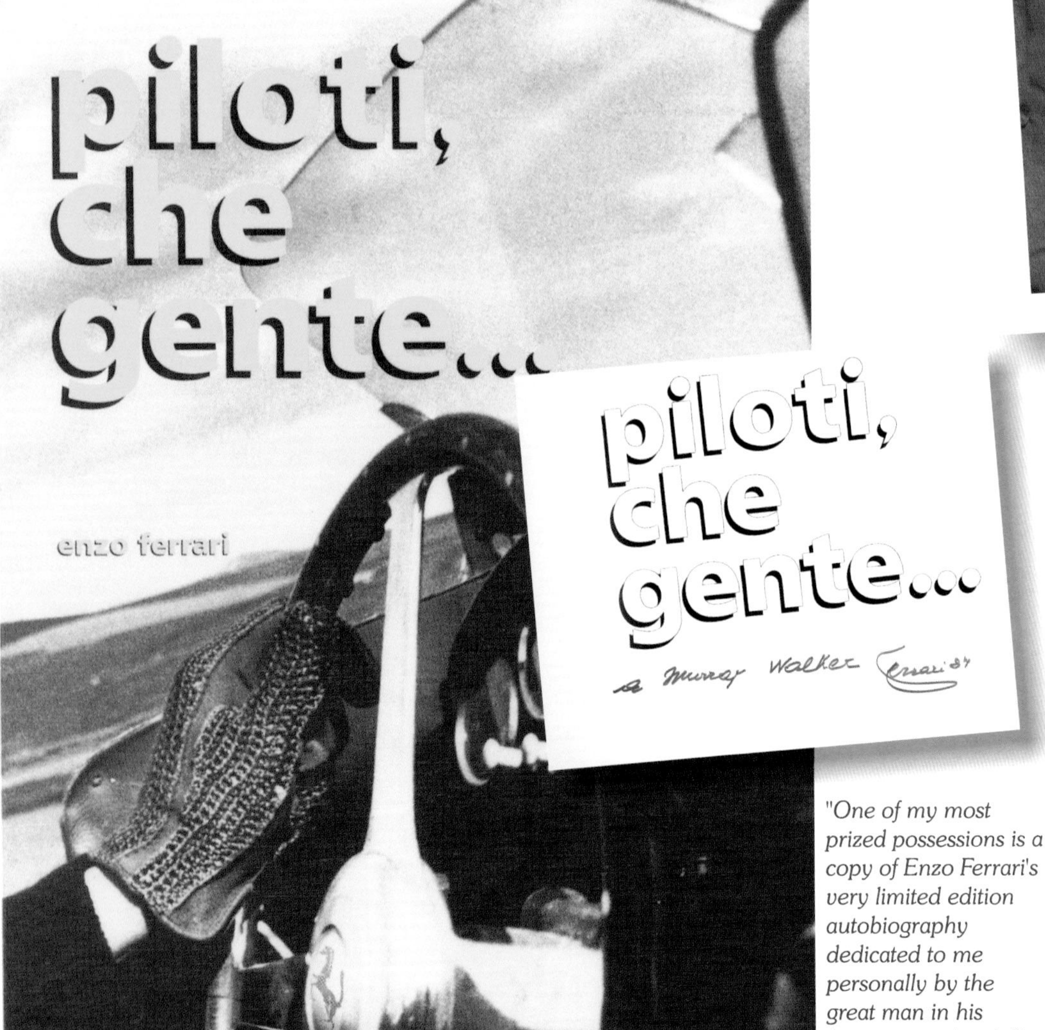

"One of my most prized possessions is a copy of Enzo Ferrari's very limited edition autobiography dedicated to me personally by the great man in his famous purple ink."

Autograph Hunting

Murray Walker

"In 1984, I was staying at the hotel at the Austrian Grand Prix, where the Ferrari team were staying. I had just got a book on Ferrari written by Alan Henry. I thought it would be nice if I could get the Ferrari people to sign it for me. So at dinner one night, I went round the tables. I got Michele Alboreto to sign it for me but wanted Mauro Forghieri, the very famous and talented Ferrari designer. I was just walking across to the table to ask when he reached across to this very pretty girl he was with, took her hand, kissed it and looked deeply into her eyes. I said to myself, 'Murray, I don't think that Mauro Forghieri is going to welcome you now'.

"So I walked across to the next table, and having dinner there, were Senna and Alex Hawkridge, the boss of the Toleman F1 team, who Senna was driving for. They were actually having a row about Senna not having told Hawkridge that he was going to be driving for Lotus the following year and breaking his contract. I sort of barged in, which broke the ice a bit. 'Oh', said Alex, 'you want to get the Old Man to sign it'. I said, 'What Mr. Ferrari himself? I can't do that, I don't know him and don't know how to get to him.'

"Alex took it over to Marco Piccinini, who was the Ferrari team manager, but he said there was no point giving it to him. 'Mr Ferrari won't sign anything that his employees have already signed, but Marco said he would try and help.'

"At the next race, Peter Gethin, who was the Toleman Team Manager, says, 'I've got something for you in the motorhome, Murray'. The something was a copy of Ferrari's limited edition autobiography, called *pilote, che gente...*, which means 'drivers, what heroes', I think. Fabulous book, and written inside it, in purple ink, which was Ferrari's trademark, is 'to Murray Walker, Enzo Ferrari', and it is dated."

Murray's Coup

Roger Moody

"We were in Portugal in 1984, when Lauda and Prost were going at it hammer and tongs for the Championship. In those days, there was no press conference after the race and my job was to get an interview with the winner before any other stations – the Germans, French, Italian, Portuguese – and I would grab Murray by the scruff of the neck, as soon as he'd finished commentating and say, 'Right Murray, you're coming with me', and we'd rush across or under the track and grab whoever we could for interviews. Murray would gather up all his notes and beetle along after me.

"The whole of the world's press were after Lauda and Prost but we, Murray and I, just grabbed the two drivers and set up the interview for the BBC, Murray did his interview and got it back to London, and the whole of the world's press quoted from Murray's interview.

"Murray was not a young man then but he would never complain. He was like a spring chicken."

Hunt's Roguish Charm

Owen Thomas

"I used to look after the commentary box.

"James's attitude as a commentator used to drive Murray absolutely bananas. Murray would just bite his lip but after a few races he'd say, 'Look James, you really ought to get here sooner so we can discuss things'. And James would go, 'Yeah, yeah, okay Murray,' and totally ignore his opinions and carry on as only James could.

"You couldn't help but like James. Because I was in charge of the commentary box, he used to get me into trouble. The producers would want to know where he was. Then he'd walk in carrying four pints of lager and say, 'Those two are for me and those two are for you as a peace offering'. He totally disarmed any bollocking you were about to give him. That was James."

"In 1986, I wrote Murray Walker's Bedside Quotes, *a book of my humorous motor sport anecdotes. I thought they were anyway. As usual, there were bookshop signing sessions to get sales moving."*

Murray revving up for Adelaide GP

AS CULT figures go in the mega-dollar world of grand prix racing Murray Walker is an unlikely hero.

The 63-year-old doyen of BBC motorsport commentators — the man with the friendly Friar Tuck looks — has an Australian fan club that rivals anything mere drivers like Nigel Mansell, Nelson Piquet or Alain Prost can muster.

For the past seven years he's entertained, informed, amused and occasionally infuriated Australian motor racing fans. His style is distinctive, his enthusiasm unbridled, his gaffes nothing short of legendary. In fact, it's said of Murray Walker that he'd talk under 40 feet of wet cement.

All of which has endeared him to grand prix followers, who've run off special edition T-shirts immortalising his oft-used and most famous quote:

"Unless I am very much mistaken . . ." it says on the front. And on the back: "Yes, I *am* very much mistaken . . ."

It would be fair to say Mr Walker is one of the most maligned, abused — yet somehow liked — personalities on television:

"I get a lot of criticism from viewers," he said in Sydney last week, en route to the Adelaide Grand Prix, "but most of it is uninformed and unreasonable. I have a chap who regularly rings me from Australia for a personal debrief after every race. Why did you say this, why didn't you say that, why don't you ever mention so and so. . ."

But despite the gaffes, the mistaken driver identifications and the missed incidents, Australia has adopted the BBC man and his co-commentator, the acidic former World Champion James Hunt.

"We're total opposites," says Walker, "but the combination seems to work very well."

Indeed, while Walker is pounding up and down pit lane filling his voluminous notebook with information, Hunt adopts a rather more cavalier approach, lounging in an air-conditioned VIP motor home or raising hell with his famous off-track partying.

Walker, like most of the huge international press contingent that will descend on Adelaide this week for the World Championship decider, is hugely impressed with the work of the Australian Grand Prix organisers:

"I don't want to sound patronising, but we were flabbergasted with the professionalism of last year's event. It richly deserved all the awards it won as the best Grand Prix of the year."

Walker's commentary career began in 1949 on BBC radio as a hobby. He was, until 1982, a director of the multi-national advertising agency D'Arcy, McManus & Masius.

He's been using his legendary gift of the gab in Sydney launching his new book, *Murray Walker's Bedside Wheels* and entertaining visitors to the terribly British Jaguar/Rover stand at the Sydney Motor Show.

Come Wednesday though it'll be back to work for the Beeb's most famous talkster, the man with the encyclopedic knowledge of motor racing. Who does he think will take out the three-way championship decider?

"Nigel Mansell is obviously the favourite, but I have a feeling in my bones that Alain Prost, very much the underdog, will win his second championship."

● **Alan Jones column – P74**

● **Grand Prix TV cover – P107**

MURRAY WALKER: cult figure.

EXCLUSIVE by Murray Walker

MR Motor Racing, Murray Walker (left), will be back in his commentary position on Sunday when the Brazilian Grand Prix in Rio gets the new Formula One season underway with a bang.

Birmingham-born Murray is an authority on the sport — and perfectly qualified to give his views on Britain's-own Nigel Mansell.

A tragic burst tyre in Adelaide robbed Mansell of title glory last year, but now he's back and more determined than ever to take over Alain Prost's mantle.

Here, in an exclusive article, Murray gives us an insight into Mansell the man — and his chances of realising a dream in 1987.

Get up and go for it, Mansell

He's got the car—and he's got the guts

On lap 64 of last November's Australian Grand Prix Nigel Mansell captured the hearts and minds of the British people.

In the closing stages of the last event of the year, when all he had to do to become Britain's first Formula One World Champion since James Hunt in 1976 was to stay in his unchallenged third place, his left rear tyre spectacularly exploded to destroy his dream of achieving the ultimate goal in motor racing.

As a fellow Brummie (I was born in Hall Green where Nigel lived for many years) I've followed his career with interest and enthusiasm since his earliest Formula Ford days.

Saved By The Ladder

Roger Moody

"We were at the Portuguese GP one year and we were doing all our pieces after the race had finished. This was at Estoril and the track had cleared and all the drivers and the mechanics had rushed off to Lisbon to catch their planes, and Murray and I and the BBC engineer were still working.

"When we came to leave, the BBC commentary team were the only people left in the circuit ... and we were locked in! We were right up at the top of the grandstand and we couldn't get out. We looked over the edge, at the back, and, as luck would have it, the Portuguese fire brigade were just packing up. They shoved up a long ladder and we were able to climb down, which was definitely one-up for Murray!"

"In my opinion, Jackie Stewart is one of the greatest personalities, and achievers, in the history of motor sport. Amongst his many skills is raising money for the Grand Prix Mechanics' Trust, which he founded. One of the ways he used to do so was to organise a fabulous, three-day clay pigeon-shooting competition at Gleneagles between Formula One sponsors, their teams and the media. I captained the Media team in 1987. My partners in crime, left to right, were Maurice Hamilton, Mike Doodson, myself, Jeff Williamson, Nigel Roebuck, Derrick Alsop and the great Walter Hayes, who was responsible for the initiation and funding of the immortal Ford Cosworth DFV V8 engine, which won 155 Grands Prix."

An Echo, Echo, Echo

"At Kyalami one year, I got into the commentary box and started talking about the race, and I was hearing everything I said through my headphones, a sentence after I said it. So I would say, 'There goes Villeneuve into Crowthorne Corner,' and carry on talking, and I would then hear myself say, 'There goes Villeneuve into Crowthorne Corner'.

"I cannot tell you how distracting this is. I tried to cope with it but, in the end, I just took the headphones off and carried on. James was completely thrown, took the headphones off and stormed out of the box, because that was the way James was, and we never saw him again. I subsequently found out that the BBC engineer involved in doing the wiring had joined two wires incorrectly. As a result, when I spoke my commentary was going all the way to London and then back again to Kyalami to my headphones. The time lag meant it was about a sentence behind. These things happen!"

The Cult Of Murray

Mike Doodson

"I had regarded him as just another professional working in F1. James Hunt was the public face of the BBC's TV coverage, and the target of autograph hunters, but F1 was a bit slow getting off the ground TV-wise and even he was comparatively low-key. It wasn't until Australia got its GP at Adelaide in 1985 that we were confronted with the Cult of Murray.

"The credit for this belongs firmly with Channel Nine. The enthusiasm and professionalism which they brought to their F1 coverage made the BBC broadcasts look horribly dull. Where the BBC just used the FOCA feed and one camera in the paddock, Nine had dozens. And since Nine had agreed to pay Murray a supplementary fee, he was kept exceptionally busy. Strangely, though, the finest example of the Cult of Murray did not involve him personally.

"One year, for the 'bumpers', which lead in and out of the commercial breaks, Nine used a hilarious short film sequence involving a buxom young woman wearing a 'Murray Walker Fan Club' T-shirt, with no underwear to restrain her assets. She is seen running toward the camera, bosoms bouncing in delicious slo-mo, with the quote, 'If I'm not very much mistaken' written on the front of the shirt.

"She then stops, with still lots of movement going on, grins and turns round. Written on the back of the T-shirt are the words, 'And yes, I am very much mistaken'."

"Moët et Chandon Champagne ambassador, Jackie Stewart, releases the bubbly at the 1987 British Grand Prix Fun Run whilst I apprehensively wait to get a face full - which I did."

WATCHING ON TV? HERE'S HOW TO SPOT THE CARS BEFORE MURRAY WALKER.

2.30 pm, Sunday July 12th.

The lights will flash from red to green and twenty six of the world's top drivers will unleash over twenty thousand horsepower on one of the fastest Grand Prix circuits of them all.

Silverstone.

Once again it's time for the Shell Oils British Grand Prix.

For those of you who can't be there, the whole race will be televised live, with the incomparable Murray Walker and James Hunt doing their double act as usual.

So, to add to your enjoyment, here's a quick guide to the circuit, the cars and the drivers.

As sponsors of the race, Shell Oils naturally wish them all luck. But especially World Champion, Alain Prost, and his able team mate Stefan Johansson, whose Marlboro MP4/3 TAG Turbo cars will both

In fact, they rely on Shell Gemini technology to lubricate their engines. Shell Gemini, the oil that stays in grade whatever the pressure or temperature, is available at Shell garages throughout the U.K.

Fuel, too, will play an important part in this race because the cars are only allowed 195 litres and the high speeds at Silverstone make fuel consumption critical.

So you'll be interested to hear that the Shell fuel used by the team contains the same 'Spark Aider' ingredient designed to improve the combustion efficiency of the fuel you use, Formula Shell.

So watch out for Prost and Johansson. They may not start from the front row of the grid, but, if the team's past form is anything to go by, they may well be at the front at the finish.

You can't be sure of much in Grand Prix racing.

MurrayismMurrayismMurrayism

"This has been a great season for Nelson Piquet, as he is now known, and always has been."

The Murray Curse

Nigel Mansell

PP: "Did you suffer any hostility from the other drivers because they felt Murray was biased towards you?"

"No, I think at times they rejoiced in it because when sometimes his bias got over enthusiastic, and it wasn't just to me, invariably our bloody cars failed!

"I know a number of drivers, including Keke Rosberg and myself, would say, 'Murray, with six laps to go [and heading for a win], just don't talk about us. Leave us alone.' You know the famous sayings, 'There's no way Keke Rosberg can't win this race,' and the engine would blow up or a wheel would fall off, you know. I suffered that same fate a number of times!"

Being A Fortune Teller

Murray Walker

"At Adelaide in 1986 Nigel Mansell looked to be a dead cert to be World Champion. It was the last race of the year and Nigel only had to finish third or higher. His team mate was Nelson Piquet and his chief rival was Alan Prost in the McLaren. I had to appear on Channel Nine's breakfast show and the chap interviewing me said, 'Well Murray, who's going to win the Australian GP?'

"Everybody was saying Nigel Mansell was going to win. I said, 'I will tell you this in confidence. Alan Prost is going to win the Australian GP and will thereby become World Champion.' 'Well there's a turn-up for the books, Murray. I wouldn't have thought you would say that.'

"Off I went, forgot all about it, did the commentary on the race and this was when Nigel had the famous tyre blow out. Alan Prost, who thought he was running out of fuel, won the race and the World Championship. I had to interview him immediately after the race. He said, 'You are fantastic, Murray'. I said, 'How do you mean?' He said, 'I was watching the television in my hotel room this morning and I saw you say Alan Prost will win the race and become the World Champion and even I myself did not think that. You are incredible!'"

"The brilliant Channel Nine production team at the 1987 Australian Grand Prix in Adelaide. That's me in the red trousers in the front row. Co-commentator, Jackie Stewart, on my left and the utterly inspirational Australian producer, David Hill, on my right."

Dodgems In Adelaide

Martin Brundle

"I remember having dinners with him, but I never really got to work with him much because they just never seemed to have any airtime for interviews. I remember in '85, after the Adelaide Grand Prix, we all went out for lunch down on the beach and I was driving him. We were flying home that day, the Monday after the Grand Prix. My wife Liz was with me and Murray was in the car. We stopped for fuel at this big junction and I had worked out that there was a point where the lights for all four roads were on red and I could bolt across to go where we needed to go. But I was wrong! And we ended up in the middle with cars coming at us from every direction! I remember Murray sitting there, looking a bit uncomfortable, and me feeling a bit embarrassed. As we headed to each of the four exits from the intersection, the cars facing us started to move. Murray was going, 'Not that way Martin, not that way, not that way' - we ended up pointing back in the petrol station again, licking my wounds!"

How Murray Lost Nigel The Championship

Mike Doodson

"It's October 1986 and the two leading contenders for the world title are Nigel Mansell and Nelson Piquet, sworn enemies, both driving for Williams-Honda. With two races to go we're in Mexico. Nigel, sensitive soul that he is, has decided that the best way to avoid upsetting his tummy is to eat only the food which he's brought with him from New York. He's living on biscuits, cheese and bottled water.

"Friday night, though, is Murray's 63rd birthday, and Nigel has quietly promised the BBC that he'll make a surprise appearance to help celebrate the occasion. The BBC man, Roger Moody, has organised dinner at a nice French-style restaurant in the Zona Rosa. Murray is in the dark because it's a birthday surprise. A couple of hours late, Nigel shows up and chats politely to a delighted Murray. Then he spots the succulent joint of beef we're all enjoying. "No harm in a slice of that, surely?" says Murray. So Nigel draws up to the table.

"Next day, in qualifying, Nigel is far from well. Getting round the Autodromo fast has taken on a whole new importance. No sooner has he done a lap than he's sprinting to the khazi. It doesn't take Nelson Piquet long to see what's happening with his team mate. It's too great a temptation for him to devise a cruel trick. When nobody's looking, Nelson nips into the team's private bog [toilet] and snaffles every scrap of toilet tissue. When Nigel's alimentary disaster strikes again, Nelson is out on the circuit.

"Call it mischievousness or irresponsibility, that was Piquet all over. It certainly seemed to have put Nigel on edge. Come Sunday, starting from the second row, behind Senna's Lotus-Renault and Piquet, he somehow overlooked the usual precautionary check to ensure that first gear was engaged ...

"Miraculously, everyone managed to avoid hitting Nigel's car as he staggered away from the line. And even though he fought through to a magnificent fifth place, it wasn't enough. To this day, everyone remembers that famous blow-out at Adelaide, two weeks later, as the moment when the title slipped out of Nigel's grasp and into the hands of Alain Prost. Prost scored just two points more than Nigel. And they were lost in the tension that followed that fateful dinner in Mexico.

"Is there still something on Murray's conscience? He insists not. But perhaps there should be...!"

MurrayismMurrayismMurrayism

"I can't imagine what kind of problem Senna has. I imagine it must be some sort of grip problem."

"In 1987 my friend Roger Chown persuaded me to write Murray Walker's Grand Prix Year. *It ran very successfully for 11 years after Richard Poulter, of* Autocourse, *took over the publication. It was great fun and I loved doing it."*

TV Mail

Oh for a breathless hush!

IN one of his books, Woody Allen writes about a man overcome with self-loathing who contemplates suicide — by inhaling next to an insurance salesman.

I have recently become convinced that the really desperate viewer might also be able to achieve final extinction by overdosing on Murray Walker.

Mr Walker is the antithesis of the ideal television sports commentator, who should combine the taciturnity of a Noh actor, the judgment of a Lord of Appeal, and the imperturbability of Buddha.

Not so Mr W. So loud was his shouting from the commentary box in **Grand Prix** (BBC 2, Sunday) that it was sometimes difficult to hear the whine of the racing cars above the whine of Murray. You can imagine him in the commentary box, his fillings pinging off the mike, as he works himself up into a supercharged turbo-driven lather.

The impression given is that if he was actually driving in the grand prix he is describing he would burn out his engine on the first lap.

His is a voice and style that harks back to the old Pathe newsreels. He has a staccato, machine-gun urgency. Even explaining the fact that the Swiss Grand Prix had been moved 80 miles into France to Dijon because of the Swiss ban on the sport was made to sound like a breathless war dispatch.

In contrast, the rather languid James Hunt provided a perfect mix of coolness and expertise. But then he is a former world champion and Walker will never be.

The chief problem commentators face concerning sport is the language they use to talk about it. The fun and the skill dribble away as they wallow in a rich gravy of metaphors about struggle, collapse and victory.

The practitioners of televised sport tend to assume that without their prattling attention the game is somehow diminished. Sport is seen as a TV event and not something which survives, even thrives, when the cameras aren't there.

ON **Grandstand** (BBC 1) yesterday, Frank Bough went so far as to hint that the Almighty was somehow intimately involved in the BBC's sporting output.

For the rest of us, rain interrupted play at Headingley mid-afternoon, but optimistic Frank saw in the showers divine intervention. 'Well, at least the showers are fitting in more or less with our plans,' he said as he handed over to racing from Ripon.

So now all the poor drenched spectators cursing under their umbrellas and looking up at the lowering clouds over Leeds know who to blame for their discomfort. It's all part of a BBC scheduling ploy. Mike Murphy, the editor of Grandstand, obviously has a direct line to God and the weatherman, and can call up rain at will when it's time to switch to another sport.

In commentaries, it is better to have things suggested rather than spelled out relentlessly. When every unimportant detail is hammered home, imagination loses the desire to use its own wings.

But give them their due: between showers, Richie Benaud and Jim Laker did give evidence that their views are weighed before they are phrased, and they seem aware that with pictures giving viewers most of the information, they don't have to say too much.

All this said, I don't suppose commentators will ever shut up and let the game do the work like the great Henry Longhurst used to do in golf. But I wish they would.

ON the theme of letting the picture tell the story, it is good to welcome back all those grainly old Interlude films that the BBC are showing all this week as part of their 60th anniversary.

Yesterday they showed that two-minute gem from the Sixties, **Messing About on the River** on BBC 1, and later there are more in store with the climax on Friday, that oft-seen masterpiece London to Brighton in Four Minutes.

The additional attraction, of course, is that unlike the majority of sports commentators, they remain gloriously and resolutely silent.

To The Point

Nigel Mansell

"One story which millions of those viewing will remember is when I won the race in 1987 in Austria and the driver of the vehicle, when I did my lap of honour, almost decapitated me when I hit my head on a low bridge. In the interview afterwards, I had a big bump on my forehead. Murray poked his finger at the lump and said, 'Does that hurt?' [Famously, Nigel recoiled in agony!] It made everybody laugh!"

Of The People

Roger Moody

"That was typical of Murray. The viewers could equate with him, that's what everybody loved about Murray. He is one of them – everyone feels they know him, as their brother, father, whatever. He really is a man-of-the-people. He was like an older brother to me and we had great fun."

Interviewing Fangio

Murray Walker

"In 1987, Pirelli, the tyre manufacturer, asked me to host a lunch in London in honour of Juan Manuel Fangio. As a part of this, they asked me to go and interview Fangio. I didn't need asking twice because Fangio is, in my opinion, the greatest F1 driver who ever lived. I know it's arguable, I know it's debatable, but that is my opinion.

"To be asked to go and interview the great man was a gigantic privilege. So I go trotting along to the Hyde Park Hotel, and up to his suite, where I am greeted politely and deferentially actually by this man, who was a god to me. He didn't speak any English but we had an absolutely first class interpreter. Now my image of Fangio up to then, based on what I had heard and seen of him when he was racing, was that he was a rather introverted, uncommunicative chap. So we sat down and had this long interview with the interpreter doing the business. I was absolutely fascinated because Fangio was anything but uncommunicative.

"In a one-to-one situation with no distractions, he was absolutely fabulous, authoritative, friendly, cheerful, helpful and the thing that absolutely amazed me was that he had total recall, seemingly, of every lap and every turn of the wheel of every race that he had driven in. I was particularly quizzing him on what is, undoubtedly, one of the greatest motor racing drives of all times, his victory at the 1957 German Grand Prix at the Nűrburgring when he was driving a Maserati, and up against Mike Hawthorn and Peter Collins in the Ferraris. He had started off with a light fuel load, very modern actually, but it wasn't in those days, made that now legendary pit stop to change tyres, which took a hell of a long time. He started, something like a minute behind them, and caught and passed them, and won the race. It was the last F1 race that Fangio won. I was absolutely spellbound because he described the whole race to me in minute detail, where he changed gear, what the revs were, what the lines were he was taking, what his mental attitude was, how exhausted he was at the end… Very, very great man."

"In 1988 the great Ayrton Senna joined Alain Prost at McLaren to form a virtually unbeatable partnership. They dominated the Championship which Senna won and, for me, one of the most stirring races of the season was the British Grand Prix at Silverstone where, in foul weather, Senna finished first ahead of Nigel Mansell`s Williams-Judd. This picture shows Ayrton leading Mauricio Gugelmin`s March-Judd which took a fine fourth place. My admiration and respect for Senna is not as unconditional as most people's for I felt he often took his determination to win too far, adopting tactics which were ruthless to the point of being unnecessarily dangerous." (John Colley)

"At times in 1987 James Hunt and I were not overly complimentary about the efforts of Ayrton Senna's hard-trying Lotus team mate, Japan's Satoru Nakajima. But Lotus didn't get all agitated and offended about it; they had these T-shirts printed with a satirical Jim Bamber cartoon showing an embarrassed looking James and I sitting on Nakajima's back wing with Satoru saying, 'It's not the camera that's the problem, Senna San!".

MurrayismMurrayismMurrayism

> **"There's only one second between them! One! That's how long a second is."**

Nothing But Respect

Owen Thomas

"The audience used to see Murray as the chap who got it wrong. If you ever walk down the pits with Murray, which I did on many an occasion, just to chat to team managers and drivers, in the two hours preceding a race, the one thing that came across was that everybody, in every team, held Murray in the highest regard. At no time did any team think he was a bumbling commentator. They all thought that he was the bee's knees and the best. And the respect that the teams used to show Murray was just phenomenal, and I haven't seen anybody, then or since, given the respect that Murray was given.

"The public don't see that side of it.

"In the days when there used to be pit walks, I've seen really big name F1 drivers standing there and there's a bigger crowd around Murray, asking Murray for his autograph. than the drivers. He is an absolute legend and he was such fun to work with."

The Biter Bit

Murray Walker

"James Hunt and I were invited to drive against each other at a stock car race at Wimbledon. The way these races worked, when there was just two cars, was that you started at opposite sides of the track and the object was for one driver to catch the other. The one who caught the other was obviously the winner. I was in an old Ford Anglia and James was in something equally decrepit and we lined up under the floodlights – thousands and thousands of people there.

"The flag dropped and James adopting an unfair advantage as they all do in F1 just drove across the middle of the track and kept right behind me, but he went off on the next lap and got the nose of the car stuck in a gap in the barrier so I drove up behind him and pushed him right into the gap so he couldn't possibly get out, then went round and completed the lap and won it! There am I being interviewed by Simon Taylor with a quizzical looking James in the background. And Barry Sheene had been there to see the fun. It was a great night!"

"At right, I modestly explain to commentator Simon Taylor how I blew World Champion James Hunt (centre) away. On the right, Barry Sheene is obviously reserving judgement."

"James Hunt? Bring him on!"

Interviewing Enzo Ferrari

Murray Walker

"I have been lucky enough to achieve two of my ambitions, one of them being to interview Fangio. The other one happened like this. In 1988, the BBC said to me, 'We want you go to Maranello and interview Enzo Ferrari'. 'What's that again? What time does the plane leave?' This was beyond my wildest hopes and dreams and aspirations. So I go to Maranello and I am taken with an interpreter into Mr. Ferrari's office, just the three of us. There was Enzo Ferrari, sitting behind his famous desk. On the desk was a black glass prancing horse, which had been given to him by Paul Newman. On the wall opposite him was a painting of his beloved son, Dino Ferrari, after whom the car was named. The whole room was full of memorabilia and pictures of famous people from the past like Ascari, Nuvolari, Varzi… I was totally overawed.

"The interpreter had said to me, 'Three historical questions, Mr Ferrari like historical questions'. I thought to myself, 'I haven't come here to ask Enzo Ferrari three historical questions and go home. I am going to take a flyer at it.' I sat opposite him, and he always wore dark glasses. He was well into his 80s. This man, probably the most famous man in the history of motor racing, had been interviewed 100s, probably 1000s of times, not just by foreign people, but by Italians, and they would have asked him every question that is possible to ask. What can I find that is new? First, I have got to find some way of getting his attention.

"He looked at me and I said, 'Mr Ferrari, you don't know me, but you knew my father'. 'Oh,' he said, 'how is that then?' I said, 'Well, my father was Graham Walker and when you had a motor cycling racing team, sir, and not many people know you had a motor cycle racing team, you used Rudge Whitworth motor cycles and you brought them from my father, because he was sales director.' I could see he was starting to pay attention because it wasn't going to be just another conventional interview. So, I then dived into the interview, and I was with him for about half an hour I suppose. I must be honest, it wasn't the greatest interview I had done, and I am sure it wasn't the greatest interview he had done. I was overawed; he was probably bored. But when we edited it, to put it out on the BBC, it came out very well indeed. It must have been one of the last interviews the great man did because not so very long afterwards he died."

Letting My Hair Down!

Murray Walker

"We English are a very funny lot. What the Continentals must make of us, I really don't know. At the Spanish Grand Prix in '88, it was Herbie Blash's 40th birthday. Herbie Blash is now one of Bernie's right hand men. Bernie is marvellous with his people. Charlie Whiting, who is the Race Director, was the Chief Mechanic at Brabham and Herbie Blash was with Brabham They are all in important positions now, thanks to Bernie, and deservedly so.

"Anyway, Bernie gave a vast wad of money to Charlie and told him to organise something. The whole of the top storey of a very upmarket restaurant near the circuit was booked. We all went there and had dinner. There were about 100 people and it all was going very well indeed. Then, they brought in an enormous cake. Nelson Piquet started cutting the cake. Then, somebody started throwing bread rolls about the place. Before we knew where we were, the whole of this cake had been dismembered and was being thrown around the room.

"Everybody stood up. A gigantic water fight erupted. I remember Bernie was standing in the middle of the restaurant, in his immaculate white shirt and black trousers, directing operations. He was standing behind a very large bloke. Someone chucked an ice cooler full of water at this bloke who ducked … and Bernie got the whole lot. Absolutely nonplussed!

"This finally petered out and all these Champagne-soaked, cake-sodden British mechanics and F1 executives were trooping out of the restaurant - we had to go down the stairs, where all these decorous local citizens were having an expensive night out in their finery - we all trooped out saying what a marvellous evening it had been. What they must have thought of us, I really can't imagine. We were looking very dishevelled, to put it mildly!"

'Muddly' karted off

Britain's best known voice in motor sport, commentator Murray Walker, or Muddly Talker as he is sometimes known by fans for his excited commentaries, tried this kart out for size when he opened the 30th Racing Car Show which runs at Olympia 2, London, until January 7.

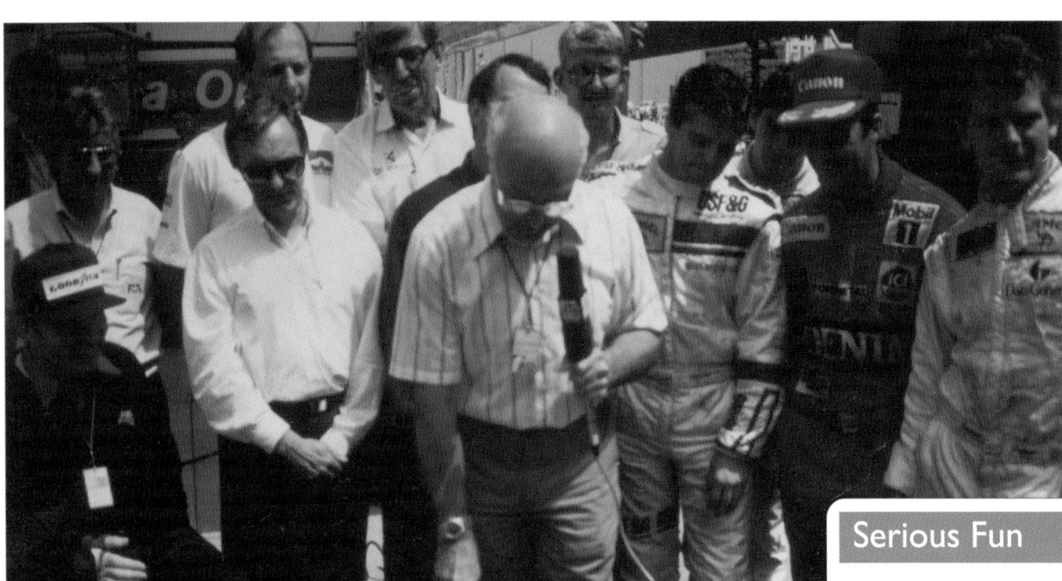

"Cutting the cake at Monaco 1988 in front of an angelic-looking Bernie Ecclestone. Little did I know what was about to happen - see 'As Scripted By Bernie' on the next page!"

Serious Fun

Herbie Blash

"Bernie arranged a surprise 40th birthday party for me at Jerez in Spain. There was my Brabham team and a lot of people I have met in F1 over the years, including Nigel Mansell and Nelson Piquet, who were both driving for Williams. They didn't get on so it was quite a coup to actually have them there together, and of course Murray was there.

"I don't really know how it started but it turned into one almighty bun fight, with water, food, wine, beer, cakes. Murray was very sporting. I remember seeing Murray walking out with a cream cake stuck on his head and his glasses just full of cream. You could see that he had really enjoyed it. It was a really stupid, crazy but fun-filled evening. Murray had been participating and acting out his youth!"

As Scripted By Bernie

Murray Walker

"1988 was the 10th anniversary of the BBC TV *Grand Prix* programme and the producer had a special 10th anniversary cake made for it and he wanted to do an in-vision piece of me cutting the cake with the notables of F1 behind and we were going to raise a glass of Champagne and drink to the health of the programme.

"So I said before the shooting began, 'Look I am going to be facing you and when I say, "So here we are on the 10th anniversary of the *Grand Prix* programme," you are all to say "Happy Birthday, *Grand Prix*," and we did a rehearsal. In the background are Frank Williams in his wheelchair, Herbie Blash, Bernie Ecclestone, Ron Dennis, Ken Tyrrell, Jackie Oliver, Peter Warr, Derek Warwick, Nigel Mansell, Jonathan Palmer...

"When I turned round to do the piece, I was aware of Bernie saying something but I took no notice. When we got to the cue they all shouted, 'Bollocks!'"

MurrayismMurrayismMurrayism

> "Unless I'm very much mistaken ... I AM very much mistaken!"

"The Australian Army always have a recruiting drive at their Grand Prix. In 1989 I went back to the old days by driving a German Leopard tank a whole lap of the Grand Prix circuit. And the tank commander, top right? My old mate, Australian World Champion Alan Jones, who shared the commentary box with me that year."

The Irreplaceable James

Mark Wilkin

"Probably my first race was about the worst James got. It was '89 Monaco and I was pretty new to the whole thing. I didn't really know anything about James, apart from he'd been a hero of mine when I was at school with his brother. I didn't see him for the whole weekend until race time, and it was two minutes to the race. The crews were just beginning to leave the pit lane when I saw this figure, in a pair of shorts, no shirt, no shoes, slightly hunched shoulders, long blond hair, ambling between the cars, on the grid. He then had to jump over a barrier and find his way round and up to the commentary box, which was alongside the start-finish straight at Monaco.

"He was almost unable to walk. He had a bottle of wine in one hand, as he walked in, and I took the wine and replaced it with a bottle of water and he was so drunk he didn't even notice. So, he spent the first 20 minutes of the race drinking water and then he perked up a bit. So he started commentating.

"But that was pretty well the last time that ever happened. He got himself sorted out very quickly after that, when he met Helen and stopped drinking so excessively. He discovered all sorts of things. He discovered the Press Room. He said, 'Do you know, they have all this information. They have lap times for every lap. That's fantastic. I've said for years that Patrese's a third rate driver. Now I can prove it.'"

Woops

Charlie Whiting

"I was standing beside Bernie, who had owned Brabham, and Murray was interviewing him. 'So Bernie, in the 17 years since you bought McLaren, which of your many achievements do you think was the most memorable ?'

"Bernie just smiled and said, 'I don't remember buying McLaren!'"

ISSUE 54

NOVEMBER 1990

COBRA

THE ALTERNATIVE F1 MAGAZINE

He's been accused of talking pure gibberish

He's been lampooned for his hysterical outbursts

He's had to sit next to James Hunt for ten whole years

Now, Murray Walker has had enough...

MurrayismMurrayism

"Mansell is slowing down, taking it easy. Oh no he isn't! It's a lap record!"

"Nowadays, those of us who are lucky enough to be part of the Formula One paddock scene revel in its own magazine, the humorous and irreverent Red Bulletin *but its predecessor was the even more irreverent, in fact on the verge of libellous,* Cobra*, which loved sending up F1 people - especially me!"*

MURRAY WALKER: You've heard him on TV, now see him in the flesh! This internationally known Grand Prix commentator will be at the Killarney clubhouse tomorrow night for an informal get-together.

GP's 'voice' Walker will visit Killarney

Hunt On The FIA President

Jim Reside

"I was responsible for the British GP as the host broadcaster. I remember, with a shiver in my spine, where we cut to a shot of the guy who used to run motor racing, Jean-Marie Balestre, a Frenchman, and as we cut to this shot, James said, 'Ah, you are looking at the picture of a cop-out'.

"There had been some political machinations that James had disagreed with leading up to the weekend of the GP and as he said that, I just thought, 'Hey James, you can't say that'. Fortunately, Bernie Ecclestone was becoming the person that ran the show, so it was the end of the era of Balestre.

"He was terribly outspoken but he did say what people were thinking at home. Because he was very articulate and eloquent, he was able to describe things in a very straightforward manner and everybody was left in no doubt about what he thought.

"He was probably one of the first experts brought into television who had previously competed who actually laid the ground rules for the future."

Brundle To The Rescue

Jim Reside

"There were the memorable James moments when he used to slide into the commentary box as the green light was coming on. Everybody had been spending the last 40 minutes wondering where he was and if he would turn up.

"There was one day at Spa and we were saying [from London] to Roger Moody, 'Is James there? Is James there?' He cut it so fine, he didn't appear at all. That was the day when we thought, 'Jeepers, creepers, we've got Murray for the whole two hours. That'll send the nation completely off their heads.' As luck would have it, Martin Brundle was driving that day and retired very early on and Roger was able to send a message to Martin and get him up to the commentary box, and that was the first time Martin Brundle was used as a commentator. So, don't let ITV tell you they discovered Martin Brundle!

"That was an eye-opener because Martin Brundle, without any forewarning or any training or any thought about it, came in and was very, very good. We always thought, here was a guy who was going to be perfect."

Murray speechless

IT IS not often that Murray Walker is left speechless, but without words he indeed was as he presided over the awards ceremony at the Guild Of Motoring Writers' 42nd annual dinner at London's RAC Club last Wednesday.

Muddly dished out the new Rover Group Award to Geoff Howard as Motor Industry Writer of the Year; the new Vauxhall Trophy to Tony Curtis for the launch of his new magazine *Car Design & Technology*; the Pierre Dreyfus Award to Brian Laban for his Masterpiece series in the *Supercars* partwork; the Pemberton Trophy to veteran Gordon Wilkins, the Michelin Award to Anthony Gould; and yet another Rootes Gold Cup to the indefatigable Tony Dron in recognition of his 10 race victories this year in cars as diverse as a Ferrari 750M and a Ford Fiesta.

He then handed over the Rider of the Year trophy to the representative of sidecar aces Steve Webster and Gavin Simmons, the Driver of the Year trophy to Ann Bradshaw on behalf of an absent Nigel Mansell, and the President's Trophy to Victor Gauntlett. When he came to the Timo Makinen Award for motorsport reportage he announced former victor Alan Henry, but was amazed when the latter took the microphone and said: "As usual, you've cocked it up again, Murray. Read it properly and you'll see the winner is... Murray Walker!"

Murray had found his voice again by Sunday night's *Autosport* bash, but it was the quietest he's ever been with a mike in hand. A nice touch, and an award well deserved.

Otherwise Engaged

Roger Moody

"At Spa one year, when we had appalling weather, we were waiting for James to appear in the box, and he never turned up. Throughout the race, people kept retiring – Martin Brundle, Johnny Herbert, etc. Murray would say, 'Well James has obviously been held up, but never mind, we've got Martin Brundle…'

"We had a succession of drivers and it wasn't until the end of the race that we learnt that he'd rather a good time with friends, shall we say, the night before. But that was James and we learned to grow to accept his idiosyncrasies and we wouldn't have been without him."

"Someone somewhere arranged for graphologist Barry Branston to assess my personality just from reading a, to him, anonymous specimen of my handwriting. I have to say, he got frighteningly close on many aspects of myself."

All my life I've been a traveller — in the work, in my job and with my hobby — and I've loved all of it!

MurrayismMurrayismMurrayism

"Anything can happen in Grand Prix racing and it usually does."

Barry Branston Mem. Sc. G. (England)

Scientific Graphologist

BBC Radio 2

(Gloria Hunniford Show
Wednesday 17 January)

NO.15

You are a practical person, self-reliant, with a matter-of-fact attitude and a talent for technical details.

Observation is a strong point, as is also an awareness of the importance of dealing with minor tasks; this is the way you keep up with things that need to be done, also realising your responsibilities and obligations.

I would think people would know you as being reserved, sentimental, and having a motherly disposition. However, if anyone were to show you affection, you would go on the defensive to protect yourself, even though it's really what you emotionally need.

Your interest is in things rather than people; therefore you don't have to compromise in any way. I am not saying you don't like to share: it's a problem you had to face during your early life that has inhibited your response for fear of being emotionally hurt.
Could it be a religious upbringing which was not fully explained to you?

Your common sense is well developed and you are intelligent, but I would say you have reached the height of your ambitions and are now content to stay as you are.

A very useful person to have around.

Bagging A Pair

Mike Doodson

"Sometimes, when Murray and I had been in place for a good half hour or more, waiting for the start, the producer would ask, from London, 'Anyone seen James yet?' Murray would usually reply, 'Well, we hear he's in the country'.

"The worst race for these shenanigans was the Belgian, because James's birthday fell around that time and he'd be partying harder than ever. He once arrived at Spa, direct from the previous night's birthday celebrations in England, leaving his hire car steaming in the car park and getting to his seat with literally seconds to spare. 'Hi, Doods. Who's on pole?'

"Another time at Spa, when he was hitting the booze and the drugs harder than ever, he told me that his friends had seen him the previous evening with 'a pair' - two likely women - on the way to the chalet where he was staying. That was the race that he actually missed. I think 'Gastric 'flu' was the excuse that someone came up with for his absence. Later James filled out the story for me as far as he could. 'I honestly don't remember a thing about it,' he reported. 'Funny thing is that when I eventually woke up there was sufficient evidence to suggest I had satisfied both of them...'"

"It was my genuine pleasure to introduce Prime Minister, John Major, when he opened the new Lola factory in his Huntingdon constituency. We actually got him into a Lola single-seater, but Cobra seems to think I was not over-impressed with the august visitor."

The Premier International Formula One Magazine

CONSERVATIVE PARTY TRAINS UP NEW NATIONAL HERO

Blimey! This geezer's got more crap opinions than James Hunt. How much longer to lunch, I wonder?

British Grand Prix Special Edition

ISSUE 57 JULY 1991

G.A. PRITCHARD-GORDON

25th January, 1991

GAP-G/NP

Dear Mr Walker

My apologies for disturbing you at home yesterday - I was loathe to take up any of your valuable time but Weatherbys, the Secretaries to the Jockey Club, insist on the approval of well-known people when horses are named after them!

Can you therefore, write me a couple of lines confirming that you are happy for the two year old colt by TRACK BARRON out of MINK HAT to be named "MURRAY WALKER". He will probably run in my name and colours and from what I have seen of him so far, there is every chance that he will win a race. Come what may, it will give Julian Wilson and Peter O'Sullevan something to talk about !

If you are ever in the Newmarket area, please feel free to call in and see your name-sake - there is always a drink or some lunch at Trillium Place.

With best regards,

Yours sincerely

GAVIN A. PRITCHARD-GORDON

> **"This is lap 26 which, unless I'm very much mistaken, is halfway through this 58-lap race."**

An Unexpected Début

Martin Brundle

"The first time I worked with him as such, was a day in Spa in '89 when they couldn't find James Hunt. He had a bit of a heavy night, the night before, shall we say. Murray was up in the com box alone and so they dragged me up there. A lot of people said after that, 'You and Murray make a good pair and you seem quite handy at that commentating lark,' which was interesting, but I never gave it a second thought."

Berger's Sense of Humour

Murray Walker

"There isn't a lot of humour in F1; it's a serious business. Frank Williams memorably said F1 is a sport from two o'clock on Sunday afternoon until 3.30 and the rest of the time it is a business. So it's very nice to come across a bit of humour. One of the people you always could guarantee finding a bit of humour, indeed often too much, was Gerhard Berger. His association with Senna was legendary. Senna was very, very serious. Gerhard was very, very light-hearted.

"There was an occasion once when a friend of mine, Eric Silbermann, who was doing Gerhard Berger's press releases, was going somewhere in Rio with Gerhard in a car. He said, 'There is a dreadful smell in this car, Gerhard'. 'Zat vill be zee fish,' said Gerhard. 'What do you mean, it will be the fish?' He said, 'I vill show you'. So he stopped the car, got out, walked round to the back, opened the boot and there was a box of rotting fish heads and fish tails. This was 40°C temperature in Rio.

"So he closed the boot lid, and drove to the hotel. He then blagged his way into Senna's bedroom, and distributed all this rotten fish, under the bed, on top of the wardrobe, inside the television set, round the back of the wash basin. You can imagine in that heat!

"There was another occasion when Gerhard was in his bedroom and the telephone rings. Senna's voice says, 'Are you responsible for all these frogs in my room?' 'How many have you found?' said Gerhard? 'Twelve,' says Senna. 'Zere are still four more.'"

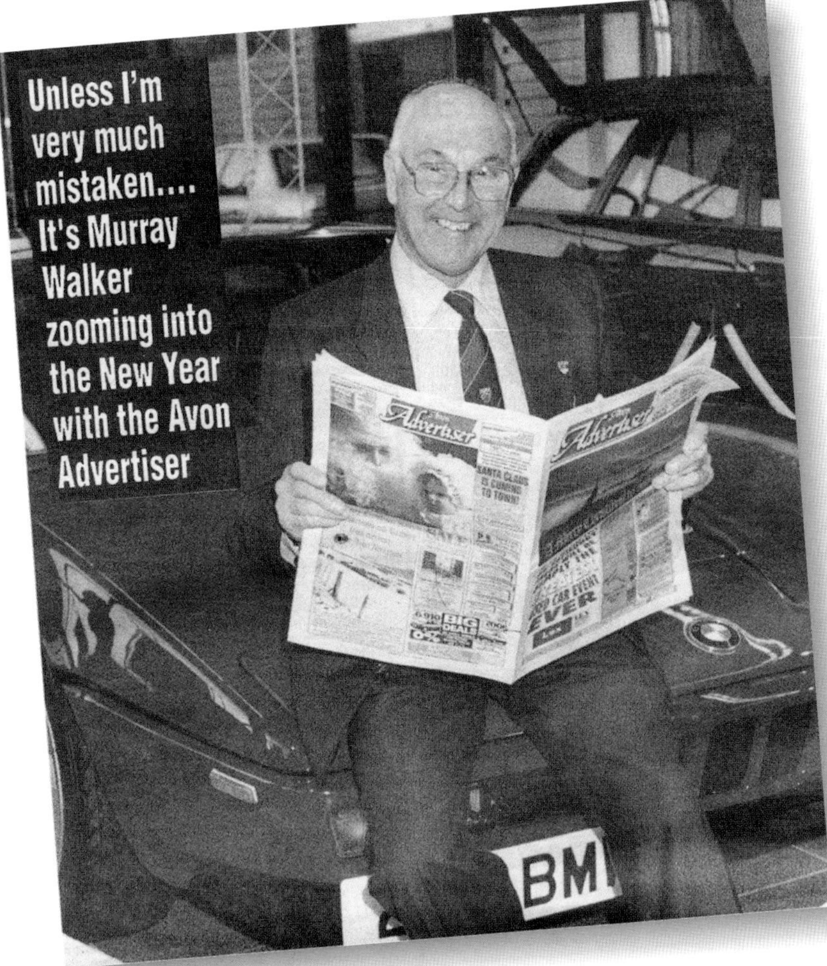

Unless I'm very much mistaken.... It's Murray Walker zooming into the New Year with the Avon Advertiser
BM

Top Cop slams TV's Mr Motorsport

MURRAY IN 'I DRIVE AT 85' STORM

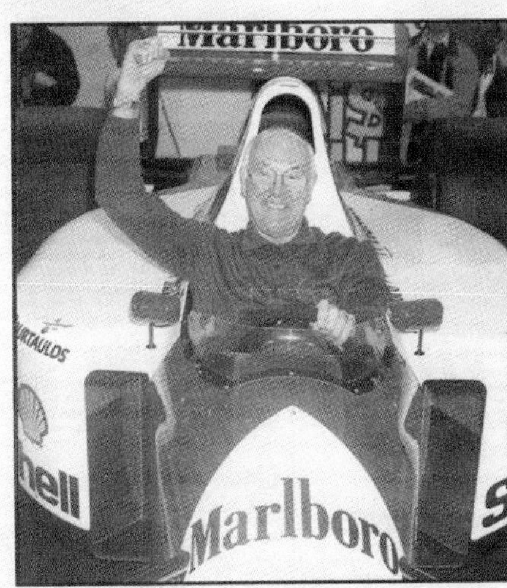

SPEEDY: Murray at the wheel of a 200mph race car yesterday

TELEVISION'S 'Mr Motorsport' Murray Walker has crashed headlong into a furious speeding row... after admitting he drives at 85 mph on the motorway.

The top Grand Prix commentator was yesterday branded 'totally irresponsible' by police and safety officials.

They fear his Murray in a hurry admission will encourage others to break the 70mph motorway limit.

Last night a defiant Murray, who is appearing at the giant motorsport show at the NEC in Birmingham this weekend, said: 'I am being honest.'

Example

He added: "People might argue that I am not setting a good example but I am telling the truth. I could just lie and say I do 70mph but that would not be right."

The veteran commentator, who owns an exclusive 130mph BMW sports car, has also revealed that he was once stopped for speeding but escaped punishment on a technicality, despite being guilty.

He has steered himself into a storm after revealing his high speed driving in a magazine interview. The TV celebrity, who like Grand Prix ace Nigel

EXCLUSIVE
By
STEFAN BARTLETT

Mansell, was born in Birmingham, said that in good weather on an empty motorway he drives at 85mph.

Asked how fast people should be allowed to drive in good conditions he told an auto magazine: "As fast as your car will happily go. Why not?"

He has been blasted by Britain's top traffic cop, Peter Joslin, the Chief Constable of Warwickshire.

Mr Joslin, chairman of the Association of Chief Police Officers traffic committee, said: "It is totally irresponsible for Mr Walker to say something like this.

"He is in the public eye through his association with motoring and his views are respected by many people.

"This will no doubt have the effect of encouraging people to speed.

"Because of who he is Mr Walker should curb his desire to speed. Otherwise he may have a rude awakening when new speeding equipment is brought into use.

"For years senior police officers took the view that the speed limit should be raised to 80mph. However we have now reversed that because of

● Turn to page 2

Sowing The Seeds

Lord March

PP: "Did Murray act as a catalyst in your enthusiasm for motor sport?"

"I am sure he did. I hadn't watched the [F1] races for years, and it was only in the late 80s and early 90s that I really got into it all again, and really started watching it religiously every weekend. So, in that sense, he did get me back into it and this was before we were thinking of doing the Festival of Speed. Obviously he was, and is, Mr. Motor Racing."

Catching Up On His Sleep

Roger Moody

"French GP, blisteringly hot. I used to say to James, 'James, I want you to walk up and down the pit lane, get as much information as you can and when you join Murray in the commentary box, you are well versed in what's going on'. Of course, he took not a blind bit of notice of that, and always used to amble into the commentary box at the end of the formation lap, by which time Murray was doing his nut. He would be commentating on the formation lap and then pulling his mic away from his mouth and whispering to me, 'Where the hell is James?'

"As the last car took up its position on the grid, James would saunter in, sometimes no shoes, cut off short jeans, smoking a cigarette, and a bottle of Coke, and sit down and he was off and running.

"But on one occasion, I think he'd had a bit too much drink, or it was very hot in the commentary box – while Murray used to stand, James would sit – on this occasion, James fell asleep. As it was so hot, everyone had their shirts off. Murray was perspiring freely and, as my wife Diane pointed out, was soaking James who slept though it all."

Dear mr. Walker,

we watched your tribute to James Hunt as a family, and were moved to tears.

We will be watching the Grand Prix next weekend. Not wondering who will win but sending you – as will thousands of others – our support and love and heartfelt best wishes.

Pat & Garry Lewis & Family

Dear Mr Walker

I am nearly 80 and lover of Motor Racing. I am so desperatly sad to hear of the death of James Hunt.

I have listened and watched your commentries for ten years and also of course last Sunday. I cannot believe he could die at such a young age.

My wife died 3 months ago from Cancer and she loved the racing also.

I just want to tell you how sorry I am to have lost a friend who I have never met

Please place my condolincies as is appropriate

Yours sincerely

John Blacker

MurrayismMurrayismMurrayism

"...the lead is now 6.9 seconds. In fact, it's just under seven seconds."

"For me, the weekly magazine Autosport *is virtually my bible. It was founded by that great Scottish character, Gregor Grant, in whose memory this award was created. I was the privileged winner in 1993. Gregor was an ebullient character who was not averse to the odd drink or two, and his presence very much enlivened any gathering. There are a 1001 stories of his exploits, but sadly most of them are not repeatable. Not here anyway!"*

The Important Switch

Nigel Mansell

"We once did the most fantastic interview in Brazil. It was one of the longest interviews I had ever done with Murray – something in the order of about 20 minutes – and it was brilliant, and he said so himself and all the rest of it. We had a lot of laughter and levity. We were just chatting and I was giving opinions about different things.

"Then, some two hours later, he came back to me very sheepish and said the interview was absolutely fantastic but there was one slight problem. He said, 'I hadn't turned the microphone on'!

"So, we had to redo the whole damn thing again, which was actually quite challenging and quite difficult because it wasn't as spontaneous as the first one. It was very funny because only Murray could get away with doing something as pretty awful as that!"

Olde World Courtesy

Louise Goodman

"I started working in F1 as a press officer, initially, and he was always so charming. When I moved from Leyton House, which was the team I had originally been working with, to Jordan, Murray sent me a letter, which I thought was so sweet – a little handwritten note, saying, 'Congratulations. So pleased to hear about this new job, I think it will be a really good move for you'. I think for somebody of Murray's stature to do that was amazing. I don't know whether it was his background in advertising but he has always had a great skill for making everybody feel important, be it a driver, some team principal or a mechanic – I don't think Murray sees any difference between social strata. He is charming and engaging with everybody."

June 16, 1993

Murray Walker
c/o Grand Prix programme
BBC TV Centre
Wood Lane
London W12 7RJ

Dear Murray,

I was shocked and deeply saddened to learn of the death of James Hunt on Tuesday. I have been an avid fan of televised grand prix racing for thirteen years, and in that time I have come to feel as if Murray Walker, James Hunt and grand prix racing are a single entity, an irreplaceable piece of glamour, colour and daring in an often all too drab world.

James Hunt was a unique character. Not only was he a great racing driver, he was a great personality too. I'm sure he culd be difficult, obstinate and opinionated, just like the rest of us, but few great things are achieved without these qualities.

So for me, grand prix racing has lost something immensely valuable. I hope, though, that you will be able to find another co-commentator and continue the celebrated commentating double-act that has kept us all entertained for years. Grand prix racing, like any other sport involving money, attracts cynics. Genuine enthusiasm is beyond price. I feel that no other commentators could have brought to the sport what you two did.

James Hunt was unique. So is Murray Walker. Because there is one thing I am sure of — the popularity of grand prix racing today is almost solely due to your energy, enthusiasm and commentating skills. Please don't ever stop, because grand prix racing needs you.

Yours sincerely,

Rod Lawton

David Cones

5th July 93

Dear Murray,

I've just watched your tribute to that great friend of yours, James Hunt in an absolute flood of tears. It was a very touching and caring tribute to a man who has been a hero of mine since I was a schoolboy.

I'll miss hearing you two work together every other week-end, but please dont ever stop!

Best wishes

David Cones

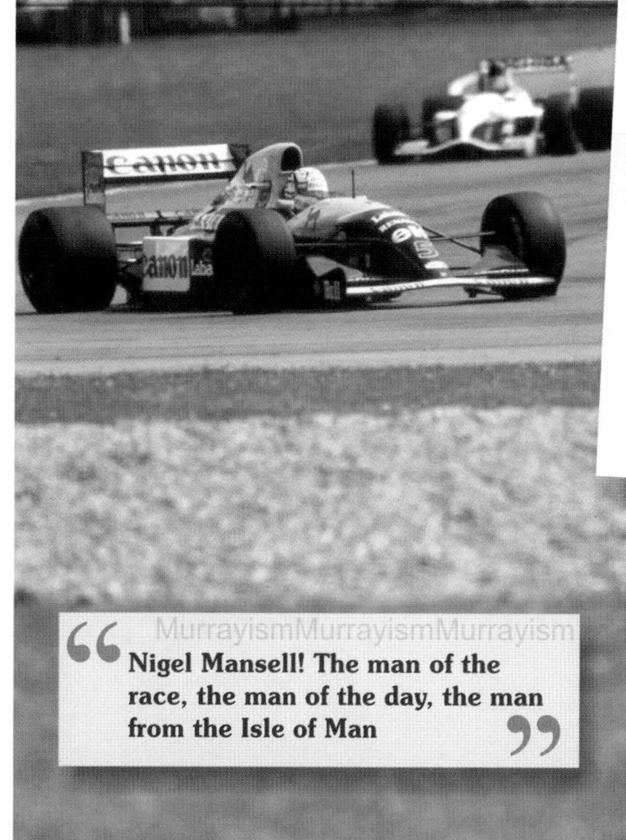

MurrayismMurrayismMurrayism

"Nigel Mansell! The man of the race, the man of the day, the man from the Isle of Man"

"'Who's your favourite driver then?' people ask me and, without hesitation, I reply 'Nigel Mansell'. He isn't everybody's cup of tea because he was never slow to complain if he felt he had been wronged, which he frequently did, but he was never anything but kind, considerate and thoughtful with me and I spent a lot of time with him, his charming wife Rosanne and his children Chloe, Leo and Greg. Never, in my entire career, did I meet anyone with greater self-belief and determination, and it took him to a well-deserved World Championship in 1992. He won nine races that year and this shot shows him in his Williams-Renault, winning the British GP at the place where they loved him the most - Silverstone." (John Colley)

"I spent 13 years of my life, from 1980 to 1993, with James Hunt as my BBC TV commentating partner. We were together 16 weekends a year for four days at a time and if you multiply 13 by 16 by four, you get a very big number. We were very different attitudinally and temperamentally but after we had learnt to live with each other, we got on extremely well and it was a sad, sad day when James died of a massive heart attack at the tragically early age of 45. I received literally hundreds of letters from the public we had both talked to for so long, all of them deeply touching in their different ways."

Sobering Thoughts

John Watson

"James made his trip to Damascus and started to sort out his own personal life, and check a lot of the excesses he had used or lived with, certainly through the '80s. Gradually, and ironically, he began to enjoy the job he was doing much, much more and, in a sense, started to understand why Murray was the man that he was and doing the job the way he did it. It was quite an interesting, if you like, conversion for James to ease up on the excesses and to realise there is a significant and very important value to having a live microphone covering Grands Prix. It doesn't mean you have to subjugate your personality but it gives you the opportunity to keep your presence and your name and your persona in the public domain, which is very important if you are a sports personality and you wish to continue an association with that sport."

Walker v. Hunt, Hunt v. Walker

Mark Wilkin

"I remember at Spa, they both came to me during the course of the weekend and said, 'I've been listening to the commentary on the past races and it's not fair'. Each reckoned the other one was doing more than him. James used to think his role was to do the replays. 'Tell him, I do the replays.'

"So, at this race, James came to me and said Murray was doing too much and Murray came to me and said James was doing too much. So I said, 'I think you're absolutely right, Murray is doing too much,' to James. And I said, 'I thing you're right James is doing too much,' to Murray. I said to both I'd have a word with the other.

"Anyway, I didn't say anything. After the race, they both came up and said, 'I don't know what you said, but it was much, much better. Thanks very much. You've clearly sorted the problem.'"

16th June 1993.

Dear Murray,

I was very sad to hear of your commentating partner's death yesterday. I've known James since he raced Marches & Heskeths in the early seventies when I was a mad keen motor racing enthusiast and more recently when he helped Mika with constant good advice while I've worked at Lotus. It is very hard to forget Mika's comments and facial expression as he described a visit to James' home and James' walking barefoot around amongs't the.... in his budgie cage!

There were times when I didn't agree with James' views but I always enjoyed his company and his cheery wit was very rarely absent even when he had much personal adversity to cope with.

He will be very much missed by all who knew him. I do wish you and all the production team luck in finding a worthy successor which will be hard.

I don't think I will be at Lotus much longer as the situation has become very unpleasant so do please keep in touch with Yumi & I at my London home address.

Please don't feel obliged to reply to this as I'm sure you will be inundated.

With sympathy.

James Penrose.

BRITISH MOTOR RACING MARSHALS CLUB LIMITED

FOUNDED 1957 RECOGNISED BY THE RAC

SAFER MOTOR SPORT

15th June 1993

Dear Murray,

I cannot think of the late Jim Clark without remembering the utter shock that I felt when I heard of his death. I couldn't believe that Graham Hill could be dead – a new career in front of him, and suddenly, no more. But I didn't know these men, nor had I worked with them, but I respected and admired them greatly. How much worse then, had I been friends of these two, had I built up a rapport with them, how we had a 'team'. Now you have lost James, and I can't believe it. I'm sure that you are a great deal ahead of me in this sentiment.

On behalf of us all – I haven't spoken to more than two or three members since the news broke, but all were unanimous – please accept our sincere condolences at the loss of a friend, a character, a team mate. You are not like Morecambe and Wise – you will never be the sad stooge that Ernie Wise has now become – but you had that team presence on an equal basis, but yet we know you were "the boss"! You'll be fine – all fans are behind you. Bear up.

Sincerely, David

PRESIDENT Murray Walker

VICE PRESIDENTS: Derek Bell, Keith Douglas, Mrs Graham Hill, Jack Lambert, The Hon. Gerald Lascelles, Jonathan Palmer, Tom Walkinshaw, John Webb

REGISTERED IN ENGLAND No. 962892 ● REGISTERED OFFICE: SILVERSTONE CIRCUITS, NEAR TOWCESTER, NORTHANTS ● VAT No. 273 9867 02

MurrayismMurrayismMurrayism

> **"And we have had five races so far this year, Brazil, Argentina, Imola, Schumacher and Monaco!"**

The Subtlety Of Alan Jones

Murray Walker

"Alan Jones, the great Australian World Champion of 1980 who, allegedly, Frank Williams and Patrick Head still regard as the best racing driver they ever had because he is a down-to-earth, no-nonsense chap like they are, went on to race in other F1 teams and went back to Australia, raced in touring cars and did a lot of commentary work. When I went to Australia for the Australian Grand Prix, Channel Nine always used me as their commentator but I often had somebody else with me and on this occasion it was Alan Jones.

"So, I was excitedly talking about the battle going on between Jean Alesi in the Ferrari and Michael Schumacher in the Benetton. This had been going on for some time, and Alesi wasn't letting Schumacher past. I said to Alan, 'I wonder what Alesi is thinking now, with this battle going on'.

"He said, 'I will tell you what he is thinking, Murray. "I am not letting you past, you dirty little Kraut."'

Dear Mr Walker,

I am writing to you regarding the death of Formula One World Champion James Hunt.

As he had retired before I was born, I never had the opportunity to see him as the great racing driver that he was.

I have always admired both you and him as two great commentators, and for me, Grand Prix racing will never be the same without him.

Please send my deepest sympathy to all his family and friends.

Yours faithfully

Prashil Goricha

Master Prashil Goricha

Murray Walker Esq

A CELEBRATION OF THE LIFE OF

JAMES HUNT
(1947-1993)

at

THE CHURCH OF ST JAMES'S,
PICCADILLY, LONDON W1

WEDNESDAY, 29 SEPTEMBER, 1993

at 3.00 p.m.

(Admission from 2.15 p.m. - 2.50 p.m.)

This card is for row .... Seat ....
FRONT

Needs Must

Mark Wilkin

"After Nigel had won the World Championship in '92, we were all waiting to get *the* interview. The room was absolutely packed to the rafters. All the press were there. Time was ticking by and ticking by and ticking by, and it became clear we were going to have to do some pieces to camera, which we had to do at some point. We were going to have do them then because we wouldn't have time afterwards. We were also in pole position to get the interview by the door where Nigel was about to come out so we couldn't afford to go anywhere.

"So I said to Murray, 'We're going to have to do them here, right now, in front of all these people, in this packed place. We can get a decent enough shot so are you happy to go?'

"Of course Murray says yes. It's shoulder to shoulder and Murray turns to camera and starts off in his broadcast voice. Absolute silence just descended on the place. He did his piece, we stopped filming and the place just erupted into applause. It was absolutely extraordinary."

Murray Walker Esq

Following a Service of Celebration
of the Life of

JAMES HUNT

at St James's Church
Piccadilly, London W1
on Wednesday, September 29, at 3.00pm

JONATHAN MARTIN

Head of Sport and Events Group
BBC Television

invites you to tea at 4.15pm at the
Royal Automobile Club, Pall Mall, London SW1
by kind permission of the Chairman

RSVP Sir Roger Cary, Bt
Room 613, Henry Wood House
Langham Place, London W1A 1AA

Taking The...

John Watson

"Towards the end of James's life, the actual sincerity of the friendship between Murray and James changed considerably from being one where they were two people doing a job and there wasn't a lot of interaction outside of what they did in the booth. In fact, in the booth sometimes it was almost as if there was a war. On one occasion it got close to a punch-up. I can understand the exasperation you would feel if you were going down the Murray route and your partner was, literally and metaphorically, taking the piss!"

Desperate Measures

Mike Doodson

"There was a memorable incident during that one-off GP race at Donington Park in 1993. James hadn't bothered to check the location for the BBC's special commentary point, which was a wooden hut on stilts overlooking a corner from the outside, and he barely made it before the off. It was raining, he was soaked ... and he badly needed a pee.

"'Where's the nearest khazi, Doods?' he demanded.

"'No idea. We're in a public area so you'll probably have to queue in the mud.'

"His eyes lit on two or three empty soft drinks cans which somebody had discarded. With great dexterity, and hardly spilling a drop, he managed to re-fill them. I've never been able to look at a can of Lilt the same way again..."

MurrayismMurrayismMurrayism

"And the first five places are filled by five different cars."

Microphones At Dawn

Mike Wilkin

"At the European GP at Donington, I had a film crew in the box because I didn't have any pictures of Murray and James commentating.

"James would hold out his hand when he felt he had something to say. Murray would see and finish his sentence and pass the microphone over. They only had one mic because otherwise they would have both talked through the entire race without letting the other one get in.

"So he held out his hand but Murray carried on. So he held out his hand a bit more vehemently but Murray carried on. So he held out his hand in a sort of 'shaking it right in front of Murray's eyes' way. Murray kept going so James just snatched the microphone out of his hand in mid-sentence. James started trying to speak and Murray tried to grab it back. James raised the microphone about his head as if to use it as a hammer on Murray's head, at which pointed I dived in between the two of them and separated them like a boxing referee.

"All the while, I was aware that there was a camera recording this. We had to be very careful what happened to that tape."

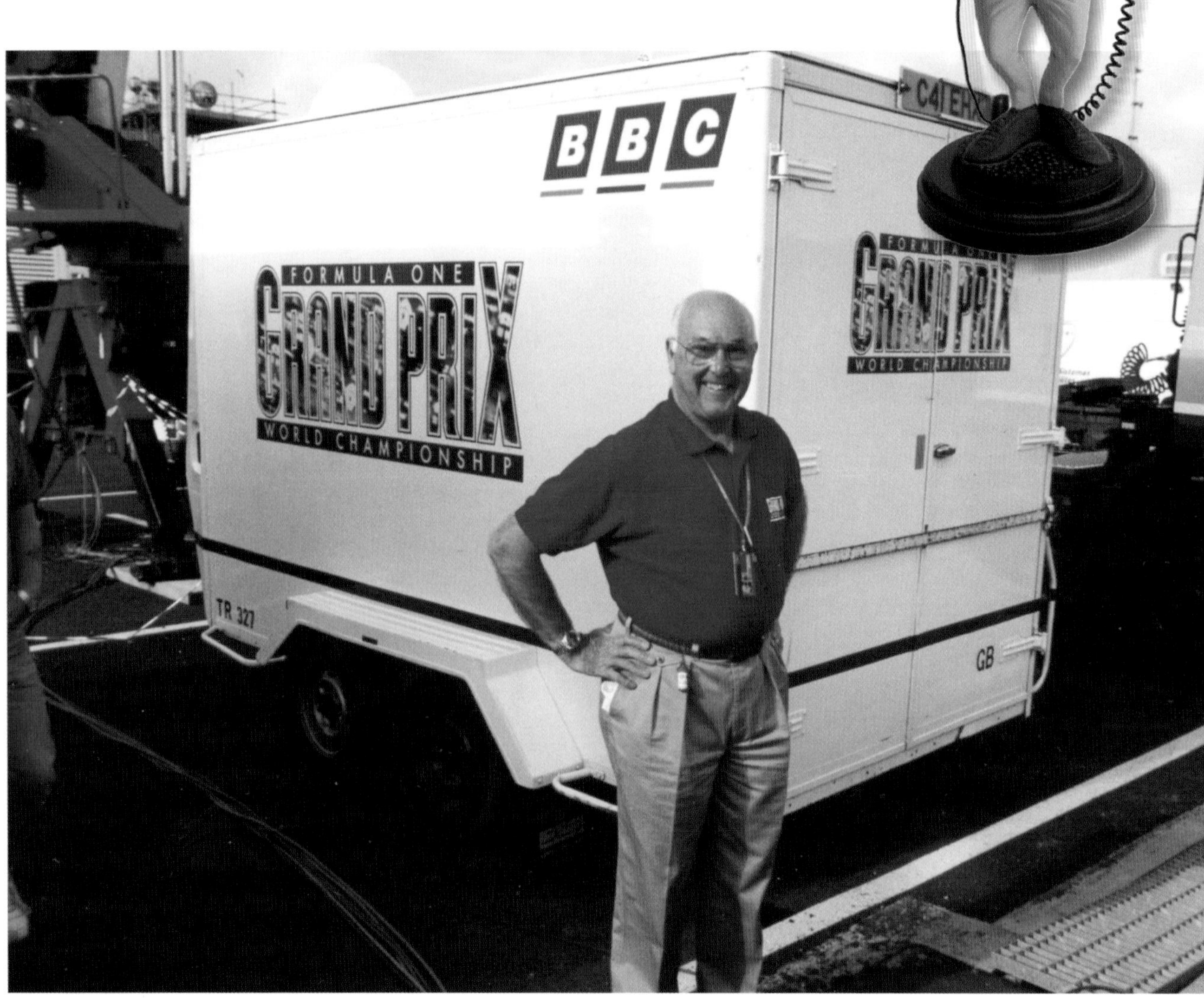

"This was the BBC TV production trailer that the stalwart Bill Fivez pulled all around Europe behind the mobile scanner. Great for its time, but very modest compared with the lavish facilities that ITV later provided. But what matters is that it did the job very well."

MurrayismMurrayismMurrayism

"So now you're looking at the battle between Frentzen and Herbert for seventh place. Heinz Harald Frentzen in the Sauber Mercedes behind Johnny Herbert, behind him Johnny Herbert in his first race in the Ligier Renault..."

Famous Last Words

Mark Wilkin

"James said to me on the Friday before he died on the Monday night that he felt like he'd been born again. Life was starting from now. He had just cleared up all his divorce stuff, which was a horrible, long, messy process and he was so happy with Helen, and he said, 'I really feel I've been born again, this is where it all starts from today'."

FROM HEAD OF SPORT AND EVENTS GROUP, TELEVISION.

BRITISH BROADCASTING CORPORATION
KENSINGTON HOUSE
RICHMOND WAY, LONDON W14 0AX
TELEPHONE: 081-895 6174/6703
FAX: 081-749 3466

21st November, 1994

Mr. Murray Walker,
Ashford Water,
Sandleheath,
Nr. Fordingbridge,
Hants SP6 1PQ.

Dear Murray,

I could not let the end of this particular Formula One season pass without writing to thank you for the marvellous job you have done in the commentary box throughout the year.

You don't need me to tell you what a variety of challenges you were posed in the live hot-seat. Imola was awful, but dealt with in the most professional and sympathetic way. By Jerez, Japan and Australia we were back where we like to be - as viewers - thrilling to the racing.

Your work and contribution, my dear Murray, continues to give pleasure to millions - and especially to me as I fondly remember our working times together in the early days of 'Grand Prix'.

Thanks again, and best personal regards.

Yours as ever

Jonathan

Jonathan Martin

P.S. I was back from holiday 'just in time' - by hours - for Adelaide!

Jon

"I commentated on every Formula One race in the amazing Michael Schumacher's career from his début with Jordan in Belgium in 1991 until the USA GP at Indianapolis in 2001 which was my last. 1994, the year of his first World Championship win with Benetton, was one of non-stop contention, especially at the British GP here where Michael was black-flagged for a rule infringement but he got there in the end. Like Nigel Mansell, Schumacher arouses extremes of opinions but, again like Nigel, I rate him as a top man for he was never anything other than friendly and helpful as far as I was concerned." (John Colley)

On Not Getting Too Close

Murray Walker

"I did the address at James Hunt's Memorial Service, at St James's Church in Piccadilly. There were hundreds of people. I have known a lot of racing drivers in my time, and one of the loveliest in terms of fun, charisma and personality was the Scot, Innes Ireland. He won Team Lotus's first ever Grand Prix. I was sitting next to Innes. On his right was his wife Jean, who had been Jean Howarth, Mike Hawthorn's fiancé. People were getting up and doing a bit. I remember one of James's sisters stood up and did a bit from Winnie the Pooh which James had been fond of when he was a child. Somebody played Purcell's Trumpet Voluntary, which I had seen James playing at the Albert Hall at some pre-Grand Prix thing - James played the trumpet very well indeed.

"Anyway, I was sitting next to Innes, and he was going to get up and do a piece from Rudyard Kipling's 'If'. I noticed his hands were shaking like a leaf. His time came, and he got up and he walked to the lectern to do his piece. I lent over to Jean and asked, 'What's the matter, Jean? Why the shaking hands?'

"She replied, 'He is absolutely petrified, Murray, about standing up and talking to several hundred people'. I thought how very odd that someone with all the guts and courage you need to be a racing driver, and someone as forthright and outspoken as Innes, could be worried about something like that. What I didn't know was that he was in hospital in the last stages of cancer and had discharged himself for the day, specifically to go to the church and do this thing in honour of his old friend. He went back to hospital and died. I thought how very, very sad.

"That is the trouble with knowing so many racing drivers and racing motor cyclists, so many of them that I have known very well over the years have gone or been killed. Mike Hailwood was killed in the most tragic circumstances, on a public road in an accident that was not his fault. James dying very early as he did. Innes Ireland. Jim Clark. So many of them. You actually get to a stage where you almost prepare yourself not to get too close to them because of the risk of something dreadful happening to them. It is a terrible analogy but it's like having a dog as your faithful pet that you have known for 12 years and is part of the family and then, as dogs do, they die young and you've got all the tragedy of bereavement. It's the same thing if you're close to motor sport."

Great Team

Vern Schuppan

"I used to love his commentary with James Hunt. That was a very special time. It was just so entertaining. When James disappeared, it was a big loss, I must say. Obviously, Murray can do that job without anybody supporting him but I felt that was a special team at the time."

MurrayismMurrayismMurrayism

> "Either the car is stationary or it's on the move."

"I must confess that I had a rather superior attitude to the CART single-seater racing championship in America until I met Nick Goozee, who was the boss of Roger Penske's car design and manufacturing complex at Poole. After he had read me the Riot Act, in his kindly but forceful way, Nick and I became great friends and I enjoyed Penske hospitality at the fabled Indy 500 and at Nazareth. This shows Nick and I at the Penske Christmas party in 1994, following Emerson Fittipaldi's legendary defeat of Nigel Mansell."

MURRAY WALKER

19.9.94

ASHFORD WATER
SANDLEHEATH
FORDINGBRIDGE
HAMPSHIRE SP6 1PQ
Phone & Fax: 0425 654236

Dear Rick,

I have to confess and say that I went to bed when I got home but now, after a few hours kip I feel the difference and am fully refreshed.

I cannot tell you how much I enjoyed the trip and your kindness and hospitality. For my vocabulary isn't adequate but it is no exaggeration to say that I will remember every hour of it with great warmth and that I deeply appreciate your kindness. To meet Dr Penske, Emerson, Al, Paul and all your colleagues was a great experience and I shall now be able to recount with pride my commentating experience on American nationwide TV!

I fear that Formula One is going to seem a bit humdrum after 185MPH and twenty second laps of Nazareth but I'll do my best to pep it up a bit!

I'll be in touch but, until then, my very best regards

Murray

MurrayismMurrayism

> "... and Edson Arantes di Nascimento, commonly known to us as Pele, hands the award to Damon Hill, commonly known to us as... um... Damon... Hill."

The Value Of James

Jonathan Martin

"James was quite a worry all the time. I think he called Brambilla 'a mobile chicane'! I used to remind James that the courts were waiting for the potentially slanderous things he would say. James played games with everybody. His criticism was not because he wanted to be critical, it was because he was being straightforwardly honest in his opinion. He was frank and forthright. He didn't actually deliberately create waves to make a stir and be a controversial star. He was just being himself and he would say on the air the sort of thing he would say to you or I if one was sitting next to him in the grandstand.

"James's skill was in reading the race."

Mobile Chicane

Mark Wilkin

"At the British GP one year Murray was driving me to the circuit for the race. It was very early and we'd worked out this route through a load of lanes from our hotel about 20 minutes away to avoid the traffic. His driving style was a little like his commentaries in many ways – it was slightly erratic and often quite quick.

"We were haring round these country lanes and we went round a completely blind corner to be faced with a milk float coming towards us on a single track road with absolutely nowhere to go. I thought, 'There's only one way this is going to end'.

"Anyway, Murray swerved, skidded up onto a grass verge, got it back together, milk float went past us, we jumped back on to the tarmac and carried on without actually having hit anything at all.

"Murray said [in all seriousness], 'Bloody hell. He was going a bit quick wasn't he?'

"I said, 'It was a milk float, Murray!'"

"British Racing Drivers' Club Annual Dinner at the Grosvenor House Hotel, 1994, with Lady Alexander Hesketh and award-winner, Damon Hill, with not a grey hair in sight!."

"'For once, Johnny Herbert, I'm talking to someone who is shorter than me.' 'That's because you're standing on a box, Murray.'"

Pole Vaulting

Jim Reside

"At Silverstone in the mid-90s, when Damon was driving for Williams, Patrick Head said to the BBC, 'We've got the technology now and we could hook Murray up to talk to Damon. Obviously not during the race but what about final qualifying just after his hot lap as he crosses the line, we'll hook you up and Murray can talk to him.'

"So Damon came round, crossed the line and, lo and behold, he was in pole position. We said, 'Murray, you can talk to Damon, stand-by, and cue.' 'Damon, Damon, congratulations you're on pole position for tomorrow's British Grand Prix, how does that feel?'

"There was then a massive noise because the technology wasn't that good and he was probably still doing 160mph around Copse Corner, but you could just hear Damon's crackling voice, 'Well actually Murray…' and as he said those words, Prost came round and took pole, and Murray went, 'I'm sorry to interrupt you Damon, you've just lost pole position'. (much laughter)

"Damon was slightly deflated and there was just this noise, 'zzzzzz', and we thought, 'Yea, maybe not such a brilliant idea after all!'"

The Human Senna

Martin Wilkin

"We went to Brazil the year Ayrton died. He was brilliant. He invited us down and we spent three or four days with him. We went all over the place with him and he showed us huge courtesies and spent a lot of time with us – came back to the hotel, sat in the bar with us just chatting, which was lovely, very relaxed and informal. This was the race before Imola.

"Murray had decided to call him 'I-airton' [which is the more correct pronunciation]. He tried to call him that throughout the Brazilian GP but by the end it had gone back to Ayrton again because it was difficult to do all the way though in high stress circumstances. So, at Imola on the Friday, we had an interview with Ayrton and his first words to Murray were, 'So what's happened to the 'I-airton' then?'

"Afterwards, Murray said to me, 'Do you know, that means he obviously watches the highlights after the race'. That meant his commentaries weren't just going out to the public; they were going out to the people he put on pedestals. That he found extremely humbling, and not a bit terrifying."

"A tremendous day at Mercedes-Benz, Stuttgart, in 1995 included a blast in the great Stirling Moss's 1955 Mile Miglia-winning 300 SLR with its famous starting time number, 722. That's my long-suffering BBC TV producer on the right."

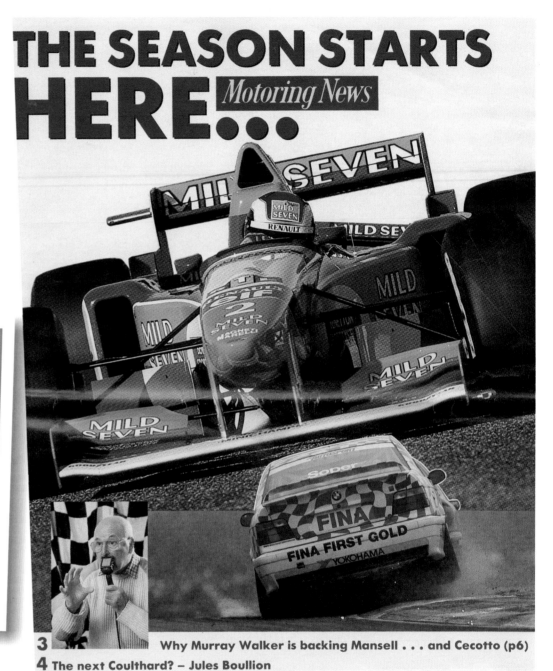

THE SEASON STARTS HERE...

Motoring News

3 Why Murray Walker is backing Mansell . . . and Cecotto (p6)

4 The next Coulthard? – Jules Boullion

8 Last chance for Johnny Herbert?

1 Have you ever tried to punch Frank Sytner? BTCC Mastermind

3 BTCC gets its wings – but how much difference will they make? Ian Flux finds out

The Benetton/Renault Team Choice

Pat Symonds

"Our favourite Murrayism was when Michael [Schumacher] was driving for us in the Benetton and Murray said, 'The Benetton is handling superbly as ever. Williams have worked very, very hard on this car at the beginning of the season.' We all enjoyed that and quite regularly reminded the Williams guys about that one!"

The Way It Worked

Jim Reside

"I was in London and beside Murray, at the track, was another producer. Roger Moody and later Mark Wilkin were what we called the onsite producers and they sat beside Murray and had local information which they fed in his ear. I was the executive producer in London who spoiled the party by constantly interjecting and saying, 'I want you to say this, I want you to say that because you've got too close to it'. People onsite at all sorts of sports events got too close to it, not just motor racing, and it's the job of the producer in London to consider what the viewer at home is thinking and wanting.

"I'm sure I was very irksome and irritating in Murray's ear. As I pressed the button, he would think, 'Oh no, it's that fellow in London interrupting my enjoyment!' But that was my job."

"A great team to work with, BBC TV's finest with, alongside me on my left, my friend Nick Goozee who joined us for the 1995 Portuguese Grand Prix. Model maker Nick Christodoulou is second from the right."

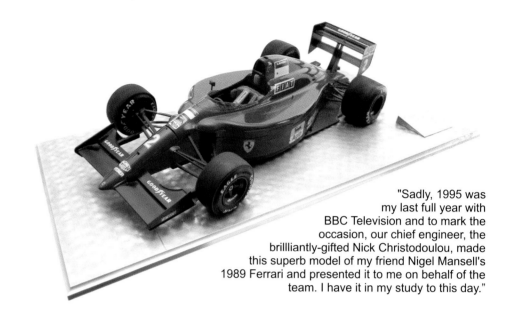

"Sadly, 1995 was my last full year with BBC Television and to mark the occasion, our chief engineer, the brillliantly-gifted Nick Christodoulou, made this superb model of my friend Nigel Mansell's 1989 Ferrari and presented it to me on behalf of the team. I have it in my study to this day."

Imola Sensitivity

Jonathan Martin

"Murray could also broadcast in a very human way about the human aspect of the sport. I remember the day that Aryton Senna was killed, and Murray's humanity in dealing with it. This was very shortly after the BBC had decided to invest in having our own cameras. It was lucky that we had because we were able to cut away from the trauma that was on the screens and the Italian director at Imola was less reticent about.

"Murray got the tone right on those occasions. He was a sensational broadcaster in the sense that he would make you stand up and listen, but at moments of real trauma, such as that, he certainly wasn't sensational. He was extremely humane and caring. Traumatic was certainly the word for his broadcast that day."

MurrayismMurrayismMurrayism

> **"Jean Alesi is reborn. Last year he was driving a car that he couldn't have done well in even if it had had two engines in it, never mind one."**

TV's voice of motor racing may be silenced

BY JOHN GOODBODY
SPORTS NEWS CORRESPONDENT

MURRAY WALKER, the much-parodied voice of motor racing, may soon be without a microphone after the BBC yesterday lost its contract to screen Formula One grands prix.

ITV has scooped the rights to the next five seasons beginning in 1997 for a record £60 million — ten times the present BBC contract price. The corporation is already reeling from the loss of the FA Cup final for the first time for 60 years.

Mr Walker, 72, who has commentated on grands prix for 47 years, was reticent about whether ITV could cover the sport without him. Asked whether he would be prepared to work for them, he said: "I really do not know. I have only just heard the news."

He added that he was disappointed that the BBC was not given the chance to bid for the championship. However, it is extremely unlikely that the BBC would have been prepared to match the money that ITV, having lost many top sports events to Sky, was offering the Formula One Constructors' Association.

Mr Walker once said about his commentating: "I do not make mistakes. I make prophecies which immediately turn out to be wrong." Some of his most famous utterances have included: "Nigel Mansell — the man of the race — the man of the day — the man from the Isle of Man" and "an Achilles heel for the McLaren team this year, and it is literally the heel because it is the gear box."

The only person who was happy yesterday about the possibility that he may not be heard on television was his wife, Elizabeth. She said: "Whoopee, now I will see more of him at home."

A BBC spokeswoman said: "We are deeply disappointed at the news. It came out of the blue. We had no notice of it." It televised its first British Grand Prix in 1949 and covered the world championship every year since 1978.

Walker: screech to a halt?

WALKER'S VIEW

MURRAY WALKER GIVES HIS REACTION TO THE LOSS OF FORMULA 1 ON THE BBC

'I'm at the end of my career rather than at the beginning. I've been doing it for 47 years continuously, so there obviously isn't a hell of a lot left in terms of years to go.

Murray: 'shocked'

'How much longer I could have gone on would in any case depend on physical condition and mental reflexes. Fortunately, both those are perfectly all right at the moment, but both are going to get worse rather than better, and I don't know how much longer I would have been able to go on anyway.

If I stop commentating, I would revert to what I was originally, which was an enthusiastic spectator, and do a bit of writing. I've got a lot of motorsport-associated books in my head and I would like to do my autobiography. I hope I've got a lot to say, so I'm not exactly looking at being at a loose end.

'But it was a bit of a shock. I was doing an after-lunch speech. I got in the car at four o'clock on the day of the announcement, turned on the radio, and it was the second item on the news.

'Then all hell broke loose, with people 'phoning, one of the first of whom was the BBC's head of sport. He heard the move was being made at 12 noon, and the public announcement was being made at 12.30. If that was the case, it seems a very harsh way to treat an organisation that has done F1 and motorsport consummately well for many, many years, and covered F1 for 17 of them, and has built an audience of record levels – which, of course, is why ITV want it.

'I did a Radio Five Live phone-in the following day, and the pity is that everybody was saying the BBC do a better job on sport in general than ITV.

'But the BBC can't have F1 because the BBC doesn't have the money. Sky has a subscription, ITV has gigantic advertising revenues, but the BBC is dependent on the licence fee.

'Whenever anybody talks about putting the licence fee up, there is a national outcry, with questions asked in the House of Commons. You can't have it both ways. If people want BBC quality, then they have to pay for it. Money rules, and the BBC hasn't got enough of it.

'But it's not the end of the world. If ITV are making such a large investment, I presume they are going to be prepared to do it properly. But commercial breaks are a problem, because they disrupt the action in a continuous-action sport where continuity of commentary and presentation is desirable.'

'However, against that background, we've still got 1996, which I'm looking forward to enormously because I expect it to be a super season.'

ITV deal could mean end of the road for Murray

THE DEAL THAT TOOK FORMULA 1 AWAY FROM THE BBC HAS STUNNED THE COUNTRY. BUT ITV'S HEAD OF SPORT SAYS F1 IS TAILOR-MADE FOR THEM. BY ANDREW BENSON

Murray Walker looks likely to make his Grand Prix commentating swansong next season after ITV snatched the contract to broadcast Grands Prix on British television from under the BBC's nose last week.

Walker, whose seat-of-the-pants style has made him possibly the most popular commentator on British TV, said last week: 'I would imagine that 1996 is going to be my last season. I hope it isn't, but I think it probably will be. I would love to go on, but you can't go on forever.

Ecclestone: dealer

'Everybody is saying: "Will you go to ITV?" But I don't know whether ITV would want me. One point of view probably would be: "Christ, this old buffer's being doing it ever since God, we want to start with a clean sheet of paper." I would be the last to say that was wrong.'

ITV has scooped a five-year contract to televise GPs, beginning in 1997. It is believed to have cost £60 million – up to 10 times what the BBC paid for its present contract. And the result should be more motor racing on network TV than ever before.

The negotiations – between Bernie Ecclestone, boss of the Formula 1 Constructors' Association, and ITV Sport's Marcus Plantin – have provided for ITV to broadcast live all 16 Grands Prix for all five years, as well as showing race highlights.

There will also be a new programme featuring the build-up to each Grand Prix, including coverage of the qualifying sessions. ITV is also committed to show the International Touring Car and Formula 3000 Championships.

Plantin said: 'We want the glamour and excitement of the big event, and you certainly get that from F1. Much of the race coverage is provided for us, so there are limits to how much we can change the show you already see. But you will see a difference in our pre- and post-race programming, and in the highlights shows.'

Asked how and when ITV would cover the ITCC and F3000, Plantin said: 'We will present them in a way which properly builds their appeal and shows off the action and personalities to best advantage, and at a time when motorsport fans are most likely to be available to view.'

Ecclestone said: 'We've agreed a minimum amount and we're working out the rest now.' He added that the races would not be shown at unsociable hours.

The deal is a huge blow to the BBC, which has recently lost the FA Cup Final, one-day cricket and Ryder Cup golf. Now, ITV has deprived it of one of its sporting staples.

The BBC, which has run its *Grand Prix* programme since 1977 and broadcast its first live GP in 1953, was told it had lost the contract only half-an-hour before the new deal was announced.

A BBC statement said: 'We are extremely disappointed. We had no notice of the deal and were not given an opportunity to bid. Our disappointment is deepened by the fact that Grand Prix motor racing is a sport which BBC TV has nurtured and promoted to our audience, particularly over the past 20 years.'

> **"I would imagine that 1996 is going to be my last season. I would love to go on, but you can't go on forever"**
> MURRAY WALKER

Sources at the BBC say that it is worried about being squeezed out of sport's coverage by the price war between the commercial stations.

Ecclestone said: 'We thought the deal was in the best interests of the sport. It's not my style to conduct an auction. They came to me with a proposal, and said: "If you want to accept it, do so now." If I'd said no and gone back to them later, they might have said it was too late.'

He added that ITV was obliged to broadcast the shows in all regions of the UK. It is understood that Ecclestone received more guarantees about coverage, on F1, ITCC and F3000, than he could have from the BBC, which would certainly not have been able to afford the highly-inflated fee.

The BBC has bequeathed ITV an already large audience for F1, with viewing figures this year higher than ever before. Audiences peaked at seven million during the European GP in October.

In many ways the deal can be seen as positive for motor racing – and especially for F3000 and the ITC – but question marks remain.

In particular, it remains unclear how ITV will explain the apparent shift in its policy on tobacco advertising and sponsorship on TV.

Previously, it had been proud of its record of showing as few sports with tobacco sponsorship as possible. Now it will be showing as one of the centrepieces of its sports programme something in which tobacco advertising is a key part of the fabric.

Whatever, the deal will swell FOCA coffers considerably. The fee been increased enormously, but Ecclestone is thought also to have demanded a slice of ITV's advertising and programme sponsorship proceeds. ■

Walker column, page 134

Working With Murray

Derek Warwick

"Regarding the so-called cock-ups and gaffes, I have never seen them as cock-ups and gaffes. I have always seen them as over-enthusiasm. It is easy when you are so excited about something and so passionate, to get red and blue confused. He almost goes into his subconscious and that's why he is able to commentate as he does.

"I've had the privilege of co-commentating with him twice and both times I just stood in awe of this guy, flexing his muscles, doing press-ups, flailing his arms around, pulling his legs up and doing breathing exercises leading up to the opening of the show to get himself limbered up before he starts speaking. Then when they counted him down – 3 – 2 – 1 - he's straight into it.

"You only had to touch him on the shoulder and he'd finish off whatever he's saying and hand the mic over. He was never selfish to the extent that it was his mic. Although he considered it his mic, he was very generous to the people who worked with him."

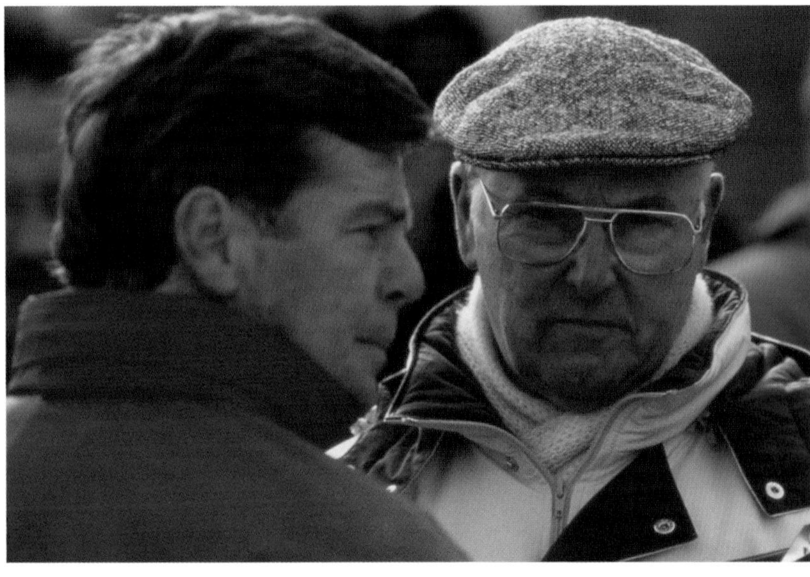

"One of the men I have most admired in my entire Formula One career is Derek Warwick, although neither of us look too happy about it here."

Equal Among Equals

Martin Wilkin

"Murray didn't realise how famous he was. Part of his enormous charm was that he expected to be treated like anybody else. He'd try and help out with the equipment, carrying boxes when we'd finished. He was absolutely delightful – no side to him at all, no prima donna-ish, 'I'm the big star' – he genuinely believed that the guy who twisted the wires together was just as important, because if he didn't twist the wires together properly, Murray wouldn't be heard in England, Australia, South Africa and all round the rest of the world. He completely believed the team was the team – every member of the team was equally important."

A Gentle Hint

Derek Warwick

"I always remember we were in Canada when I co-presented with him and when we came out after the race – remember I had just retired from being a F1 race driver – the punters were looking for his autograph, not mine. I thought, 'I am standing by an icon, a guy who is admired and respected by every enthusiast in motor racing throughout the world, not just in the UK – it was worldwide.

"What I cannot understand is why he has not been knighted. He should be Sir Murray Walker."

MurrayismMurrayismMurrayism

> **"Twenty four points for Schumacher, 23 points for Hill, so there's only one point between them if my mental arithmetic is correct."**

Sad day when Walker is driven to scrapyard

AND so we must prepare to bid a fond farewell to Murray Walker, past-master of turbo-charged hyperbole and the 'famous last word'.

From 1997, watching Formula One motor racing on television can never be the same again (for a start, we should be able to hear the roar of the engines above the roar of the commentator). But though ITV's cameramen might be able to match their BBC counterparts in terms of images from Silverstone, Monaco or wherever, no-one is capable of replacing the familiar high-octane screech that is Murray Walker when the lights change to green on the start line.

Like Dan Maskell, Henry Longhurst, John Arlott and a few, precious others, Walker has a unique voice and a unique delivery — not to mention a unique misunderstanding of the intricacies of sport which he translates on screen for us; just as the drivers can easily make a slip at 185mph, of course, so, too, can Britain's most accident-prone commentator. And that is why we treasure him so dearly.

"The lead car is absolutely unique," he told us from Monza one year, "...except for the one behind it, which is identical.

"Do my eyes deceive me or is Mansell's Ferrari sounding a bit rough?

"Michael Andretti's hopes, which were nil before, are absolutely zero now.

"Whatever is wrong with Piquet's engine would be irremediable in the time it takes to do it."

Even in last year's official BBC Grand Prix 95 magazine, Walker was making an endearing fist of things in an article predicting the season ahead. Tipping Nigel Mansell to win the world drivers' championship ahead of Michael Schumacher and Damon Hill, Walker opined: "McLaren, Mercedes and Mansell — what a partnership! I'll be amazed if they don't win this season." Not only did Mansell fail to win the title, he failed to win a single point before driving away from F1 in a huff.

So let us savour the season to come, which begins in March, after which the voice of motor racing will be fitted with a silencer.

"And that's the benefit of having a clean windscreen," screeched Murray after what seems a lifetime of Saturday afternoons ago on *Grandstand* as a small Hillman Imp took the chequered flag in a saloon car race at a mud-splattered Brands Hatch. As if on cue, at that precise moment the winner skidded straight off the course into a grassy bank.

□ Do you have a favourite example of the 'famous last word' (real or imagined)?

Usual prize (i.e., zilch) to the most off-target entry and a few examples to keep the mind ticking over during the restive season:

"I can beat the fat kid on the best day he ever had"... Arnold Palmer talking about Jack Nicklaus.

"This will be the best heavyweight contest in the history of the division"... Joe Bugner before trading 'blows' with Frank Bruno.

"Zola Budd will become a great British athlete... her heart lies here"... *Daily Mail*.

"It would be nice if we could recover our reputation in soccer and once again become the gentleman of Europe"... Margaret Thatcher's New Year speech in 1988.

"Billie Jean [King] is a great player for a broad. But no woman can beat a man who knows what he's doing. I'll put her and all the other women's libbers back where they belong — in the bedroom and kitchen"... the late Bobby Riggs before being beaten in straight sets by King in the 1973 'Battle of the Sexes'.

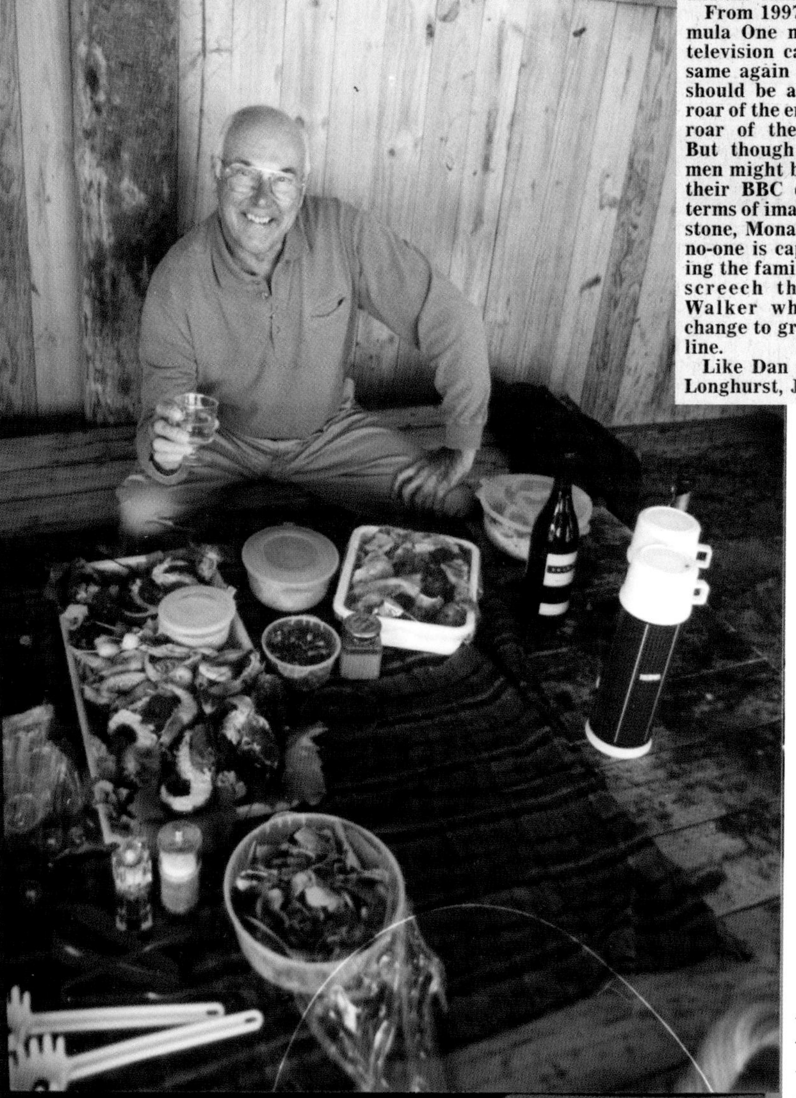

"It isn't all work, you know. This was a picnic lunch at Australia's Kangaroo Island, and I've never had a lunch like it."

Forms Of Fame

Nick Goozee

"I took Murray to Goodwood in 1994, which was his first experience of the Festival of Speed. In those days, Murray was *one* of the BBC commentators. The BBC seemed to have a policy of not making anybody more famous than the Corporation. You had a lot of commentators who were household names in their own fields but they weren't particularly famous. Murray *was* well-known and he was besieged.

"We sought refuge in the Mercedes hospitality area. Stirling Moss came in. Murray turned to me and said, 'I never really knew Stirling Moss'. Murray had never commentated on Moss, though he had followed his career closely. He said, 'Now Stirling is very famous for being Stirling Moss'.

"I didn't think any more about that until much later when Murray had started working for ITV. Being much more of a market orientated organisation, ITV realised very quickly that the key to their success was utilising, to the maximum, their household name, gifted to them, Murray Walker. The whole programme was built around Murray and he was getting much, much greater profile. He was better known than most of the people who were actually driving. ITV started taking him all over the world and used him as a marketing tool.

"I said to him around about 2000, 'Murray, remember you telling me about Stirling Moss? Do you realise you are now becoming famous for being Murray Walker?'"

The Senna Accident

Murray Walker

"I have actually been commentating about four times when someone has been killed in my vision, not necessarily the audience's vision. The worst one, indeed the worst one ever, was Senna's fatal accident during the San Marino GP in 1994 because Senna was a colossus, a god like figure in Japan, Brazil, in a lot of the world.

"I had seen Alboreto, Piquet and Berger all survive dreadful accidents at the Tamburello Corner, so when Senna crashed I was not expecting him to be killed. However, it very rapidly became obvious to me when they stopped the race and the body language of people around the car, and the general feeling of doom and gloom, which percolates through the commentary box, that all was not well. It's a commentator's dilemma because we stayed with the race, and you couldn't say, 'Don't worry folks, I am sure he is alright'. You couldn't say that because you didn't know that it was true, nor could you say, 'This is terrible, I think it's terminal', because you don't say that sort of thing on television.

"So you have to walk the tightrope between those two things, but saying something, which I managed to do. Actually, Jonathan Martin, who was the Head of Sport at the BBC, afterwards phoned me and said, 'That was your finest hour, Murray. You dealt with that absolutely magnificently because you didn't put a foot wrong, and you didn't create alarm, nor did you create false optimism.' That was undoubtedly the worst thing that ever happened to me in my career in television commentary."

"Yet another seat of the gods, and this time it's Michael Schumacher's Championship-winning Benetton."

"Table 41 at the BRDC Dinner at the Grosvenor House Hotel, scene of Louis Stanley's unsettling speech. Louis is far left, then clockwise, Lady Hesketh, Geoffrey Rose (I believe), myself, Jackie Stewart, Jean Stanley, Alexander Hesketh and Helen Stewart."

Louis Stanley

Murray Walker

"I was the master of ceremonies at the BRDC dinner at the Grosvenor House Hotel in 1994. There were probably about 1000 people there. Louis Stanley, who could be the most pompous, self-opinionated, superior bore you have ever met in your life and was very conscious of his self perceived status in life, was to give a speech. His main claim to fame, apart from running BRM into the ground, was, and this was greatly to his credit, that he had been the instigator of the Grand Prix Medical Unit, which was the predecessor of everything that Professor Sid Watkins has done so magnificently to promote safety in F1.

"So Louis Stanley was giving his speech, and this was to a mixed audience, when everyone is supposed to be having fun and enjoying themselves, and rambled about the medical unit, and ghastly casualties that they had taken, and that they had had to pick up someone's head out of a ditch, and reunite it with his body. There were people shouting, 'No more. Stop.' He went on, and on, and on. I was thinking that I must do something about this because everybody would be walking out.

"I was just about to wait for an appropriate moment, and I was going to stand up and say, 'Ladies and gentlemen, Louis Stanley', round of applause. But [Lord] Alexander Hesketh, who was sitting opposite him, and who he is nothing if not outspoken, leant forward and said, 'Louis, in the name of God, sit down.' Louis sat down. It was a pretty fraught occasion."

Murray's Hip Problems

Mark Wilkin

"His biggest concern was that he wouldn't be able to fulfil his duties. Often commentary boxes are on the top of the stand and that meant 100/150 steps. So we were always very careful to manage his schedules, to make sure he had enough time to get up there without having to rush. Part and parcel is to make sure the performers, because that's what they are, are in a comfortable position. So you work out what their routines are. Some people like to be in the commentary box an hour before and to have complete silence while they mentally rehearse things, other people want to get there two minutes before and not have too much time to mull stuff over.

"You get to know who likes what. Some people like to have a row. Famously, David Coleman would like to argue with everybody because it got him excited and pumped up and his adrenalin running. He would be having a screaming row with somebody seconds before going on air. That was how he fired himself up to perform.

"When Murray had his hip problems, we just had to make sure he had more time to get into position."

"Renault naturally wanted to emphasise their motor sport involvement with publicity shots like this of their BTCC Renault saloon and the Renault-powered Formula One Williams." (BTCC Archive)

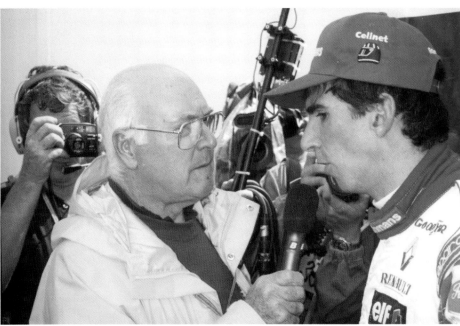

"Damon Hill was under colossal pressure in 1996, his Championship-winning year, and there were times when it looked as though it was getting to him during our frequent interviews. Hardly surprising."

Bemoaning the loss of a high-pitched salesman

SIR—I must make clear my annoyance at the latest actions of the Federation Internationale d'Autosport (FIA). It has been demonstrated to us once and for all that they are more interested in commercialism and money than the interests of the sport.

If they were at all concerned about the many fans of Formula One in the English-speaking world, they would not have been so ignorant as to remove the contract for the television rights from the BBC.

We will lose Murray Walker, the master of the art of commentary, and 30 years of experience in covering grands prix; and above all, us fans will have to put up with several commercial breaks during the course of what could be a very important and exciting race. At last, we have seen the true colours of the FIA.

SIR—Perhaps this is as good a time as any to remind Bernie Ecclestone, the head of the Formula One Constructors' Association, that blaming salesmen for failing to promote a dodgy product successfully is self-deluding.

Murray Walker could sell electric blankets in Barbados. Is Bernie not aware that the only real interest left in watching these two-horse processions is to enjoy the enthusiasm and wonderment of Murray Walker.

Try listening to commentary on Eurosport. They have all the technical knowledge, expertise and jargon that any viewer could wish for. However, it is delivered in a manner reminiscent of my algebra teacher.

Get the product right, Mr Ecclestone. We want motor racing, not party games like 'Which team can change a set of wheels fastest?' Blue Peter did that.

SIR—What a disaster the decision to move coverage of Formula One from the BBC to ITV will prove to be. Their coverage of sport is woefully substandard. They did their best to ruin our enjoyment of the rugby World Cup and the football World Cup's coverage could not even be compared with the BBC's.

Will ITV ruin motor racing coverage, with a succession of advertisements and clueless commentators, as they have all of their attempts at sports coverage? I would like to think not, but I very much doubt it.

SIR—Like your correspondent (Referee blows the whistle on Dark Blues, Dec 12), I, on the whole, applaud the performance of the referee at Twickenham last Tuesday.

However, there is an irony in the result of his interpretation of the advantage rule. He played the advantage in favour of Cambridge against Oxford's off-side infringements. Fair enough. When Cambridge failed to take this advantage, and knocked the ball on, he awarded a penalty try. This gave Ashforth a chance of converting from between the posts and, effectively, gave Cambridge the game. Had they not knocked on and scored in the corner, then nothing in Ashworth's previous form would have led us to believe he would have converted the goal.

Cambridge therefore won the match as a direct result of their own foul.

The Consummate Professional

Alan Fearnley

"One of the Monaco GP weekend broadcasts was done from an exhibition I had one year at Mike McKee's studio just off Casino Square. Murray was chatting away to a group of us, had a tap on his shoulder, swung round, did a piece to camera without notes or, seemingly, any rehearsal, finished, swung back and carried on chatting."

Royal Appointment

Owen Thomas

"We were at Silverstone in what used to be the Dunlop Tower and were on the second floor. The floor below was the BRDC hospitality area in those days. Jackie Stewart always used to host the box down below us and used to have all the VIPs in there – various royalty and so on. Jackie would always pop up, just five minutes before the race and say, 'Do you mind if I bring them up to see Murray commentating?'

"Just to the left of us was the In-vision area with Steve Rider. Murray was in full flow and we had Princes William and Harry up there. I don't think William could have been more than 10 and they were sort of playing with the camera and they were fans of Murray's and they were watching Murray.

"At the end of the race, the Princes had gone back downstairs with Jackie and Murray just said, 'Who on earth were those boys?'

"I said, 'That was William and Harry, Murray'. 'Oh, what did they want? Did they want to come and meet Steve Rider?' It just didn't dawn on Murray that the two Princes had actually come up to see him. It wasn't in Murray's ego to even contemplate that."

The Supreme Golden Egg awarded to
MURRAY WALKER
for a lifetime devotion to the glorious cock-up

Murray made several appearances on Noel Edmonds's top-rating BBC TV 'Late Late Breakfast Show' and was humorously awarded the Supreme Golden Egg, as the citation says, for services to broadcasting

A Young Visitor

Murray Walker

"Silverstone and the British Grand Prix. I got very agitated and excited when I was commentating because I stood up and walked around the commentary box and gestured, looked out of the window and looked at the monitor. At one point I was about to do something and there was a movement by my elbow. I looked down and there were two little boys standing there, so I turned round. I wasn't best pleased because the BBC commentary box is a hallowed place and the people who are in there are the commentator, the co-commentator, if there is one, the producer, maybe somebody else to help and that's it. You can't bring your wife, and friends and family and mates in. So I wasn't best pleased about these little boys being there. When the broadcast had finished I said to Jim Reside, 'What the hell were those children doing in here?' 'Prince William and Prince Harry,' he said. 'Oh,' I said, 'how nice!' They were both motor racing fans and I believe Prince William now has a motor cycle."

The Odd Couple

Murray Walker and James Hunt: not always the best of friends.

For the first two years of Grand Prix on BBC, Murray was on his own. Then James Hunt retired in 1979 and was invited to join in. It was to prove an inspired choice, for Hunt's rich voice and outspoken comments went down a treat with the public. Although the former World Champion was there to add expert colour, Murray initially felt his own position was under threat.

"Basically, as far as I was concerned, James was then an arrogant, self-opinionated Hooray Henry who drank too much and took drugs, and I didn't respect him for any of those things. I'm quite sure he thought I was a pompous old fart who talked too much! But our adverse opinions of each other were certainly never reflected in the commentaries.

"There was something about the chemistry of James Hunt and Murray Walker which worked very well, but actually in the early days – I can say it now, and I don't mean it with too much disrespect – he was an idle bugger. He would arrive five minutes before the race began and, as soon as the chequered flag came, it was as though it was synchronised with a spring up his arse, because he would stand up and disappear from the box instantaneously!

On one notorious occasion in Belgium, Hunt failed to turn up at all, blaming "food poisoning" for his parlous state. He would continually frustrate Murray, who would sometimes turn things to his advantage.

"I would be jabbering away and sometimes, out of sheer devilment because he was sitting there doing nothing, I would ask him a question. I always knew I could get reactions from James by making complimentary remarks, at various stages of our careers, about certain drivers – first of all Nelson Piquet, then Riccardo Patrese – especially Patrese – and then Nigel Mansell.

"We shared one microphone, and James would instantly gesticulate for it, and a torrent of invective would pour from him about the uselessness of Patrese, or the fact that Nigel Mansell had let the side down by going to Indy racing, or that Piquet was a wanker – he actually said on one occasion that, 'The trouble with Jean-Pierre Jarier is he's a French wanker, always has been, always will be ...' Thank you James!

"We almost used to come to blows sometimes. I had him pull the microphone out of my hands, and the producer literally had to stop me from hitting him. I'm not easily roused, but one year at Silverstone I was bloody furious, and I actually had my fist above his head ready to hit him ..."

Over time, the two became close friends. Hunt died suddenly in June 1993, the day after they'd covered the Canadian GP from the London studio. The following week Murray paid a tearful tribute on Grandstand.

"I dare say we both changed to accommodate each other's attitudes. James actually became a lot more responsible about the broadcasts, for all sorts of reasons. Firstly, he got more interested in it, and secondly he produced a couple of sons. He was a marvellous, loving, caring, doting father, and I think he realised he had to get stuck in and make a living, and the world no longer owed him one. He started to work much harder at it, he started writing columns, and because he became a maturer chap altogether he became much more fun to work with. I'm genuinely happy to say that we parted company as good friends and work mates. And I miss him."

> "James then was an arrogant, self-opinionated Hooray Henry, who drank too much and took drugs."

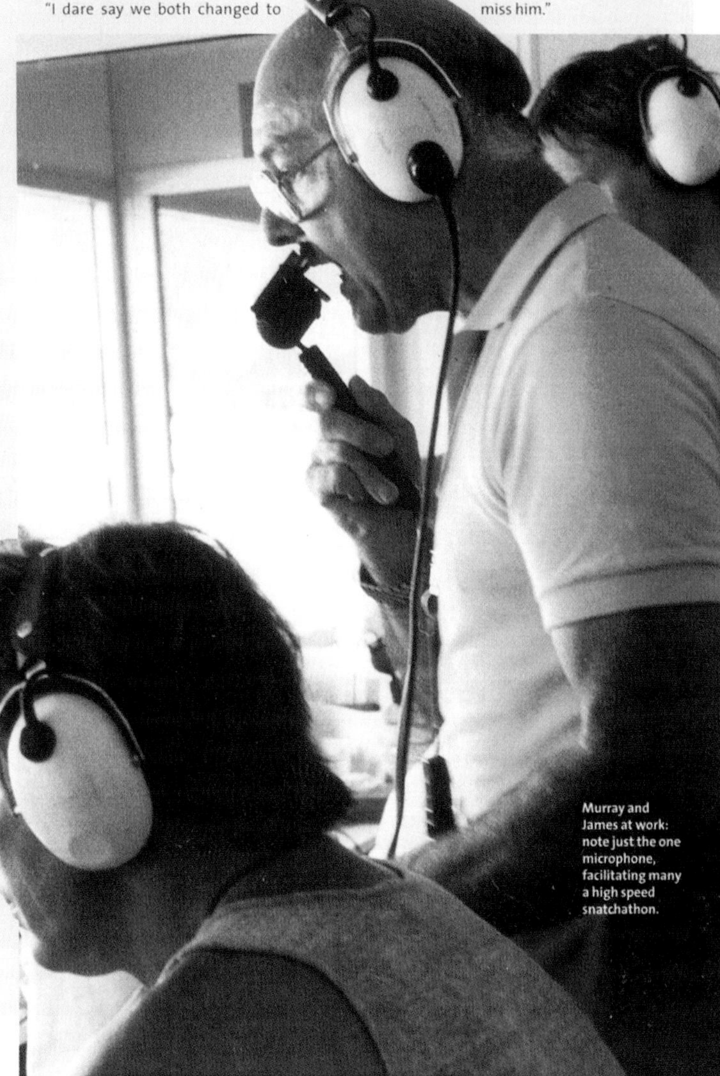

Murray and James at work: note just the one microphone, facilitating many a high speed snatchathon.

10 DOWNING STREET
LONDON SW1A 2AA

From the Principal Private Secretary

2 May 1996

IN CONFIDENCE

Dear Sir,

The Prime Minister has asked me to inform you, in strict confidence, that he has it in mind, on the occasion of the forthcoming list of Birthday Honours, to submit your name to The Queen with a recommendation that Her Majesty may be graciously pleased to approve that you be appointed an Officer of the Order of the British Empire.

Before doing so, the Prime Minister would be glad to be assured that this would be agreeable to you. I should be grateful if you would let me know by completing the enclosed form and sending it to me by return of post.

If you agree that your name should go forward and The Queen accepts the Prime Minister's recommendation, the announcement will be made in the Birthday Honours List. You will receive no further communication before the List is published.

I am, Sir
Your obedient Servant,

Alex Allan

ALEX ALLAN

M Walker Esq
Ashford Water
Sandleheath
Fordingbridge
Hampshire
SP6 1PQ

MurrayismMurrayismMurrayism

> **"And Alesi spins there ... spins out of the race, surely... Yes! ... NO! Alesi manages to keep the engine, does not stall, but of course he will have lost the place, I think. No!"**

In A Different League

Murray Walker

"Jonathan Martin, who was the brilliant BBC Head of Sport for many years, used to say, and these are his words, not mine, that in his opinion F1 was the hardest sport in the world to comment on because virtually all other sports are in the eye of the beholder in the grandstand – football, cricket, athletics, swimming, boxing, tennis – you can sit there in the grandstand and see the whole thing.

"Goal posts at each end, 22 people, you've played the game at school so you know the rules. F1 is entirely different, you have this gigantic technologically-orientated sport which is not just down to the driver, but down to the driver and the cars and the tyres and the mechanics and the technicians and the designer and the people who do the telemetry and the people who make the strategy and the people who implement the strategy and talk to you. It is a great big team effort and if any member of the team drops a ball the whole thing is blown apart.

"If you are sitting in the grandstand they go past you and then 1min 20sec later they go past you again, you almost certainly cannot hear the public address, you may or may not have the big screen nowadays to look at and relate to, you can't read the numbers on the cars because they are so small so the sponsors can get their name in, the positions are constantly changing lap by lap – that is ok for the first 10 laps, then they start making pit stops and unless you are sitting there completely obsessed and probably making a lap chart and probably using a stop watch at the same time, it is very difficult to read a race. Now that's what a TV commentator has to do in motor sport and according to Jonathan Martin, that is the hardest job to do in commentary."

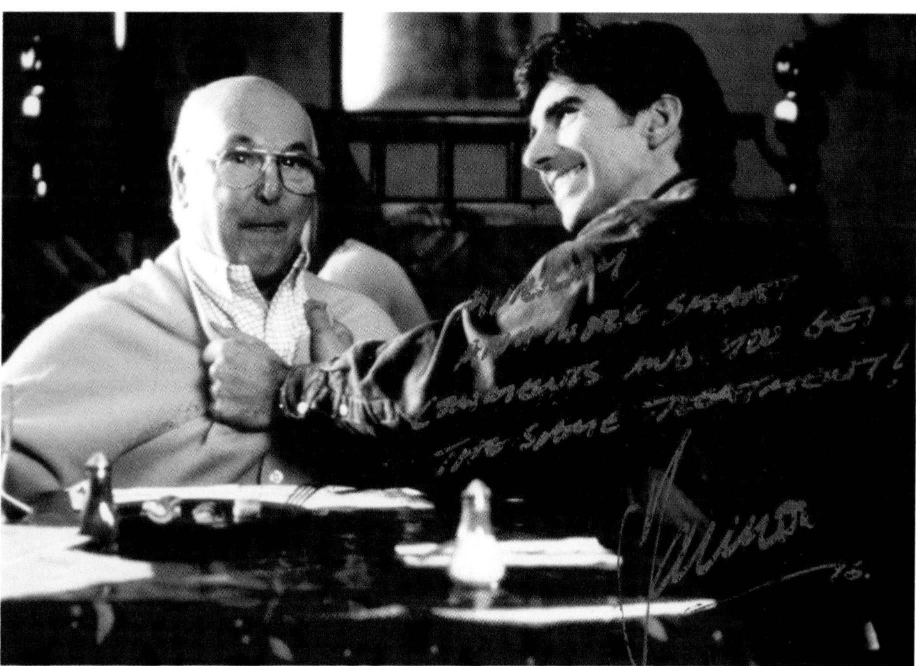

"Damon and I made a brilliantly-successful TV commercial for Pizza Hut's peperonni pizza with stuffed crust in his Championship year. I took the part of his hysterical companion, commentating non-stop, as we enttered the restarurant to Damon's intense irritation. Here's a still which Damon sent me on which he's written, 'Any more smart comments and you get the same treatment!'"

The Beeb Losing Out

Murray Walker

"In 1995, the BBC were negotiating with Bernie for the renewal of their five year franchise to cover F1 racing. The bloke who was doing the negotiation was my BBC mentor, Head of Sport, Jonathan Martin. Things were going well, he thought, until one day the telephone rings, 'Hello Jonathan, it's Bernie'. 'Oh hello, Bernie. How are you?' 'I have rung you to tell you that you have lost the contract and that we are making the announcement in half an hour's time.'

"So when Jonathan picked himself up off the floor, because this was a major, major setback as far as he was concerned, he said, 'Gosh Bernie, you might have given us the opportunity to put in a counter-bid'. Bernie said, 'Unless you have been cheating me all these years, there is no way you can pay what they are paying, so there was no point in talking to you'. So that is another indication of Mr. Ecclestone's nature. He was absolutely right, of course. But not many would have adopted as hard-nosed an attitude as that."

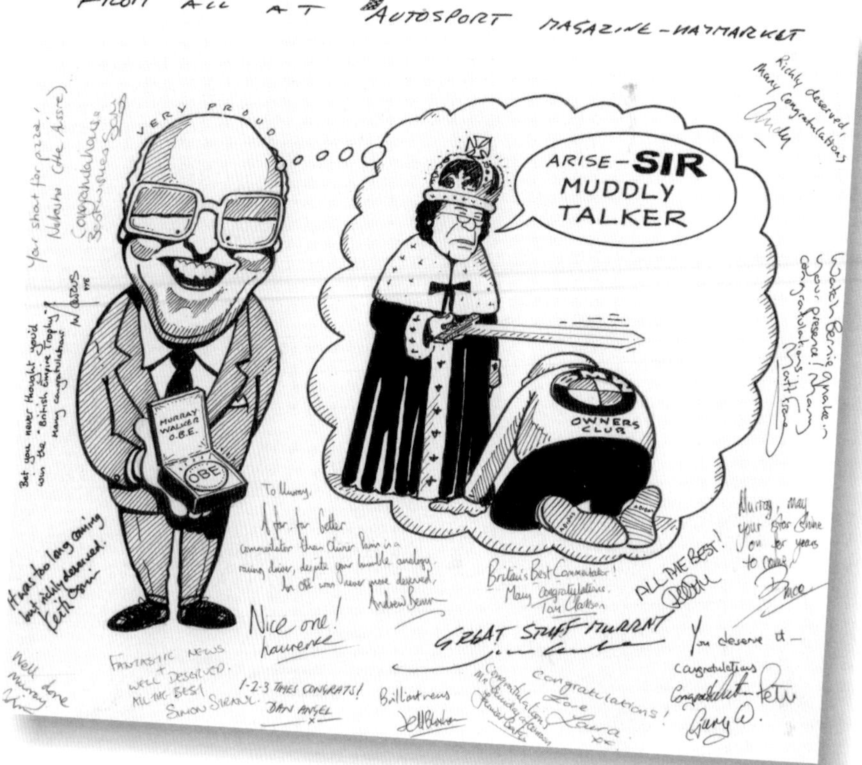

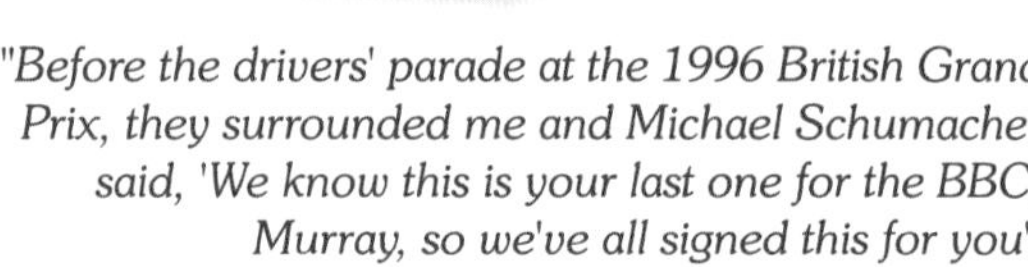

"Before the drivers' parade at the 1996 British Grand Prix, they surrounded me and Michael Schumacher said, 'We know this is your last one for the BBC, Murray, so we've all signed this for you'.

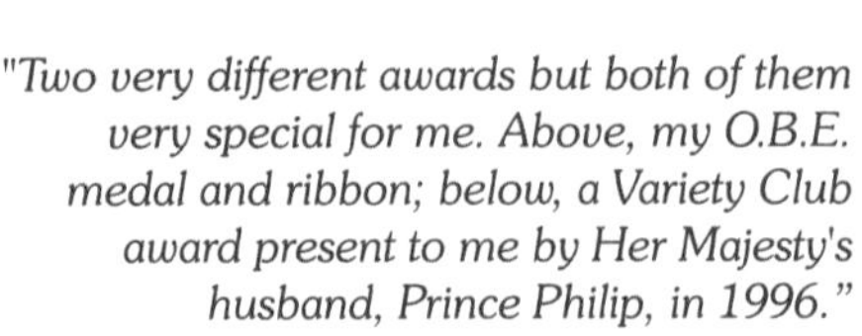

"Two very different awards but both of them very special for me. Above, my O.B.E. medal and ribbon; below, a Variety Club award present to me by Her Majesty's husband, Prince Philip, in 1996."

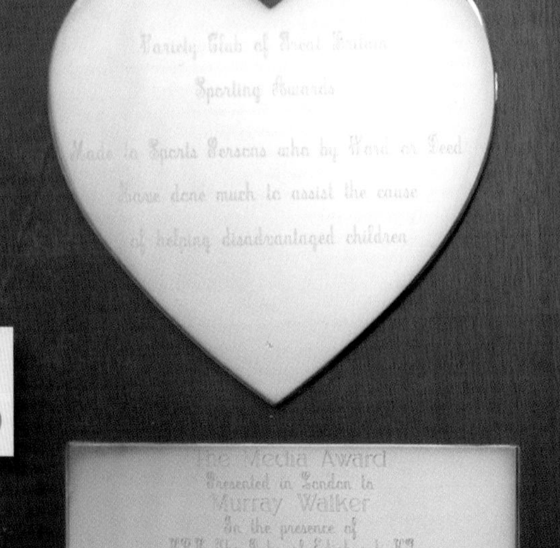

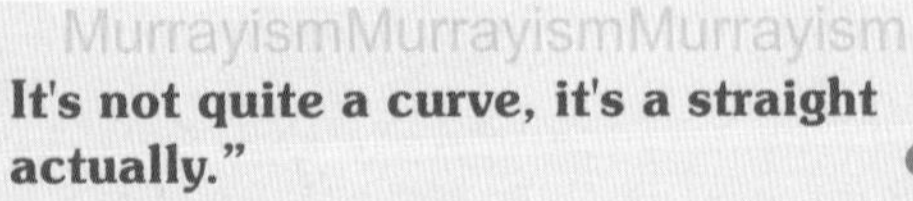

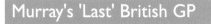

MurrayismMurrayismMurrayism

"It's not quite a curve, it's a straight actually."

Murray's 'Last' British GP

Jim Reside

"Bernie said to me, 'We need to do something for Murray to mark his last British Grand Prix. I've got an idea. Ask Murray to come and see me.'

"Murray went over to Bernie's darkened-window bus which used to sit in the prime position in the paddock and people used to think, 'Oh God, I've got to go and see the headmaster'.

"Murray went over there. 'Murray, Murray, Murray, come in, come in. Your last British GP, I thought there ought to be something memorable for you personally so I've arranged for you to go round the circuit in Damon Hill's car.'

"And Murray said, 'Ooh Bernie, I don't think Damon will be too keen on that idea. Surely it's all set up for him.'

"And Bernie said, 'Not his race car. The drivers' parade car.' And he arranged to go with Damon Hill on race morning when all the drivers paraded round the track on open-backed trucks and waved to the crowd. Honestly, you'd have thought Murray was the driver. The reception he got was absolutely fantastic. Bernie always tells that story with a slight twinkle in his eye."

Honours list is a thriller for novelist Rendell

Ruth Rendell: CBE

By Colin Randall, Chief Reporter

RUTH RENDELL, the creator of Inspector Wexford who-dunnits, joins the rock singer Van Morrison and the master of motor racing commentary, Murray Walker, among more than 1,000 people on the Birthday Honours list published today.

Rendell becomes a CBE in recognition of the doyenne status she has achieved without following the well-worn crime writer's route of applying knowledge gained from a related career or painstaking research.

She has never met a murderer — having turned down one invitation — or interviewed a policeman to obtain an insight into the minds of criminals or their pursuers.

News of the honour arrived as she worked on her latest Wexford novel at her Suffolk home.

"It's wonderful. It is very satisfying to feel appreciated, although I am appreciated by such a large number of readers," she said.

"Van the Man" Morrison's OBE for contributions to music is one of 401 "people's choices" — those made on the recommendation of members of the public in line with John Major's crusade to make the honours system "more classless".

The Prime Minister accepts that such awards, this year accounting for a record 40 per cent, may now have peaked. One of his favourite novelists, Joanna Trollope, receives an OBE.

The OBE for Murray Walker, 72, honours the remarkable second-string career of an advertising man whose enthusiastic, high-octane style of commentary became a fixture of BBC coverage of motor racing. He said: "It is a great honour and I am very flattered.

"I have enjoyed every moment of my career and receiving the OBE makes me feel very humble."

Although ITV's purchase of the rights to screen Formula One from next season raised doubts about his future, Walker has been in talks about a continuing role.

Reports and list: Pages 4, 10 & 11

Royal Presence

Owen Thomas

"On another occasion, same place [commentary box at Silverstone] and Jackie's brought somebody up. I was sort of aware of somebody standing over my shoulder and turned round and there was King Hussein of Jordan who was watching Murray flailing his arms around and gesticulating at the screen, and there were tears in his eyes, he was laughing so much at the way Murray was commentating. And Murray, bless him, was blissfully unaware and King Hussein must have been there for about 45 minutes. Murray was in his own world.

"To this day, I'm pretty sure Murray never knew that King Hussein had been in the box."

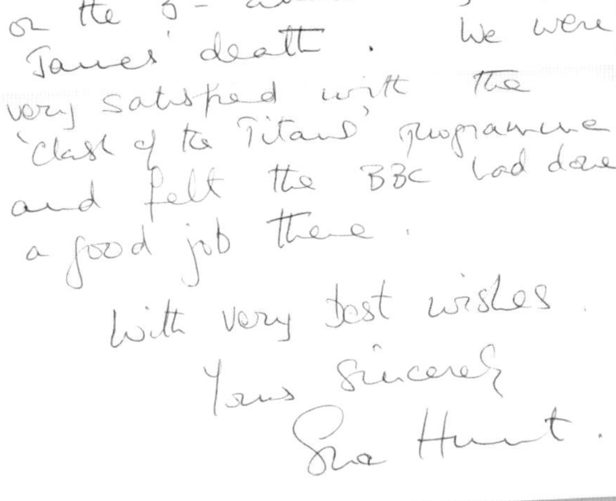

Mr. & Mrs. Wallis Hunt.

17th June 96

Very many congratulations on your appointment as O.B.E. Wallis + I were absolutely delighted when we read the news – curiously enough on the 3rd anniversary of James' death. We were very satisfied with the 'Clash of the Titans' programme and felt the BBC had done a good job there.

With very best wishes

Yours sincerely

Sue Hunt.

This letter is from James Hunt's parents

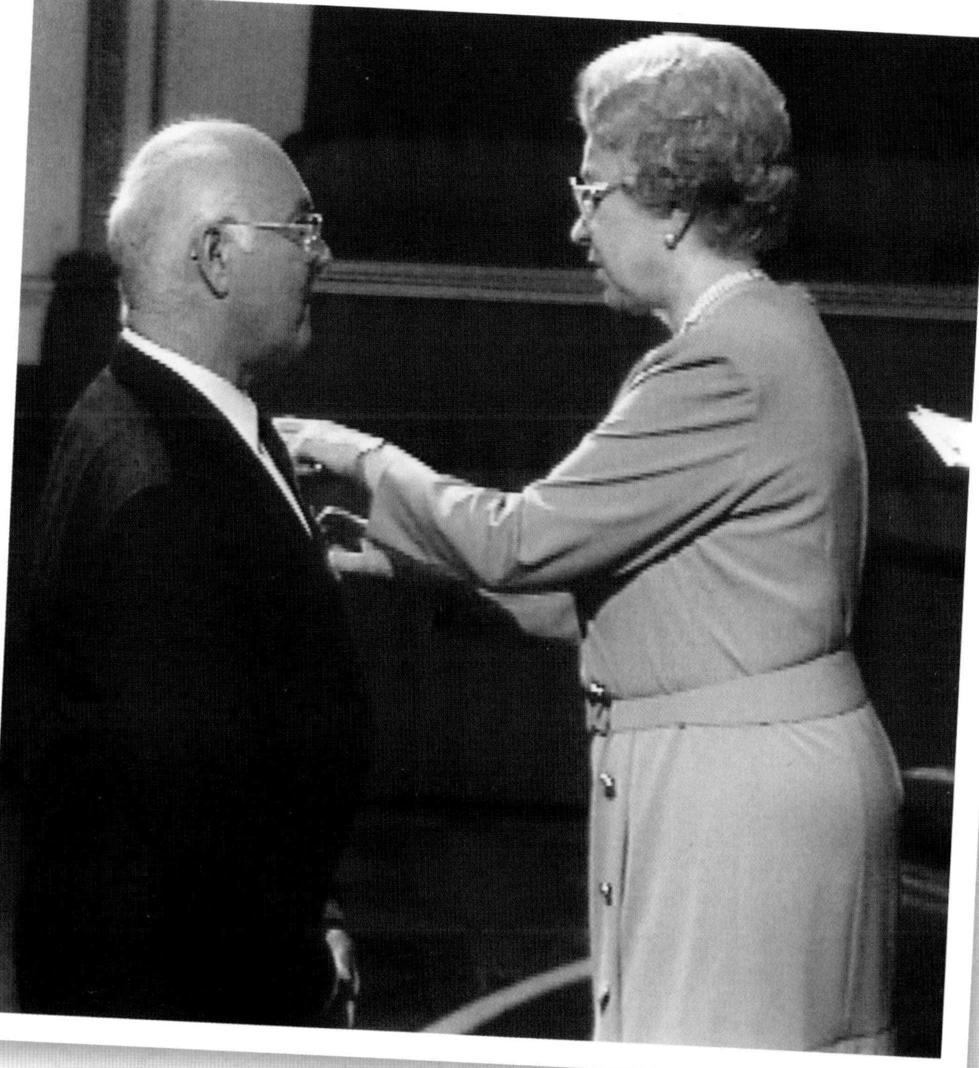

"Her Majesty, The Queen, presents me with my O.B.E. honour at Buckingham Palace."

Fan Club Committee

Murray Walker

"When Bernie said he wanted me to go in the parade car, the Rolls-Royce, with Villeneuve and Damon, I went to the driver's briefing at 11am. To my surprise, when I came out, they formed a ring round me and Schumacher came out carrying a magnum of Champagne and he said, 'Murray, we know this is your last British Grand Prix for the BBC and we have all signed this'. I said, 'Thank you very much' but it wasn't Schumacher, it was Bernie Ecclestone who put them up to it.

"I have said that Bernie has always been very good to me and that is an example."

The Murray Factor

Jim Reside

"At the Barcelona Olympics in 1992 Linford Christie and Sally Gunnell had won gold medals and one of them was expected to win the *BBC Sports Personality of the Year* award, and Nigel Mansell won it. Four years later, Redgrave had won his fourth gold medal at the Atlanta Games but Damon Hill beat him.

"I think both those results prove that Grand Prix racing, whilst some people said it was tedious, and indeed it could be, was extremely popular. Murray made it all so exciting that the BBC audience watched in very large numbers and I think the Sports Personality of the Year with so many motor racing winners (over the years) proves the breadth of the interest. I think Murray was partly responsible for those shock results."

I hope you will enjoy seeing it at the Palace it is quite an occasion.
Many Congratulations again
Affectionately
Bette

British Motor Racing Marshals Club

FOUNDED 1957 RACMSA RECOGNISED

'The Marshals Club'

Dear Murray,

'DUE RECOGNITION'

It is heartening to know that from time to time, due recognition is given to those who truly deserve it.

On behalf of all of the members of the club I am delighted to note your receipt of the Order of the British Empire and offer our heart felt congratulations.

Few people have done so much for motorsport and especially in such an honest and open manner despite the difficulties and tragedies that you have had to endure especially in the past few years.

We are proud to have you as our President and continue to make strenuous efforts to uphold the high standards that you expect and recognise.

I believe that a number of marshals have joined this and other clubs as a direct result of your evident passion for motorsport.

We look forward to enjoying many more occasions when your lively and enthusiastic involvement, together with your indepth knowledge will bring motorsport into the homes of the nation.

Our congratulations once again, together with our very best wishes for the future.

Yours sincerely,

Peter Roberts
Peter Roberts
Club Secretary

"I was deluged with all sorts of congratulatory notes when I received the O.B.E. and none of them was more welcome than that from the great Graham Hill's widow, Bette, who is also, of course, Damon's mother. As well as being a lovely person, she is truly unique for no-one else has been married to, and the mother of, a Formula One World Champion."

The Venerable Society of North Devon Savages.
Dear Murray, 14. 7. 96.
Congratulations on your well deserved GONG.
We enjoy you better than the Racing!
You are the very best, AS WE SAY AGAIN!
There is only ONE Murray Walker,!!
All good wishes Murray,
Woofer Crouch PRESIDENT.

Working With Jonathan Palmer

Murray Walker

"Jonathan Palmer and I didn't get on badly. We didn't have the same rapport but it's no reflection on Jonathan and I hope it's no reflection on me. Jonathan did a very capable job from his expert pundit point of you. He did tend to go on at inordinate length about fuel loads and tyres and so on which, ironically, would be a lot more relevant now than it was then. Jonathan and I had the remainder of the 1993 season together, plus the 1994, 1995 and 1996 seasons.

"During 1996, Martin Brundle was driving for Ligier and sharing a car with Aguri Suzuki. When Suzuki was driving the car, Martin had the time off and hadn't got anything particular to do. Mark Wilkin had the brainwave idea of bringing him into the box with Jonathan and me. To put it bluntly, Martin revealed himself as an absolute natural straight away, and subsequently ITV decided they would rather have him because he retired at the end of 1996.

"I always felt very sorry for Jonathan because he actually did a bloody good job. I don't think it bothered him because he's gone on to much greater things now, running MotorSport Vision which he does well, to put it mildly."

Damon Hill

4 July 1996

Dear Murray,

Many congratulations on your OBE. I can't stand it - I acted my socks off in the ad and you're the one who got the OBE. It's just not fair!

Many, many congratulations - you thoroughly deserved it.

With best wishes.

Brigitte Hill.

pp Damon Hill
(Dictated by Damon Hill and signed in his absence).

"I am a 100% dyed-in-the-wool royalist and my admiration and respect for Her Majesty, The Queen is unbounded. It was a genuinely inspirational experience for me to meet and talk to her at my 1996 investiture."

BMW (GB) Limited

CW/js

Press & Public Affairs
01344 480109
20 June 1996

Dear Murray,

A brief note to offer my sincere congratulations on your O.B.E. I heard it first on Radio Le Mans and there was a universal grin of satisfaction on the faces of my journalist guests.

You have brought so much pleasure to so many motor racing enthusiasts, this accolade is truly deserved and it is pleasing to think that this is recognized at the highest levels.

I hope to see you at Goodwood and I will ring to arrange a lunch before I go on holiday.

With warmest regards.

Yours,

Chris

Chris Willows
Public Affairs Manager

"Prince Michael, Damon Hill and my great friend, Chris Willows sent much-appreciated congratulations, but no - O.B.E. does not stand for 'Old Bald 'Ead'!"

Telemessage®

SOT2762 MSA6183 PFC0019 P052 BUCK0019 18 JUN 1996/1445
BUCKINGHAM PALACE
LONDON
SW1A 1AA

18 June 1996

TELEMESSAGE
MURRAY WALKER, ESQ.
ASHFORD WATER
SANDLEHEATH
FORDINGBRIDGE
SP6 1PQ

FROM: H.R.H. PRINCE MICHAEL OF KENT.

ALL MY CONGRATULATIONS ON YOUR OBE.

PRINCE MICHAEL.

Dear Murray,

Congratulations on your OBE
(As Mike said of Stirling's – 'Order of the Bald 'Ead'!)
Terrific stuff indeed and very well deserved.

Chris.

Damon's Triumph

Murray Walker

"People say to me what are the most memorable things that happened to you in your F1 career. I have been asked it so often that I trot out a standard reply. The first that comes immediately to mind is Damon Hill winning the World Championship by winning the Japanese Grand Prix in Suzuka, in 1996. This meant an enormous amount to me because I had known his father, Graham. Graham, double World Champion, had done commentary with me for the BBC.

"I had known Damon, and Brigitte and Samantha his two sisters, and of course his mother, Bette, for years. Damon and the family were very, very hard hit when Graham was killed because it transpired that Graham's plane's Certificate of Airworthiness had not been renewed. As a result of which the insurance was invalidated, as a result of which there was only one place the creditors could go for money and that was the family. They were really on their uppers, and had a very, very hard time. Bette brought the children up magnificently.

"I had seen Damon go through motor cycle racing, Formula Ford, F3, F3000. Not an obvious superstar, because he wasn't in any of those categories. He didn't win any championships - he won races - apart from a clubman's motor cycle championship at Brands Hatch. Then he got into the Williams team by sheer persistence. So, when he won the World Championship, it was very big indeed. When he crossed the line at Suzuka, I said, and it was entirely spontaneous, 'I have got to stop now, I have got a lump in my throat'. I did stop because I did have a lump in my throat. People have subsequently accused me of having thought that up beforehand, and trotting it out at the appropriate moment. But it really did come from the heart."

Visiting Buckingham Palace

Murray Walker

"I received the OBE from the Queen at Buckingham Palace in 1996. I was there with captains of industry, sports people and all sorts. We were all gathered together and told how to conduct ourselves. A Colonel in the Guards said, 'You will line up, and you will go to Her Majesty one at a time, and when your time comes you walk forward, and you turn to face her and she or may not say something to you. If she does say something to you, you address her as Your Majesty. If she continues talking to you, which she won't necessarily do, you will then address her as Ma'am, as in jam, not Ma'am, as in jarm. When she holds out her hand, it's time for you to get on your bike.'

"So I went and stood in front of Her Majesty and faced her, and she is very well briefed, incredibly well briefed, with someone who mutters a few words to her, and probably said, 'Murray Walker, motor racing commentator'.

"She said to me, 'I have been listening to you for a very long time'. I said, 'I am very pleased to hear that, Your Majesty'. 'How long is it?' she said. I replied, 'Well, it's over 50 years'. 'That is a very long time,' she said. 'Yes, thank you, Ma'am', as in jam. And she held out her hand and I got on my bike."

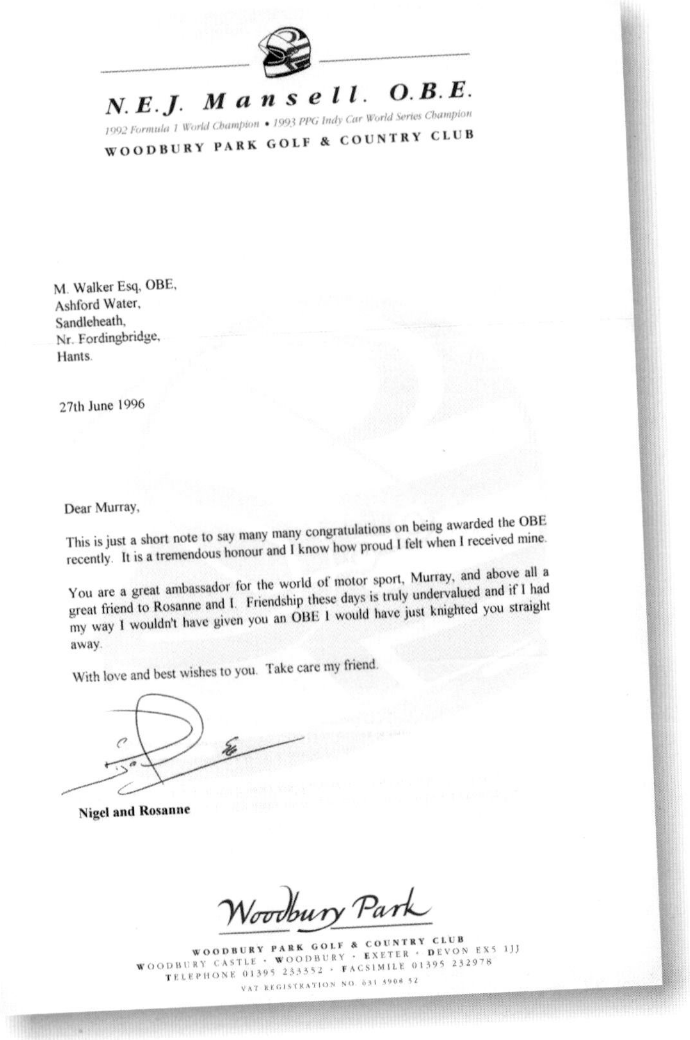

N.E.J. Mansell. O.B.E.

1992 Formula 1 World Champion • 1993 PPG Indy Car World Series Champion

WOODBURY PARK GOLF & COUNTRY CLUB

M. Walker Esq. OBE,
Ashford Water,
Sandleheath,
Nr. Fordingbridge,
Hants.

27th June 1996

Dear Murray,

This is just a short note to say many many congratulations on being awarded the OBE recently. It is a tremendous honour and I know how proud I felt when I received mine.

You are a great ambassador for the world of motor sport, Murray, and above all a great friend to Rosanne and I. Friendship these days is truly undervalued and if I had my way I wouldn't have given you an OBE I would have just knighted you straight away.

With love and best wishes to you. Take care my friend.

Nigel and Rosanne

Woodbury Park

WOODBURY PARK GOLF & COUNTRY CLUB
WOODBURY CASTLE · WOODBURY · EXETER · DEVON EX5 1JJ
TELEPHONE 01395 233352 · FACSIMILE 01395 232978
VAT REGISTRATION NO. 631 3908 52

"Needless to say, for probably the most important single occasion of my life, I wore my best suit, my old school tie, the gold tie chain that Elizabeth and I bought in Vienna and the gold and diamond cuff-links she gave me as a very special present. Oh, and I had my hair cut as well."

A Peer Amongst Peers

Roger Moody

"I worked with a lot of the BBC commentators, in those days, and the presenters. As well as being the producer of *Grand Prix*, I was the producer of *Match of the Day* and *Sportsnight*, and worked on programmes like *Grandstand*, as well as World Cups and Olympic Games. But Murray, for me, always stood head and shoulders above everybody else – a brilliant professional to work with and a lovely person to know.

"For me, that made my life at the BBC very enjoyable."

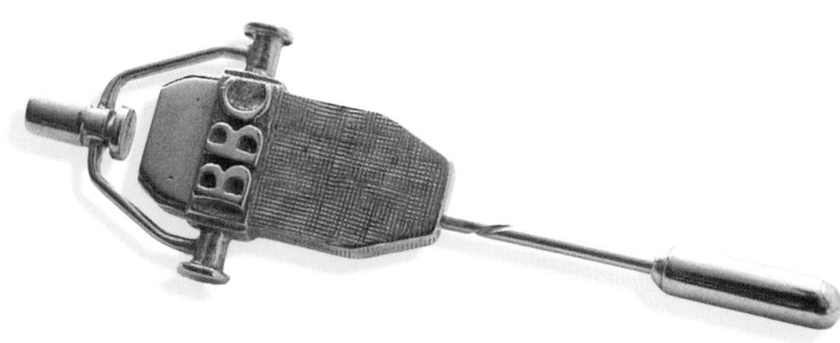

"Above left is the gold 'BBC microphone' lapel pin given to me by Bernie Ecclestone (see 'Bernie'). Bottom left is the great man himself, with the equally great Ken Tyrrell and myself at the 'Good-bye BBC TV' party at the Portuguese Grand Prix in 1996. Above right, Damon Hill tells me what it's like to be World Champion at the 1996 BRDC Dinner."

MurrayismMurrayismMurrayism

"And will Jacques Villeneuve be racing with Williams next year? Well, we will only know that in the future."

A Fair Dinkum Pom

Vern Schuppan

PP: Why is he so popular in Australia?

"It's his total enthusiasm. The odd one has tried to copy him but nobody ever comes close really. I don't know how he makes it so exciting. You hear other commentators and so many just drone on and miss so much. I don't know of any other person in any sport that comes close to the excitement that Murray puts into it."

"Motor sport is lucky to have been recorded by some gigantically talented artists, including Alan Fearnley and Juan Carlos Ferrigno (second and third from left) and Craig Warwick (third from right). Amongst others present at this Grand Prix Sportique function with myself were Prince Michael, Stirling Moss, Derek Bell and Lord Alexander Hesketh."

The Technophobe

Mark Wilkin

"Murray acquired a mobile phone and proudly showed it to me one day. I said, 'Oh good, I've always wanted to be able to get hold of you, when I need you, rather than having to wait till I found you. What's the number?'

"He said, 'Oh, I don't know. Don't be silly. I can't possibly remember all that.'

"Two or three months later, I'd still been asking for it and still hadn't got it, he declared at dinner one night, 'I'm going to throw this bloody thing away. It's absolutely useless. Nobody ever calls me.'"

"It's interview time again. Ralph Firman Jr, right, and Frank Williams, left, at the 2003 BRDC Dinner."

Pieces To Camera

Mark Wilkin

"Pieces to camera were generally scripted. I would say, 'You've got to do the hello and welcome, and lead us into an interview with Damon Hill'. That was how much information he'd get from me. He would then work out, in his head or on paper, roughly what he was going to say. He didn't memorise, he just knew he had to say it was the 15th race of the year, the Championship was going down to the wire and here's Damon Hill's thoughts on it.

"He was very good at it. There's many people you are doing 26 takes for a one-liner. He wasn't the best, but he did it very well. His performance was always right; he'd sometimes stumble over the words. Other people you had to work much more on the performance to get the emphasis the way you wanted it. He had no problem with that. Sometimes he'd just stumble or forget that it was Damon Hill he was going into!"

Murray Walker Esq.,
c/o B.B.C. Sports Department,
B.B.C. Broadcasting House,
London W1A 1AA.

Dear Mr Walker,

It was with great sorrow that we have received the news that the B.B.C. Formula One Grand Prix broadcasts are to be discontinued as a result of commercial pressures.

We understand that the races themselves will, in future, continue to appear, in some form or another, on one of the independent channels, but this will hardly remedy our sense of loss. For us, the pleasure of the entire event of a Grand Prix was provided by your professional, sincere and, on occasion, highly entertaining masterminding of the commentary and presentation, and the excellent coordination and liaison you achieved with the other contributors, sometimes under very difficult circumstances. We rather suspect that Grand Prix commentating is, by its very nature, one of the most skill-demanding of all commentating tasks and we would wish you to know that we recognise the high level of skill you displayed, with apparent ease, in this difficult field.

We write, therefore, to thank you most sincerely for the many hours of enjoyment you have provided during our years of watching your Formula One transmissions, and to wish you all happiness and success in whatever future tasks you undertake.

We shall miss you,

Yours sincerely,

The Rev. M.R.M.Ramsay,

on behalf of himself and

Dr. A.C.A.Ramsay, C.P.O. A.J.D.Ramsay, R.N.

and the ladies of the family.

BRITISH BROADCASTING CORPORATION
ROOM 5106
TELEVISION CENTRE
WOOD LANE
SHEPHERDS BUSH
LONDON W12 7RJ
TELEPHONE: 0181-225 8755 / 6644
FAX: 0181-749 3466

Dear Murray,

Just a short note to mark the end of your involvement in our Grand Prix coverage – and sadly ours. Your contribution to our Formula One coverage has been simply immense – and I am glad we had such a fitting close to the season last weekend.

I look forward to seeing you on November 19, to discuss your future involvement in our Touring Cars Championship output next year and beyond.

Meanwhile, best wishes and thanks for an outstanding contribution to a special part of BBC's sporting history.

Regards

Brian Barwick

"When I retired in 2001, the British Racing Drivers' Club, of which I am a proud member, presented me with its rarely-awarded Gold Medal. Sir Jackie Stewart did the honours at the British Grand Prix where I was privileged to join the few previous recipients, Bernie Ecclestone, Sir Frank Williams, the legendary Ken Tyrrell and Sir Stirling Moss. I am also the equally proud holder of a British Automobile Racing Club Gold Medal."

"I have been lucky enough to work for some truly outstanding people in my career, including Jack Wynne-Williams at Masius, and Jonathan Martin and Brian Barwick at BBC TV. Brian later became my Head of Sport at ITV and is currently Chief Executive at the Football Association. They were all inspirational for me."

Boundless Enthusiasm

Mark Wilkin

"His greatest attribute, I always felt as a producer, was that he was so enthusiastic. This enthusiasm would translate into what he was saying and how he was saying it.

"We used to sit in traffic jams endlessly, getting into European races and particularly at Imola. There was a dreadful motorway system with tolls and then small roads to do the last three or four kilometres into the circuit. We'd sit in these ghastly traffic jams at ridiculous times in the morning and Murray would say, 'Isn't this fantastic?'

"You'd go, 'Well actually no, it's seven in the morning Murray, we had a late night, the traffic jam's awful and I just want to get there so we can have some coffee'.

"And he'd say, 'No. All these people. All these people love what we love as well. Isn't it great?' And that sort of endless, childish, boy-like enthusiasm was how he lived every day – it wasn't just when he was broadcasting."

The All-Rounder

Charlie Whiting

"He knows so much about the sport. He's not just a Formula One person, that's what's so great about Murray. He has such a wealth of vast experience. There aren't many people in F1 who have that sort of knowledge and he was incredible in that respect."

ITV
THE NETWORK CENTRE

MURRAY WALKER JOINS ITV

Veteran BBC motor-racing commentator Murray Walker is to join ITV when the channel takes over television coverage of Formula One next season, it was confirmed today.

Murray has signed a two-year deal to be ITV's principal commentator for the Grands Prix.

Speaking at 'Setting The Pace', an event to launch ITV's 1997 programme schedule to advertisers and agencies, Network Director Marcus Plantin said, "I'm delighted to be able to end recent speculation and welcome Murray to ITV. Public support and affection for him is enormous. He is a wonderful ambassador for the sport, and viewers and those in the Formula One community have tremendous respect for him.

"All of the production companies which tendered for the ITV contract supported Murray for the lead commentator's job, and I'm delighted he's agreed to join us."

Murray Walker said, "It'll come as no surprise to anyone that Grand Prix motor racing is my absolute passion. Naturally, I'm overjoyed that I'm going to be able to continue to communicate my enthusiasm to the English - speaking world as part of ITV's Formula One team.

"I've been really impressed with ITV's exciting ideas to make a great sport even greater. I'm convinced that next year's coverage of Formula One is going to be outstanding and am greatly looking forward to working with ITV".

"The guests at the BRDC Dinner are a daunting audience to address because just about anyone who is anyone in motor sport is sitting there in front of you in the Great Room at the Grosvenor House Hotel."

JACKIE STEWART, O.B.E.

25 September 1996

Dear Murray.

I read with great happiness to-day in the Daily Express that you have agreed the deal with ITV. I am thrilled for mostly you, but certainly also for ITV, who I am sure are very happy to have you on board.

All best wishes and many congratulations.

Yours sincerely

Jackie

I See No Note

Roger Moody

"Murray would not stop talking. We always liked the pictures to tell the story, which was alien to Murray, because he always thought the words tell the story, as much as the pictures. Very often I would write a note for Murray, during his live commentaries, saying, 'Shut up, Murray'! I would jab Murray very viciously in the ribs and shove this piece of paper under his nose. He would stop for a nano-second, look at the piece of paper, look at me, and then go on. He wouldn't take a blind bit of notice. That was Murray."

"When BBC TV lost the Formula One coverage franchise in 1996 and I switched to ITV, Autosport published this typically perceptive and humorous Jim Bamber cartoon."

Happy To Be Public Property

Vern Schuppan

"He is such a genuinely nice bloke. He's always got time for everybody. He'll sit and chat away with anybody who wants to talk to him, but many in that position would just want to avoid contact with the public at that level. He never seems to shy away from it."

Dear Murray,

My wife and I, like many more people in England, were up to listen to you at 4.45 on Sunday morning and we just felt that we had to write to you after what was a very emotional day.

So often commentators are accepted as part of the furniture and are not given praise enough for their contribution to significant sporting events that we witness.

We would like to thank you for bringing the whole race into our lives and charging us all with such emotion. Two of your comments

"I am afraid I am going to have to stop talking now as I have a lump in my throat".

"To viewers in New Zealand, South Africa .... because thats our boy"

I believe will go down in the annals of television history. They bring the same level of excitement to me as the famous Ken Wolsenholmes "they think its all over".

However having watched the Grand Prix live and then again at 8.00am we then stayed up to watch the Grand Prix at 10 o'clock at night.

A lot of people would have missed this programme and not fully appreciated your own personal feelings being the end of a long and incredibly distinguished career with the BBC and especially the Grand Prix programme for the last 20 years. This was a very significant day for you also.

"It was typical of Bernie Ecclestone, who was responsible for BBC TV losing the Formula One franchise to ITV, to ease the pain with a wonderful party at the Portuguese Grand Prix where he presented the BBC with this superb silver trophy. Damon Hill, David Coulthard, Martin Brundle and Johnny Herbert enjoyed the occasion as much as I did."

BBC BROADCAST

DIRECTOR OF TELEVISION
AND CONTROLLER BBC1

To: Jim Reside

cc: Jonathan Martin
Brian Barwick

GRAND PRIX

Many people have mentioned to me this week how much they'll miss the BBC's coverage. Suzuka was a fantastic race to go out on and the highlights of the programmes history felt very appropriate on Sunday evening. Its a very sad moment, but its good to see so many people recognising the quality and superiority of the BBC's coverage, which almost everyone recognises will not be matched by the competition. You and the Grand Prix team have done a superb job.

Best wishes.

(Michael Jackson)

Media Award

Murray Walker

Most people in this country shut their eyes and by sound only immediately recognise the voice of Murray Walker, undoubtedly the doyen of all commentators connected with motor racing. Murray injects such excitement into his commentaries that even when there is a clear leader in any Grand Prix, he keeps people glued to their screens, expecting something to happen at any minute. A worthy winner of our Media Award.

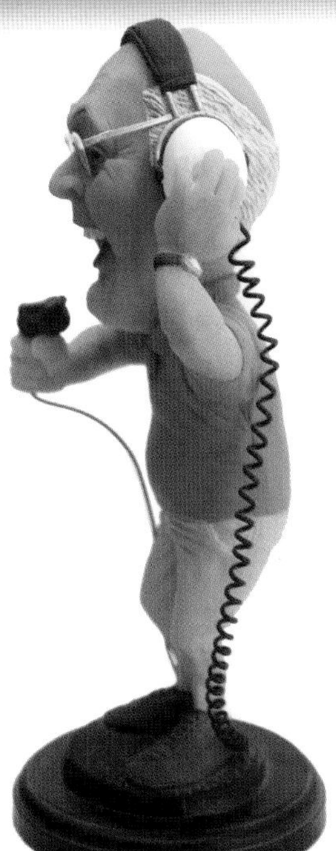

Several figurine manufacturers have featured Murray strutting his stuff. This one brilliantly captures his 'trousers on fire' commentating style

Daily Mail, Friday, September 20, 1996

Murray keeps pole position in TV switch

MURRAY WALKER will continue to commentate on Grand Prix races when they move from the BBC to ITV next year.

Walker (above) has agreed to work for the production company MACh 1, which yesterday signed a £15million deal to cover the Formula 1 Championships for five years from 1997.

The 72-year-old has commentated on Grand Prix since 1949 and is so closely associated with the sport that three of the four companies who submitted bids to make the programmes believed he was vital to their success.

Former Formula 1 champion Nigel Mansell and commentator Steve Rider may also join MACh 1 after this year's final Grand Prix in Japan next month.

MACh 1 was formed by the Anglia and Meridian TV companies, and independent producer Chrysalis Sport.

Bernie

Murray Walker

"Bernie is a hard man, a tough man, but he is also a good-hearted man with a very good sense of humour and loves winding people up.

"One year I was walking round Monaco, by myself, before the race on the Wednesday. A Fiat limousine drew up alongside me, and a dark tinted window at the back went down, and a pair of horn rimed glasses looked at me, and a voice said, 'Do want a lift?' So I said, 'Thank you, Bernie', 'cos that's who it was. I got in the car, he asked where I was going and took me to the paddock. I got out and thanked him.

"I was a bit surprised when he got out as well and walked to the back of the car, and he produced a piece of tissue paper from his pocket. He said, 'I was walking down Bond Street and I saw this in a jeweller's and I thought you might like it'. I undid the bit of tissue paper and it was a 22 carat gold pin, an exact reproduction of the old BBC table microphone, the octagonal one with BBC across the middle of it. I was absolutely bowled over by this. I said, 'Gosh Bernie, I don't know what to say'. He said, 'Well, you are the BBC aren't you?'"

F1 With ITV

The change, in 1997, from BBC to ITV was a radical one to say the least. Competition is a very healthy thing and ITV would certainly raise the standards considerably. There were those who felt the coverage by the Australian TV stations had, as with cricket for example, raised the bar considerably and the BBC had been rather left behind. The upside of the switch was that ITV invested heavily in improving the TV coverage with an expanded team of presenters, greater coverage and various technical advancements. The downside was the adverts but something had to pay for the improvements.

ITV very wisely employed Murray as main commentator and equally wisely brought in Martin Brundle as the resident expert. Apart from Murray's unique abilities behind the microphone, retaining him gave ITV the continuity it required as it stepped into a completely new field. Recruiting Martin was another masterstroke because, as he had proven with his occasional appearances on BBC, he was an absolute natural and the two gelled superbly. Indeed, ITV even started a programme on Grand Prix weekend Saturday afternoons entitled *The Murray and Martin Show*.

The initial ITV team was completed by journalist and broadcaster, James Allen, in the pits, supplemented by former journalist and PR lady, Louise Goodman. Additional expert comment came from Tony Jardine and Simon Taylor, and the presenter was football commentator Jim Rosenthal.

The announcement regarding ITV winning the contract was made by Bernie Ecclestone with one final year of the BBC's contract to run. To all the world, therefore, this looked like the end of Murray's career. There was uproar in many quarters and the media took great delight in stoking the debate. The *Daily Mirror* even ran a "Save Our Murray" campaign and others ran headlines such as, "ITV motor racing deal leaves Walker in pits". In actual fact, Murray had signed a deal with ITV soon after that first announcement but was sworn to secrecy and had to play along with all the rumour, speculation and even the tributes!

During 1997 something rather different, and very surprising, happened to Murray. He was the victim on the long-running television programme, *This Is Your Life*. It must have been very difficult to squeeze all Murray's achievements into a half-hour slot.

Just as the BBC coverage had followed on from James Hunt's winning of the World Championship, so ITV began their coverage after Damon Hill's similar feat in 1996. Sadly, success was thin on the ground for British drivers during Murray's four-year reign with ITV. The British constructors, though, were more successful and Williams drivers, Jacques Villeneuve and Heinz-Harold Frentzen, occupied the two top spots, respectively, in 1997. Mika Hakkinen took the 1998 Championship in his McLaren from Michael Schumacher who was gradually succeeding in rebuilding the Ferrari team around him. In third position was David Coulthard for the second year running.

The following season Hakkinen made it a brace of Championships but, due to Schumacher's leg-breaking accident at Silverstone mid-season, it was Eddie Irvine who stepped in to take the role of number one in the Italian team and very nearly annexed the ultimate prize. Frentzen was third in a Jordan.

In the year 2000 Schumacher added to his trophy cabinet by taking his third world title, chased by Hakkinen and Coulthard. Once again Schumacher dominated in 2001, this time followed by Coulthard in second place and Michael's loyal team mate, Rubens Barrichello, in third spot.

Following an unwarranted and unkind attack in a national British newspaper, the sensitive Walker's mind turned to thoughts of retirement. Though famous for his gaffes, or Murrayisms as they became affectionately known, or Muddly Talker, as he was also fondly known, Murray was enormously admired and respected, having found a place in the hearts of many millions of viewers. Rather than be vilified for his occasional slip, as some sensation-seeking journalists suggested he should be, he was only loved all the more for being Murray. Ironically, many of the so-called gaffes are, actually, apocryphal!

This is an age of grey people and the media, surely, are responsible for this. National figures, from politicians to sporting stars to TV personalities, live in dread of saying or doing the wrong thing, which has drained the personality out of most such people, at least in public. Characters are a rarity, an endangered species. Murray is a character, able to combine pre-eminent professionalism with his very personal human elements.

To leave when you are at the top of your profession takes strength of character and courage. We have often seen personalities who have clung on too long, witness certain racing drivers. Murray was determined not to fall into that category. Though he disappointed many, from Bernie down, he announced his impending retirement at the end of 2000. The plan was to do one more year, sharing commentating responsibilities with his designated successor, James Allen, who would do five of the 17 races. One thing, thus, was guaranteed – Murray would have an amazing final year as the motor racing world, quite rightly, paid due homage to the man who, together with Bernie, had transformed motor racing by bringing the sport to many, many millions, giving untold pleasure in the process.

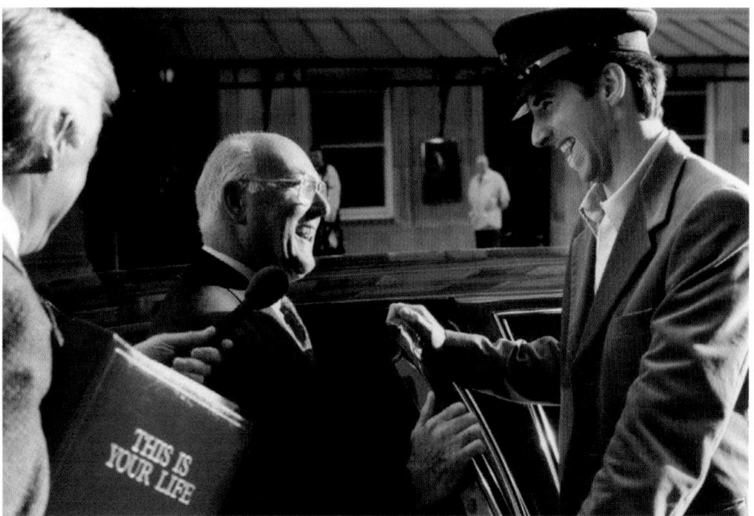

"With a smiling Michael Aspel holding the Red Book, my 'chauffeur', Damon Hill, ushers me into the Volvo for our ride to Shepperton Studios."

Working With Martin Brundle

Murray Walker

"It was very different (from working with James) with me and Martin Brundle because we got on extremely well as individuals. Martin has a very well-developed sense of humour – he has been there and done that in terms of being a racing driver, World Sports Car Champion, he has driven for eight Formula One teams, he's been on every step of the podium except the top one, he knows what he's talking about, he is a good politician and, most importantly from my point of you, he was, and is, a team player and would defer to me, as I would defer to him when it was necessary from my point of view. Probably Martin had to make quite a lot of the accommodations when he started off in the box with me, because I was very dominant as I had been doing it for years."

MurrayismMurrayismMurrayism

> **"This will be Williams' first win since the last time a Williams won."**

"On stage with me at my 'This Is Your Life' programme were so many of my friends, including Simon Taylor, Tony Jardine and my ITV successor, James Allen."

"Martin Brundle explains to Jonathan Palmer, Elizabeth and I how we swayed from side-to-side together in the commentary box 'like a couple of windscreen wipers'."

"On my right my life-long friend, Brian Emerton, alongside Damon Hill. I've had a lot of emotional experiences in my life but having so many people who meant so much to me, singing my praises was a real tear-jerker."

How It Came About

Martin Brundle

"In '95 I was sharing a drive with Aguri Suzuki in the Ligier Mugen Honda thing. So I would fill in. On the Saturday I'd do Eurosport and on the Sunday I would do BBC. I wasn't always that welcome to the resident experts at the time. I forged, I guess without realising it, a working relationship with Murray. Then, at the end of '96, when ITV got the deal, everybody assumed that I was going to do it, much to my annoyance because I expected to carry on Grand Prix driving. I ended up really with nowhere else to go apart from signing the ITV deal. It was a sort of a self-fulfilling rumour really."

The Young Apprentice

James Allen

"I wanted to work in television, I wanted to work on the programmes that Murray was making, that's what I'd wanted to do since I was a kid at school. I had been cutting my teeth with various cable channels, encouraged by Andrew Marriott. When ITV took over, I was involved from a very early stage.

"We always got on well because, although he is at least 40 years older than me, mentally he has always been a young man, and still is. Apart from the genes that he inherited from his mother's side of the family, I think it is his greatest strength that he has always kept himself very young. He has always hung around with people who are a lot younger than him."

"Martin Brundle and I at our first British Grand Prix together for ITV in 1997. The commentary box isn't the luxurious place a lot of people think it is."

"A thrilling race for me. Alan Fearnley's wonderful painting shows race winner, David Coulthard (McLaren), giving it plenty as he leaves the pit lane just ahead of Jean Alesi (Benetton), who finished second, less than two seconds behind the Scot."

Mutual Admiration Society

Murray Walker

"Martin said that he made a policy decision that if old Murray can stand up for the whole race then I certainly can. He used to stand just behind me with his hand on my shoulder. I was a lot freer [with the microphone] with Martin than I was with James. During my commentary, it would be obvious where I wanted him to pick up. I would physically look at him or point. We also had a system of hand signals. If he really wanted to say something, and I was boring on, he would give me a really, really good shake. We worked very well together. We didn't need a lot of prompting or interrupting because neither of us was selfish with the microphone.

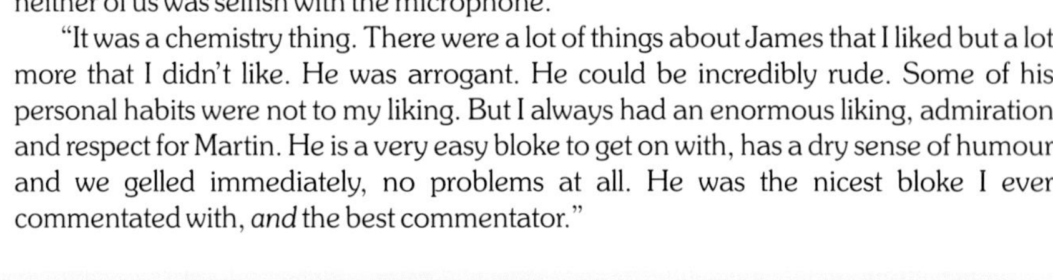

"It was a chemistry thing. There were a lot of things about James that I liked but a lot more that I didn't like. He was arrogant. He could be incredibly rude. Some of his personal habits were not to my liking. But I always had an enormous liking, admiration and respect for Martin. He is a very easy bloke to get on with, has a dry sense of humour and we gelled immediately, no problems at all. He was the nicest bloke I ever commentated with, *and* the best commentator."

A 'Close' Relationship

Martin Brundle

PP: "You seemed to have a mutual respect for each other instantly. There was rivalry with James, but there is no hint of that with you at all."

"No, absolutely not. We had a microphone each, we had a system to take over next time either of us drew breath, and it worked. I found him very genuine. I think, as soon as he realised I wanted to work with him, and not try and dominate or push myself, he became very generous.

"I think one of the smartest things I have ever done in either of my two careers was to choose to stand up and talk to Murray and I think that formed a bond. We talked to each other, with a few million people listening in. We looked at each other when we were conversing and I thought, 'If it was good enough for him, it's good enough for me'. And he's right, you can deliver better anyway when your lungs are not restricted when you're sitting down. So, from the first moment of first qualifying I stood and that created a relationship which obviously endured for five years.

"We had a show together, the *Murray and Martin Show*, which was like a magazine style thing. We were flat out all weekend. There'd be the qualifying show, the *Murray and Martin Show*, the race show - more than we've got now in many respects. All weekend we were trudging all over the venue trying to find different backdrops for a new link - down town or out with the fans or whatever. Saturday afternoon, particularly, was frantic.

"I smashed my feet and my left ankle badly in the Tyrrell in '84 and I struggled to stand sometimes, especially if the broadcast was extended by a red flag situation or wet weather. So I would have to rest my foot on something, otherwise it gets too painful.

"Once, I got my foot caught round a cable to his headphones without realising it. I went to shuffle position to ease the pain in my ankle a bit and I have this vision of Murray coming towards me! I was dragging him across the commentary box by his headphones, without realising it.

"I think I had the audience with me and I could gently rib Murray, because he did say some funny things, and not always intentionally, but it was always done out of endearment and respect. There was this sort of sub-plot going on where we could, in a gentle way, enjoy some of Murray's idiosyncrasies and bloopers, as such!"

BRINGING A FEMININE VOICE TO GRAND PRIX

Has Louise got the formula to keep Murray on the right track?

THIS is the woman who will bring the feminine touch to Formula One. Louise Goodman is one of the stars of ITV's new Grand Prix motor racing commentary team.

She joins veteran presenter Murray Walker — poached from the BBC — former driver Martin Brundle and Jim Rosenthal.

The line-up was revealed yesterday as ITV previewed its Grand Prix coverage. The channel snatched the sport from the BBC in a £70million five-year deal.

Miss Goodman, 33, who is single and from Oxford, will file pit lane reports.

An ITV spokesman said: 'She is blonde, but she's no bimbo. She knows everything there is to know about motor racing.'

Miss Goodman has covered the sport for Irish television and has been a press officer for the Jordan racing team.

She said: 'A lot of women think they need an intimate knowledge of the mechanical side of racing, but they really don't.

'Many women are passionate followers of Formula One and I think the audience will continue to grow.'

ITV's coverage starts on March 9 with the Australian Grand Prix — when viewers can find out if Miss Goodman can help Walker avoid his famous verbal slip-ups.

Walker: Slip-ups

Louise Goodman: Will report from the pit lane

"Two very important women in my life - on the left, my beloved mother, Elsie, on her 101st birthday and above, Louise Goodman, such an outstanding presence in the pit lane and paddock for ITV. Both of them the greatest of fun with very strong personalities and enormous charm."

Keeping Pace

Murray Walker

"I have a fax and a computer and a mobile phone and all the rest – not because I am particularly good with them – my wife is infinitely better - but because if you do what I do you have to have them. I couldn't live without emails, a mobile or a fax because if everyone communicates like that with each other and you haven't got one you are unable to communicate with them or they with you, and life today is all about communication. So, I am a reluctant technophile."

Coping With The ****** Commercials

Brian Barwick

"I worked for the BBC from 1979 until 1997, ending up as Head of Sport, and from ITV from 1998 until 2004 as Director of Sport. At the BBC I was mainly involved with football, but at ITV I became very involved with our motor sport coverage and thus came into direct contact with Murray.

"You couldn't reconstruct Murray's commentary style because the word unique does not do it justice but I was able to help him, even in the autumn of his career, just to be a better commentator than he already was. I often used to draw diagrams for him. One was of a graph with an ascending line from left to right and then that line goes vertically down – like falling off a cliff face. When you go to a commercial break on ITV, which he had to get used to doing, his commentary should end anti-climatically. It should not be, '...Mika Hakkinen is ahead of Damon Hill and this is going to be the most amazing tussle between them,' and then go for a break. You could feel the whole of the nation throwing cushions at the telly!

"By the drawing I tried to explain to take words d-o-w-n rather than up. And he tried his damnedest to do it."

"My friends, the stars - part seven. Above, on the left, Gary Anderson, the enormously talented Formula One designer who, for a variety of reasons, was never able to exploit his knowledge and ability to the full, and to the right, the irrepressible Eddie Jordan, whom I knew and worked with from his time as a Formula Ford driver to his retirement as an outstanding Formula One team owner."

"Five friends together on the Cunard's QE2 liner on their way to New York, prior to the 1997 Canadian Grand Prix. Two of Formula One's top journalists, Nigel Roebuck and Alan Henry on my left and right, with touring and sports car star John Fitzpatrick (white shirt) and the great Jo Ramirez, then McLaren's Team Co-ordinator."

"Margaret Thatcher's redoubtable Press Secretary, Sir Bernard Ingham, presents me with the Television and Radio Industries Club Special Award in 1997."

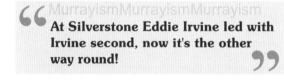

MurrayismMurrayismMurrayism

> **"At Silverstone Eddie Irvine led with Irvine second, now it's the other way round!"**

The Production Angle

Neil Duncanson

"We inherited the F1 contract at the end of the 1996 season. There was a national press campaign by the *Daily Mirror*, a 'Save Our Murray' campaign, and it was unthinkable that we would carry on without him. We did want to make quite a lot of quite significant changes to the way the coverage was done but working without Murray we couldn't countenance. So, it worked out extraordinarily well and, to be honest, he was one of the key pieces of continuity that enabled us to make such a good running start to our coverage of F1 on ITV.

"We had another stroke of luck in that Martin had retired as a driver at the end of the '96 season and was interested in getting involved in TV. I don't think he realised how good he was going to be but the two of them hit it off straight away.

"They were always quite amusing to watch in the commentary box. Murray stands up to do all his commentary and because he gets so involved he tends to sway backwards and forwards. And Martin started to do it as well and they looked like a pair of well-worn windscreen wipers after a while!"

"I think this explains itself but just in case it doesn't the caption says, 'Congratulations on 50 Glorious Years from the only magazine that's ever managed to shut you up'. Under the inspired leadership of Editor, Matt Bishop, F1 Racing was a breath of fresh air in Formula One and became the top-selling publication of its type in the world. I enjoyed contributing on many occasions, one of which sadly included bitterly offending the charming Peter Sauber."

Relaxing The Troops

Neil Duncanson

"The first Grand Prix was a good memory. I was editing the programme and there was a degree, as you would expect, of nervousness with our first race, live from Melbourne in March, 1997. We were all sitting down at breakfast on the morning of the race, quite early, before we strolled across Albert Park.

"No-one was saying very much, and Murray came in. There was a breakfast buffet bar and Murray walked up to it, and started commentating on what he was going to have for breakfast. 'What will Murray have? Murray will have cereal, with fruit…' and on he went. Everyone was laughing and it just completely broke the ice. We all relaxed instantly and we had a very good day."

> MurrayismMurrayismMurrayism
>
> **"I've no idea what Eddie Irvine's orders are, but he's following them superlatively well."**

Number One

Murray Walker

PP: "Are the drivers, by nature, very self-centred people?"

"I think all racing drivers, all sportsmen are almost certainly self-obsessed and unbelievably selfish because they are in a gigantically competitive environment. Life is like a pyramid and the higher you go, the less room there is. At the top there is only room for one and everyone is clawing at your feet to replace you with themselves. When you think about these chaps who made their way up to F1 through karting, Formula Ford, Formula Renault, F3 and they are obsessed with winning. If Nigel Mansell was playing tiddly-winks with his children he would have to win because that it is the way they are made. In order to win, you have to be selfish on occasion and you have to bear in mind that the first person you have to beat is your team-mate because he is the only one who has the same equipment. So, yes they are and I don't see how they can avoid being unbelievably selfish. They can be nice people as well – David Coulthard, Stirling Moss – you couldn't meet nicer blokes."

More Advice

Brian Barwick

"I also said that if there were two Ferraris going into the first corner, just say there are two Ferraris, don't try and name them. You can only be right or wrong, but if you are wrong, you are absolutely wrong. Sometimes just take a breath, just pause, before you absolutely identify who's in the car. It is not easy to identify the cars these days with all the sponsor stickers all over them. The days of a large number are gone and often you use the driver's helmet to recognise who it is. And although TV slows them down, they are still going bloody fast.

"Never be scared about making a mistake - because that was part of Murray's make-up – but don't celebrate the mistakes, let them happen but don't build them into the commentary style."

This Is Your Life

James Allen

"I had got Michael [Schumacher] to do a piece to camera for Murray's *This Is Your Life* programme. I spoke to his press officer and I explained I needed Michael to do a little, 'Sorry I can't be with you, Murray, but you've had a fantastic career…'

"So I went and saw Michael and he did a great piece, a very affectionate piece, saying, 'You've been in the sport a long time and I've got great respect for you…' and that meant a lot to Murray."

"Trying it for size while Trials superstar, Sammy Miller, looks on. Sammy and I go back a long way to the beginning of his incredible career during which he won over 1000 Trials to become, in my opinion, the greatest ever. Sammy now masterminds his superb motor cycle museum at New Milton (Hampshire), which is a Mecca for any true enthusiast."

"I really can say I was a man with a golden mic because this one was presented to me to celebrate 50 years of commentary at the Prescott Hillclimb in 1998 at a special Auto Windscreens function."

Bournemouth University

At a Ceremony held on 11 November 1998

Murray Walker

being a person distinguished in eminence and by attainments was duly admitted to the degree of

DOCTOR OF ARTS

honoris causa

Chancellor

Vice-Chancellor

Chancellor

Murray is too modest to mention it but he has been awarded honorary degrees from four different universities and says he feels rather guilty that he got them all without any studying whereas most people have to do so for years

Fever Pitch

"With Murray, as soon as something was happening – you could be in another room – you could just tell something exceptional was happening by the pitch of his voice. If you'd gone to the loo, you'd certainly know you'd missed something by Murray's style of voice."

Being A Brick

Neil Duncanson

"Murray was much like a father-figure to me. He was terrific on guidance and advice if ever I had any problems. I would bounce things off him and he was marvellous to me in what could have been a very difficult period. We had many different factions – BBC resources and ourselves, an independent production company, plus the ITV Sport guys. Pulling that all together could have been quite difficult but he was tremendously helpful in making sure we all worked nicely together."

PRIDE: Murray Walker, honorary Doctor of Arts at Bournemouth University Picture: Richard Crease

Podium tears for F1's Murray

TAKING pole position on the podium yesterday, Murray Walker OBE, became an honorary Doctor of Arts at Bournemouth University.

The famous voice of Formula One motor racing, Mr Walker was attending the first day of the Bournemouth campus graduation ceremony, at the Bournemouth International Centre.

Watched by nearly 450 graduates in their gown and mortarboard finery, and hundreds of proud parents, the veteran BBC broadcaster said: "I have never been given such a great honour as the one you have bestowed upon me today and I wish you every success in the lives ahead of you.

"I am the first ever member of the Walker household ever to have received a degree without having to go through years of slog and backbreaking, like you have."

He went on to say that his uncle, however, had been a professor of South African history at Cambridge.

And there were tears in his eyes when Mr Walker, of Fordingbridge, said that a two-minute silence –observed in the hall only moments earlier in memory of the Armistice – had really moved him as he had driven a tank in the Royal Scots Greys, during the Second World War.

Students walking to the stage to collect their hard-earned certificates from the University's senior staff included journalism, PR and media production graduates.

Of those graduating from the journalism, seven out of 10 have already found work in the newspaper industry.

Dr. Walker shows his pleasure on receiving his honorary degree at De Montfort University

Murray's Quirks

Brian Barwick

"Seven times out of 10, they added colour, and three out of 10, they were a pain in the butt! A good example of a bad one would be where he'd do a one-to-six (race positions) and, A. he'd never get to six, and, B. by the time he got to number six, the positions had changed!

"I said to Murray and Martin, 'If you start a one-to-six, your responsibility to the viewer is to finish it'. But Murray would get to number two and give you a life story of the guy in second and forget he had to get to numbers three, four, five and six. I also told both of them it was a neutral way of getting into the break.

"Now it's very easy for me to say this - they had a producer shouting in their ears, the cars were going round very fast, they were checking lap times and all the rest of it, but that's what they were paid to do.

"Having said all that, Murray was an absolute diamond of a commentator and was a pivotal part of ITV's success in Formula One. ITV cleverly took Murray on board. Murray weighed it up and decided he loved F1 more than he loved the BBC. Everyone at the BBC was aggrieved for 20 minutes but then understood it. Murray was the entry point for lots of viewers to F1 motor racing and the familiarity of his voice meant that ITV got off to a flying start. Also they discovered that Martin Brundle was a fantastic analyst for that sport and I think, to this day, including my old profession [football], he is one of the top three sports analysts in British television.

"The combination was brilliant because Martin found a polite but firm way of putting Murray right when Murray was on a flight of fancy! They became a formidable commentary team – Murray with his huge affection, love, knowledge, enthusiasm for the sport, and Martin had been in the cars and had a younger brain. The combination was dynamic."

October 23 1999 - No. 18 - £2.50
•JAPANESE GP PREVIEW•
F1 news
WHAT'A MISTAKE'A TO MAKE'A!
Marlboro
MURRAY WALKER
76 NOT OUT & STILL HOLDING A STRAIGHT BAT
PANIS FOR McLAREN?
FRENCH GP IN TROUBLE
puts the fun back in formula one

In 1997 celebrated china manufacturer Royal Doulton commissioned Stanley James Taylor to model this amusing, limited edition 'Toby Jug' as a tribute to Murray`s achievements

A mug with character

Murray Walker, the motor racing commentator, always reckoned he knew enough about the sport to prevent anyone making a mug out of him.

Now, however, it has happened to the man who throughout Britain is known as "the voice of motor racing." Furthermore, it is happening in the heart of the Midlands.

For the Royal Doulton factory in the Potteries' city of Stoke-on-Trent is producing a new addition to its international best-selling range – a Murray Walker mug, officially styled "character jug".

The jug, which will be made in a limited edition of only 2,500, is decorated by hand in the John Beswick studios of Royal Doulton at Stoke.

Modelled by one of the firm's top ceramic artists, Stan Taylor, Murray follows in a long line of sporting stars, politicians, royalty, entertainers and other distinguished celebrities who have been featured on similar styles over the years.

Collectors around the world have formed extensive collections of them and many of the earlier ones now out of production, fetch large sums today.

In addition to his smiling features and unmistakable spectacles, the handle is decorated with a chequered flag and, of course, a microphone.

Presented with one of the first likenesses to come from the works, Murray said: "Working so closely with such gifted Royal Doulton craftsmen and women has been an amazing experience. It has been wonderful to watch how their creativity and care has brought the entire character jug to life."

The Murray Walker character mug is available from Lawley's By Post and costs £59.85. To order, call 0345 023444.

The McLaren Two-Seater

Murray Walker

"Going out in the McLaren two-seater was absolutely fantastic. McLaren had built this car and the performance was virtually identical to the then F1 car because, although it carried two people, they compensated for the extra weight by having a smaller petrol tank. So it didn't weigh very much more than the normal car. They said that this car is going to take a maximum, ever, of 130 people in it. I was the first!

"We went to Silverstone, Martin and I, to do a thing for ITV but first I had to have a major medical with X-rays and getting on the treadmill to check heart rate and all that sort of thing to make sure I was fit enough to do it. I was very pleased because I passed but one of the leading daily journalists, who was half my age, failed.

"We get to Silverstone and it's actually quite a daunting experience. You get into the back of this car and you are belted in and you've got all the kit on - the racing underwear, racing boots, three-layer suit, crash helmet, neck brace and all the rest of it. You sit in the back seat and then you have to splay your legs open as wide as you can. In the gap they put the driver's seat, so your knees are under his elbows. In order to support the back of the driver's seat, they put in a big carbon fibre bar and it bears right up against your chest. You've got the choice of either putting your hands on your knees underneath the bar or your hands on your chest with the bar forcing them into your chest. I decided I would put my hands on my chest in the naive belief that, if anything went wrong, with one mighty bound I could fling my arms out and spring free.

"I said to Martin, 'What happens if we spin and go into the bank backwards? You'll have a spring up your arse and you'll be straight out of the cockpit and I'll be trapped and won't be able to get out.' He said, 'Won't happen, Murray'."

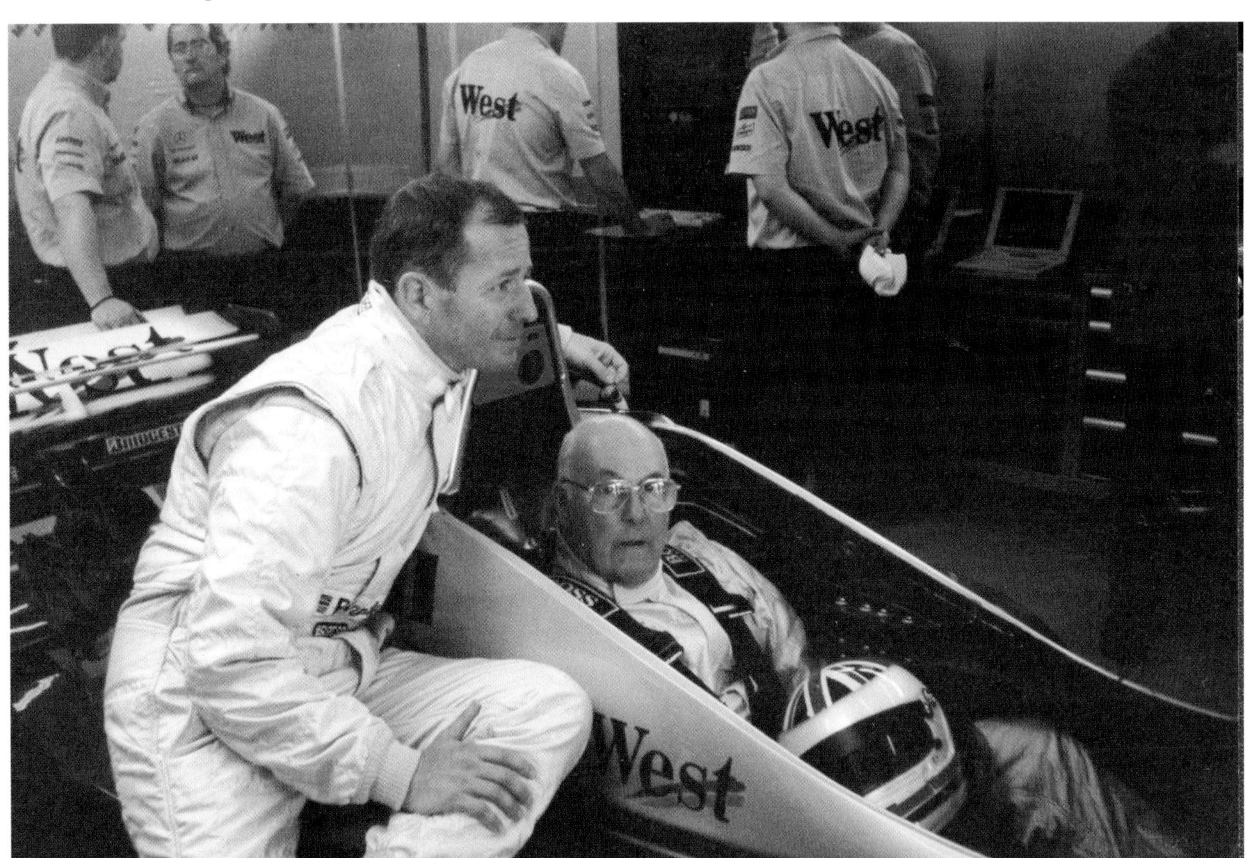

"Another day of my life I'll never forget is the fabulous ride I had in the Formula One McLaren two-seater in 1998 with my co-commentator and ex-Grand Prix star, Martin Brundle, at the wheel. It wasn't so much the speed that impressed me as the unbelievable G-forces. Five continuous laps was more than enough for me."

Formula One Experience

Murray Walker

"The experience was unbelievable. It wasn't so much the actual speed, even though we were doing about 190mph down the Hangar Straight on the way to Stowe Corner, because I had been very quick in other things being driven by other people. It was the unbelievable G-forces - braking, acceleration, sideways through corners.

"I had a kind of cylinder in my hand and it had a plunger. As long as I kept the plunger pressed, a red light in front of Martin would not go on, but if I let go the plunger this big red light was going to come on, and it was supposed to tell him to stop. Whether he would have or not, I don't know.

"You can't see very much because you have got the driver's headrest in front of you, but if you tipped your head to the right or the left, you could just see a bit in front of you. As a passenger, you really can't see where you're going, you don't know when he's going to be braking, you don't know when he's going to be accelerating. You're trussed up like a chicken, you can't move and it's a gigantically stressful experience.

"McLaren had said no-one is ever going to do more than three laps, and as far as I know, no-one, other than me, ever did do more than three laps. But this was the first day and we went out in the morning, and it was wet and we did three laps. When we came in Martin said, 'Well that wasn't very exciting'. I thought it was bloody exciting. He said, 'If it's dry, we will go out in it again this afternoon'."

And After Lunch...

Murray Walker

"So we had lunch and it *was* dry. Martin said, 'Look, do you think you can stand five laps Murray, because if we did five laps, we'll do an out lap, three quick laps and an in lap'. I said, 'Martin, I will stand five laps if it kills me, because I am never going to be able to do anything like this again', experiencing something of what it is really like at speed in a proper F1 car of today. I had driven a McLaren F1 car at Silverstone in 1988, but that had a DFV engine producing about 450hp. This was a full-blooded V12 Mercedes-Benz knocking on 1000hp. So we did five laps, and if Martin had said to me over the intercom on the fifth lap, 'Would you like to do another lap Murray?' I think my pride would have made me say, 'Yes Martin, I'd love to', but in actual fact I didn't want to do another lap at all.

"I was so absolutely shattered with the noise, the vibration and the G-forces that I had had enough. It increased the enormous respect I already had for F1 drivers. Imagine doing it at Monaco, two hours of that non-stop, trying to get past the bloke in front, trying to stop the bloke behind from getting past, coming in and making pit stops, changing tyres - I mean quite amazing. It was an experience I would not have missed for the world."

"'Martin, my old chum, that was fantastic.'"

Come In Louise, Come In James

Louise Goodman

"I suppose the most famous cock-up with me was at the Canadian GP. Twice he got my name wrong when he threw down to me. On the second occasion, he said, 'Right, we're going down to Louise Allen in the pits...'

"I did my report and at the end said, 'Right, back to Murray Brundle', just to take the mickey out of him.

"At the Belgium GP of '98, there was the big shunt at the start, and it was obviously going to take quite a lot of time to clear up the track. So James decided to nip off and have a quick pee while there was a bit of a break because once the race started, we were going to be full on. He had just availed himself of the facilities but luckily still had the headphones on, when, 'Right James, what's happening down there?'"

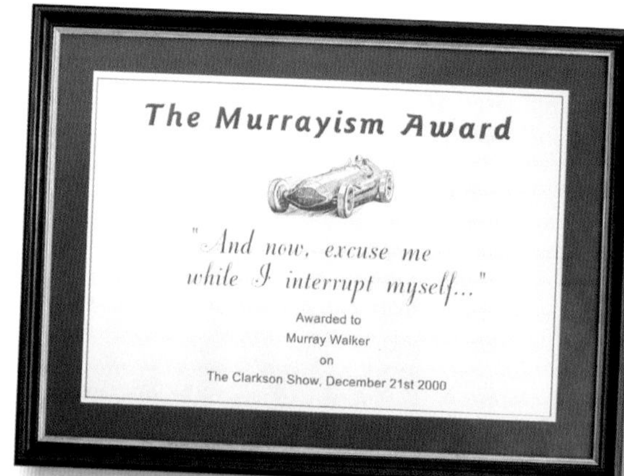

The Murrayism Award
"And now, excuse me while I interrupt myself..."
Awarded to
Murray Walker
on
The Clarkson Show, December 21st 2000

Live From The Gents

James Allen

"Murray always had a producer in the box, who was in touch with the editor, who is the boss in television terms, and he would hold up boards, telling Murray when to go to a break or there was a report from myself or Louise to throw to. Part of the reason for that was Murray used to quite often throw to us [James was nearly choking with mirth as he recalled this!] without any warning!

"So, at Spa while the clearing up was going after the accident, I reasoned it was probably a good time to go to the toilet as I wouldn't get another chance for two and half hours. I was in a portaloo on the outskirts of the paddock somewhere and I had one-piece, fireproof overalls on – this is probably more detail than you need – but I obviously had to remove this but I kept my headphones on so I could listen to what was going on. You can picture the scene. And Murray threw to me!

"The etiquette was that I would tell the editor I had something to say and the editor tells Murray via these 'cheat boards' and Murray throws to me. But, he went and threw to me anyway.

"So I was scrabbling around on the floor, grabbed my microphone and made some sort of report off the top of my head. It was, by far, the most extraordinary circumstances I have ever broadcast in!"

Career Inspiration

Herbie Blash

"I remember the name Murray Walker more than I remember any other name when I think back to my childhood. It was so important to me – watching the scrambling on Saturdays. That was inherent in my falling in love with, and becoming involved in, motor racing. For me, Murray was a very big name, very much a star."

"In 1999 I took my courage in both hands and not only competed in one of the motor cycle races but started it as well (don't ask). This is a very apprehensive me, worried about how to stay upright in the wet, chatting with Trials and road racing genius, Sammy Miller, who wouldn't have been at all worried."

"Goodwood Revival. Damon Hill (who, not many people know, actually started his competition career as a successful motor cycle racer) does a bit of hand-language about riding his Manx Norton and, yes, that is the great Barry Sheene behind me and, of course, he won the race."

Respective Roles

Martin Brundle

"I always say starting to do sports commentary with Murray Walker is a bit like having Pele teach you how to play football, starting with the best. So I was very lucky I could learn from the maestro, and what I particularly enjoyed was that he could talk for England - he always had something to say with great enthusiasm and genuine passion.

"This gave me the chance to step back and think about what was going on in the race. We have two distinctly different jobs. One is the colour commentator – 'The sky is blue, the crowd is big, it looks like a great race today…' Then there is the expert witness, if you like, which is my role - what is significant about the sky being blue, the track will be hot and how is it going to affect the cars.

"So, whilst you work together, you actually have very different roles to play to complete the picture. It was great because we never trod on each other's toes really. His job was to pump up the event, my job was to put the viewer behind the steering wheel or on the pit wall. He was obviously the dominant one, he was the primary guy picking it up, and then I could come in when I wanted to.

"There is all this talk about Murray being greedy with the mic and certainly I have always said I could have crept out the back of the commentary box and gone home, and I don't think Murray would have noticed until the end of the race because he was so engrossed in, and so genuinely passionate about, what was going on."

The Challenge Of Fame

Murray Walker

PP: **"**Is it a downside that one is recognised?"

"Yes! It is very flattering when people come up to you in the street wanting to talk to you or when you are at the British GP and you are besieged with people wanting autographs. But it is also gigantically frustrating, because you are trying to do a job and they are there socially and they subconsciously expect you to have the time and inclination to talk to them and it's not that I am reluctant to talk to them, but if I am on my way to interview Michael Schumacher, I haven't got time to give 50 autographs or to have a cheerful chat with normal enthusiasts.

"So, I can well understand the attitude and points of view of F1 drivers and famous sportsman who brush their fans off, notwithstanding the fact that I always say to them, 'Look, they are the people who are your bread and butter, enabling you to make the massive salaries and income you do and enjoy the life you have, so be nice to them and talk to them and let them have their photo taken with you and give them your autograph'. But when the boot is on the other foot, I can see what is bugging them. Their attitude is, 'I am here to be a racing driver'. It's not that they don't like people. They don't want to be distracted and it is the same with me.

"You are walking through the paddock at Silverstone and someone comes up and asks for an autograph. They are very pleasant and you stop. Then others see and suddenly you are surrounded by maybe 200 people. You then get to the point where you can't go on so you say something like, 'I can do five more then I am sorry I have to go'. Then the sixth person says, 'So, I'm not good enough for you?' And you say, 'Of course you are, you are no different from all the others I have been signing for and I would like to continue, but you don't seem to realise that I am working here. I have a job to do and I have to give priority to that.' My problem was that, like the drivers, the public saw me as a personality because I was the bloke who talked to them out of the box about their interest in life. If I were a mechanic, they wouldn't have known who I was and wouldn't have wanted my autograph."

"In 1999 I drove Damon Hill round the British Grand Prix parade lap at Silverstone in a vintage Rolls-Royce. Well, I say I drove Damon Hill but he was actually the world's worst backseat driver!"

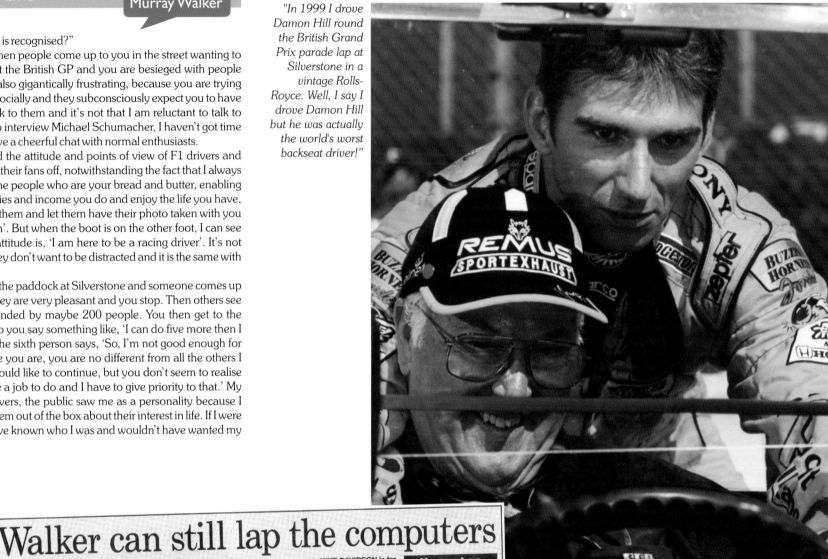

Walker can still lap the computers

IS Murray Walker a motor-mouth as Mike Davidson suggested in *Sportsmail* on Tuesday? Or is he still the viewers' favourite? We asked for your views and the vote was a decisive 68 per cent in favour of Murray keeping his Formula One microphone. Here is a selection of your views.

He must stay

MURRAY is a sports TV icon working in the toughest broadcasting environment — live sports. He is a hugely valued member of ITV's award-winning Formula One team and long may he remain so. Murray and Martin Brundle did a great job describing one of the most action-packed races in recent memory — a race which was so sensational, the F1 computers at the circuit couldn't keep up with what was going on. Even they crashed!
Paul Tyrrell, Head of Press and PR, ITV Network Ltd

ON MANY, many occasions 'Hurry Talker' has been far more entertaining than the actual racing.
Ray Mitchell, email

F1 RACING without Murray Walker would be like Eric Morecambe without Ernie Wise: possible, but not entertaining.
R Dixon, Great Bookham, Surrey

I TOTALLY disagree with your paper's stance regarding Murray Walker. It is quite true to say that he makes his share of mistakes but, then again, so does Michael Schumacher and no-one is suggesting he should retire.
Dominic Jones, email

MURRAY WALKER should not stop doing what he does, because he does it brilliantly. He injects his commentary with enthusiasm, speed, excitement and yes, the odd mistake. But that's what makes it so special. He's like an excited schoolboy who is at his first Grand Prix.
Joanne Davies, Darlington, Co. Durham

MURRAY retire? No way! We all sit in front of the TV yelling at him to be quiet but who could do it better? He should go on forever. His knowledge is outstanding and his humour is the best. Don't give in Murray — stay in the fast lane, not the pits.
Colleen McNaughtan, Plymstock

He must go

MIKE DAVIDSON is far too generous in his article re: Murray Walker. Walker has always been an irritant, his hypermanic hyperbole has driven me to distraction for many years and when ITV took over from BBC I thought at last we would see the last of him. Sadly, not to be.
CJ Cooper, Beverley, East Yorkshire

MURRAY WALKER'S voice is excruciating. I bet he never auditioned for the job. Walker reached the sound barrier years ago. He should retire gracefully.
Ed Burrows, Wilmslow, Cheshire

AT LAST someone has had the courage to come out and say it. Murray Walker should go, go, go — in his own words at the start of every race.
Mrs VP Harris, Wokingham, Berkshire

WHAT a breath of fresh air when Murray Walker was missing. He speaks without thinking and makes gaffes.
Pat Feltham,email

MURRAY WALKER is a Schumacher apologist and should go as he is in Bernie's pocket.
George Baird, email

I couldn't agree with your article more. Our family adore F1 — and try not to miss one minute of it. But, we all seriously suffer from Murray Rage — the man is a menace.
Peter Rowcliffe, email

The Power Of Television

Murray Walker

PP: "You were more famous than a lot of the drivers."

"Yes, that is a function of the fact that my voice and my face have been on the box and if you are on the box in someone's living room you are their friend because if you are not their friend, they can turn you off. So if you are their friend, and have been for 60 years or so, they have grown up with you. You know there were a lot of people who, until I retired, had never heard anyone but me talking about F1 on radio or television so it is not surprising that they were going to like me or loathe me. Thankfully more people liked me rather than loathed me!"

Non-Mutual Recognition

James Allen

"He was upgraded to First Class on the way to Australia one year and he was sitting next to this *very* pretty girl and she was talking to him, and obviously knew who he was, which is not unusual for him. And he said, 'Oh, and what do you do?' And she said, 'I'm a singer'. He said, 'Oh, that's nice', and they had a chat for a while.

"It was Kylie Minogue, and he had no idea who she was!

"On the one hand, you wouldn't say he was 'hip with the kids' but neither was he the uncool old grandpa. Mentally, he was tuned into modern culture and I think a large part of that came from his advertising background. Obviously, when you are in advertising, you need to be fresh with ideas. He always wanted to know what the latest thing was. On the way home in the car, he'd say, 'So, what have you learnt today, James?'"

"'Don't worry, Murray' says Sammy Miller, who was about to get on his four-cylinder Gilera, 'All you have to do is lie flat on the tank, open the throttle and you'll blow us all away'. Fat chance!"

"No wonder I looked so apprehensive on my Manx Norton at the 1999 Goodwood Revival - that's John Surtees's fire-breathing scarlet four-cylinder MV Agusta alongside me with Formula One winner, Gerhard Berger, on his supercharged BMW Twin in the background."

MurrayismMurrayismMurrayism

"A battle is developing between them ... I say developing because it's not yet on."

The Fun Of The 'Fare'

Neil Duncanson

"Because Murray was the only person to commentate on Formula One, people didn't realise how difficult it was – it's not like a cricket match or a football match where there is an ebb and a flow, and even a half time. This thing flies past you at 200mph and Murray tried to follow it at the same speed. Inevitably, the odd glitch crept in! But incredibly, he was able to make a virtue of it. We had a lot of fun with him mis-identifying people, mispronouncing things and getting his phrasing round the wrong way but no-one seemed to mind too much. We had a lot of fun with him."

Murray, The Magician

Stirling Moss

"People laugh at his mistakes, but really he is a very knowledgeable person. He actually does know a lot about motor racing - not only in the past, but what goes on now.

"He is one of the few things that makes F1 really quite exciting. Listening to his commentary, one could really think something is going on. Then, when you look at the picture, it doesn't match! That is something I have always admired about him."

THE WORLD'S BEST-SELLING FORMULA 1 MAGAZINE

F1 RACING

itv SPORT www.itv-f1.com

F1 2000 www.EASports.com

APRIL 2000 £3.40

SUITS YOU!
MURRAY'S BRITISH GP SPECIAL P67

The new season kicks in
All the news, views and action from Melbourne

Villeneuve vow
More progress and less politics – then he'll stay

PLUS

ON BUTTON
Jenson gets that *TFI Friday* feeling

TRICK TRUCK
F1 lorries cost half a mill. Here's why

BARRICHELLO
Writes exclusively on his Ferrari debut

JARNO AND FISI
Who will end Italy's 40-year title wait?

9 771361 448039 04>

"My friends, the stars - number eight. The world's only Formula One car and Grand Prix motor cycle World Champion, John Surtees demonstrates full lock to an astounded Stirling Moss and myself. Can you see a likeness between Stirling and I? Lots of people seemed to and, if there is one, I'm very flattered."

"'Now look here, Minister of Pensions, Alistair Darling, I think you ought to do more for old chaps like me.' But of course, he shuffled off to become Chancellor of the Exchequer before he had time to."

The Mechanics' Friend

Jackie Stewart

"Murray had a wonderful relationship with all the mechanics because at the end of the day they are the surest form of clear and deep information on a driver's behaviour or the manner in which he uses a car. So he had a very good relationship with them. One of Murray's great skills is his ability to communicate. He gets on with everybody. It doesn't matter who it is or from what background they come, Murray is the same Murray for everybody. I think he got a lot of respect from the mechanics on that basis."

"The start of my McLaren 'teach-in' at Woking in 2000 - left to right, my great friends Neil Trundel who is McLaren's top gearbox man, the charismatic Jo Ramirez and (blue shirt) George Langhorn, ex-McLaren tyre man who now runs the team's superb paint shop. This was a great fun day and taught me a lesson in the nicest possible way."

"The McLaren rear wing end plate which was presented to me at the end of my memorable factory tour and which had been signed by every member of the team."

Apolitical And Admissible

Ross Brawn

"My impression of Murray is of an absolute consummate professional. His enthusiasm gives him a certain air but underneath he is actually a very professional guy, who always made a great deal of effort to make sure he had the right information and knowledge about what was going on.

"He was also somebody who seemed to rise above the politics and nonsense, a lot of which goes on in the Formula One paddock, which meant he was always welcome wherever he went.

"He had great judgement about knowing what to get involved in and what not to get involved in. You will find that with every other television commentator or other media journalist, there will be somewhere in the paddock they are not welcome or don't go because they have had a fallout at some stage in the past. It was to Murray's credit and due to his professionalism that he could go anywhere he wanted and be made very welcome. That was what I always admired about Murray, that he was part of the F1 circus but he never seemed to offend anyone but still did a very informative job. I don't think he ever got caught up in any of the gossip and scandal that's pretty rife in Formula One most of the time. He still managed to keep people entertained and wanting to watch F1."

Being Turned By McLaren

Murray Walker

"In the year 2000, I was being pretty eulogistic about Ferrari and McLaren got fed up with this. Instead of taking me aside in the paddock and saying, 'Look Murray, for God's sake, stop talking about Ferrari all the time. We're British, we're trying hard and we're doing well,' I got a letter, an absolutely charming letter from Martin Whitmarsh, the managing director. The gist of it was, 'Dear Murray, Like you, we at McLaren are great respecters of the Ferrari tradition and their achievements. However, the fact that we have been trying very hard and are not that unsuccessful in F1 seems to have passed you by. Could I therefore invite you to come to our factory at Woking and have a tour, and talk to your many friends. We hope to hear from you.'

"So, naturally, I wrote back. When I arrived at Woking - this was the old factory - I walked into the showroom where they have all the trophies and cars lined up. There was a reception committee to meet me. It included Neil Trundel, who had originally formed Rondel Racing with Ron Dennis - he is now the gearbox shop manager at McLaren - the legendary Jo Ramirez, who is a great friend of mine and I've known for years, and George Langhorn, who was one of the McLaren mechanics, and is now in charge of their paint shop that does all this fantastic work on the cars. They took me all round the factory, and everywhere I went, when I went into a new area, as if by magic, someone who I knew very well would appear. 'Hello Murray, what are you doing here?' I said, 'I've come to see the factory'. 'Oh, let me show you what we do here.'

"When I got to about the fourth one, I said, 'I know why I'm here you know'. Whoever I was talking to said, 'Oh, why is that Murray?' I said, 'To be brainwashed!' 'Yeah, that's right,' he said. Anyway, we had lunch and then we had tea in the canteen with all the people and George Langhorn appears with something behind his back. He produced a rear wing end flap from a McLaren F1 car, and they had got everybody in the factory to sign it, and it is now in my study, and I hope I have always given McLaren due recognition since."

My Day Job

James Allen

"Every year Renault UK host a dinner for the British press and it was always one of Murray's favourite evenings of the year. He once gave me a lift from the hotel to this event in his black BMW and it was the first time I had ever been driven on the road by Murray. For some reason, I thought he'd drive like a grandad. We absolutely flew like a rocket. I couldn't believe how quickly he drove.

"We got there, parked the car round the corner from the restaurant, walked through a gang of kids – youngest five or six, oldest 12 – probably about a dozen of them standing on the street corner – it was in a village, so it was not a threatening environment. Anyway, we walked through these kids and, of course, Murray got mobbed. They all wanted his autograph.

"A few minutes later, I realised I had left something in the car, so I asked Murray for the car keys and went back outside. I walked through the crowd of kids and, just as I turned the corner, I heard one of them whisper to another, 'That's Murray Walker's driver'.

"In 1998 it made me laugh so much. I thought, 'Fame, at last!' But that gives an indication of the esteem he was held in."

"On the Saturday of the 2000 Goodwood Festival of Speed, I (number one) demonstrated my father's 1928 Ulster Grand Prix-winning works Rudge Whitworth. On the Sunday, I dislocated my hip. Not funny."

THE JURY IS STILL OUT ON MURRAY

Is it time to switch off Murray's motor?
NO
YES

YESTERDAY'S Mirror

THE future of Murray Walker as the voice of Formula One has produced one of the biggest responses in the history of Mirror Sport.

We asked whether the undoubtedly unique style of commentary should continue, or whether the veteran broadcaster should step aside after half a century in the sport.

The reaction was staggering, with hundreds of faxes and e-mails flooding in.

Many were aghast at the thought of F1 without Murray, claiming it would not be the same. "The cock-ups make it more fun to watch and I find it sad that people have to find fault with his commentating," wrote Marie Hoffman.

Others believe it is time the microphone was finally switched off. Megan Smith said: "I cannot endure his commentary with his endless mistakes and have to resort to watching it without the sound. Stay as an expert opinion but please let Martin Brundle do the commentary."

Love him or loathe him, Murray is certainly not someone who can be ignored.

DON'T MISS OUR MURRAY LETTERS SPECIAL ON SATURDAY

TALKING POINT: Murray Walker

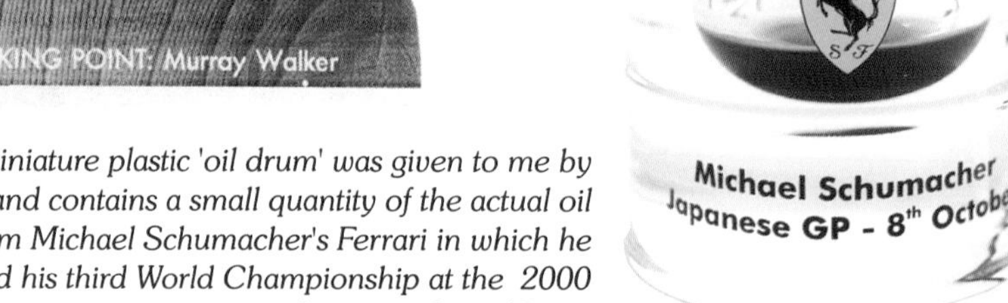

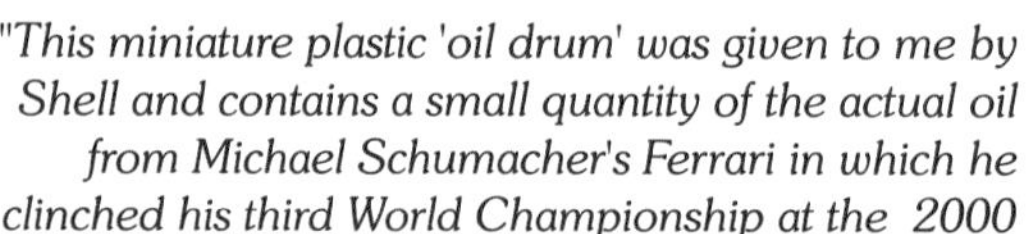

"This miniature plastic 'oil drum' was given to me by Shell and contains a small quantity of the actual oil from Michael Schumacher's Ferrari in which he clinched his third World Championship at the 2000 Japanese Grand Prix."

"We had enormous fun on a Formula One-themed cruise on the P & P ship Oriana in 2000 - 'we' being (left to right) Ian Phillips, Capt. Hamish Reid, the ship's master, and authoritative BAR Honda race engineer, Jock Clear."

Murray And Martin

Ross Brawn

"Having the foil of the racing driver who has a really intimate knowledge of some aspects was important but Murray always had the enthusiast's view. It is often very difficult for people like myself, or drivers, to really understand [that aspect] because we are deeply involved and engrossed in the business and we don't have the enthusiast's perspective on things. So, ideally you have the intimate knowledge of the racing driver balanced by the enthusiast's approach and I think they worked very well together."

Murray Interviews Bernie For 'F1 Racing' Magazine

MW: "There are people – and I'm not one of them – who look back and say, 'Those were the days. That Bernie Ecclestone,' they say, 'has taken all the soul out of F1. It's all about business now'. What do you say to that?"

BE: "There are not many people who could look back like we can and say that. Most of the guys who are around today weren't around then. They don't know what had to happen to make them what they are. But they are probably completely right: because, if you asked me whether I preferred the era that we're talking about – the '60s – or today, I'd probably have to be quite honest and say that it was much nicer in the old days. Many more friends. For example, when I owned Brabham, if we had a problem with the gearbox, we'd go and tell Colin Chapman from Lotus that we needed a second gearbox. And he'd say, 'Yeah, no problem'. It couldn't happen today because all the cars are different. It just wouldn't work. But I'm quite not sure that if it could, it would."

VOICE OF F1 MURRAY WALKER TO STAND DOWN

AND I'M OFF!

PETER INNES

MURRAY Walker, Britain's legendary Formula One commentator, will retire at the end of 2001.

Walker, 77, who has been commentating on motorsport since the late 1940s, has captured the imagination of racing fans all around the world with his exuberant style.

He said: "I don't actually want to stop, but I've always said I will do so while I'm still ahead with the viewers.

"I have a purely gut feeling that now is the time to wind down. I'm already looking forward immensely to the start of the new season, which will be gigantically emotional and important for me."

Walker has gained international respect in the F1 paddock and has developed strong friendships with a number of world champions, including Nigel Mansell and Damon Hill. They were among many who lavished praise on Walker earlier this week.

Mansell said: "He's a wonderful man and friend. His retirement will be a great loss to the sport."

Hill added: "Murray has to be a big reason why so many people watch motor racing."

Walker's current commentary box sidekick Martin Brundle said: "He's a superb professional and a special broadcaster. It is a privilege to work with him."

James Allen, who subbed for an injured Walker at this year's French GP, is favourite to take over his commentary duties.

Full story & reactions Page 3
Comment Page 11

"He is a wonderful man and friend. His retirement will be a great loss to the sport"
Nigel Mansell (left) on Murray Walker

TORQUE TALK: Walker had a strong rapport with '96 champ Damon Hill

WORLD RALLY REVIEW
How title was won and lost ● Top 10 drivers ● The teams ● Technical review ● Gp N ● Stats and facts – Pages 26-34

Schanche quit threat rocks rallycross Page 23

CLASSIFIEDS: Everything for race, rally and road – Pages 40-51

Dear Murray,

You will have thousands of these after your announcement but it needs saying:

In the 'without whom' column of people who provided the inspiration to make me do what I do today, your name is nearer the top than you'd ever credit.

Festive greetings
for Christmas and
the New Year

Thankyou for inspiring rather more than a generation of us – for your insight, humour, compassion and unwavering professionalism. Your guts, too.

Believe this if you believe anything: if you live in Britain, there is not a man in F1, not a driver or team-owner – whose retirement from the sport will hit as hard as yours. But God knows you've earned it.

Have a fantastic final season.

All the best
Andrew

17 December 2000

Dear Mr Walker

We are currently travelling in the USA and heard news today that you intend to retire next year. Please don't. We have both enjoyed your unique commentary for Formula 1 for several years and are sure that the future broadcasts will be considerably less interesting should you be missing. We both very sad to hear that will retire. Even when some of the races in the last few years have gotten a little monotonous, you always manage to keep our attention. Please, please, please stay for a few more years if ~~you~~ (and that, as well all know, is F1 backwards) you really can't keep commentating can you get ITV to use a recording of your "Go! Go! Go!" at the start of all the races? We are returning to the UK on the 1st Feb and would really love a couple of signed photographs of you.

If you really must go, we would like to take this opportunity to thank you for your service to F1. It will never be the same.

Thank you, and good-bye for now

Steve Sharkey and Hannah Westcott

"Two of the many letters I received when I announced my forthcoming retirement which both meant a very great deal to me for different reasons - the one from Andrew Frankel because I have enormous admiration and respect for his journalistic work, and whom I know well, and the other from Steve Sharkey and Hannah Westcott whom I have never met but were representative of the millions that I had the pleasure of talking to for so long."

Wrong Scot

Jackie Stewart

"The thing is when he did make a mistake it wasn't an, 'Oh my God, that was terrible'. I think that was the nice thing about him.

"I would always say to him, it must be very difficult for you, Murray, with Martin Blundell and Mark Brundle. Because that is what you would expect him to say - to get it the wrong way round. Two of them working on the same programme. The names are so alike, it is just the sort of a thing Murray would come up with.

"He has called me Jim Clark before now! I was looking around to see who he was talking to."

Murray On Paper

Matt Bishop

"Murray was extraordinarily co-operative and hardworking in the time that he wrote a column for *F1 Racing*. He wrote a regular race preview column and, even though we were paying him next-to-nothing by his standards, and the benefit it was bringing to his profile was a drop in the ocean compared with the enormous profile he already had, and the enormous profile he was adding to via fortnightly appearances on ITV, he still threw his heart and soul into it.

"Written Murray is just like spoken Murray. It has the same passion, the same friendliness, the same unmistakeable tone and, in fact, you can't read aloud an *F1 Racing* column of Murray's without trying your best to do the Murray Walker voice!"

"We took several outstanding historic racing cars on our 2000 Oriana Formula One-themed cruise. One of them was this Maserati which was driven by my all-time hero and ultimate Grand Prix driver, Tazio Nuvolari."

"IT WAS A RETIREMENT PRESENT FROM BERNIE ECCLESTONE,OFFICER"

MurrayismMurrayismMurrayism

"He's obviously gone in for a wheel change. I say obviously because I can't see it."

Formula One And Sandwiches

Louise Goodman

"Obviously Murray comes from a different era to me and I remember at the British GP, a piece appeared in one of the newspapers, basically being totally disparaging about women in motor sport. He was quoted as saying the Formula One pit lane was not a place for women. I pointed it out to him and he said, 'Oh, no, no, I don't mean you, dear. Don't mean you.' 'Well, I'm a woman working in the pit lane, Murray!' (much laughter)

"That goes back to his earlier era when nice ladies didn't get involved. Although having said that, back in the sixties women were quite heavily involved, but they had their little niche. They would be doing lap charts and making the sandwiches, as opposed to actually getting involved in broadcasting or something like that.

"On a personal level, he was always incredibly welcoming but I think, deep down, he does really believe that women shouldn't really be in the paddock, in the pit lane, other than perhaps in a decorative role, or functional – like making sandwiches!"

Direct Line 01908 329

Date 11 January, 2001 | Our reference CL234L/sb

Your date | Your reference

Dear Murray

It hardly seems that the next F1 season is only a few weeks away and I know that for you it will be a very special and memorable and without doubt a very emotional year.

Over the years I have worked with a great deal of "celebrities", models, royalty, rockstars, actors, sports personalities a complete mixture of personalities and I can say without fear of contradiction that working with you has been one of the most pleasurable aspects of my job. Quite honestly, I have never worked with a more professional, honest and interesting person. I know throughout this year you will be honoured by numerous associations and maybe a trip up the Mall will beckon. All of it will be quite deserved.

I would like to thank you for all the help you have given me and I will always remember the lunches we had when we were working on projects. I always found them very interesting and rewarding. I was in London the other day with my young son and I was casually pointing out Big Ben, the Houses of Parliament, Trafalgar Square and by the way over there is the restaurant I had lunch with Murray Walker. He was very impressed as he is a big fan. I'll also never forget your generosity and kindness when I came to see you at your new magnificent house in Hampshire when you very kindly gave me a Ferrari book. It still has pride of place on my bookshelf.

I know you'll be very busy throughout the year but if you have a spare lunchtime slot, I would be delighted to buy you lunch and you can give me all the latest gossip from the paddock. Enclosed is a small token of my appreciation to one of life's great gents. Have a great year enjoy every moment and I am thoroughly looking forward to walking through Waterstones doors sometime in the near future to buy your autobiography, I just know it is going to be a great read.

Thanks again and I look forward to your first race.

Kind regards.

Yours sincerely

Chris

Chris Love
Communications and Company Promotions Manager

Enc

Mot
Fleet T

SCANIA (GREAT BRITAIN) LIMITED
DELAWARE DRIVE, TONGWELL
MILTON KEYNES, BUCKS
MK15 8HB
ENGLAND

Telephone
Nat. 01908 210210
Int. +44 1908 210210

Scania (Great Britain) Limited
Registered Office: Milton Keynes,

An Honorary Aussie

Louise Goodman

"He is massively popular down in Australia. At Albert Park there is quite a long distance between the television compound and the paddock. They are on opposite sides of the track. Murray would get absolutely mobbed and I always got the impression it got a bit much for him. I know from my own smaller example of that when you are going from A to B, and you're trying to get your head round what you're going to say when you get there, to have people constantly coming up, or occasionally in my case, it can be very distracting.

"I always felt for Murray because half of him probably wanted to turn round and say, 'Can't you piss off? Can't you see I'm working?'

"There were occasions when I think he basically used to just pretend he hadn't heard them, which was entirely plausible because Murray does have somewhat selective hearing!"

"On a visit to Ferrari at the end of the 2000 season, Ferrari technical boss, Ross Brawn said to me, 'Stay on a day, Murray, and I'll give you the Heineken Tour (the parts other people don't reach). I did so and that evening, we had a fabulous dinner at Ferrari's restaurant, The Montana. Back row - Ross Brawn, Ferrari's brilliant South African designer Rory Byrne with recently baby born and bottom row, right to left, team boss, Jean Todt and my friend Nick Goozee."

The Ferrari Treatment

Murray Walker

"In 2000, we did our end of the year programme from the Ferrari factory at Maranello and Ross Brawn said, 'If you can stay on for another day, Murray, I will take you on the Heineken Tour - show you the parts other people don't reach'. So I did stay over another day and he took me all round everything - the race shop, the factory, the road car factory and, most importantly, the wind tunnel. During the afternoon, when I was going round the road car factory, I was being shown a map of facilities and everything, and my guide said, 'And this is the wind tunnel but nobody, even at Ferrari, who doesn't work in there, is allowed to go in there'. I said, 'I was in there this morning'. He said, 'I find that very hard to believe'!

"Anyway, that evening Ross said, 'Right we are going out to dinner, Murray. Most people go to The Cavallino, which is the restaurant opposite the main gates, but it's turned into a bit of a tourist trap, so I'm going to take you to the real place.' We went to a restaurant called the Montana, which is between Fiorano, the race track, and the factory. It is actually a public restaurant but it is basically the Ferrari F1 Canteen. It's fabulous food. I love Italy and I love Italian food. The whole place is stuffed with memorabilia - there is the nose cone off Gilles Villeneuve's Ferrari, and stuff Alberto Ascari used, signed napkins which have been framed and put on the wall... And you've got this wonderful atmosphere, and they're all Ferrari people, nearly all of them in race uniform. There was Ross Brawn, Nick Goozee, my friend who had gone out there with me, Rory Byrne, the Ferrari designer, and Jean Todt who joined us with his then girlfriend. We had an absolutely fabulous evening talking about the thing closest to our hearts, in a wonderful atmosphere."

Stark Contrast

James Allen

"When Murray, Louise and I would be driving to Germany, we'd cross the Rhine and Murray would say, 'Now, pay attention you two. I sweated blood to cross this river in 1945.' I always enjoyed his war stories. He didn't volunteer them, you had to coax them out of him.

"Occasionally he would remind us that here we were wafting across a bridge being directed by sat nav to our hotel somewhere and the circumstances of him crossing that river 50 years earlier had been somewhat more arduous. It was quite sobering."

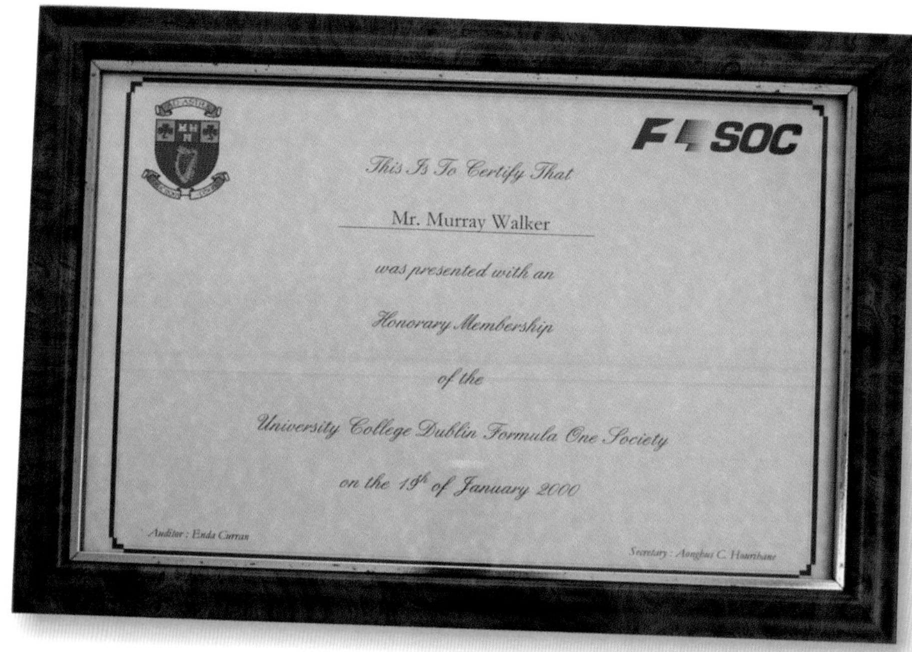

F1 SOC
This Is To Certify That
Mr. Murray Walker
was presented with an
Honorary Membership
of the
University College Dublin Formula One Society
on the 19th of January 2000
Auditor: Enda Curran
Secretary: Aonghus C. Hourihane

MurrayismMurrayismMurrayismMurrayismMurrayism

Murray: "First man out is Marques in the Arrows. Of course he's going out early to generate some media interest."
Martin: "I'm sure he would generate some interest if he went out in the Arrows because Marques drives for Minardi."

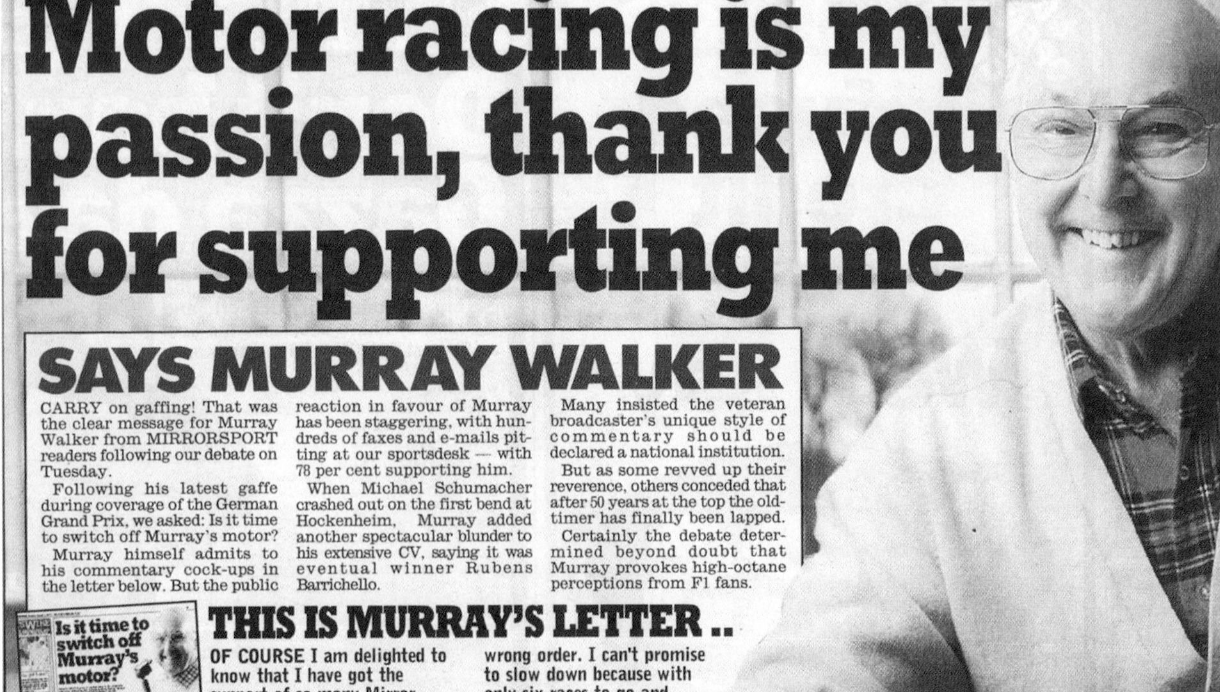

Motor racing is my passion, thank you for supporting me

SAYS MURRAY WALKER

CARRY on gaffing! That was the clear message for Murray Walker from MIRRORSPORT readers following our debate on Tuesday.

Following his latest gaffe during coverage of the German Grand Prix, we asked: Is it time to switch off Murray's motor?

Murray himself admits to his commentary cock-ups in the letter below. But the public reaction in favour of Murray has been staggering, with hundreds of faxes and e-mails pitting at our sportsdesk — with 78 per cent supporting him.

When Michael Schumacher crashed out on the first bend at Hockenheim, Murray added another spectacular blunder to his extensive CV, saying it was eventual winner Rubens Barrichello.

Many insisted the veteran broadcaster's unique style of commentary should be declared a national institution.

But as some revved up their reverence, others conceded that after 50 years at the top the old-timer has finally been lapped.

Certainly the debate determined beyond doubt that Murray provokes high-octane perceptions from F1 fans.

Is it time to switch off Murray's motor?

NO YES

FRANK'S DESTRUCT BUTTON

THIS IS MURRAY'S LETTER ..

OF COURSE I am delighted to know that I have got the support of so many Mirror readers and I am really grateful to them for speaking up for me.

Motor racing is my passion and I try hard to share it with the viewers, so it is great to know they like the way I do it.

I am the first to admit that in my excitement the words sometimes come out in the wrong order. I can't promise to slow down because with only six races to go and just 10 points covering the top four in the championship, we are in for a fizzing climax to the season and I am really looking forward to talking about it.

So thanks again . . and stay tuned.

MurrayismMurrayismMurrayism

Murray: "How do they do that, Martin? How does a man talk calmly and especially to his team boss, when Damon in the situation he's in?"
Martin Brundle: "Well, you press a little button on the steering wheel and start talking, Murray."

Heart To Heart

Tony Jardine

"We had a few dinners, just Murray and I together, where he was agonising over 'Should I, shouldn't I' over his retirement. He was saying, 'Tony, I want to go while I'm on top. I don't want them to say, "Oy, Walker, you're past your time now. I want to go with dignity," etc. I actually pointed out to him, 'Murray, I think the reason you're so young in everything you do and your spirit and your looks and everything is because of your love for this game. I can honestly sit with you now and say that I don't think you make any more mistakes, cock-ups, than you did two years ago. It's the same level, the same balance, and people love you for that. It's not you becoming a clown or dropping off or anything.'

"I think it was purely that, as the calendar increased and you had more back-to-back events, the pressure was on him and all the flying when you are getting into your late seventies - it is heavy-going. I think that, more than anything else, got to him but I personally said to him, 'You've another two or three years. Keep going. It's brilliant.'"

Sad People

James Allen

"There was a degree of jealousy among certain people in the Press Office. I think they found it difficult that Murray got so much airtime and was talked about so much and was so revered. There always was a touch of jealousy amongst some of the senior journalists, more and more towards the end of his career. But that's Formula One, you get that."

MurrayismMurrayismMurrayism

"And Michael Schumacher is actually in a very good position. He is in last place."

ITV BOSSES take note that Murray is a true legend to the sport. I hope he continues for many good and exciting years to come. I hope I speak for the majority of viewers of the sport – *DAVID SAMUEL, Leeds.*

I TOTALLY agree with Charlie Catchpole that Murray's emotion and noise makes the Grand Prix what it is and give viewers F1's alternative to shouting at football refs when he make blunders during the race. Martin Brundle does the perfect job of correcting mistakes and giving technical info, if only Murray would keep quiet while he is doing so – DIANE DAVEY, Bexleyheath.

I HAVE been watching F1 for 20 years and it would not be the same without Murray Walker. He is the voice of F1 with a voice that encourages excitement. Just ask Mansell and Hill. It would be like sacking Harry when Frank Bruno was around and we all know what happened to him...panto – *TOMMY GILCHRIST, via e-mail.*

IN RESPONSE to the negative comments about Murray in The Mirror, I respond: Dominic who? – ROBERT McCANN, via e-mail.

AS A huge Formula One fan, I have to agree with all the others who say F1 would not be F1 without Murray Walker. Who are you to speak about mistakes? – *CAROLINE PRIOR, aged 16, via e-mail.*

MURRAY should definitely keep commentating, even at the age of 75. It's not just that he's "the voice" of motor racing, he's the only real fan on TV. He is the voice of the true petrol-head motor racing fan, and mistakes or not, I salute him – STEVE WILLIAMS, via e-mail.

YOU must keep Murray Walker because Formula One would be like a football match without a football – *GORDON PAOLOZZI, via e-mail.*

I HAVE met Murray. He's very kind and should carry on being the voice of F1. Martin Brundle is really good too, but nowhere near as enthusiastic. Murray enjoys himself and is the heart and soul of F1 – VIVIENNE ECCLES, via e-mail.

I LIKE Murray. He has a shiny head and makes the races challenging – *ANDY SIMMONS, via e-mail.*

I AM 14, and have only been watching Formula One for a year, but I don't think that it would be the same without Murray commentating. His mistakes give you something to laugh at. I cannot think of another person who could replace him – STUART LOWIS, Darlington.

DOES Dominic Hart actually watch F1? It doesn't seem like it! He ought to get a fun life and just enjoy the mistakes – *PAUL MOSLEY, via e-mail.*

I THINK Murray should stay behind the mike for as long as he, and the public, want him to, hopefully for a long time yet. He is an inspiration to all – MICHAEL HARDY, aged 15, via e-mail.

I WOULD like to hear Dominic Hart commentate on F1 and make it half as interesting and exciting as good old Murray. So he makes the occasional gaffe, don't we all. The man is a walking F1 encyclopaedia – *RICHARD HUDSON, via e-mail.*

FORMULA ONE without Murray is like Punch without Judy and it will never work. I say keep Murray in front of that mike for as long as possible – LAURA MILLER, aged 17, Maidstone, Kent.

MURRAY represents the acceptable face of the British eccentric. Sky Sports has its own characters but none have the appeal, enthusiasm or warmth of our Murray – *JIM MEATON, via e-mail.*

IT'S not Murray's mistakes that annoy me when I'm watching the Grand Prix, it's the adverts. I don't want them – *BARBARA IRWIN, via e-mail.*

MURRAY deserves to go on until he drops – *BRENT McMURRAY, via e-mail.*

WHY spoil the entertainment? For the first few laps Grand Prix racing is OK. But after that it becomes so boring and predictable that it's Murray's clangers that become the focus of interest. I have now switched to watching motorbike racing – *PETE CAVE, via e-mail.*

FINAL VOTE: 78.5% SAY: STAY STAY STAY 21.5% SAY: GO GO GO

MURRAY, please call it a day! It's got nothing to do with age, it's a style thing. The French Grand Prix was much more enjoyable without that constant whining in the background (and I don't mean the cars). There is a time for all of us to call it a day and yours is now – *GARY BURLING, via e-mail.*

IT is time for him to go. He makes too many mistakes, sounds like a banshee and repeatedly interrupts Brundle only to make more mistakes – DAVID G BANYARD, via e-mail.

MURRAY Walker should have been made to retire 20 years ago. He completely spoils F1 for me with his constant gaffes, wishful thinking and airing his views and opinions. The rest of the commentary team do a cracking job and would do an even better job if they did not have to carry Walker all the time and constantly rectify his mistakes – *F.DIXON, Mablethorpe, Lincs.*

PLEASE get rid of him ASAP. He is so far behind what is happening on the track, he has become an embarrassment – STEVE MEDWAY, via e-mail.

PERHAPS Murray should pop into the pit lane and get a few screws re-tightened. The best commentary in many years of following F1 was a month or so ago when his hip went the same way as his brain – *B C EDWARDS, via e-mail.*

SORRY Murray but it's time to finish, I for one do not relish all the mistakes and the repeating of a word such as GO! five times on the trot. We need to keep Brundle as he gives a great insight into the world of F1. GRAHAM HOLMES, via e-mail.

YES, Murray Walker should go, he is long overdue for retirement . His gaffes spoil the races – *JOE HEATHMAN, via e-mail.*

COME ON Murray, give a younger person the chance you once had – KEN MOORE, via e-mail.

IT'S about time Murray Walker was given the blue flag, and give way to Martin Brundle and Co. He is way

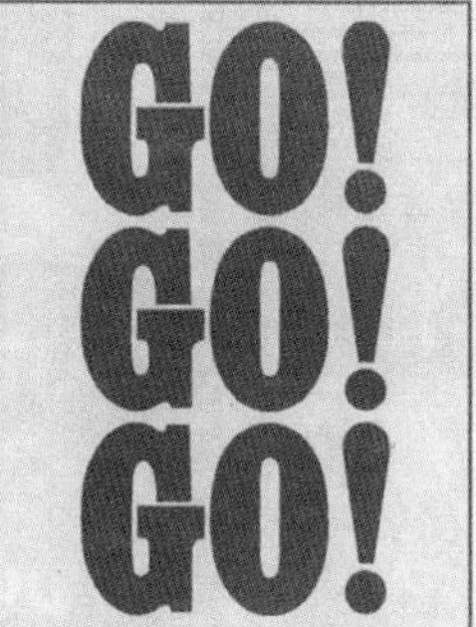

past his sell-by date. The mistakes he makes are so embarrassing they are beyond a joke. *JOHN DORKEN, via e-mail.*

I THINK Murray does extremely well for his age but it is time for time to move over and let the others have a go – MEGAN SMITH, via e-mail.

I QUITE agree with Dominic Hart when he says real F1 fans shouldn't have to watch with the sound turned down. What a difference it was watching the French Grand Prix when Murray Walker was laid up with a bad hip. It was great viewing, with excellent commentary – *M SAUNDERS, Cornwall.*

MURRAY WALKER drives me up the wall every Grand Prix. He definitely must go – TJ POLLARD, via e-mail.

ITV made a huge mistake when they hired Murray Walker. He is very annoying and spoils the races. Get rid of him – *ROBERT JAMES, Liverpool.*

YES, I say get rid of Murray Walker. He has been good in the past but now he is beyond a joke. He really spoils the racing for me now. It was a pleasure to listen to Martin Brundle and James Allen commentate on the French Grand Prix.

LET'S have more of Martin Brundle and James Allen and less of the comedy of errors – JUNE YOUNG, via e-mail.

GREAT MAN 2000

"Sounds, in his quieter moments, as if his trousers are on fire." So wrote Clive James of Murray Walker. But for sheer heart and soul and love of motor sport there's never been anyone remotely like the vital 77-year-old, who has decided to give up his ITN commentary at the end of next year. I'm already looking forward to Murray's British GP, where he's certain to tour the track in an open car, sitting between Schuey and Hakki, while the crowd roars his name rather than theirs. How he'll keep control of his ever-present emotions as he calls his last GP I can't think. They're not naming Murray's replacement yet, but the jockeying has started. Tell you something, though. To have any chance of filling the great man's shoes, the new ITV race caller had better be a fundamentally nice person, a true gentleman. Or he won't have a prayer.

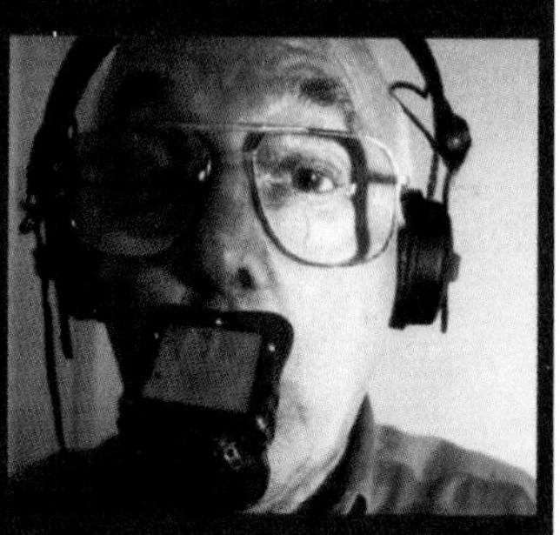

Facsimile

To	Murray Walker	Fax	
Company	Formula One Guru		
From	Tony Sinclair		
Date	1 March 2001	Total Pages (with Header)	One
Subject	Au revoir, not goodbye		
cc			

Channel Seven Sydney Pty Limited
ACN 000 145 246
Mobbs Lane
Epping
New South Wales 2121
Australia
Telephone
(02) 9877 7424
Facsimile
(02) 9877 7881

Dear Murray,

What a year you're about to have!! Like a conquering hero, you will be given the royal salute all round the world. You'll probably even give HRH a run in the popularity stakes – even in her jubilee year!!

Extraordinary is the only way to describe your career. Like Dan Maskell and John Arlott, you've become more than a commentator on the game – you've become part of the fabric of the sport.

For me, nobody will give it the welly that you have. I guess the great thing about archives is that they will always link your voice with some of the most memorable moments in motor racing. Testimony enough.

I hope this week in Melbourne, and for the rest of the long season, you remain in good health…I know you'll be in good spirits, and I'm sure you've earned every glowing tribute that comes your way.

We will all miss your warmth, sincerity, enthusiasm and above all, professionalism. My best wishes for the year, and for the many years after your last chequered flag.

Sincerely yours,

Tony Sinclair
Network Head of Sport
Seven Network (Operations) Ltd.

Do Tell

Louise Goodman

"I don't think Murray's great sense of humour comes across. He can actually be quite devilishly wicked about people. He has a sort of 'butter wouldn't melt in his mouth' perception but he can be quite naughty, some of the stories he will tell and some of the things he will say about people. He is such a brilliant raconteur."

Going With Dignity

Brian Barwick

"I helped him retire. He'd needed somebody to tell him it was the right time to retire, and I was that person. We thought about it and discussed it together and came up with, what I think, was a great scheme. He didn't retire one October; we announced his retirement a year ahead. So he had a fantastic year and I was so pleased for him. Everywhere he went, he was feted. It was great to be part of that and to make sure everyone enjoyed the last vestiges of the great Murray Walker's commentaries.

"The sport was very lucky to have a guy like Murray, who made it so accessible. In the last year, if he did cock-up, people would just say, 'Ah, good old Murray'. If he had gone on another five years, people might have had a different view.

"Murray would be right up there in terms of being one of the doyen commentary voices – the Dan Maskells, the Peter O'Sullevans, the Richie Benauds – the names that have made their sport come alive through, sometimes their lightness of touch, like Dan Maskell – speak at the end of every game, not on every point - to Murray's speak on every second of every lap! Top bracket people who, in the end, become absolutely synonymous with their sport, and the specialist viewer enjoys their commentary and the generalist is brought in by their commentary. I think that's the uniqueness of Murray, and a fine, upstanding gentleman he is too."

Undue Power And Influence

Murray Walker

"For *F1 Racing* I used to do a preview of the season each year. I would go through all the teams, all the drivers, all the technicians and give my opinions on them. One particular year when I got to the bit about Sauber, which was headed up by Peter Sauber who is Swiss and an extremely nice bloke, I said, 'Well, Sauber are making up the numbers; they are not going to do anything. They will be lucky if they score any points. It is not surprising because their chief designer is a chap called Willi Rampf, and if Willi Rampf rode through my study on a one-wheeled bicycle, I wouldn't know who he was.' It was, I have to say with shame and hindsight, a rather uncouth, unpleasant and totally unnecessary thing to say. I didn't do it nastily. I meant it as a bit of fun.

"At the Malaysian GP, Peter Sauber was so incandescent about this that he went round all the teams collecting all the copies of *F1 Racing* that he could find and putting them in the dustbin. I had an instruction that I was to meet Mr. Sauber and talk to him, which I was a bit queasy about to put it mildly. By now I had realised I had put my foot in it; I hadn't been at all diplomatic and I had been rather unpleasant. Quite unnecessarily. So he takes me into his office, at the Sepang circuit and remonstrated with me about this and it wasn't fair and it wasn't justified.

"I said, 'I'm extremely sorry. I realise it was quite the wrong thing to say, and I do apologise. I didn't mean it in quite the way that you have taken it, but I can well understand you have taken it the way you have taken it.' He said, 'I don't think you realise how important you are'. I said, 'I am not important at all Mr. Sauber. I am just a commentator and I do a bit of writing.'

"'No, no,' he said, 'you are extremely important. People listen to you and regard you as *the* man in F1 and that's why I was so offended when somebody that so many people respect writes something unpleasant about my team.' If I felt bad before, I felt terrible after that. Needless to say, I didn't say anything unpleasant about Sauber ever again."

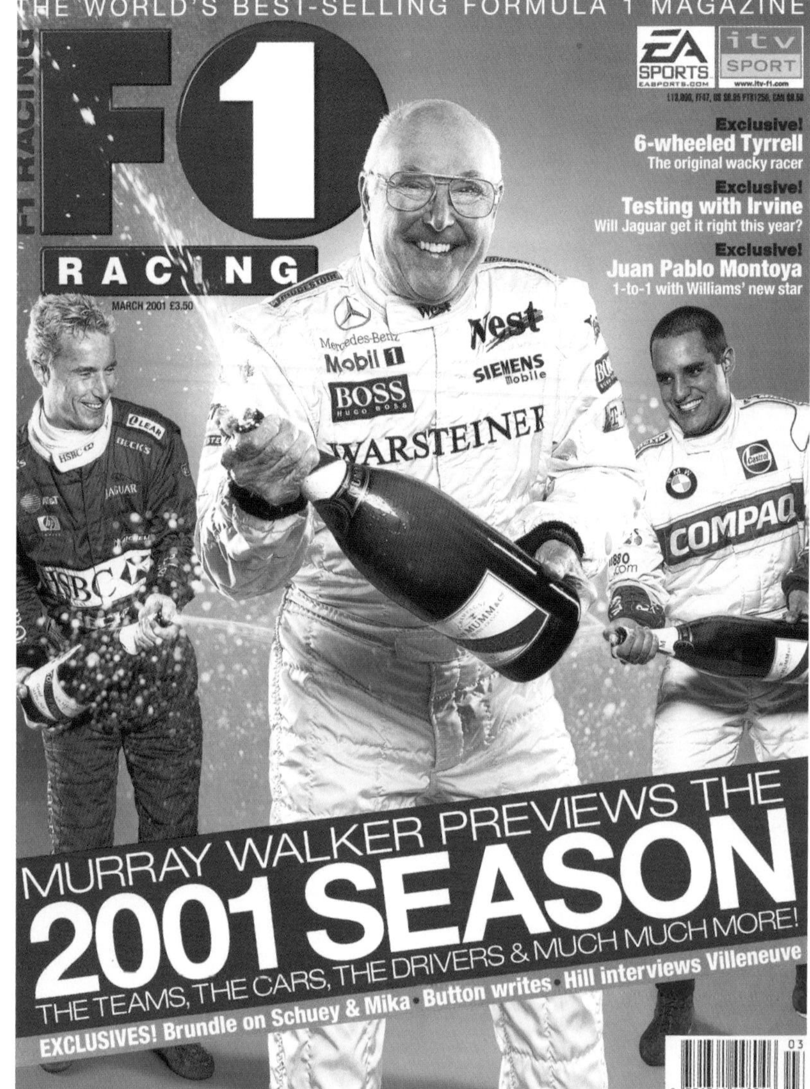

Fairly Detailed

Christian Horner

"I think he is scrupulously fair. Even when there's been a Brit in the running for a championship or a result, he's always been very balanced in his opinions and his commentary, even in the later years with Damon Hill and Michael Schumacher slugging it out for the Championship. What I particularly like about Murray is the amount of interest he takes within the teams – the chief mechanics, the truckies, the guys that are the nuts and bolts and fabric of the teams. It's not just about the drivers and the team principals. He's interested in the workings behind the teams - you can clearly see that reflected in how much time people have for him when he walks up and down the paddock. There's not been a commentator since, that I've seen, that's put as much effort into the research and background detail that Murray presents."

Finger On The Button

Jenson Button

"I have a favourite story about Murray. You know how, in qualifying, people say, 'Start the stopwatch'. Murray famously said, 'Stop the start-watch!'"

All the best in your retirement from everyone at Benetton Renault! 24.09.01

Remember the 20% you owe me!! Del Boy

Best wishes Hope the book goes to plan. Won't be the same without you

Thanks for many years of enjoyment All the best for the future. Pat Symonds

Good luck Grandad! Regards John Button

Goodluck & best regards the 21 year old "teenager"! Jenson

"This one from four-times World Champion Alain Prost."

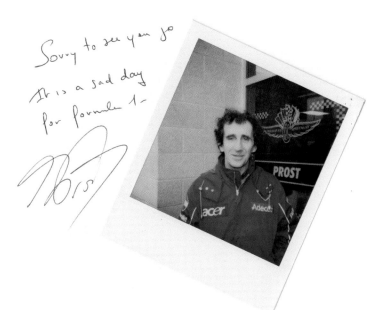

Sorry to see you go. It is a sad day for Formula 1 –

"And this one from David Coulthard. one of nature's gentlemen."

I hope you have as much happiness in retirement as you have brought to us all in your commentary. Best wishes David.

"I've been lucky enough to win quite a few awards but by far the most significant was my Lifetime Achievement BAFTA."

THE BRITISH ACADEMY OF FILM & TELEVISION ARTS
SPECIAL AWARD
AWARDED TO
MURRAY WALKER
2001

"In the weeks up to my 'retirement' in 2001, the wonderful Sally Blower, who faultlessly, humorously and endearingly organised every move of the ITV team, patiently plodded round the paddock collecting tributes that anyone was prepared to contribute to a 'Farewell Murray' album. They were all deeply touching for me because they were made by people whom I had worked with and revered for many, many years."

They think it's all over!

Don't stay away too long We'll miss you

"Some very kind words from top banana salesman, Ross Brawn!"

Commentating To Himself

Louise Goodman

"You would sit down at breakfast with Murray and he would commentate on what he was doing. He would be discussing with himself, 'Is Murray going to have banana on his porridge today or is Murray going to have honey on his porridge?' You'd think, 'What's he going on about?' That's just Murray!"

Dealing With A Murrayism

Martin Brundle

PP: "How did you react when he produced a Murrayism on air?"

"Sometimes, I just stood back and watched him in full swing and out of amazement really. I would, literally, just stand and watch him. I would either try and gently smooth it out, or square it up, but I would always try and do it with respect. I think I am famous for often saying, 'I think you might find, Murray, that…'

"He would be at full 19,000 revs on the rev limiter and of course he would say something that even he didn't mean to say. I'd make mistakes as well; we all make mistakes. I think we are on air 60 hours a year or something and you say things that are wrong. He was fine about it; he would have a wry smile sometimes. I think, well I know, I always tried to do it without scoring points, because there was no point in trying to score points off him. It was about working together and telling the story and, even today, he has forgotten more about sports broadcasting than I know. There would be no point trying to be smart about it. There was almost a sub-plot with the audience, I think, sort of coming along with me, almost gently putting a few things back on the rails.

"He had got the constitution of an ox. We used to walk the track, but I would have to stop halfway round because my feet hurt too much."

I love your chest too. Missing you already. Big Kiss Carmel x

"'But not half as much as I love yours, Carmel' (opportunity's a fine thing!)."

JACKIE STEWART, O.B.E.

JAGUAR RACING LIMITED
BRADBOURNE DRIVE TILBROOK
MILTON KEYNES MK7 8BJ ENGLAND

02 January 2001

Dear Murray

Thank you for your kind letter of 16 December. I was going to write to you at that time and then I thought it would be nicer for me to call and I am glad that we got the chance to speak.

By now you will have read all of the nice things that everyone has been saying about you and the fact that they are going to miss you in your retirement, which I think goes for everyone.

The fact that you are taking a slowing down year is nice for us all and I am sure correct for you. I myself will only be doing about seven or eight Grands Prix in 2001. The BRDC is taking up so much more of my time than I ever thought it would - it will take some fixing up with all the new plans that are afoot but it is going to be a good challenge which I think is well worth taking on.

Thank you for coming to the EGM, it was very nice that the members gave it the enormous support and backing that they did.

You are very kind and generous with your time and that is of course why so many people are so fond of you and will continue to be strongly behind anything you do.

Murray, it goes without saying that I wish you a very happy, healthy and prosperous 2001 and that comes from the entire Stewart family as they all are Murray Walker fans!

All the very best, and I look forward to seeing you soon.

Yours sincerely

Jackie

Pains In The Derrière

Paul Stoddart

"Murray's biggest critic is always Murray. Towards the latter years of him commentating, he always felt that if he dropped one of his bloomers or Murrayisms or predictions that turned out wrong, that people would think less of him. In actual fact, people just loved him. The few arseholes, and I use that quite meaningfully, the few arseholes who did write in and complain about when Murray got something wrong were in such a minority and yet I saw the effect it had on him. It certainly, in my book, forced him into premature retirement. I have no doubt he could have still been doing it today."

Murray

From the moment I first stepped into the paddock you've been nothing but supportive, helpful & kind and made me feel welcome.... even though I was a girl!! Its been a privilege working with you. I shall miss your fabulous stories - both on & off the telly. Take care & don't be a stranger because I'll miss having you around.

All my love Louise

"Louise Goodman has made her own very special mark on ITV's Formula One coverage. Against massive competition, she's always the first with the interviews. Not bad for a girl!"

Being Mobbed

Paul Stoddart

"It happened many times in Australia that we would go into a restaurant and everyone stood up and clapped. I've been with him in airports where there'd be drivers walking through and Murray would walk through and all the autograph hunters just ran over to Murray.

"Many, many times over the years, we had to literally escort him. I remember after one of the races in Germany, at Frankfurt Airport, we had a major problem trying to get him through. Another year at Nice Airport, after Monaco, we walked into the terminal and obviously because we are a private flight we have a way of getting through pretty quickly. The plane was almost delayed because we couldn't get Murray through the terminal.

"At Graz Airport when the A1 Ring was active in Austria, we landed and we had a pretty healthy reception for the drivers we had on board but then Murray appeared and they all just mobbed Murray. So we got him out and then coming out on the Sunday night we actually had to shepherd him into a VIP room to try and get him through the back way because there were so many autograph hunters and so many well-wishers standing out the front. Murray's such a lovely guy, he'd stand there all night signing autographs and we wouldn't get back to the UK."

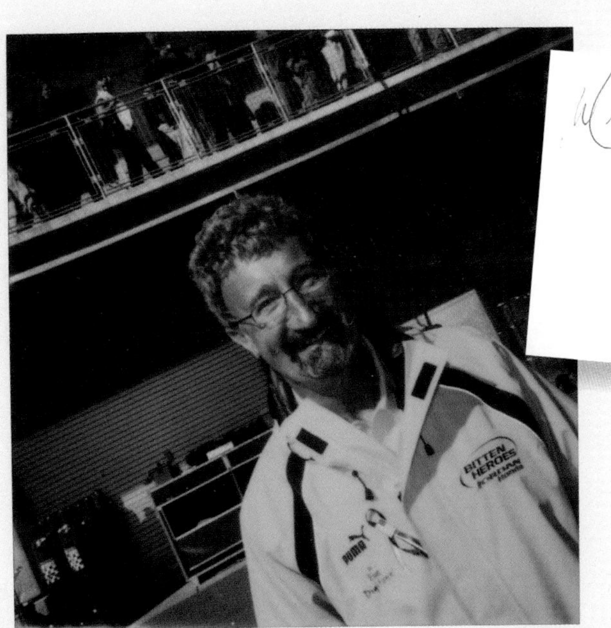

Murray

33 years without saying a bad word about Jordan – that must have been difficult!

Love ya Man

Eddie

"How 'could' anyone say a bad word about Jordan? It was the most fun-team in Formula One, always gave us journalists unlimited hospitality and was headed by, not just one, but two incredible characters, Eddie Jordan himself and his irreverent lieutenant, Ian Phillips."

"There's an 'oldtimer's' run for veteran and vintage machines at Beaulieu in honour of my father every year and whenever I'm in the country I present the prizes. Number 72 carries the sidecar that my father designed and which he took to second place in the 1923 Sidecar TT."

Self Doubt Sown

Murray Walker

"In the year 2000, the *Daily Mail* published a piece which I thought was very unfair, basically saying, 'Murray Walker is past it and he should get out'. It raised a storm of controversy, 'for Murray' and 'against Murray'.

"It sowed the first seeds in my mind that I had been doing it for a very, very long time and that I had got to stop sometime, and maybe now was the time to do it. I am not saying that this actually caused my retirement, but it led to the state of mind that made me feel that now was the time to get out while I was still ahead."

An Arduous Schedule

James Allen

"He just had a spectacular amount of energy. That was just remarkable. Doing the same job as him, and covering the same ground, and I'm 43 years younger than him, it takes a lot out of you, especially with all the long hauls at the beginning and the end, and in the middle of the season. It was quite noticeable, in the last couple of years, that he was feeling it by September."

"Even Michael Schumacher chipped in with a few, very appropriate words - I was back sooner than he expected!"

See you soon
I'm sure !!!

'Twinkle Twinkle little star How I wonder
why you are quitting - you lazy git - I told you
there's at least another good five years left in the
voice box and now you decide to desert us - temporarily
I hope - We expect to work with you at some Races next
year when you are not a) promoting your book
b) earning mega bucks from appearances
c) cruising on big ships
After 24 yrs of working with you from team + media side of things
it has been GIGANTICALLY FANTASTIC.......
from 'TWINKLE TOES'

"'Teach' of course is the enormously likeable Tony Jardine. For years, he was BBC TV's and ITV's Formula One pit lane reporter and then he became Jim Rosenthal's pundit partner in the one million pound ITV paddock presentation suite. Behind all his witticisms, cracks and jokes, there was an immensely hard-working and knowledgeable chap, who was also a real joy to work with."

"One of my best friends in Formula One was the incredible Paul Stoddart, boss of European Aviation and Minardi F1. This is the painting he gave me on my memorable last flight back from Monza in 2001 with his airline. It shows the BA111 in which we flew and the teams we flew with - Tyrrell, Arrows, Jordan and Minardi, and was beautifully painted by top artist, Andy Kitson."

The End Of The Brand

Martin Brundle

PP: **"**Did you think it was right for Murray to retire when he did?"

"In hindsight, I think it was too early. But it's always better to leave them wanting a bit more. Some other legendary commentators have gone on too long. I wasn't involved in the decision so I don't know how it came about. We had a good brand, the 'Murray and Martin' brand. We were working extremely well. Unquestionably there were times in wet races, with a flurry of pit stops or a really complex situation going on where you could see Murray beginning to struggle to stay on top of a busy race. Where he came into his own was in a very boring race because he could make a boring race interesting. That was when he was absolutely brilliant."

Dear Murray,

While I didn't get much of a chance to work with you in Formula One, I did want to add my congratulations to the thousands of others you have received following your retirement announcement.

You will forever be remembered as the voice of Formula One.

To Murray.

Welcome to the ranks of the "Retired"

What a great time you have had!!

What a great time you have given all of us in F1!!! ooo

Jackie

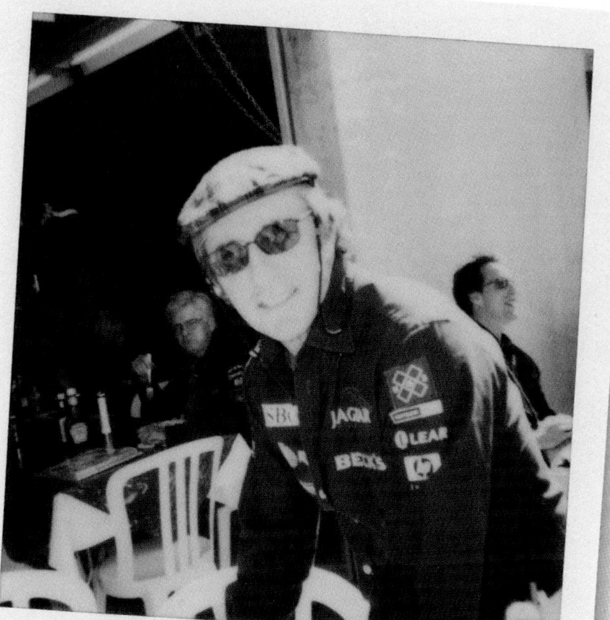

"Thank you, Jackie, and I'd say just the same about you."

Ecclestone And Brundle Banter

Murray Walker

"Martin was doing his grid walk and he accidentally, or on purpose, bumps into Bernie Ecclestone and they exchange a bit of banter because Bernie is gigantically, terrifyingly quick-witted and likes getting a rise from people, as does Martin. So Martin, as the ITV presenter, said, 'Anything particular you are doing then, Bernie?' and Bernie says, 'I am just trying to arrange this deal with Sky Television!' Martin came straight back with, 'Is that the one where you bring a friend and you double the audience!' He definitely got the better of Bernie and that doesn't happen very often."

Goodbye Murray

from all your friends and fans

in the F1 Paddock

Don't forget you are on a gap year

Bernie

"I'd love to think I was, Bernie, but sadly you can't go on for ever and I've had a fabulous innings."

MurrayismMurrayism

"He's here again for the first time."

Formative Influence

Jenson Button

PP: "Your father tells me you watched GP racing from an early age. Would it be correct to say Murray was part of your upbringing, part of your education?"

"Definitely. Through my younger years, when my father was racing, I was obviously watching a lot, but also when I started racing in Formula One, Murray's thoughts and comments meant a lot to me. Obviously the whole world got to hear what he had to say and his opinion was very important."

An Appreciation

Pat Symonds

"A generalisation, but an incredibly important generalisation, is that those who work in Formula One on the non-PR side of things – the mechanics, the people who are on the dirty side of it – are generally very hardworking people. I think we often look over the fence at others from the PR and journalistic side and think that life's pretty easy [for them] and, in many, many cases, it is. And it appals me to read a lot of journalists who have very little opinion – they are note-takers. They will interview someone, they will write down the thoughts of that other person and just get paid as if they were their own thoughts. They spend very little time trying to get background to set the scene.

"True journalism is setting the scene for people to understand, it is forming opinion, it's passing on opinion. Now, very few do it. Murray absolutely was not one of those people. One of the things I loved about Murray was that he was the guy who was there before all the action was happening. He was there early in the morning, he was there late at night. He was there on Thursday. He was walking around. He was talking to everyone. He didn't have his favourites – his professionalism was way beyond that. He'd talk to anyone. He didn't care if they were a mechanic. He didn't care if they were World Champion. He'd speak to them in very much the same way and he would build *his* picture of what was going on. And that was the picture that he was so able to get across in his commentaries.

"So, my generalisation is that one of things I liked about him was his work rate. That work rate would have been admirable for someone in their 40s or 50s. To be in your 70s and still be working like that - that was passion - and that conscientiousness and that honesty – I hope that I can do the same. I so much admire him, I really do."

MurrayismMurrayismMurrayism

"The battle is well and truly on if it wasn't before, and it certainly was."

Murray,

It's been a great pleasure working with you these last 5 years. Thank you so much for all your encouragement, advice and, most important, public support. It is greatly appreciated. As I am constantly being reminded, you are a one-off ~~a~~ great character, a great broadcaster and a great friend. I shall miss you.

James

"I guess one of the nicest things that can happen to you is for your successor, in what is a fiercely competitive business, to be as generous as this about you. Thank you, James."

„Die Autos fahren im Kreis, ich brülle"

Seit 50 Jahren kommentiert **MURRAY WALKER** die Formel 1. Seine Analysen sind fast immer falsch, aber gerade deshalb lieben ihn die Briten

Out To Lunch

Louise Goodman

"Murray never quite got to grips with technology. We used to have to have a little scout trotting along behind him everywhere because if you needed Murray for something, you could never find him. You could call his phone but he never answered it. At the French GP once, he memorably walked into the production office and somebody said, 'Oh my God, there you are. We've been trying to contact you.' He said, 'Well, I've got my phone with me', and pulled it out, and it was ringing. 'Ah. Okay'!"

A Plane For One, Sir?

Murray Walker

"For years I flew to GPs with Paul Stoddart's airline, European Aviation. Paul Stoddart is the charismatic Australian who owned Minardi. The airport from which they flew their BA111s was at Bournemouth. Paul would send a driver to collect me at my home, which is about 20 minutes from the airport, drive me there, not to the airport but to the aeroplane. No customs, no immigration. I would get out of the car and walk up the steps of the aeroplane. There was me, the flight crew and about five air hostesses. We would then take off and fly to Coventry where we picked up the Jordan team or the Arrows team or whoever it was, and fly wherever we were going.

"When any normal person gets on a aeroplane they have with them either their wife or business colleague, and that's who they will know on the aeroplane, full stop. When you got on this plane, you'd know everybody on the aeroplane because they are all going to be F1 people. So you get a wonderful atmosphere – like-minded people going to the same thing. You would get up and walk about and talk to each other, and drink and eat meals together.

"One of Paul Stoddart's party tricks, with chosen people, was as follows. You take a plastic-coated safety instruction card out of the back of a seat and stand on it at the front of the aisle, with your back against the door that leads into the cockpit. When the plane takes off, you go straight down the middle of the plane. Strictly forbidden."

Dear Murray
Many great moments -
but none better than wearing that
dress on the plane
Best Wishes
Mick

MurrayismMurrayismMurrayism

> **"Schumacher is either coming into the pits on this lap or he's not."**

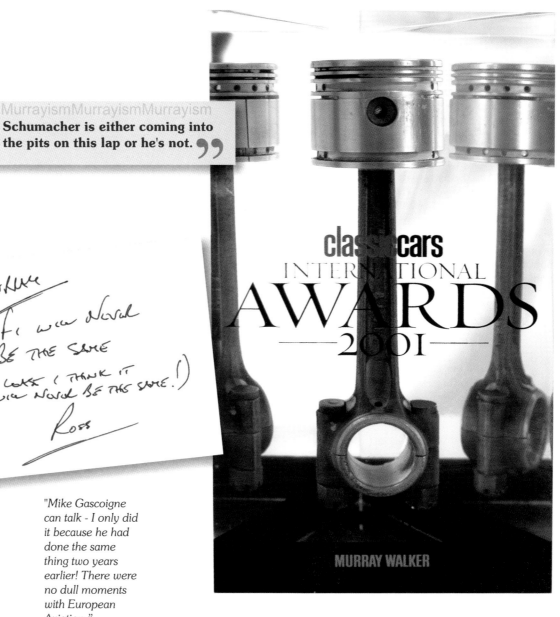

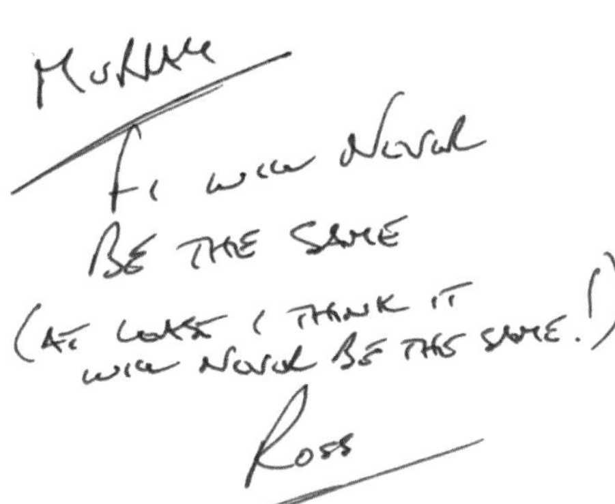

Murray
F1 will never
be the same
(At least I think it
will never be the same!)
Ross

"Mike Gascoigne can talk - I only did it because he had done the same thing two years earlier! There were no dull moments with European Aviation."

The Physical Ordeal

Louise Goodman

"In the last couple of years, I think he was finding it a strain, physically, to travel to all of the races. On and off planes all the time, and in air conditioning all the time – he had a cough that wouldn't go away for a long time. We would try and carry his bags for him, without him noticing."

What A Brick

James Allen

"One thing I saw him receive which really meant a lot to him was the brick from the yard of bricks at Indianapolis. That happened at the Farewell Murray event, which was an amazing occasion in the Paddock Club. Everybody was there, including Michael Schumacher. Bernie Ecclestone and Tony George were there, plus a good chunk of the drivers, certainly all the British drivers, and a lot of senior team people, as well as from the media centre. I've been to quite a few send-offs now for people who have served a long time in F1 and Murray's was, by some margin, the best attended in terms of the seniority of the people there, and it meant a lot to him. It was very, very special, especially when Schumacher got up and did a little routine about the boot being on the other Schumacher!

"Someone had said to me, 'What's the best way to get Schumacher involved in Murray's thing? Will he get up and speak?' And I said, 'No, he won't want to do that. I think the best thing to do would be to get Michael, and the other drivers, to read back some of the classic Murrayisms he's come out with about them'. It was bloody funny, it really was!"

Dear Murray,
all the best to you.
I hope to see you
here and there and
we all will certainly
miss you!
Yours Norbert

Go digital everybody else has.
Best wishes
Ron

"They look like a couple of elderly Hell's Angels who have lost their bikes but they are actually two of the most important people in the paddock - McLaren's Ron Dennis and Mercedes-Benz's Norbert Haug."

$3.5m puts Murray on grid

HIS glamorous jetset career may have ended, but the life of luxury is definitely not over for the very excitable Murray Walker (right).

The retired voice of Formula One has landed the largest fee ever paid to a Briton in sport as an advance for his book, provisionally titled *Unless I'm Very Much Mistaken*. Walker closed a $3.5 million deal with publisher HarperCollins, 20 per cent more than the contract that Manchester United manager Sir Alex Ferguson signed for his autobiography.

What is more surprising is that the former television commentator negotiated the contract, signed without him having written a word, himself without an agent, hence saving himself having to pay away 15 to 20 per cent of the fee.

The book will be published next September.

I can't believe we won't see you again!
Nigel

Boa sorte!
It's all I can wish you
Barrichello
2001

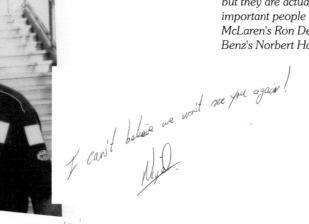

"Hopefully Rubens meant well!. As ever, he was absolutely wonderful to work with when we subsequently both wore Honda team colours."

"In the happier times of 2001 Ferrari's Nigel Stepney was rightly regarded as Formula One's top Chief Mechanic. Sadly for him, and Formula One, it was all to go pear-shaped six years later and I wonder whether we will ever know the true full story."

Standing Down Under

Paul Stoddart

"The Drivers' Winners' Trophy that's presented in Australia is a very famous trophy which is in the shape of an old steering wheel from the '50s. These are very prestigious trophies. There are trophies and there are trophies that are presented at the various Grands Prix around the world – some of them are great and beautiful, and some of them are somewhat mysterious, to say the least! But this Australian trophy is one that is well recognised and well-liked and Murray was given one. Not only was he the guest of honour at the Grand Prix, but he was given one of these trophies which was presented at the Gala Ball on the Friday night in front of some 3000-5000 people. He had not only a standing ovation but they wouldn't sit down!"

Cover Boy

Matt Bishop

"Interestingly, during my 11 years as Editor-in-Chief for *F1 Racing*, the three issues that had Murray Walker on the cover weren't in positions one, two and three in terms of highest ever sales, but I think all three were in the top five, even though we've had people like Damon Hill, Michael Schumacher, Mika Hakkinen, Jenson Button, Fernando Alonso and latterly Lewis Hamilton. The person who was the safest cover image of all on the UK newsstand was a man in his 70s, now 80s, which is an astonishing statistic, and said something quite extraordinary about his powerful and enduring personality."

JAGUAR
Daimler

FROM THE OFFICE OF STUART DYBLE DIRECTOR COMMUNICATIONS AND PUBLIC AFFAIRS
Jaguar Cars Limited, Browns Lane, Allesley, Coventry CV5 9DR, England

Dear Murray,

It was a pleasure to see you again at the Retirement Dinner held in your honour at the National Sporting Club, Café Royal, on November 22nd.

To commemorate your retirement from Grand Prix commentating, it gives me great pleasure to present to you on behalf of Jaguar Cars and Jaguar Racing this signed, mounted nose cone from one of our Jaguar R2 Formula One cars.

In the short time Jaguar has been involved in Formula One, we appreciated the support you gave the brand over two difficult seasons and I know you wish the race team future success.

While I am sure you will enjoy a well-earned retirement, I am confident that we will see you around sometime soon at a Grand Prix in the future.

Yours sincerely,

Stuart

Stuart Dyble
Director, Communications and Public Affairs
Jaguar Cars - Jaguar Racing

With very best wishes Murray and thanks for everything.

TELEPHONE 44 (024) 7620 2869
FAX 44 (024) 7640 5395

Registered Office: Browns Lane Allesley Coventry CV5 9DR Registered in England No 1672070

"A typically kind and generous note from Martin Brundle, the best co-commentator I ever worked with."

Dear Murray and Elizabeth.

I hope you are enjoying your Cruise. Well earned after a hard long year although I know the eagerly anticipated book must march on.

Murray thanks for your lovely note that you sent recently. I was pleased for BEN on the evening and I thought the turnout was once again a great tribute to you.

I'm sure we'll see plenty of each other in the future but I must thank you at the end of this, our final year working closely together, for helping me so much.

It seems 5 minutes since our first preview show in Melbourne, with you looking up Marilyn Monroe's dress!

Since then you have been so free with help and advice and given me such a springboard into sports broadcasting. You have been so generous to all of us and your many kind words about working with me haven't gone unnoticed.

Take it steady and pace yourself next year. It sounds very demanding even for a man with his "trousers on fire".

Love to you both

Martin and Family.

Wishing you
a very Merry Christmas
and a Happy New Year
from

Martin, Liz, Charlie + Ali

Christmas 2001

F1's Master Salesman

Pat Symonds

"There are good and bad aspects of Formula One. There are plenty of things about F1 that could be better but I think Murray took the positive aspects and emphasised them. Throughout the English-speaking world, here was this guy who was taking this sport a little beyond its true level. Murray made it reach a level that it probably didn't deserve but he was so convincing that people took it on board and they went with it. That's a helluva of a thing to do.

"It's like his advertising. It's what advertising is about, isn't it – it's making the world believe that something is just a little bit better than it really is. Maybe that's what he managed to do with Formula One."

Leaving Party At Indianapolis

Murray Walker

"There were about 300 people who came to this on the Saturday after qualifying when they would normally have been working on the cars. So I was very flattered that they turned up. One of the people that turned up was Michael Schumacher. Tony Jardine, who was running it, was getting people like Bernie Ecclestone and David Coulthard to come out to the front. He'd give them a piece of paper, on which there was something I was alleged to have said. They had to say it the way I would have said it, so they had to imitate me.

"David Coulthard said, 'Well I will do it, but I'm not going to do it in public'. There was a big lectern there, and he went and got inside the lectern, so that no-one could see him! Then Tony brings Michael Schumacher out, and he gives him his piece of paper, and he's written on it – 'Here comes Ralf Schumacher, son of Michael Schumacher'. Now would I have said that? Of course I wouldn't. Michael looks at this and says, 'I don't understand. What I am supposed to do?' Tony said, 'You say that, like Murray said it'.

"Michael said, 'But when Murray says it I'm in the car and I don't know how says it'. So I put my arm round him. 'Come on Michael, we will do it together.' So we both said, 'Here comes Ralf Schumacher, son of Michael Schumacher'.

"I thought that was marvellous of Michael Schumacher. This thing lasted about an hour and a half, and he sat there and he took it all in. He said to me afterwards, 'I don't understand Murray. This party was in your honour after so many years of TV commentary, yes?' I said, 'Yes'. He said, 'But they spent the whole time making fun of you'. I said, 'Well that's just the way we are'.

"He said, 'Oh, is it your English sense of humour?' I said, 'Yeah, I suppose that must be it, Michael!'"

"I've got a study full of memorabilia and things from my long career which mean an enormous amount to me in terms of happy memories of wonderful people and wonderful places. I think one of the most unexpected, and certainly most appreciated, of them all is this actual brick from the original Indianapolis all-brick Speedway which was presented to me at my retirement party by Indianapolis Motor Speedway boss and owner, Tony George."

V.I.P.
MURRAY WALKER
00-2004-37-0590

A very, very special red pass, given at the discretion of Bernard Ecclestone Esq.

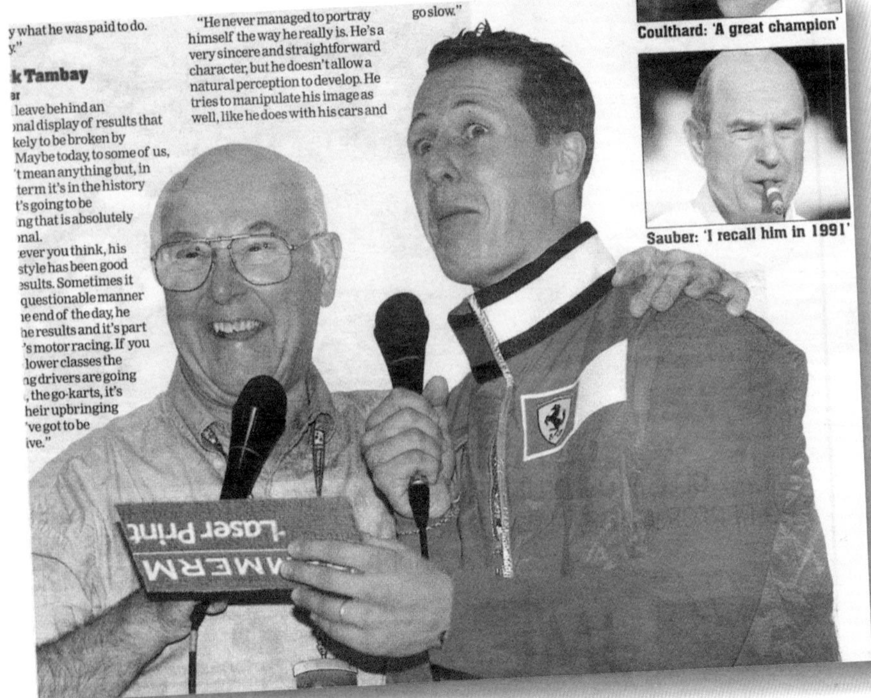
y what he was paid to do.
y."

k Tambay

leave behind an onal display of results that kely to be broken by Maybe today, to some of us, 't mean anything but, in term it's in the history t's going to be ng that is absolutely onal.

ever you think, his style has been good esults. Sometimes it questionable manner e end of the day, he he results and it's part 's motor racing. If you lower classes the ng drivers are going , the go-karts, it's heir upbringing 've got to be ive."

"He never managed to portray himself the way he really is. He's a very sincere and straightforward character, but he doesn't allow a natural perception to develop. He tries to manipulate his image as well, like he does with his cars and go slow."

Coulthard: 'A great champion'

Sauber: 'I recall him in 1991'

"Anyone who says that Michael Schumacher has no sense of fun doesn't know what they are talking about. Here he is at my retirement party joining in inexplicably saying, 'Here comes Ralf Schumacher, son of Michael Schumacher!'"

Grand Prix Bus Pass

Murray Walker

When we had this wonderful party at Indianapolis, Bernie, bless his heart, came. When his time came to say something, because Tony Jardine was asking all the really important people like him to say something, Bernie stood up and said some very nice things about me and then he said, 'And he's going to get a red pass'. Now this is very special because, as far as I know, only retired World Champions and people of that status get a red pass. So every year, I just drop Bernie a line and say I am going to be at the Grands Prix this year, and he sends me one on these marvellous red passes. *Very* nice to have."

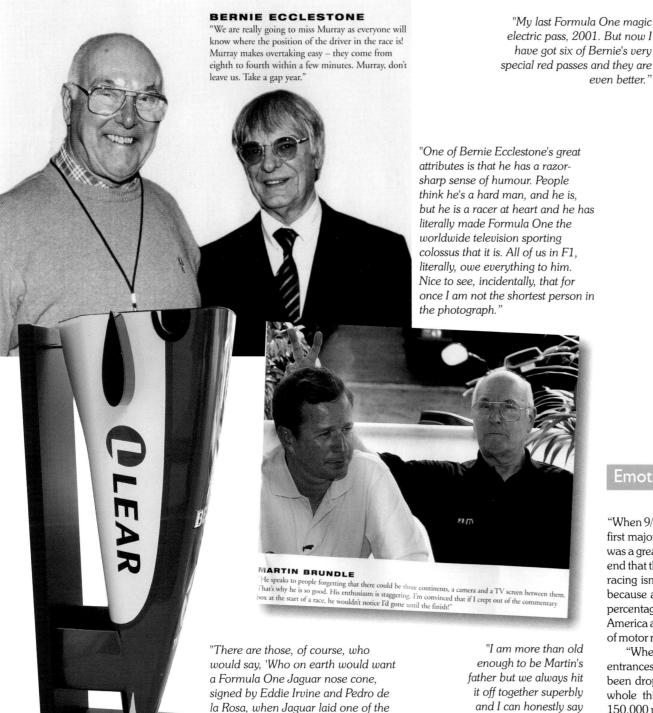

BERNIE ECCLESTONE
"We are really going to miss Murray as everyone will know where the position of the driver in the race is! Murray makes overtaking easy – they come from eighth to fourth within a few minutes. Murray, don't leave us. Take a gap year."

"My last Formula One magic electric pass, 2001. But now I have got six of Bernie's very special red passes and they are even better."

"One of Bernie Ecclestone's great attributes is that he has a razor-sharp sense of humour. People think he's a hard man, and he is, but he is a racer at heart and he has literally made Formula One the worldwide television sporting colossus that it is. All of us in F1, literally, owe everything to him. Nice to see, incidentally, that for once I am not the shortest person in the photograph."

MARTIN BRUNDLE
"He speaks to people forgetting that there could be three continents, a camera and a TV screen between them. That's why he is so good. His enthusiasm is staggering. I'm convinced that if I crept out of the commentary box at the start of a race, he wouldn't notice I'd gone until the finish!"

"There are those, of course, who would say, 'Who on earth would want a Formula One Jaguar nose cone, signed by Eddie Irvine and Pedro de la Rosa, when Jaguar laid one of the biggest eggs in the history of the sport?' Well, I would actually. I appreciated a very kind gesture from publicity boss, Stuart Dyble, and it's in my hallway in my home."

"I am more than old enough to be Martin's father but we always hit it off together superbly and I can honestly say that we never had a cross word. That just shows how tolerant he must be!"

Emotions In The Aftermath

Murray Walker

"When 9/11 happened, all sporting events were stopped altogether in America, and the first major sporting event that *was* held was the US Grand Prix at Indianapolis. There was a great deal of discussion as to whether it would be held or not. They decided in the end that they would hold it. F1 in America is not terribly important to Americans; motor racing isn't terribly important to Americans. But you get a big crowd at Indianapolis because although the percentage that are interested in F1 is very small, a very small percentage of the American population is a lot of people. So they come from all over America and from all over the rest of the world to Indianapolis, which they call the home of motor racing. So there was a big, big crowd.

"When we arrived on the morning of the race, they were handing out at the entrances little plastic American flags. I was given one. I actually picked one up that had been dropped on the ground and I had them in the commentary box with me. The whole thing was a gigantically emotional experience, because there were about 150,000 people there, I suppose, and the Americans are very good at these emotional, tear-jerking presentational things. They did the *God Bless America*. Everybody was very fraught about 9/11, obviously, and they all stood there singing *God Bless America* with their hands on their hearts. Then 'Mari' Hulman George, the daughter of Tony Hulman, who saved Indianapolis in 1945, did the 'Gentlemen, start your engines' thing and away went the race and away went the commentary. It was a tremendously emotional, memorable day for me."

No Nonsense

Louise Goodman

"After Murray's final US Grand Prix, we were all flying out of Indianapolis that night so we'd gone back to the hotel to have a shower before we got on the plane but we hadn't kept all the rooms. So Murray and Elizabeth came back to my room to have a shower. It was a bit odd to have the great Murray Walker padding about with a bathrobe on.

"Whilst he was in there, I said to Elizabeth something about, 'It's been a big, big weekend for Murray, emotionally, as well as everything else'. She said, 'Don't know what you mean'. I said, 'Well, you know, a lot of emotion…'

"She said, 'All he does is stand around and talk about cars. He would do that anyway without you paying him'! She's lovely. I love Elizabeth."

"Prince Albert of Monaco follows in his father, Prince Rainier's footsteps as a very keen supporter of the most famous Grand Prix of them all. Rightly so because it contributes untold wealth to the principality's coffers."

"In 2001 the great Tom Wheatcroft, owner of the Donington Circuit and the fabulous Donington Collection of historic racing cars, commissioned this exact duplicate of the memorial to DKW motor cycle racing star and brilliant pre-war Auto Union driver, Bernd Rosemeyer, and installed it outside the museum entrance as a tribute to a truly great driver. Typically, Tom persuaded the original stonemason out of retirement to carve it."

LEADING FORMULA 1 figures surprised commentator Murray Walker with a party to celebrate his final F1 race at the US Grand Prix. Walker was also presented with an original brick from the Indianapolis Motor Speedway. See feature, p50

"Absolutely true because how's this for a line-up, from left to right - Ross Brawn, Flavio Briatore, myself, Tony George, Bernie Ecclestone and Eddie Jordan."

A Third Career

Louise Goodman

"The European Aviation planes were based at Bournemouth, which is not too far from where Murray lives. The plane would start in Bournemouth and then fly up to Coventry, pick the team up and fly out to wherever the race was. But Murray would get on board in Bournemouth and so Murray would have this entire plane and all the hostesses to himself for the first leg. Of course, they would all be all over him and looking after him, and making sure he was okay. And I can just imagine Murray loving every second of it, but pretending not to!

"Because he had always flown out to all the races with 'Stoddie-air', Paul [Stoddart] laid on something special for his last European race. We had this whole subterfuge going on because Murray wasn't supposed to know it was happening. Paul had got special decals on the side of the plane.

"Paul had us all stood by with party-poppers. At the last minute, one of the pilots came flying out of the plane and said, 'For Christ's sake don't let those off or we will never get this plane off the ground'. You can imagine, having all those bits of paper flying around an airport is probably not a good idea!

"So, we set off and it was just a crazy flight. The party piece was Murray putting on a hostess's outfit and serving us the food. That was just so incongruous – I never really saw Murray as a cross-dressing air hostess!

"It is not in keeping with his style but he entered into the spirit of the whole thing totally."

A Worthy Challenge

Paul Stoddart

"That flight was just after 9/11. We'd already decided to do it and then 9/11 sadly happened and the amount of effort it took for that still to happen at that airport that night, where we managed to get not only the plane decaled with 'Murray – Thanks for the memories' but also managed to get a 50-strong guard of honour, all in T-shirts lined up on the tarmac, that took some organising. And we still kept it a surprise.

"There were just three of us on the bus. He still had no idea and I kept talking to him, and then there it all was!"

"This is where it all began - Vox Villa - the startline commentary box at the Shelsley Walsh hillclimb in Worcestershire. My first broadcast of any description was at a mixed car and motor cycle meeting there in 1948 and it led to my subsequent BBC audition at Goodwood which in turn led to my first BBC broadcast at the 1949 British Grand Prix."

"And this is where it all finished. An imminently tearful Murray Walker, choked with emotion, at the end of the 2001 US Grand Prix at Indianapolis. Martin, bless him, rests a comforting hand on my shoulder."

"The Midland Automobile Club gave me my first chance by letting me do that 1948 public address commentary at Shelsley Walsh so it was a very real pleasure to do the after-dinner speech at their centenary dinner in 2001. To my right, is Ian Harper and to my left is John Moody (exciting motor cycle commentator Toby Moody's dad). Amongst those attending the dinner was Philip Porter, my co-author and a Life Member of the MAC."

McLaren

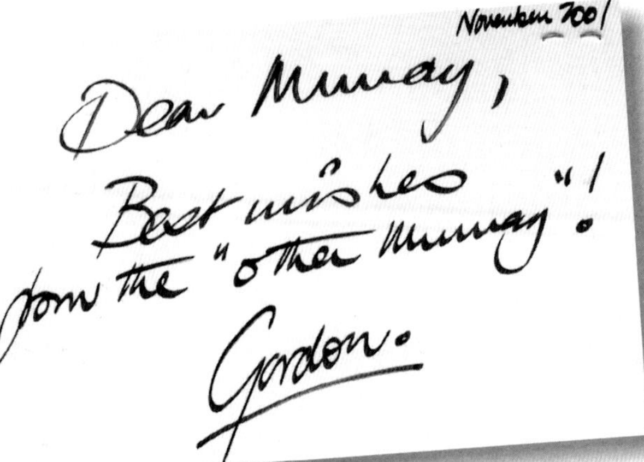
November 2001

Dear Murray,

Best wishes

from the "other Murray"!

Gordon.

28th November 2001

F.A.O - Murray Walker
C/O National Sporting Club
Café Royal
68 Regent Street
London
W1B 5EL

Dear Murray,

I am writing to thank you very much for the great evening last week and also in appreciation for everything you have done for our sport. It must make you immensely proud when you look back on your career and of course alongside this you must have an amazing amount of good memories of friendships & fun!

I hope you will keep in touch one way or another and I wish you happiness in your retirement.

Best wishes,

Gordon Murray

"Gordon Murray was not only a brilliantly innovative designer of outstandingly successful F1 cars for Brabham and McLaren but was also responsible for what, in my opinion, is the greatest road car of all time, the McLaren F1 as well as the exciting Yamaha-engined Rocket."

(Custard) Pie In The Sky

Murray Walker

"When I did my last European Race at Monza in 2001, we came from the circuit after the race, checked in at the airport, and we started going out to the plane. Paul Stoddart and Sue Aston, who was his partner, said, 'Now we will wait here Murray and go later. Let the others go and get on first.' So all the others got the coach and disappeared onto the aeroplane. Then, about 30 minutes later, Paul and Sue and I, got in a small people carrier, and it was dark, and drove to the aeroplane. As we got nearer the aeroplane, I could see that there was a whole long line of people in white T-shirts.

"I said to Sue, 'Look at that. What the hell are they doing?' When we arrived, I saw that it was all the people that would be travelling on the plane with me. They had all got on a special T-shirt with an outline of the aeroplane, and underneath it, 'Murray - thanks for the memories'. On the side of the aeroplane there was an enormous picture of me, sitting in a Mercedes, with 'Murray - thanks for the memories'.

"They formed a welcoming line. So I walked all down the line, shaking people's hands and talking to them. Then I did my, 'Thank you my people,' business and got on the aeroplane. The aeroplane has a great big oak table in the middle of it, and on it there was an absolutely marvellous cake with 'Murray - thanks for the memories'. The whole of the inside of the aeroplane was festooned with balloons and party poppers. We had Champagne when we got on the aeroplane. Just before dinner, Kerry, one of the airhostesses came to me with a European Aviation stewardess's dress and said, 'You know what you have to do, Murray'. So I went down to the loo, and changed into the dress. I wheeled the dinner trolley down the aisle and helped serve all the meals. Then Paul, god bless him, produced an absolutely marvellous painting, which he had had commissioned specially, painted by Andy Kitson, the very famous motor sport painter. It shows the BAC111 that we were flying in, in the middle and then all around the edge there is a Tyrrell, Jordan, Arrows and a Minardi.

"We just had an absolutely hilarious time. We had a gigantic water fight on the plane, Champagne flying about. God knows what the British Aviation Authority would have thought. It was most definitely one of the most memorable and enjoyable evenings of my life.

"When we got to Coventry, Paul activated the emergency slide. We all left the aeroplane by sliding off, not getting off in the conventional way. One of the girls got so excited she took her top off and set off down the slide with everything showing which got a gigantic round of applause!"

Fund benefits from Murray's big night

Legendary motor racing commentator Murray Walker OBE nominated BEN as the charity he would like to benefit from his retirement dinner which was organised by the National Sporting Club at the Café Royal, London, in November.

More than 500 guests paid tribute to Murray on the night, including four F1 World Champions: Sir Jackie Stewart, Sir Jack Brabham, John Surtees OBE and Damon Hill OBE. One of the highlights was an auction conducted by Murray's fellow commentator Martin Brundle. The items on offer included the ITV F1 Sport shirt worn and signed by Murray at his last race, the 2001 USA Grand Prix.

A magnificent £60,000 was raised for BEN from the dinner. Our warmest thanks and best wishes go to Murray for a long and healthy retirement.

It's Been A Lot Of Fun

Tony Jardine

"He's never been afraid of having fun. After Murray's retirement, Paul Stoddart arranged for us to fly back together on one of his special flights. We all had these special T-shirts and it was absolutely great, but the best thing was that they got this stewardess's outfit ready for Murray and he put the whole trolley-dolly suit on and he went down the aisle and he served us all with a smile on his face and laugh. He thought it was absolutely brilliant."

The movie world has the Oscars. Formula One has the Bernies. This is Murray's of which he is intensely proud

"Cosworth's farewell gift to me was this mounted set of four titanium valves from the engine of Eddie Irvine's Jaguar at my last Grand Prix, Indianapolis 2001."

MURRAY-
THANKS FOR T

"'Thank you, my people. Let us all now enter this magnificent flying machine and make our way back to our beloved homeland.' Little did I know what was coming!"

MURRAY-
THANKS FOR THE MEMO

"This was the start of my utterly hilarious and unforgettable last flight with Paul Stoddart's European Aviation after the 2001 European Grand Prix at Monza. All the team personnel, who were flying with us, formed a guard of honour alongside the BA111 which carried my picture and the 'Thanks For The Memories' slogan which was the theme of the flight. Paul Stoddart, God bless him, who masterminded the whole thing, stands gleefully beside me."

"Bald-headed stewardess, Marie Walker (dig those hairy arms) serves his favourite Formula One girl, Louise Goodman, with her appetising four-course dinner, which was soon being thrown about the plane. Paul Stoddart, whose lap she is sitting on, can't believe his luck. When did you last see balloons in an aeroplane?"

The Bernies

Murray Walker

"I have an enormous amount of admiration and respect for, and indeed warm heartedness towards, Bernie Ecclestone. He is a very great man. In 2001 Tony Jardine instituted a thing called the *Bernie Awards*. This is like the Oscars, but instead you get a statuette of Bernie himself. It's about 14 inches high. I was one of the first recipients, in 2001. Michael Schumacher, Sid Watkins, myself and Jenson Button, I think it was, were awarded Bernies. They have subsequently been given to some of the real greats of F1. I am enormously proud to have mine."

Time To Go

Murray Walker

"I did a big interview with Bernie for *F1 Racing* in my last year there. Jolly good interview, mainly because of his answers rather than my questions. At the end of it he said, 'You're not retiring'. 'Oh yes I am, Bernie', I said. 'I am retiring after Japan.' 'No you're not,' he said. 'You've got 10 good years left in you yet and I want them.'"

"This is what an informative and authoritative female pit line reporter, posing as Louise Goodman, looks like at the receiving end of the contents of an inflight ice bucket."

"With a wonderful cake, four stunning birds and multi-millionaire as company, what more could you want? Except a pair of trousers!"

THUMP!
BRUNDLE
ITV
FIRE
NOW THE TRUTH CAN BE TOLD – THIS IS WHY MURRAY ALWAYS COMMENTATES STANDING UP!
"MURRAY TALKS AS IF HIS TROUSERS ARE ON FIRE!"
CLIVE JAMES.

Going Out At The Top

Ross Brawn

"I was always able to consider him a friend in the F1 paddock, someone who was always interesting to talk to and fun to talk to, someone who was hugely respected by everybody in the paddock. He stopped before he needed to, which I think is also a mark of someone of his calibre. It's rather like racing drivers – it's never much fun to see them fade into the sunset – but he went into semi-retirement at a time when there was huge demand for him."

In 'Retirement'

People like Murray do not retire. Indeed, he has been so active since the end of 2001, and in such demand, that it would almost take another book to recount all his latest adventures.

These have ranged from after-dinner speaking to heading up presentations for corporate clients around the world, from driving tanks to writing regularly for publications, such as the *Daily Telegraph*. He has certainly not given up commentating, nor lost his magic touch, having been retained by many overseas broadcasters and the BBC to cover such events as the GP Masters series. In writing about the South African round in 2005, a local newspaper reported that one of the few pleasures enjoyed in earlier years by the inmates on Robben Island had been the fortnightly Grands Prix they were allowed to watch as a 'privilege'. One of those was a certain Nelson Mandela.

Following his so-called retirement in 2001, Murray penned his autobiography and went on a world tour to promote the book. Hardly surprisingly, it has sold in prodigious numbers just illustrating the breadth of admiration and affection for the man who was the 'voice of Formula One' but was also much, much more than simply that.

As recounted later in this chapter, he achieved an ambition by competing in the Targa Tasmania, with Aussie legend Colin Bond, and then in the Targa New Zealand with GP great, Chris Amon. As the illustrations show, he has been fêted around the globe like no other commentator who has ever lived. Since 2006 he has taken on the role of ambassador, or 'Cheerful Chappie' as Murray calls it, for the Honda F1 team.

He has had, and continues to have, an absolute ball. Though it might seem like one endless life of fun-loving enjoyment, Murray still invests time and dedication into everything he does to achieve that level of supreme professionalism for which he will always be famous. Equal only to the professionalism is his undying and infectious enthusiasm. These two ingredients, and a handful of others, still combine to create the unique 'Murray magic' that we all love.

One Maestro On Another

Stirling Moss

"He is such a character. But the great thing about Murray, as far as I am concerned, is that he seems to have total recall of everything and of everyone when we are doing interviews or a co-hosting, as I have done with him on cruise ships and so on. He is very, very easy to work with because he has such a wonderful memory bank, full of stories and everything else. He is a really hard-working man, which I admire. He is in his 80s but you would never believe it. I have great respect for him.

"The cock-ups are very funny things. They are really amusing. I think he started his own cult, the Murray Walker cult.

"He is a man of considerable integrity and I have great affection for him."

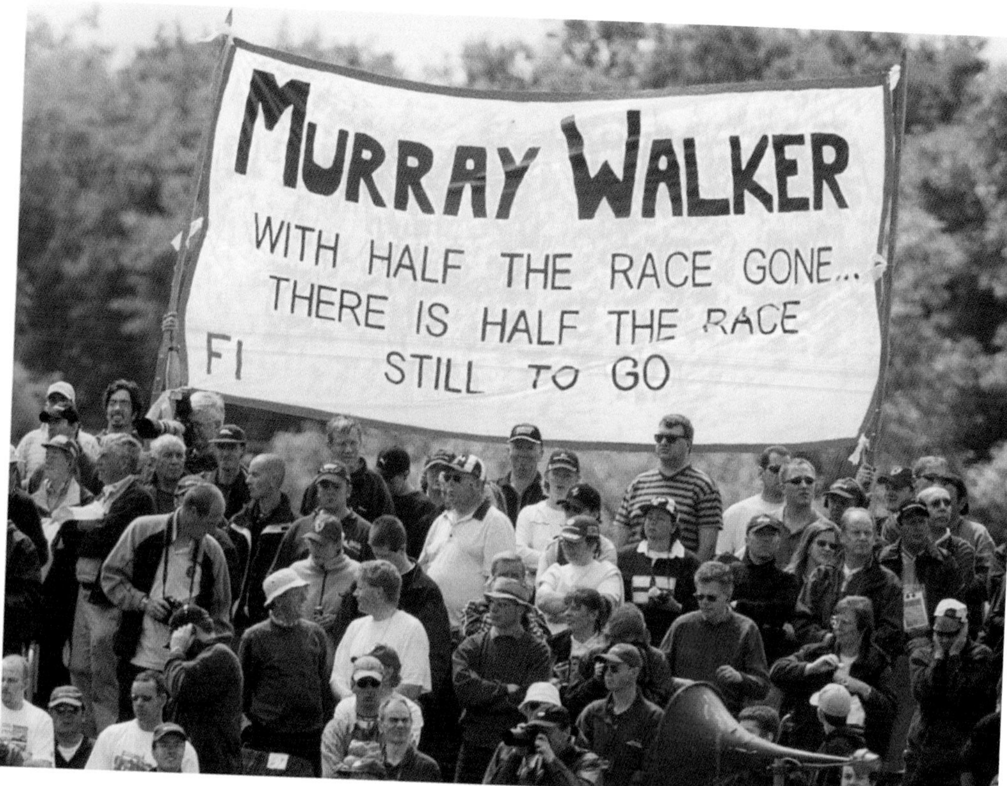

"2001 was the year that I decided to retire from fulltime commentary, although I am happy to say that it did not turn out to be a fulltime retirement. ITV really pushed the boat out at my last British Grand Prix for them and organised a 'Best Banner About Murray' competition. Needless to say, I was gigantically emotional on race day, on seeing efforts like this all round the circuit, even if I would vigorously deny having ever said what they said I said!"

"At the Goodwood Revival meeting in 1999, now aged 76, I decided to risk life and limb by racing a Manx Norton. I'm number 22, slugging it out with Norton-mounted Formula One World Champion Damon Hill and double motor cycle World Champion, the great Barry Sheene, followed by Rolls-Royce boss, Karl Heinz Kalbfell on a G45 Matchless. Pretty sensational, eh? Luckily for me, however, the picture doesn't show that all three were in the process of lapping me!"

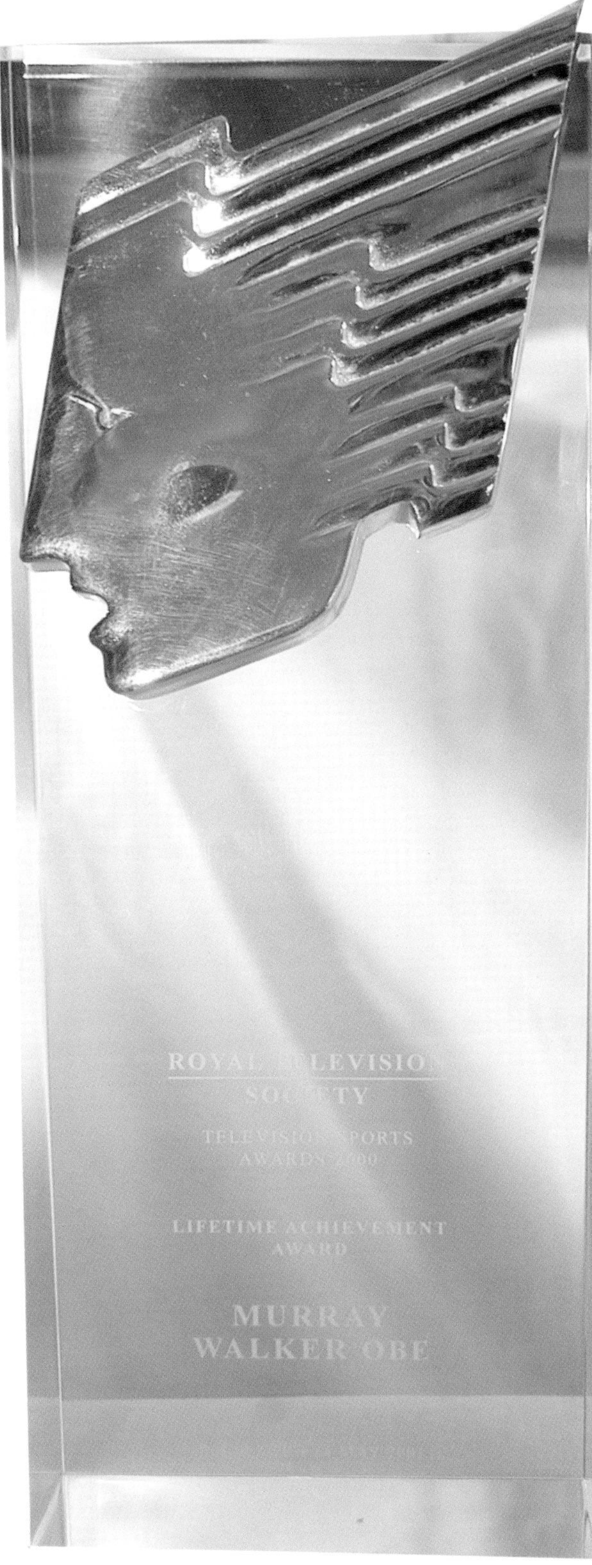

Status Quo

James Allen

"We've kept the same commentary box layout which he always enjoyed. As you know, he stood up to commentate. Although it is slightly more tiring on your limbs standing, it's more than paid back by the power and expression you are able to get in your voice. Even to this day, we are the only people who do it.

"Instead of having a production person in the commentary box, we've got Mark Hughes of *Autosport* as another pair of eyes and ears that helps us to read what's going on. Otherwise the commentary box is very much as Murray left it."

"If I had a quid for every word I've uttered standing behind a lecturn, I could buy Bernie out, but sadly the pay rates aren't that good. Here I am facing in both directions for a change at an Anglia TV sales conference."

"In 2001 I was overwhelmed to receive a prestigious Royal Television Society Lifetime Achievement Award. They don't exactly come with the rations and it made me feel very proud."

Congratulations to
MURRAY WALKER
Unless I'm Very Much Mistaken
The Number 1 Bestseller 2002/2003
from all at
CollinsWillow

"Many years ago, I said to the great Rob Walker, Stirling Moss's mentor 'When are you going to write the book, Rob?' 'What book, Murray?' he replied. 'The one about your life.' Rob was reluctant but in the end he did it and a jolly good read it is too. Maybe it was with that in mind, that I buckled down to do my autobiography which was published in 2002, the year following my retirement. Publisher CollinsWillow did a fantastic job for me, which included a three-month sales promotion tour, taking in the whole of Britain, the Channel Islands, America, Australia, New Zealand, Dubai and Singapore. I was on my chin-strap when it finished but it was all more than worthwhile because, to my utter amazement, the book became the UK's bestseller."

Murray Missed

Matt Bishop

"His retirement did coincide with the first absolutely dominant Michael Schumacher year – 2002. I think the combination of no Murray Walker and a completely dominant Schumacher was too much for some Brits and as a result we saw a diminution of interest. That is not to take anything away from James Allen, who is a friend of mine and who is, I think, a very competent broadcaster – but he isn't a legend."

Everlasting Youth And Anthem

James Allen

"Somebody asked me, when I took over, what I most admired about Murray. I said, 'His youth'. The guy looked at me and I said, 'If you knew him, you'd know what I am talking about'.

"The only piece of advice Murray gave me when I took over was, 'Watch out for the Italian national anthem – it's longer than you think'."

"I'm not really big-headed enough to wear this but I thought you might like to see the T-shirts that CollinsWillow gave the staff at shops where I did book signings. On the back, it has details of the 60 places I spoke at - and they did not include about 15 after-dinner speeches."

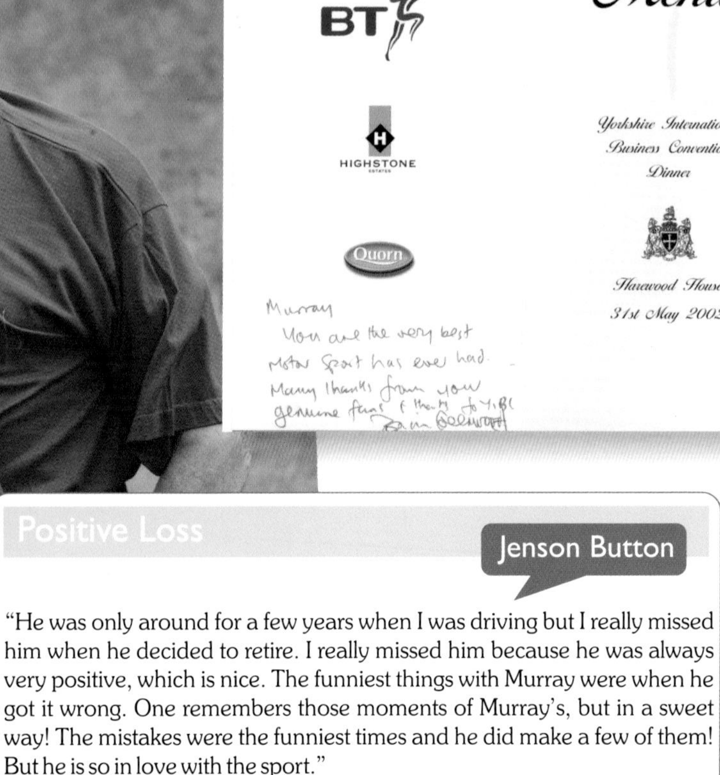

With best wishes
Thanks for a great presentation at our 2002 conference.
Menu
With Special Thanks to our Sponsors
BT
HIGHSTONE
Quorn
Yorkshire International Business Convention Dinner
Harewood House
31st May 2002
Murray
You are the very best Motor Sport has ever had
Many thanks from your genuine fans

"Now this really was pure nostalgia for me. I'm privileged to be associated with the magnificent Royal Armoured Corps Tank Museum at Bovington in Dorset, (Bovington being where I started my army career in 1942) and in 2002 I was taken out in a Sherman tank, exactly like the one I fought in. Judging from the picture, I seem to have been able to resume my role as a bossy tank commander quite well."

"Who is the most impressive man I have met in my entire life? It is, without a shadow of doubt, ex-Russian Premier, Mikhael Gorbachev. We both spoke at the Yorkshire International Business Convention at Harrogate in 2002 and I was overawed to sit next to him at the dinner which followed. I talked to him about advancing towards Berlin, from the West, in my tank in 1945, and he talked to me about advancing towards Berlin from the East, as part of the mighty Russian Army. Gorbachev went on, in effect, to sound the death knell of communism in Russia and I count it as a very great privilege to have met him. At one point, during the dinner, he made his interpreter laugh and when I asked him what the joke was, he said, 'Mr. Gorbachev says you are like each other because you are both bald and have a big mark on your forehead'. 'Ha, ha, ha,' I said, 'Please tell Mr. Gorbachev that grass does not grow on a busy street.' Oh, how he laughed."

Positive Loss

Jenson Button

"He was only around for a few years when I was driving but I really missed him when he decided to retire. I really missed him because he was always very positive, which is nice. The funniest things with Murray were when he got it wrong. One remembers those moments of Murray's, but in a sweet way! The mistakes were the funniest times and he did make a few of them! But he is so in love with the sport."

A True Friend

Lord March

"He has been a huge friend to Goodwood. He once said an incredibly nice thing. There are 16 Grands Prix, or whatever, a year and he can go to any of them. He said it wouldn't be the end of the world if he missed one but one event he wouldn't miss was *The Festival of Speed*. Coming from him, that was a pretty nice thing to say.

"He is an icon in the same way that Stirling Moss is. Two of a kind really. What he brought to the way he commentated on those races was way beyond any normal commentary. He was as important as any of the racing going on. Very rarely does anybody as a commentator, or anyone in television, actually manage to do that. I don't watch it, but I believe Peter Alliss is the same in the golf. They were all of that era, I guess, when television was at its most powerful and they were probably better-made programmes than we will ever see again."

"In 2002 my great friend, Tom Wheatcroft, who is also an ex-tank man, did me the honour of presenting me with the inaugural Tom Wheatcroft award which has also been given to such luminaries as Prof Sid Watkins, Stirling Moss and Ferrari boss Jean Todt."

2002 GRAND PRIX PARTY

BRAIN & SPINE FOUNDATION

A GALA EVENING OF STARS, CARS & GUITARS

MEDIA AND PHOTO-CALL NOTICE

IT'S "BERNIE" TIME

Michael Schumacher, Jenson Button, Murray Walker and Professor Sid Watkins...

... pick up F1's equivalent of the Oscars...

in the presence of Bernie Ecclestone

5 pm (EMT), Saturday 28th April
on location at the Barcelona Grand Prix

VENUE: Karl-Heinz Zimmermann's Motor Home, The F1 Paddock

On the eve of the Spanish Grand Prix, organisers of the 2001 Grand Prix Party announce plans for next year's **Evening of Stars, Cars And Guitars** and invite you to witness some of the sport's top personalities receiving the inaugural 'Bernie' awards for their outstanding contribution to Formula One.

These eponymous new awards, also moulded in the shape of F1 supremo, Bernie Ecclestone, will be handed to Michael Schumacher (Driver of the Year), Jenson Button (Best Newcomer), the Voice of Formula One, Murray Walker (Lifetime Achievement) and FIA Medical Delegate, Professor Sid Watkins, for his Outstanding Contribution to the Safety of F1.

James Allen & Pip Calvert

20th February 2002

Dear Murray,

I wanted to drop you a line just before I go off to Australia to thank you personally for your kind gesture at the Albert Hall last week.

As someone who has done this job for so long and clearly cherished it, you know better than anyone how much it means to me to embark on this season. It is a stiff challenge because of the great work you have done for so many years.

I would not even be attempting to follow you if I did not know that you supported me and you have always been so kind in making that support clear. Many people in your position would not have bothered or would have been downright obstructive. These last five years working alongside you have been an education and you have always been a very generous colleague on the air.

The hardest job for me now is convincing the public and your gesture at the Albert Hall will have gone a long way towards that. Now it's up to me to do the business behind that mike you gave me!

I hope you enjoy the season. Good luck with the book and I look forward to seeing you soon.

Yours ever,

James

MurrayismMurrayismMurrayism

"There's been a major malmisorganisation problem there!"

Whatever You Do, Don't Mention Murray

James Allen

"A thing we have in common is that we both have very loud voices. In Monaco, before they built the new commentary boxes, all the different national broadcasters used to be in a row in an open commentary box with only a small glass divider between us – three feet wide with a corridor behind, so you weren't in sound proof booths. The Germans had suffered quite a few times from having Murray next door, with the volume of his voice bleeding through on to their microphones.

"When I took over in 2002, after qualifying, the commentator from German TV said, 'Ve had hoped zat vith Murray retiring, it vould be quieter vor us!'"

Never Predictable

Tony Jardine

"He got on very well with Jim Rosenthal. I remember Jeremy Clarkson said, 'Who was your favourite person in Formula One?' Everyone expected him to say Alain Prost or Nigel Mansell.

"'Ummm. I think it was Jim Rosenthal!'" (much laughter)

A Right Card

Eoin Young

"I've got a framed Brockbank cartoon I made up for Murray's 79th birthday out here in New Zealand in 2002 when he came out for the launch of his book. It's the one with the ERA/Merc/Maser in the air flying towards the commentary box and we see the rear view of the commentator with mic in hand and hair on end. I think the original caption said, 'And now we pass you back to the studio'. Anyway, my words say 'Unless I'm Very Much Mistaken ... I'm 79 Today!' And Murray has signed it with his usual flourish."

"This is a joke publicity picture, showing how we even had a book signing for my autobiography in the desert at Dubai."

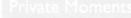

Murray Walker

"Unless I'm Very Much Mistaken..."

...I'm 79 Today

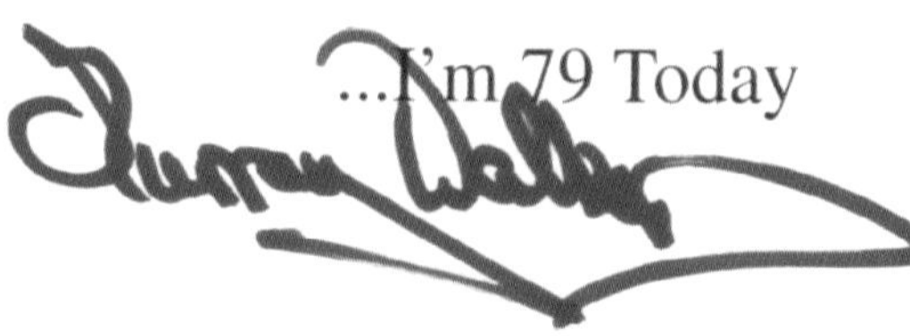

"Stirling Moss and I have done double-acts all over the place. He has a charismatic personality and is a great raconteur with an endless fund of stories about his time at the top of Formula One, racing against and beating them all, even the iconic superstars Juan Manuel Fangio and Alberto Ascari. But Stirling didn't confine his success to F1 - he was arguably even better in sports cars, as well as touring cars and rallying. In fact, I have no hesitation in nominating him as the greatest all-round racing driver of all time."

Private Moments

Nick Goozee

"In 2003 he and I went away for five days to Northern France to visit the WW1 battlefields. Murray is very proud of his military background. Being a very sentimental man, he felt these battlefields very intensely and standing amongst the war graves was very emotional for him. We would have long periods of quiet and he would sit down with a sigh. One doesn't get to meet famous people in these circumstances and see their true inner self, where they are comfortable enough to release their own feelings without worrying about what the circumstances might be.

"One day we passed the Ulster Tower, a monument raised in honour of the Ulster regiments which had fought with colossal casualties. We were ready for a coffee and we found a small museum with a little café. I asked the lady if they were open because there was no-one else around. I then went and got Murray and she took one look at him and said, 'Are you Murray Walker? Stay here, please.'

"She rushed off and brought back her husband and he had raced in Isle of Man TTs when Murray and his father were doing the broadcasts. There we were in the middle of Northern France, in a very remote museum and I don't know whether he really did remember who this chap was but he let the person believe he did. 'Yes, of course I remember you.'

"We sat, just the four of us, quite alone for what must have been two hours. Murray was always very quick to take any focus off himself. We found this Irish couple had been living there for many years on behalf of the Ulster regiment. I think, of our entire trip, that was one of the most moving moments, discovering these people and seeing how much it made their day having him come in."

The Voice

Derek Warwick

"I think he single-handedly helped to raise awareness of motor sport in general but in particular F1. He was the voice of F1. He brought credibility to F1 and without him it would all have been a much poorer place. He brought excitement during dull moments and unbelievable excitement when things did happen. I think he has this wonderful knack of being able to talk in a situation where there was a lull on the circuit or nobody going out on to the track during qualifying. You were looking at nothing but found it interesting because Murray had such enthusiasm, passion and love for F1, but not just F1, for most of the people in F1, especially the drivers. I think he had this admiration that came through in the way he spoke about us, the way he thought about us, the respect that he gave us. That made us feel very, very special.

"I felt sorry for James Allen when he took over from Murray because it's almost like stepping into the shoes of Bernie Ecclestone. Whoever steps into those shoes, basically is on a hiding to nothing because of what he has done. Although James has carved out his own little niche in F1, everyone still misses and respects the voice of Murray Walker. He could still have an 'Evening with Murray' anywhere in the world and have a sell out. I genuinely believe that. If I was anywhere close by, I would turn up just to hear his voice."

"This is at an 'Evening With Murrray Walker' at Abu Dhabi."

"As the holder of the Tom Wheatcroft Trophy it was my very great pleasure, with Elizabeth to make sure I got it right, to hand over the Trophy to the 2003 recipient, Prof Sid Watkins, who attended with his charming wife, Susan. Here we stand in front of the superb memorial to those two great South American drivers, Juan Manuel Fangio and Ayrton Senna that Tom Wheatcroft has placed on the approach to the museum entrance. Sid's contribution to motor sport is incalculable because he is the man who, with the very strong support of Bernie Ecclestone and Max Mosley, has transformed the safety of what is an extremely hazardous pastime. Sid, who has now retired, not only initiated so many of the safety procedures that are now taken for granted, but was responsible for organising and administering the hospitals and on-circuit medical personnel at every Grand Prix. Many drivers literally owe their lives to him and, if you want to know more, read either of his riveting books." (Rob Ford)

High Octane Murray

Nigel Mansell

PP: "Do you think he helped to fuel Mansell-mania?

"I think more important than that, Murray helped to fuel Formula One, period. Formula One-mania. He made Formula One the pinnacle of motor sport worldwide. I think he's the single most talented man who made some incredibly mundane races be very exciting because of his contagious commentary and occasional faux pas, for which he was legendary. While some people do faux pas on purpose, Murray's were always accidental or through over-excitement. When it's genuine, and part of the make-up of the man himself, you can carry off all sort of wondrous things. It's like Peter Alliss who commentates on golf. He gets away with murder on his commentaries and what he says at times, but it's very funny and articulate. He says things totally off the wall that you and I would get shot or fired for!"

The Missing Link

John Surtess

"Motor sports, despite being a major part of this country's heritage, have always suffered from being in a secondary spot when it comes to the mass media, and getting through to the people out there. What I think Murray has done is get motor sport, in its various forms, out to the people. And get them to sit up and be interested.

"You have a wonderful situation with Lewis who is taking Formula One out to the people and getting on to all the news pages, for the right reasons, but unfortunately you haven't got anybody projecting it in a manner which really excites people. Lewis has excited people with his racing, what he has achieved and how he presents himself but, let's face it, just imagine the dramas of the last GPs of 2007 and what Murray would have made of it. It would have been repeated and repeated.

"Murray for so long was the voice of motor sport and, if you speak to people out there, he was their link."

Honesty In F1

Pat Symonds

"Honesty is such an important word with Murray. Of course, he supported his British drivers but he was a very honest man. It sounds a terrible thing to say, but his principles were of the old school and there are so few of them around now. The world's not a better place in that respect. I just loved the honesty and the principles that Murray had.

"He would never judge anyone harshly. Can you think of two more opposite people than himself and James Hunt? He took James for what he was, he respected what he could do. I am sure he was appalled by other aspects of James's life but that didn't come out. What came out were the positive aspects. I suppose that was one of the great things about Murray. He was always looking for the positives and not dwelling on the negatives."

"I never thought I'd get to see the wonderful island of Tasmania but I did in 2003 and what's more I did as navigator to iconic Australian Touring Car Champion, Colin Bond, in a works Toyota Camry. It was an incredible experience."

CLASS AWARD

2003

This is to certify that Competitor No: 931

Driver: Colin Bond
Navigator: Murray Walker
Vehicle: 2002 Toyota Camry Sportivo

Achieved the following result in Targa Tasmania

Modern Competition
Class C
Contemporary 1998 - 2003
Showroom Specification

SECOND PLACE

Issued by Octagon Australia Pty Ltd

octagon

TARGA

Number 805 "Always Ahead" December 2003

SUNBEAM Club News

SUNBEAM MOTOR CYCLE CLUB

Published bi-monthly

Free to Sunbeam MCC members

...rray Walker astride his father's Rudge, immediately prior to presenting the prizes at this year's Graham Walker Run

Firm Friends

Nigel Mansell

"I would say we became extremely good friends. When you recognise someone incredibly professional, you actually rejoice in each other's professionalism in your different areas of work. Murray, for me, was fair, very outspoken, very witty, very wrong at times, but even if he was wrong, I don't think anybody, except a very small handful throughout the world, failed to adore or love Murray. That was a tremendous talent and I think I was one of the favoured few, and I would like to think that Murray would even call me a very good friend."

Divers Encouragement

David Richards

"The abiding memory for me of Murray is not so much of when I was a competitor but just as one of the voices I always associate with motor sport that encouraged me to become involved in motor sport in the first place. That enthusiasm and that passion that came through as a commentator is one of the things that encouraged me to get involved in motor racing.

"In later days, I bumped into Murray regularly socially at events and the lovely thing about him was that he was always so encouraging to me. I was the new kid on the block but he'd always have time to spend with me and congratulate or support or encourage, and that was always appreciated.

"Most people, if you ask them who they remember in motor racing, they still remember Stirling Moss and they still remember Murray Walker."

Targa Tasmania

Murray Walker

"I was in Sydney to speak at a dinner. There was a chap sitting next to me who said, 'I have just read your autobiography. Did you mean what you said about wanting to do the Targa Tasmania?' I said, 'Yes, of course I did'. He said, 'I am associated with Toyota and they would like you to be an official works competitor in a Toyota Camry to be driven by Colin Bond'.

"Now Colin Bond is a mega-star of Australian motor sport. We went from Launceston in the North right down to Hobart in the South. I had never seen the Targa Tasmania, but had a wonderful image of what it was like, which was dramatically exceeded by the actual event. Sitting beside Colin Bond was an absolute education because he is a brilliant driver, and has a very well-developed sense of humour. The whole thing was a magnificent experience for me."

AMON & WALKER'S TARGA TALE

Eoin Young, who has been following this year's Dunlop Targa, caught up with Chris Amon and Murray Walker at the finish of the event to talk to them about their Targa experience

PHOTOS EOIN YOUNG

"Capt Murray Walker, dressed in keeping with the spirit of the event at the 2003 Goodwood Revival meeting."

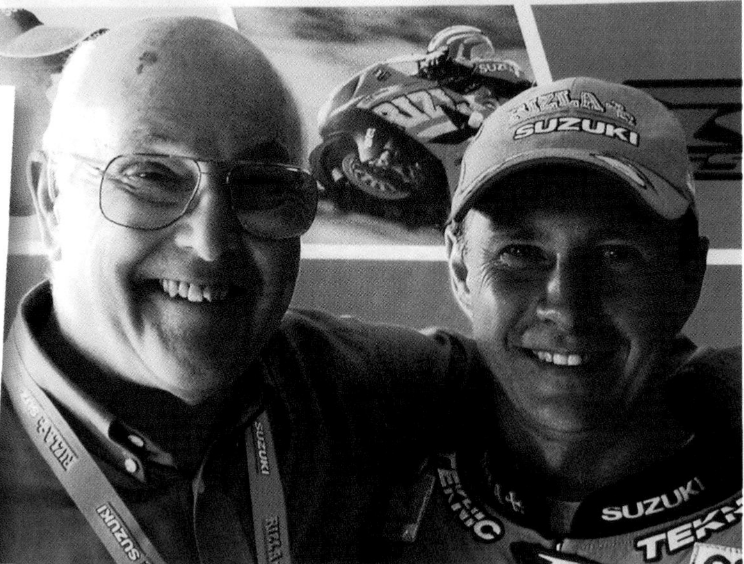

"Motor bikes are my first love and now I've got more time to go to events like the superb British Superbike Championship to be with chums like Champion Suzuki rider, John Reynolds. Since I don't have a chance to say this often, I would like to point out that John is shorter than I am!"

"The older you get, the better it becomes. As a result of not doing too badly in the Targa Tasmania, Toyota offered to send the same car to New Zealand for me to navigate the country's great Grand Prix driver, Chris Amon."

Targa New Zealand

"As a result of competing in the Targa Tasmania I was invited to compete in the Targa New Zealand by Toyota. I flew up to Auckland to meet my driver, none other than one of the truly great F1 drivers of all time, who was never really able to realise his potential, Chris Amon.

"When Chris was racing in F1, I was the BBC's motor cycle man, and although I used to go to Grands Prix, I would not have have had to temerity to go up to the great Chris Amon. So, I had never actually met him and we were going to be cooped up in a Toyota Camry, doing 120mph down New Zealand roads, for five days. I thought, 'What will happen if we can't stand the sight of each other?'

"So, we arranged to have dinner together before the event, and he is an absolutely fabulous bloke, and we got on like a house on fire. He said to me, 'You will have to be very patient with me Murray, because I haven't driven in anything competitive since 1976, and I have never driven in a rally'. I said, 'But you will have to be very patient with me, Chris, because I have only driven in one rally'. It was quite complicated with pace notes. It wasn't a kids' rally, it was very serious stuff.

"Anyway, on Day One we started off, and it was a bit tentative both from his driving and my navigating points of view. Day Two it all started to come together. You know they say if you have got it, you never lose it; it is like riding a bicycle. For the remaining three days, I sat spellbound by the side of one of the great Grand Prix drivers - just observing what he was doing when I wasn't actually navigating. Chris was inch perfect everywhere. I would say that we were doing 120mph in a Toyota Camry, along some very iffy New Zealand roads and rough stuff. We didn't win the class but we did extremely well. I have been lucky enough to have had a lot great experiences in my life. I would certainly rate that as one of them."

One Car, Two Legends

Chris Amon

"The Targa in 2003 was the first time I had met Murray. I think he started F1 commentaries the year after I retired; he told Eoin Young at some point that he hadn't really met any of the New Zealanders, i.e. Bruce, Denny or myself. The closest he had come was at Silverstone in the early '70s when he inadvertently got in Denny's way in the pit lane and was asked what the bloody hell he thought he was doing!

"I found Murray to be an absolutely delightful person and it was a real pleasure to have spent those few days on the Targa with him. Apart from being great company, he was also a very good and professional partner to have. That is the only time I have competed in the Targa. To have done it with Murray made it particularly special and I look back to the event with many fond memories.

"Murray is, of course, very well-known in New Zealand and I think it gave many people a lot of pleasure to have him here in the country and to be able to see him in person. I remember on one of the stages in the middle of nowhere a farmer had parked a truck in a paddock beside the road with the tray tipped right up and a big banner draped over it. Written on it was 'Go Go Go'!"

"I used to say that I would willingly give up all the Grands Prix to attend the annual Goodwood Festival of Speed and Goodwood Revival - alright I was exaggerating a bit but not all that much because nowhere else do you enjoy seeing fabulous machinery in such relaxed and enjoyable surroundings. Getting round 'Marilyn Monroe' wasn't too bad either. I also bumped into 'Private Walker' of the pseudo Dad's Army platoon."

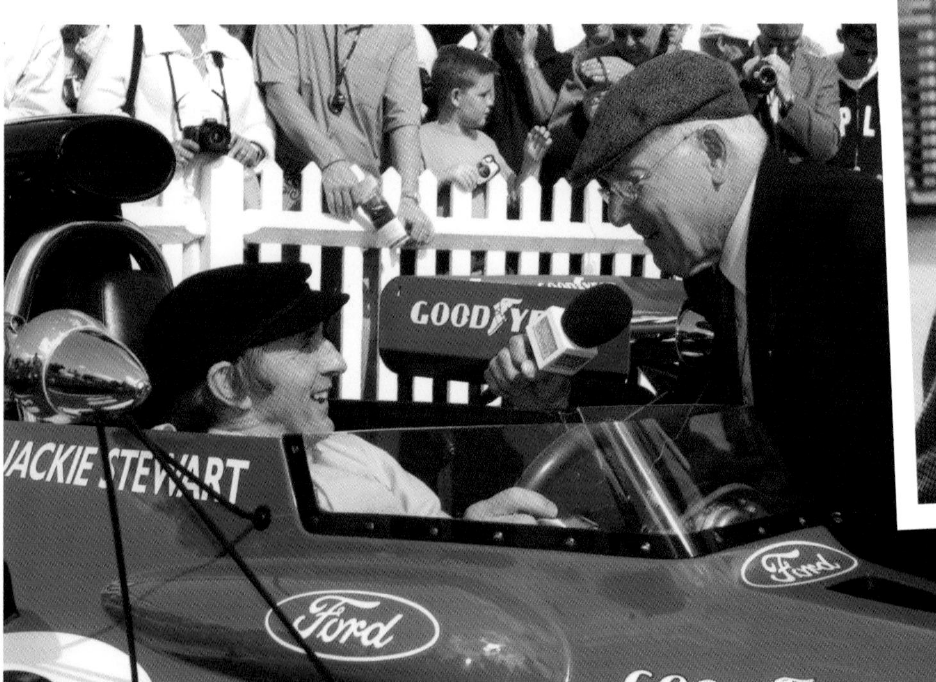

"'My God, Jackie, I thought my cap was pretty grim but yours is even worse!'"

Beckham And Me

Murray Walker

"If you are any sort of a personality these days, when the whole world seems to be personality struck, you get an enormous amount of attention. Take David Beckham. I feel desperately sorry for him. I had lunch with him at Honda this year [2007], and I thought he was an extremely nice, decent, honest, straight-forward chap but poor devil can't do anything without paparazzi all over him. It must be absolute purgatory."

Speaking Volumes

Nick Fry

"The role of [Honda F1] ambassador was suggested to us by Matt Bishop. He realised that Murray was missing F1 and had done enough gardening for a while.

"At the first GP he attended with us as an ambassador at the beginning of 2006, he was in the back of the garage (pit) during qualifying and, as it was in Australia, doing something for Channel 10. Even though the engines of the cars were running and even though we all had ear defenders on, everyone commented, and was laughing, that we could still hear Murray's high-pitched enthusiasm over everything. It was actually quite remarkable, in your own garage, to be listening real-time to the real Murray telling the world what you were doing, which thoroughly entertained us all.

"He has been a great asset and done a great job for us. At his age, his research is unbelievably thorough, his professionalism remains without comparison and he still absolutely loves it, which is a great example to us all. I think if we are all as half as enthusiastic about F1 at his age, then we'll all be doing pretty well."

Press-On Walker

Jenson Button

"You know we have the Paddock Club with about 100 guests at each Grand Prix. Murray will be interviewing me and he'll ask me a very exciting question and I'll be halfway through answering it, and the crowd will be loving it, and I haven't even fully explained my answer, and he's already asking Rubens another question! He seems to be in his own world, but he's very sweet and he means a lot to the team, and it's good to have him on board."

"On the Thursday of the Goodwood Revival meeting, there is always a cricket match between the Duke of Richmond and Gordon's XI and that of his son, the Earl of March. I am one of the umpires with Nick Goozee."

"I am told that the largest military base in Europe is the Royal Navy's training establishment at HMS Collingwood, Portsmouth. It is an incredibly impressive place at which I have given talks, as a result of which I was able to indulge myself in some simulated naval gunnery. I sank three cruisers without even getting out of my seat."

THANK you, Murray Walker, for coming back and for your delightful words and enthusiasm over the Clipsal 500 broadcast. The best attracts the best.

You added something very special to a fantastic long weekend – even if you didn't know what a rattle-gun is. Are you free next year?

D. BURGESS,
Wynn Vale.

Village Folk

Matt Bishop

"Murray is a byword for integrity and honesty. In fact, almost to an extent that when he has encountered things from the dark side of F1, he discusses them almost in an innocent way, as if to say, 'Can these nice people that I know so well, and like so much and respect so much, can they be capable of doing something less than perfect, integrity-wise?' In those circumstances, Murray seems a bit like a lost soul. Whether it be Michael Schumacher allegedly parking his Ferrari at Rascasse in 2006, or whether it be Mike Coughlin and Nigel Stepney allegedly doing what they did in 2007, all these are people that Murray has got to know in the village we call Formula One – and Murray never really saw it as a Piranha Club - he really did see it as a village. Trouble is, it is not always a very nice village."

A Producer's View

Roger Moody

"Murray and James were the perfect mix 'n' match. I doubt there will ever be a combination like Murray and James again, a winning combination. Even though Martin Brundle does a fantastic job, and his pit walks are out of this world – as we all know because he keeps on winning awards – but I do think that Murray and James were unique and, with the greatest respect to all the latter-day commentators, there will only ever be one Murray Walker."

Strong Words

Jonathan Martin

"In my career at the BBC, of nearly 40 years, I don't think I ever met a more industrious or hard-working commentator. He really was dedicated to doing as much homework as he possibly could. He would spend two days before every GP just walking up and down the pit lane. Not only would he know the name of everybody in every team, every mechanic, but he would just absorb so much knowledge. He would walk around every circuit. His energy was amazing. Anybody who worked with him not only enjoyed it but they had to be fit to keep up with him!"

"This is a 'Help The Aged' charity function at Windsor Castle. I was there as a youthful observer, you understand. Amongst the others present were 007 Roger Moore, Robert Powell, Aynsley Harriet, Lionel Blair, Cilla Black, Joan Bakewell, June Whitfield and other faces you'll know. We were all privileged to meet that very gracious lady, Her Majesty, The Queen."

"When I no longer had to be neutral, Honda asked me to be their Formula One Ambassador and I nearly bit their hand off in saying yes, for it is a fabulous job that not only enables me to enjoy the company of Jenson Button, who is a super bloke, but literally to get close to his stunning mother, Simone."

The Soothsayer

Murray Walker

In July 2007 Murray, a great Lewis Hamilton fan, was asked if Lewis was going to win the Championship. He replied:

"He's had a charmed life so far. Something could happen that will stop him finishing a race – a puncture or someone will shunt him off."

"On the left, Goodwood's brilliant mastermind, the Earl of March. Then it's Renault's Rene Arnoux, Bruno Senna and a taller (than Arnoux) Murray Walker."

Generation Swap

Nick Fry

"I was at a Variety Club Dinner prior to Christmas 2006 and a number of much younger people, including Nigel Mansell and Martin Brundle, were arguing how dull F1 was and that some of the technology was inappropriate. Much to my amazement, Murray, being probably 40 years older than those two, came up with, 'No, it's absolutely fantastic'.

"It was the wrong way around – the younger people were acting as fuddy-duddies and Murray, and in fact John Surtees, were arguing completely the opposite."

Making It Fun

Jenson Button

"It's great having him as part of the team. It's really good working so closely with him. And all the PR stuff we do with him now is always good fun. It's always good fun because the crowd love him – they really do. Everyone has got such fond memories of Murray."

We would like to thank the following for their support of tonight's event.
Axiom Communications
Aazam Ahmad
Alistair Watkins
BBC Radio Manchester
Bellagio-Time
Belle Vue Greyhound Racing
Bernie Ecclestone
Bobby Charlton Soccer School
Damon Hill
Dianne Bourne and
the Manchester Evening News
Daytona Racing
Excel Publishing
F1 Racing Magazine
Gentry Grooming Co
Granada Television
HGA Creative
Honda F1 Racing
Jim Rosenthal
Live Nation
Lowry Hotel
Manchester Confidential
Monarch Airlines
North One Television
O.K. Magazine
Pizza Hut
Silverstone Racing Circuit
Sir Jackie Stewart
Sir Stirling Moss
Skylight Photography
Sophisticars
Steve Garner
The Book People
THEMagazine
Virgin Trains
Yang Sing
variety club
the children's charity
Charity Reg No:209259
Telephone: 0161 236 0500
Variety Club (North West Region) 4th Floor,
St James's Buildings, 79 Oxford Street, Manchester M1 6FQ
varietyclubnw@btconnect.com • www.varietyclub.org.uk
sponsored by
axiom
The Book People
F1 Honda Racing Team
Virgin trains
Tribute Evening to
Murray Walker OBE
variety club
the children's charity
Charity Reg No:209259

Public Property

Nick Goozee

"He once said to me, 'It might surprise you but I don't actually have a lot of friends'. He meant friends in the sense where you could just behave normally. Just as if you and I became friends, we wouldn't talk about our work, we wouldn't talk about a single subject but a variety of things and be very comfortable doing so. Whereas nearly everybody that meets Murray, whether it's socially or at any of the functions he attends, always wants to express their opinions or remind him of certain situations. It never lets go of him. He has got nowhere to hide really."

"I was privileged to watch Bernd Rosemeyer and Tazio Nuvolari win the 1937 and 1938 Donington Grands Prix in their Auto Unions and was very excited to have this picture taken in spite of the fact that I only had one leg!"

Murray's Value

Lord March

"We have a little party after the Festival of Speed for everyone involved, on Monday, lunch for 300 people. They are all Goodwood people except that we encourage some of the big names to stay and come to that lunch because it is very good for everyone, and for Goodwood, to have them there. We have had some great people.

"This year [2007] Murray was still around, so we said, 'Why don't you come for lunch?'

"Of all the people we have ever had at that lunch, he got by far the biggest, by far the biggest, response. We usually ask the big names to sign programmes. Literally Murray's queue was out the door, round the building. That was interesting in terms of what he means to people in relation to motor sport. That was clear evidence of how much more he means than any driver."

The Invisible Driver

Jenson Button

"At the Turkish Grand Prix last year [2006] in the Bosphorus at the Palace in Turkey, there were hundreds of guests, and Murray's doing a Q & A on stage. He's been building it up, and there's so many people there, and he's really excited and he introduces me, I come up on to the stage, and then he introduces Rubens Barrichello on to the stage. Everyone was cheering for him but he didn't appear. Murray had forgotten Rubens wasn't actually coming to that event!

"I whispered to Murray, or 'mother' as we call him, in his ear that I was the only driver there! But that's Murray for you!"

FOND MEMORIES: F1 greats, driver Nigel Mansell (left) and commentator Murray Walker, at Nelson Mandela Square yesterday. PICTURE: STEVE LAWRENCE

F1 legends roar to Madiba magic

Terrible Twins

Susie Moss

"I don't remember which ship it was because it was a while ago. Stirling and Murray did this talk, and questions and answers. The next day this lady comes up to Murray on the deck and says, 'I really did enjoy that. I thought you were wonderful. I didn't think I would be interested in motor racing, but you were so entertaining and so interesting, and besides which that Murray chap wasn't bad either.'

"Murray tells that one, and it's true. We had it the other way round as well. We were in Bromley, at a car event, and Stirling was signing all these autographs, and there is a great queue of people. This lady comes up to Stirling and says, 'You know Formula One has never been the same since you gave up doing the commentary.' So it goes both ways!"

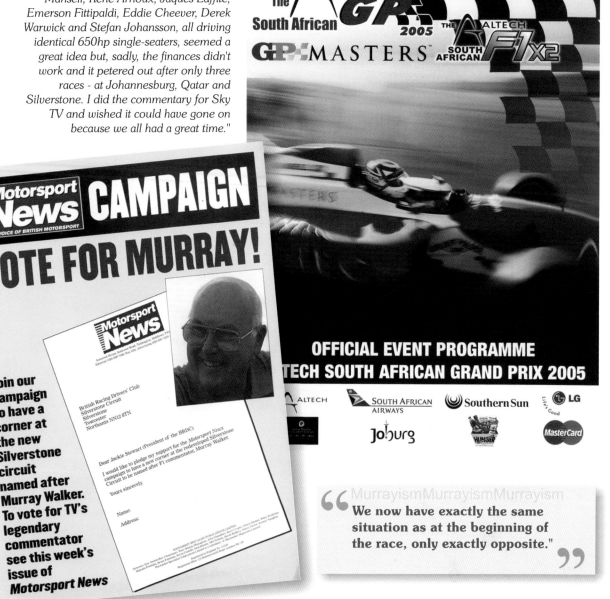

"The 2005/6 Grand Prix Masters series for retired Formula One drivers, such as Nigel Mansell, Rene Arnoux, Jaques Laffite, Emerson Fittipaldi, Eddie Cheever, Derek Warwick and Stefan Johansson, all driving identical 650hp single-seaters, seemed a great idea but, sadly, the finances didn't work and it petered out after only three races - at Johannesburg, Qatar and Silverstone. I did the commentary for Sky TV and wished it could have gone on because we all had a great time."

Motorsport News THE VOICE OF BRITISH MOTORSPORT **CAMPAIGN**

VOTE FOR MURRAY!

Join our campaign to have a corner at the new Silverstone circuit named after Murray Walker. To vote for TV's legendary commentator see this week's issue of *Motorsport News*

Motorsport News

British Racing Drivers' Club
Silverstone Circuit
Silverstone
Towcester
Northants NN12 8TN

Dear Jackie Stewart (President of the BRDC)

I would like to pledge my support for the *Motorsport News* campaign to have a new corner at the redeveloped Silverstone Circuit to be named after F1 commentator, Murray Walker.

Yours sincerely,

Name:

Address:

> MurrayismMurrayismMurrayism
>
> **"We now have exactly the same situation as at the beginning of the race, only exactly opposite."**

> MurrayismMurrayismMurrayismMurrayism
>
> **"For the second time in the very recent future..."**

No Script Needed

Bill Smith

"He gave a speech this year (2007) at the TT celebrations which was probably the best speech I have ever heard in motor sport – he didn't read it, it was from the heart."

Very Much Missed

Charlie Whiting

"He is the most apolitical chap you could meet. He just doesn't get involved in that stuff. He is a friend to everybody. I have never heard a bad word said about him, which is fairly unique in the Formula One world! He did such a great job with such enthusiasm for so many years, and undiminished enthusiasm. It must have taken a great deal of courage to bale out when he did. I don't believe he needed to. He was an impossible act to follow, same as if Bernie was to leave or croak – no-one could replace him. And Bernie was against him retiring.

"Murray is sorely missed in the F1 paddock; there's no doubt about it."

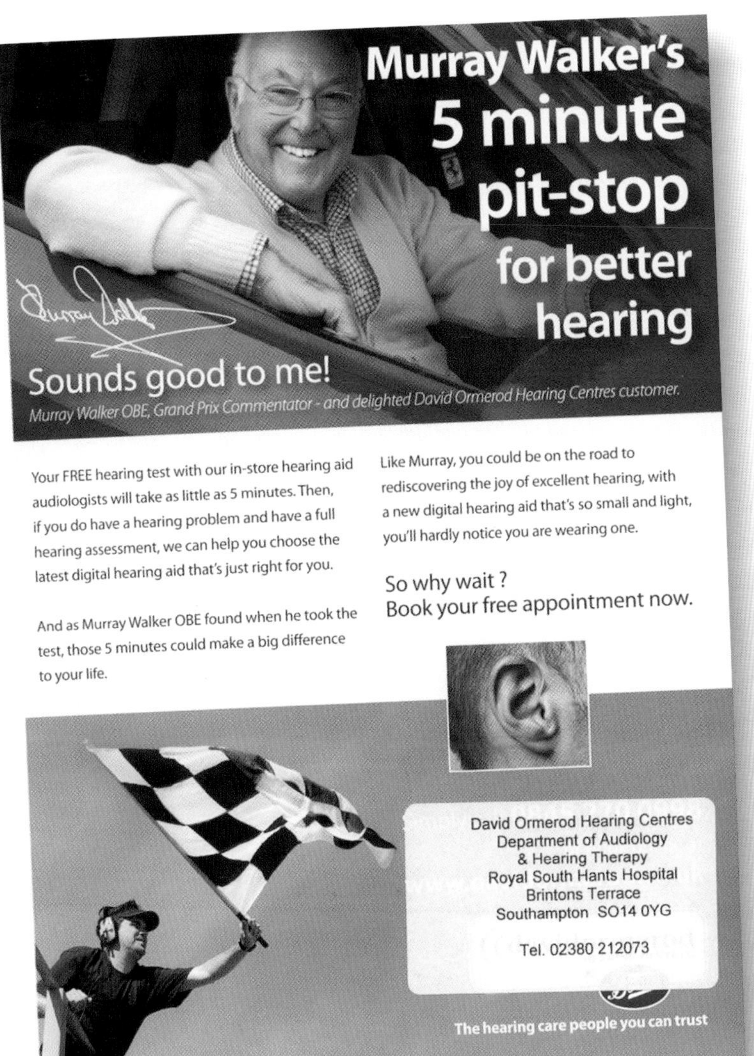

"This is the serious bit. My hearing has been severely affected by a lifetime's exposure to racing engines which is why I agreed to become the spokesman for David Ormerod Hearing Centres, whose expertise has genuinely made life much easier for me."

MurrayismMurrayismMurrayism

"The atmosphere is so tense you could cut it with a cricket stump."

"I appeared (yellow cardigan) in the 2006 'Petrolheads' TV quiz series, which was headed up by Neil Morrissey and Top Gear presenter, Richard Hammond. I was a guest on the fourth programme with James May. This is the production crew so you can see why television is so expensive - even before Morrissey and Hammond got paid!"

Another Retirement Job

Tony Jardine

"He did the commentary this year [2007] in Germany for BBC Five Live. I wasn't at that Grand Prix because I was at another function. I was coming back and my wife was with me and we turned on the radio. We laughed. Well, we so enjoyed it, brought it to life. It started raining and his comment was, 'It's not raining here, it coming down STAIR-RODS!'

"I spoke to people afterwards who'd also listened. 'Wasn't that just great?' His did all his homework as he always used to and showed his professionalism. Maurice Hamilton was with him doing the co-commentary and Maurice said it was hard for him to keep a straight face. It was just pure magic, Murray-magic at its very best."

A Natural Gift

John Button

"He used to give the kiss of death to people but he can still do it. I'm sitting down with Murray [in 2007], watching the F1 testing. Someone was going round, and Murray said, 'You know, John, sitting here watching, it doesn't look that difficult, does it?' As he said it, the guy went off and crashed! Absolute fact. He has still got the touch!"

26th July 2007,

Dear Murray,

We spoke briefly before your 'debut' on Radio Five Live last weekend. I just wanted to put on record my thanks for the terrific job you did for us in Germany.

It was a demanding schedule, an extraordinary race and you sailed through it all as if you had never been away. We were all very proud to have you on board.

I do hope we will get the chance to hear you involved again in the near future.

Best wishes.

[signature]

British Broadcasting Corporation BBC Radio Five Live Room 6200 Television Centre Wood Lane London W12 7RJ www.bbc.co.uk/fivelive

"Just when you thought it was safe to come out, I was back! I only stopped in 2001 because I wanted to do so with dignity when I felt I was still ahead but I really missed being a part of the addictive Formula One scene. So, when BBC Radio 5 Live F1 commentator, David Croft's wife decided to have a baby during the weekend of the 2007 European Grand Prix race at the Nürburgring and the BBC asked me to make a one-off return, I was only too happy to do so. And, boy, was it a great race to talk about! Full of incident, drama and excitement, including Lewis Hamilton getting it wrong for once. I was beside myself with excitement for the whole 60 laps, and it felt just like old times. Fabulous!"

EUROPEAN NURBURGRING 22.7.07 ROUND 10/17	DRIVERS: 1 HAM 70; 2 ALO 58 (-12); 3 RAI 52 (-18); 4 MAS 51 (-19); 5 HEI 33 (-37); 6 KUB 22 (-48)		CONSTRUCTORS: 1 McLAREN 128; 2 FERRARI 103; 3 BMW 56; 4 RENAULT 31; 5 WILLIAMS 13; 6 TOYOTA 9; 7 RED BULL 6	[illegible] 2006: 1 SCHUMACHER; 2 ALONSO; 3 MASSA; 4 RAIKKONEN; 5 BARRICHELLO; 6 FISICHELLA	LAP = 3.144M; 60 LAPS = 192 MILES; LR = MSC (FER) = 1M 29.468 128.714; POLE '06 = ALO: 129.519s; POLE '07 = RAI: 1m31.450
1	ALONSO (R)	26	OVIEDO: WC 05/06: 96xGP: 17x1: 16xP: 10xFL: KARTS 94-98 (WC96): F. NISSAN CHAMP '99: F3000/2000 F1 MINARDI TESTER: '01 MINARDI: REN 02-06: McL '07 07: 2x1: MAL/MON: 3x2 OZ/USA/BRIT: SPAIN 3: BAH 5: CAN 7		DWC 2/58
2	HAMILTON (Y)	22	STEVENAGE: 9xGP: 2xP: 1xFL: MULTIPLE KART CHAMP 1995-2000: F.RENAULT CHAMP 2003 (10x1): F3 EURO CHAMP 05 GP2 CHAMP '06: 07: 2x1 CAN/USA: 4x2 BAH/SPA/MAL/MON: 3x3: OZ/FRA/BRIT		1/70
3	FISICHELLA (R)	34	ROME: 186xGP: 3x1: 3xP: 2xFL: 18xPOD: KARTS/F3/DTM: F1: MIN x 8GP 96: JORDAN 97: BEN 98-2001: JORDAN 2002/03: SAUBER 04: RENAULT 05-07 07: MON 4: OZ 5: 2x6 MAL & FRA: 2x8 BAH & BRIT		7/17
4	KOVALAINEN (Y)	25	FINLAND! 9xGP: KARTS/F.REN/F3/NISSAN WORLD SERIES: 1ST RACE OF CHAMPIONS '04: 2ND GP2 '05 (ROSBERG 1ST) RENAULT TESTER '06: RENAULT '07: 07: CAN 4: USA 5: SPAIN & BRIT 7: MAL 8: BAH 9: OZ 10		8/14
5	MASSA (R)	26	SAO PAULO: 80xGP: 4x1: 3xP: 5xFL: KARTS/BRAZIL T/C/ F.REN CHAMP: F3000 CHAMP: SAUBER '02: FERR TESTR '03: SAUBER 04/05: FERRARI '06/07: 07: 2x1: BAH/ESP: 2x2: FRA/USA 3: 2x5 MAL/GB: 1x6 OZ: CAN DQ		4/51
6	RAIKKONEN (Y)	27	ESPOO: 114xGP: 11x1: 14xP: 21xFL: KARTS: BRIT F.REN CHAMP 2000: DAVID ROBERTSON: SAUBER 2001: McL '02-'06: FERRARI '07: 07: 3x1 OZ/FRA/GB: 2x3 MAL/BAH: USA 4: CAN 5: MON 8:		3/52
7	BUTTON (R)	27	FROME: 129xGP: 1x1: 3xP: MULTIPLE KART CHAMP: SON OF JOHN: F.FORD BRIT CHAMP & 1ST FESTIVAL '98: F3: F1 McL & PROST TESTS: WIL 2000: BEN '01: REN '02: BAR 03-05 HON 06-'07 07: FRA 8:		16/1
8	BARRICHELLO (Y)	35	SAO PAULO: 245xGP: 9x1: 13xP: FLx15: SENNA: 5x BRAZ KART CH: GM LOTUS: BRIT F3 CH '91: F3000 '92: F1: JOR 93-96: STEW 97-99: FER 2000-05: HON 06/07: 07: BRIT 9: SPAIN & MON 10:		18/0
9	HEIDFELD (R) BABY JODA	30	M-GLADBACH: 126xGP: 1xP: 6xPOD: KARTS 89-93: FF 94/95 CHAMP: F3 '96/97 GERM CH & MONACO 1ST F3000 98/99 CH: F1 McL TESTR 97-99: PROST 2000: SAUBER 01-03 JOR '04: WIL '05: BMW '06-'07 07: CAN 2: 3x4: 1x5: 2x6		5/33
10	KUBICA (Y)	22	KRAKOW: 14xGP: 1x3: KARTS 11YRS: F.REN '01-'03: MAJOR ROAD ACCIDENT '03: 2ND MACAU 04: REN WORLD SERIES '05 BMW TESTER/DVR '06: BMW '07: FIRST GP HUNGARY '06 07: 4x4 OZ/MAL/BAH/BRIT: CANADA CRASH: FRA 5: MON 6		6/22
11	SCHUMACHER (R)	32	HURTH: 172xGP: 6x1: 6xP: 7xFL: KARTS 14YRS: F3 93-95 (MAC 1: MON 2): F3000 JAPAN CHAMP: F1: JOR 97-98: WILL 99-2004: TOY 2005-'07 07: CAN & OZ 8TH:		15/2
12	TRULLI (Y)	33	PESCARA: 176xGP: 1x1: 3xP: 7xPOD: MULTI-KART CHAMP: F3 '95-'96 (GERM CH): F1: MIN & PROST '97: PROST 98-99: JOR 2000-'01: REN 02-04: TOY 05-07 (& ON!) 07: USA 6: MAL & BAH 7:		10/7
14	COULTHARD (R)	36	TWYNHOLM: 221xGP: 13x1: 12xP: 18xFL: 61xPODIUM: KARTS 82-88: FF CH x2 '89: BRIT F3 (2+ MACAU & MASTERS) F3000 92/93: "1ST" LE MANS 93: F1: WILL 94 (SENNA): McL 96-2004 (8YRS): RBR 05-08 07: USA 7: SPAIN 5TH:		12/4

Unique Popularity

Jackie Stewart

PP: "Murray has popularised F1 and brought it to a larger audience."

"Absolutely. The mass audience factor. And that's why Murray is so popular, that's why this book will sell well, and that's why his autobiography did sell well, because he is just so much loved, particularly with English-speaking people around the world, but it's not just the British Isles. Certainly in Australia and New Zealand, they adore him, as do the Canadians. He really was a great favourite everywhere. Everywhere he goes he is instantly recognisable. Very modest in all his mannerisms and his lifestyle. He and Elizabeth are a great couple. I have great respect and admiration for Murray.

"He must be the most popular British sports commentator that has ever lived."

Inspiring The Future

Lewis Hamilton

"Murray was 'The Man'. When I was younger I used to turn on the TV and watch the Grands Prix just to hear and follow Murray's enthusiastic commentary. He brought such passion to the sport and made it exciting for us, and I am sure the whole world, to watch. Murray was Formula 1. He is unique, can never be replaced and we all miss him."

Pure Emotion

Rubens Barrichello

"Murray has always been very kind to me. I think the way he commentates he takes over and commentates with his heart, and I very much appreciate that."

"And that's it, folks. Last page of the book. Au revoir but, I hope, not good-bye." (Abigail Humphries)

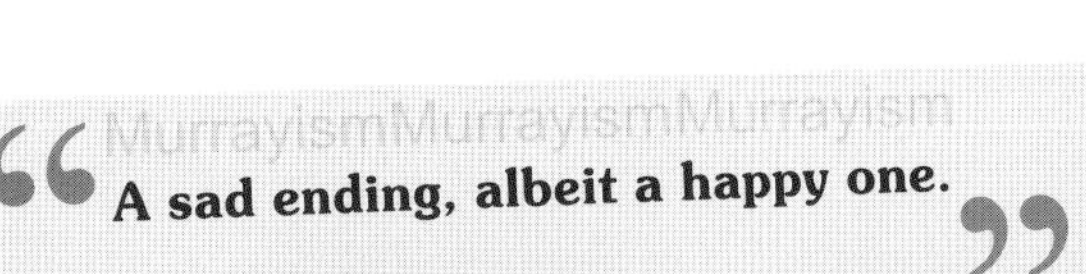

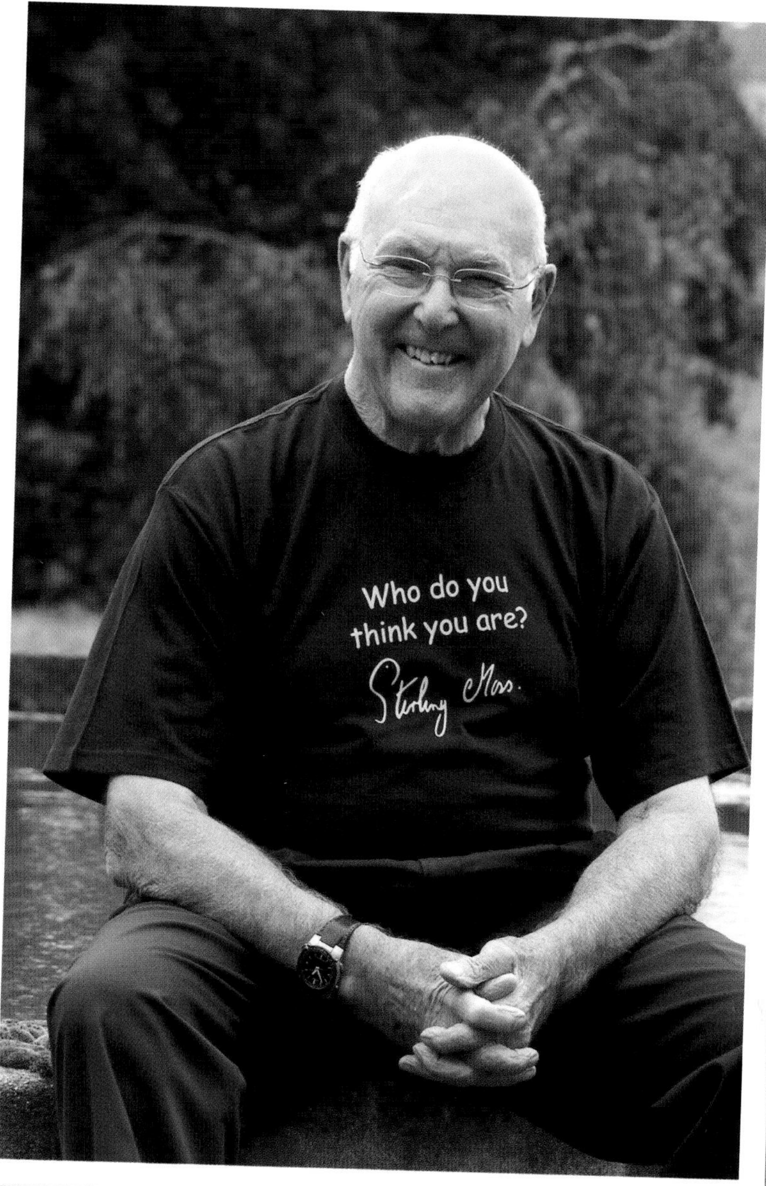

A Great Mate

Nigel Mansell

"I think the saddest day of my life was when Murray retired from commentating on Formula One. He should have more guest appearances. He is just one brilliant human being who is the finest, most consummate professional in his trade in the world, period.

"Forget our friendship, I just think he is absolutely, stunningly brilliant."

The Last Word

Murray Walker

PP: "You blend nostalgia with the modern age."

"I have never regarded myself as very good at looking back. I have never yearned for the good old days, because I have thought they weren't any better than the good modern days, just different. I always tend to look ahead at what is going to happen rather than look back at what did happen. Actually this is why this has been so satisfying and rewarding, because I have had to get out all the things you needed for the book and it has enabled me to relive some wonderful times and recreate some wonderful memories."

Cellnet
RENAULT